THE EARLY EPISCOPAL CAREER OF
ATHANASIUS OF ALEXANDRIA

Christianity and Judaism in Antiquity
Charles Kannengiesser, Series Editor
Volume 6

THE EARLY EPISCOPAL CAREER OF
ATHANASIUS OF ALEXANDRIA

by

Duane Wade-Hampton Arnold

University of Notre Dame Press

Notre Dame   London

Cover illustration, portion of London Papyrus 1914, reprinted by permission from Harold Idris Bell, ed., *Jews and Christians in Egypt* (Oxford, 1924), pp. 58-61, Plate II (LP 1914). Courtesy of the British Library, London.

Library of Congress Cataloging-in-Publication Data

Arnold, Duane W. H.
    The early episcopal career of Athanasius of Alexandria / by Duane Wade-Hampton Arnold.
        p.   cm. — (Christianity and Judaism in antiquity ; v. 6)
    Includes bibliographical references and index.
    ISBN 0-268-00925-2
    1. Athanasius, Saint, Patriarch of Alexandria, d. 373. 2. Synod of Tyre. I. Title. II. Series.
    BR65.A446A75 1991
        270.2'092—dc20
        (B)   90-45796
                                                                                                 CIP
                                                                                                 r91

To

ARTHUR MICHAEL RAMSEY

requiescat in pace

Bishop, Teacher, and Friend

Qui in Dei gloria ministrans,
Dei ad gloriam servat.

Converti me ad Athanasium legendum,
tantaque summi, et exii viri admiratio
tenuit, ut ab eo divelli non possim.
Legi duos eius libros adversus Gentiles;
namque in primo Gentile superstitionem
arguit; in secundo Crucis, ac divinae
e Incarnationis tuetur ignominiam tanta
argumentorum vi, sententiarumque
gravitate, ut agi quidem ea caussa, ut
est a plerisque acta, et in primis a
nostro Lactantio, dignius tamen, atque
divinus non posse videatur. Legi ex
ordine tres iam libros adversus Arium,
nam quinque sunt, et magni quidem:
tantaque fragrantia pietatis refectus
sum, ut nihil me legisse
meminerim, quod huic operi conferri
possit. Eminet eis literis
incomparabilis, viri venustas quaedam
tum sententiarum, tum verborum, digna
profecto, quam omnes admirentur,
venerentur, ament. Granditer enim eam
caussam, ut dignum fuerat, agit
cunctasque illius haeresis obiectiones
ita aperit, arguit, refellit, tantaque
Scripturarum sacramenta enodat, ut
exsatiari eius lectione non possim
Quid plura? Statui apud me convertendo,
igneo ac coelesti homini debitis meis me
totum dedere; si quid otii suppeditare
potuero; nihil enim illius doctrinae
salubrius, mihil ignitius reperiri posse
constanter adfirmaverim.

AMBROGIO TRAVERSARI
27 February 1424

CONTENTS

Section I
ATHANASIUS: QUESTIONS OF CHARACTER AND CONTEXT

Section II
ATHANASIUS AND THE SYNOD OF TYRE

PREFACE

This book, which began as a Ph.D. thesis for the University of Durham, England, has been written in an attempt to clarify the many complex events which took place during the first seven years of the episcopate of Athanasius of Alexandria and to explain the impact of those events upon our current understanding of the bishop. The structure of the book, therefore, has been dictated, first, by the concerns of historiography and, second, by the chronological sequence which stretches from Athanasius's consecration as bishop of Alexandria in AD 328 to his banishment by Constantine in AD 335. Within this course of seven years many accusations arose in connection with Athanasius's conduct. Although the effort has been made to comment upon each of these charges within a particular period of time, it should be noted that many of the accusations were repeated within a wide variety of settings, spanning a number of years. Whenever possible, however, I have sought to place the charges within a proper chronological context.

Certain other stylistic features of this present study should be noted. The reader will find full publishing information for all of the sources used in this study in the bibliography along with those other materials which have been consulted in the course of research and found useful. Abbreviations which are used for the works of Athanasius may be found in the preliminary pages of this work, as can those for standard works of reference, journals, etc.

Small portions of this book first appeared in *Studia Patristica,* vol. 21, pp. 377-383. Earlier versions of material presented here also are to be found in three articles in *Coptic Church Review:* "Athanasius and the Meletians" (vol. 10, no. 3); "Authority and Procedure at the Synod Tyre" (vol. 11, no. 3), "Athanasian Historiography" (vol. 12, no. 1). I would like to thank the Peeters firm in Leuven, publisher of *Studia Patristica,* and the editors of *Coptic Church Review* for their permission to allow the use of this material, now revised, in the present study.

I would like to thank those whose encouragement, advice, and assistance aided the research and writing of this present work. There have been many persons who have influenced my understanding of Athanasius of Alexandria, far too many to mention in this brief space. Some, however, have shared so generously of their time and expertise that I would be remiss not to name them. I owe a special debt of gratitude to many within the academic community of the University of Durham who assisted me along the way and provided helpful direction during the time of my research at that institution. These persons include the Rt. Rev'd Stephen W. Sykes, Mr. Gerald Bonner, Dr. C.T.R. Hayward, and Dr. Ann Loades. My special thanks is also extended to Dr. David Thomas, who guided my initiation into the realm of papyriological research and assisted me in my understanding of the Meletian archive materials.

In the academic community beyond the University of Durham there have been many others who have assisted my research by their advice and direction. The Rev'd Dr. William C. Weinrich first directed me to the study of Athanasius and has continued to show interest in my research. Prof. Charles Kannengiesser has provided helpful interaction and criticism. The late Rt. Rev'd R.P.C. Hanson, while disagreeing with many of my conclusions, nonetheless provided insightful comments on a number of critical points of interpretation within this present study. The Rev'd Canon Prof. Rowan Williams took time from a busy schedule to read and examine the thesis from which this book came and thereby earned the thanks and gratitude of the author.

I received courteous assistance from the librarians and staff of the Manuscript Room and Reading Room of the British Library; the libraries of the universities of Durham, Sheffield, Notre Dame, and Detroit; and the Wayne State University Library.

For the academic years 1983-1985 I was the recipient of the Overseas Research Student Award bestowed by the United Kingdom's Committee of Vice Chancellors and Principals. This generous award enabled me to engage in the study which stands behind this present work.

Finally, as I write these acknowledgments one person who befriended me during my time in Durham remains foremost in my heart and mind. Although his death has denied me the opportunity of sharing this final result of my research with him, the Rt. Rev'd and Rt. Hon. Lord Ramsey of Canterbury was an example of theological integrity and true spirituality and was a great encouragement to me in my work through the course of countless conversations. It is to Bishop †Michael that this book is dedicated.

D.W.-H.A.

2 February 1990
The Feast of the Presentation

ABBREVIATIONS

The Works of Athanasius of Alexandria

Ad Adelph.	*Epistola ad Adelphium episcopum*
Ad Afros	*Epistola ad Afros*
Ad Const.	*Apologia ad imperatorum Constantium*
Ad Dracont.	*Epistola ad Dracontium*
Ad ep. Aeg. et Lib.	*Epistola encyclica ad episcopos Aegypti et Libyae*
Ad Joan. et Ant.	*Epistola ad Joannem et Antiochum presbyteros*
Ad Lucif. I-II	*Epistolae duae ad Luciferum episcopum*
Ad monach.	*Epistola ad monachos*
Apol.	*Apologia contra Arianos*
C. Gentes	*Oratio contra Gentes*
De decretis	*Epistola de decretis Nicaenae synodi*
De fuga	*Apologia de fuga sua*
De incarn.	*Oratio de incarnatione*
De morte Arii	*Epistola de morte Arii*
De sent. Dion.	*Epistola de sententia Dionysii episcopi*
De syn.	*Epistola de synodis Arimini Italia et Seleuciae in Isauria celebratis*
De virgin.	*De virginitate*
Ep. encycl.	*Epistola ad episcopos encyclica*
Exp. in Pss.	*Expositiones in Psalmos*
Festal Letters	*Easter Letters*
Hist. Arian.	*Historia Arianorum ad monachos*
Or. c. Ar. I-III	*Orationes contra Arianos* I-III
Or. c. Ar. IV	*Oratio contra Arianos* IV (Pseudo-Athanasius)
Serap. I-III	*Epistolae ad Serapion* I-III
Tom. ad. Ant.	*Tomus ad Antiochenos*
Vita Ant.	*Vita Antonii*

Journals and Series

AnalBoll	*Analecta Bollandiana*
AJAH	*American Journal of Ancient History*

BLE	*Bulletin de littérature ecclésiastique*
Byz	*Byzantion*
ByZ	*Byzantinische Zeitschrift*
ChH	*Church History* (The American Society of Church History)
CRAI	Comptes-rendus des séances de l'Académie des inscriptions et Belles Lettres (Paris)
DOP	*Dumbarton Oaks Papers*
GCS	Die griechischen christlichen Schriftsteller der ersten (drei) Jahrhunderte, Leipzig and Berlin, 1898-
GS III-IV	E. Schwartz, *Gesammelte Schriften,* vols. 3 and 4, edited by W. Eltester and H. D. Altendorf, Berlin, 1959, 1960.
HTR	*Harvard Theological Review*
JACE	*Jahrbuch für Antike und Christentum.* Ergänzungsband.
JEA	*Journal of Egyptian Archaelogy*
JEH	*Journal of Ecclesiastical History*
JJP	*Journal of Juristic Papyrology*
JR	*Journal of Religion*
JThS	*Journal of Theological Studies,* 1899-1949
JThS, NS	*Journal of Theological Studies,* new series, 1950-
LNPF	A Select Library of Nicene and Post-Nicene Fathers of the Christian Church, edited by P. Schaff and H. Wace, New York, 1899-1900; Reprint ed., Grand Rapids, Michigan, 1952-1974
NAKG	*Nederlands archief voor kerkgeschiedenis*
NedThT	*Nederlands theologisch tijdschrift*
NGG	*Nachrichten von der Königlichen Gesellschaft der Wissenschaften zu Göttingen*
NTS	*New Testament Studies*
Opitz	*Athanasius Werke,* hrsg. im Auftrage der Kirchenväter-Kommission der Preussischen Akademie der Wissenschaften, vol 2, 1, 1-280: *Die Apologien,* edited by H.G. Opitz, Berlin, 1935
Opitz III, *(Urkunden)*	*Athanasius Werke,* hrsg. im Auftrage der Kirchenväter-Kommission der Preussischen Akademie der Wissenschaften, vol. 3, 1, 1-76: *Urkunden zur Geschichte des arianischen Streites 318-328,* edited by H.G. Opitz, Berlin, 1934
OrChP	*Orientalia Christiana Periodica*
PG	Patrologiae Cursus Completus, Series Graeca, 161 vols., edited by J.-P. Migne, Paris, 1857-1866

PL	Patrologiae Cursus Completus, Series Latina, 221 vols., edited by J.-P. Migne, Paris, 1841-1864
PO	Patrologia Orientalis, edited by R. Graffin and F. Nau, Paris, 1907-
RevSR	*Revue des sciences religieuses*
RHE	*Revue d'histoire ecclésiastique*
RHPR	*Revue d'histoire et de philosophie religieuses*
RSLR	*Rivista di storia e letteratura religiosa*
RSR	*Recherches de science religieuse*
SC	Sources Chrétiennes, edited by H. de Lubac and J. Daniélou, Paris, 1941-
StP	*Studia Patristica,* Papers presented to the International Conference on Patristic Studies held at Christ Church, Oxford
TP	*Theologie und Philosophie*
TU	Texte und Untersuchungen zur Geschichte der altchristlichen Literatur
TLZ	*Theologische Literaturzeitung*
ThQ	*Theologische Quartalschrift* (Tübingen)
ThSt	*Theological Studies*
ThStKr	*Theologische Studien und Kritiken*
ThZ	*Theologische Zeitschrift* (Basle)
VC	*Vigiliae Christianae*
ZKG	*Zeitschrift für Kirchengeschichte*
ZkTh	*Zeitschrift für katholische Theologie*
ZNW	*Zeitschrift für die neutestamentaliche Wissenschaft und die Kunde der älteren Kirche*

Dictionaries and Lexicons

DACL	*Dictionnaire d'archéologie chrétienne et de liturgie*, edited by F. Cabrol and H. Leclerq, Paris, 1903-1953
DCB	*A Dictionary of Christian Biography, Literature, Sects, and Doctrines*, 4 vols., edited by W. Smith and H. Wace, London, 1877-1887
DHGE	*Dictionnaire d'histoire et de géographie ecclésiastiques*, edited by A. Baudrillart, Paris, 1912-
Lampe, *Lexicon*	*A Patristic Greek Lexicon*, edited by G.W.H. Lampe, Oxford, 1961
Liddel-Scott	*A Greek - English Lexicon*, 9th edition, Oxford, 1940
LThK (first)	*Lexicon für Theologie und Kirche*, 1st edition, edited by M. Buchberger, Freiburg, 1930-1938

LThK (second)	*Lexicon für Theologie und Kirche,* 2d edition, edited by J. Höfer and K. Rahner, Freiburg, 1957-
Müller, *Lexicon*	*Lexicon Athanasianum,* edited by G. Müller, Berlin, 1952
ODCC	*The Oxford Dictionary of the Christian Church,* 2d edition, edited by F.L. Cross and E.A. Livingstone, London, 1974
RAC	*Reallexikon für Antike und Christentum,* edited by T. Klauser, Stuttgart, 1950-
RE	*Realencykopädie für protestantische Theologie und Kirche,* 3d edition, edited by A. Hauck, Leipzig, 1896-1913
Smith, *Lexicon*	*A Concise Coptic - English Lexicon,* edited by R. Smith, Grand Rapids, Mich., 1983

INTRODUCTION

In a work published in the early winter of 1988, the late R.P.C. Hanson made the following observation concerning the state of the church in the fourth decade of the fourth century:

> The Greek-speaking Eastern and the Latin-speaking Western areas of the Christian Church were now heading for a major rift. . . . The cause of this was not primarily the doctrine of Arius. Theoretically at this point the Arian Controversy had been settled. . . . The chief causes were the intrigue of Eusebius of Constantinople, the opportunism of Julius of Rome, and the misconduct of Athanasius of Alexandria, and among the three causes we must judge the last to be the most serious.[1]

The misconduct of Athanasius to which Hanson alludes as the most serious cause of the breach between the East and the West in AD 341 consists of the accusations and rumors which surrounded the early episcopal career of Athanasius and culminated in the Synod of Tyre and the bishop's subsequent banishment by Constantine. It is the purpose of the present study to examine in detail the early episcopate of Athanasius from his consecration in AD 328 to his first exile in AD 335. The allegation of Hanson, cited above, has become, as will be seen in the course of this study, an increasingly common interpretation of the early career of Athanasius and has, therefore, created the need for a balanced and critical examination of those documentary sources which provide the basis for such a statement. This study attempts such an examination.

Before the exploration of primary sources and the construction of an historical narrative centering upon the Synod of Tyre, however, it is important to note that the present opinions concerning the early career of Athanasius are also themselves a part of an historical process which cannot be viewed in isolation. For this reason Section I examines "Athanasius: Questions of Character and Context." Within this section modern critical approaches to Athanasius are compared to nineteenth-century evaluations of

---

[1]R.P.C. Hanson, *The Search for the Christian Doctrine of God*, Edinburgh, 1988, 272-273.

the bishop in order to establish a basic historiography of contemporary and near-contemporary Athanasian studies. Although it is almost impossible for such a study to be exhaustive (as may be observed in the bibliography attached to this work), the section may be suggestive of the way in which the basic approach to Athanasius has been altered in the course of the last century. The remainder of the first section is devoted to particular disputed issues in the early career of Athanasius with an emphasis upon the various viewpoints of a large number of primary sources which stand behind the debated concerns of character and context.

These important questions of character and context having been considered, Section II provides an historical narrative and examination of "Athanasius and the Synod of Tyre." Owing to the recent research of R. Lorenz, which has resulted in the redating of a number of Athanasius's *Festal Letters*, it has been possible to prepare a more exact reconstruction of those events which led to Athanasius's first exile.[2] Such a task has been aided by the editing of the Syriac index of the *Festal Letters* which was undertaken by A. Martin and M. Albert and which has provided a somewhat revised

---

[2]R. Lorenz, *Der zehnte Osterfestbrief des Athanasius von Alexandrien: Text, Übersetzung, Erläuterungen,* Berlin/New York, 1986, 30ff. The dating of the *Festal Letters* has been a developing area of study for over a century. Additional information concerning the dating of the letters, as well as textual information and comments, may be found in the following studies and translations: W. Cureton, *The Festal Letters of Athanasius,* London, 1848 (the first completed edition of the Syriac letters); the Latin translation of the letters made by Cureton may be found in J.P. Migne, PG 26, cols. 1360-1444; H. Burgess, *The Festal Epistles of S. Athanasius,* Oxford, 1845, provides an English translation which also incorporates additional Syriac fragments for the tenth and eleventh letters; A. Mai, *S. Athanasii epistulae festales,* Nova Patrum Bibliotheca 6, Rome, 1853, contains another Syriac edition; a German translation is found in F. Larsow, *Die Fest-Briefe des heiligen Athanasius,* Leipzig, 1852; the translation of Burgess has been reprinted and annotated in A. Robertson, *Select Writings and Letters of Athanasius,* LNPF, second series, vol. 4, Oxford, 1891 (reprint ed., Grand Rapids, Michigan, 1975), 503-553; L.T. Lefort, *S. Athanase: Lettres Festales et Pastorales en Copte,* CSCO 150-151 (*Scriptores Coptici* Tomus 19-20), Louvain, 1955; P. Merendino, *Osterfestbriefe des Apa Athanasius,* Düsseldorf, 1965, contains a German translation of the Coptic letters; a French translation of the important tenth letter is provided in M. Albert, "La 10⁰ lettre festale d'Athanase d'Alexandrie: Traduction et interprétation," *Parole de l'Orient,* 6-7 (1975, 1976): 69-90; the Coptic text of the sixth letter along with a French translation is provided in R. Coquin and E. Lucchesi, "Un complément au corpus copte des Lettres Festales d'Athanase (Paris, B.N., Copte 176) (Pl. III)," *Orientalia Lovaniensia Periodica* 13 (1982): 137-142; and the Coptic text of letters 39, 40, and 41 with a French translation is provided in R. Coquin, "Les Lettres Festales d'Athanase (CPG 2101), Un nouveau complément: Le Manuscript IFAO, Copte 25 (Planche X)," *Orientalia Lovaniensia Periodica* 15 (1984): 133-158.

chronology of those events preceding and surrounding the Synod of Tyre.[3] Much of this work has, of course, required a reconsideration of the standard Athanasian chronology which was established by E. Schwartz.[4] Moreover, the Synod of Tyre, as well as those events which both preceded and followed its meeting, has remained somewhat enigmatic. Questions concerning procedure and authority at Tyre have often been overlooked or dismissed as unimportant. Whether or not the final judgment at Tyre was binding or only advisory has also remained unclear. It is hoped that this situation will be redressed within the course of this study.

The principal difficulty which one has to overcome in writing a study of the early episcopal career of Athanasius—which is also perhaps the main reason why no complete modern critical biography of the bishop has yet appeared—lies in the nature and condition of the sources. Although Athanasius was a prolific writer on theological, polemical, and pastoral themes, little biographical information emerges. As will be observed in this study, many historians, both early and contemporary, based their accounts largely upon those of Athanasius himself and may, therefore, present a rather narrow perspective. On the other hand, it must be recognized that the extant fragments of Philostorgius and the lost works of Sabinus of Heraclea, as well as the Arian reports included in the works of Sozomen and Epiphanius, are far from impartial and may present an equally constrained point of view.

In the present study, however, attention has been centered upon episodes within the early career of Athanasius which have numerous sources, not the least of these being the bishop's collection of documents presented in *Apologia secunda*.[5] Beyond the sources cited above, however, a special effort

---

[3] A. Martin and M. Albert, *Histoire "acéphale" et Index syriaque des Lettres Festales d'Athanase d'Alexandrie*, SC 317, Paris, 1985.

[4] The Athanasian chronology of Schwartz and the importance of the *Festal Letters*, as well as attendant problems, were first addressed in *GS* III, Berlin, 1959, 1-29 (*Zur Geschichte des Athanasius I, NGNG* 1904) and secondly in *GS* IV, Berlin, 1960, 1-11 ("Zur Kirchengeschichte des 4. Jahnhunderts," *ZNW* 24 [1935]: 129-137). Although many questions concerning Athanasian chronology with respect to the *Festal Letters* were settled by Schwartz, other points have been given attention in V. Peri, "La Cronologia delle lettere festali di sant' Atanasio e la Quaresima," *Aevum* 34 (1961): 28-86; Mgr. Lefort, "Les lettres festales de saint Athanase," *Bulletin de l'Academie royale des sciences, des lettres et des beaux-arts de Belgique* 39 (1953): 641-656; and T. D. Barnes has considered additional problems arising out of the Index in his review of A. Martin, *Histoire*, in *JThS*, NS 31 (1986): 576-589.

[5] For the purposes of this study, the author has accepted the conclusions of H. G. Opitz concerning the unity of the text's composition which are outlined in *Untersuchungen zur Ueberlieferung der Schriften des Athanasius*, Arbeiten zur Kirchengeschichte 23, Berlin and Leipzig, 1935, 158, fn. 3, and which refer to the ms. tradition of the *Apologia secunda*. O. Bardenhewer had earlier argued that the treatise had been the result of a gradual evolution and that the main body of the work, ch. 1-88, had been completed by AD 348 with ch. 89-90 being added later,

has been made to collect even the smallest particles of information, either certain or merely probable, which might enable us to draw a more complete and accurate picture of the personality and actions of Athanasius in the early years of his episcopate. Also, particular attention has been given to some aspects of his consecration, to the treatment of the Meletians, to the circumstances surrounding the Synod of Tyre which have not received sufficient consideration, and to some sources whose information has not yet been fully integrated into current Athanasian studies. These are, to name a few: Alexandrian consecration practices after the Council of Nicaea; the large number of Meletians who gave their allegiance to Athanasius subsequent to his consecration; the similar sequence of events relative to the condemnation of Eustathius of Antioch; the effect of the Nicene canons upon Egyptian church order; the lack of Arian activities in Egypt between AD 328 and AD 335; and the possible alternate interpretations of London Papyrus 1914 in light of the confused religious situation in Egypt during Athanasius's early episcopate.

The need to clarify these particular points, especially the work of H.I. Bell on London Papyrus 1914, has been highlighted by the following comment of Hanson:

---

about AD 357 (*Geschichte der altkirchlichen Literatur* II, second edition, Freiburg, 1914, 61). Similar arguments had been put forward by A. Robertson, LNPF, second series, vol. 4, 97, who dated the main portion of the work to AD 351. R. Seiler rejected these attempts at dating and contended that the entire text was the result of almost twenty years of editing and reworking, the first instance of use being Athanasius's interview before the emperor following the Synod of Tyre in AD 335 (*Athanasius' Apologia contra Arianos: Ihre Entstehung und Datierung* [Diss., Tübingen], Düsseldorf, 1932, 1-32). P. Peeters adopted the earlier opinion of Bardenhewer, again pointing to the probable addition of ch. 89-90 ("Comment s. Athanase s'enfuit de Tyr en 335," *Académie royale de Belgique: Bulletin de la classe des lettres et des sciences morales et politiques,* series 5, vol. 30, 174). Another recent return to the thesis of Bardenhewer has been suggested by T. Orlandi, with the contention that Athanasius began to collect documents for the work following his return from exile in AD 346 and completed the main body of the treatise around AD 352/353. The entire work was then made ready for distribution with the addition of ch. 90 in AD 355/356 ("Sull' Apologia secunda [contra Arianos] di Atanasio di Alessandria," *Augustinianum* 15 [1975]: 54-56). V. Twomey, following Opitz, also argues for the unity of the text, but, making use of the repeated references to Valens and Ursacius, believes the work to have been essentially completed by AD 356 with minor alterations in ch. 89 being made by either Athanasius or another editor between AD 367 and AD 370 (*Apostolikos Thronos*, Münster, 1982, 304). Although outside of the main focus of this study, Opitz's evaluation of the text and the dating of AD 357/358 seems correct, although one must allow for a gradual process of collecting the large number of documents represented. The minor later revisions of the text suggested by A.H.M. Jones do little to alter the overall conclusions of Opitz ("The Date of the Apologia contra Arianos of Athanasius," *JThS*, NS 5 [1954]: 224-227).

H.I. Bell has published the papyrus which throws such a lurid light on the behaviour of Athanasius in his see; though this was published nearly sixty years ago the significance of it has not yet sunk in everywhere. It is astonishing to read the article in *TRE* on the subject of "Athanasius" by Martin Tetz written as recently as 1977 and find no mention of this document, so important for our estimation of Athanasius' character.[6]

The correct interpretation of this document is vitally important to our estimation of the early Athanasius, that much is agreed. It will be observed, however, in the course of this study, that the standard interpretation which has been accepted by Hanson, in concert with so many others, leaves much to be desired in terms of accuracy and clarity.[7]

It would be unrealistic not to accept that there remains much that is unknown concerning these crucial years in the career of Athanasius. This study, however, is presented in the hope that by a reasoned approach to the primary sources a new appreciation of the context, character, and actions of the early Athanasius will emerge.

---

[6]Hanson, *op. cit.*, xx. Although Hanson's study appeared as this study was being completed and, therefore, is not treated in the main body of the text, I have sought to make some comments on this fine work in the conclusion. It may be noted, however, that Hanson regards an estimation of Athanasius's character and actions in the early years of his episcopate as being crucial to the understanding of the controversies of the time. In his section on "The Behaviour of Athanasius" (*op. cit.*, 239-273), Hanson makes it clear that he follows, to a lesser or greater extent, the basic propositions of the modern critics and the standard interpretation of LP 1914 (*op. cit.*, 252-254) with very little critical analysis of the document. It is, therefore, all the more surprising that in another section on "The Doctrine of Athanasius" (*op. cit.*, 417-458) he takes issue with the Schwartzian presentation of the bishop, stating that although "an unscrupulous politician, [he] was also a genuine theologian" (*op. cit.*, 422) and that "it would be a great mistake to follow Schwartz's opinion" (*loc. cit.*). In this presentation of the bishop, Hanson has highlighted the ambiguity which seems to characterize the modern approach to Athanasius. A transcription of LP 1914 appears below, in the appendix to this study.

[7]Hanson comments upon the initial stages of the thesis put forward in this study, yet seems to contradict his remarks cited above (*op. cit.*, xx) by saying, "these papyri are by no means the only evidence for the case against Athanasius" while castigating current studies for ignoring "this document, so important for our estimation of Athanasius's character" (*op. cit.*, 252, fn. 63).

SECTION I

ATHANASIUS: QUESTIONS OF CHARACTER AND CONTEXT

SECTION I
ATHANASIUS: QUESTIONS OF CHARACTER AND CONTEXT

1. INITIAL CONSIDERATIONS

In approaching a topic such as *The Early Episcopal Career of Athanasius of Alexandria,* AD 328-AD 335, two disciplines are involved— history and theology. Both disciplines are not, of course, mutually exclusive, and each informs the other. This is true especially with regard to the character and career of Athanasius, for his entire life was shaped by the historical and theological forces of the first three-quarters of the fourth century. During the first seven years of his episcopate these forces combined to bring forward a new understanding of imperial jurisdiction as it related to ecclesiastical assemblies and judgments. This combination has often obscured the theological issues and the historical sequence of events which led to Athanasius's first exile in AD 335. Moreover, Athanasius himself was a driving force in the theological controversies of his age, and it is in his writings that one can find many of the source materials which were later employed by fifth-century church historians such as Sozomen and Socrates. The line which divides historical integrity and theological polemic in the writings of the bishop of Alexandria is very thin indeed. It is for this reason that the thoughtful observer must turn to corroborative materials in any attempt to reconstruct the theological and historical ethos of the early episcopate of Athanasius.

We must also, however, take note in the historico-apologetic works of Athanasius of the subjective elements which many readers have found and compare them with similar subjective elements which may be found in the other writings which report the events under discussion.[1] This is especially

---

[1]The question of subjectivity in the historical writings of Athanasius has been a major point of contention for modern scholars who have sought to extract a "pure" historical narrative out of the mass of material which came from the pen of the bishop of Alexandria. It is important to note at this point that the writings of Athanasius were composed in response to the particular theological and ecclesiastical controversies in which he was personally involved. Many of the

true when we endeavor to understand and disentangle the complex sequence of events which led from Athanasius's consecration as bishop of Alexandria in AD 328 to his banishment by the emperor Constantine in AD 335. Such a process is made even more difficult because certain theologians and historians of more recent times have questioned the veracity of Athanasius's writings, basing their skepticism upon what they perceive as an unjustifiably large measure of blatant literary self-interest on the part of the bishop of Alexandria.[2] Whether, in fact, this perception is correct must be examined on the basis of the documentary evidence available to us. In the course of such an examination, however, care must be taken not to impose upon fourth-century personalities either our own presuppositions or the ethical standards current in our own time. In order truly to understand Athanasius, we must allow him to speak from his own age and situation. In that many modern writers have placed their own presuppositions upon the bishop of Alexandria, especially in regard to the early years of his episcopate, a certain amount of contemporary historiography must also be undertaken to discover how such views have developed in recent times.

In asserting this contextual view of Athanasius and the early years of his episcopate, it is of the utmost importance for any serious study to evaluate, insofar as is possible, all of the varied elements which made up and influenced the theological outlook and ecclesiastical activities of this particularly controversial bishop. One must, therefore, consider the character of the man, both as a churchman and as a writer. Furthermore, one must critically evaluate the image of Athanasius which has been created by current scholarship. Only then can one proceed to examine that tangled web of events which set the banished bishop of Alexandria upon his journey to Trier in the early winter of AD 335.

---

historical narratives and records which he provides, therefore, are summoned by Athanasius as evidence for a particular point of view or partisan position. It is to this extent that we must allow that the historical writings of Athanasius do contain a decidedly partial or subjective viewpoint.

[2]Cf. O. Seeck, "Untersuchungen zur Geschichte des nicäanischen Konzils," ZKG 17 (1896): 1-71, 319-362; see also E. Caspar, Geschichte des Papsttums von den Anfängen bis zur Höhe der Weltherrschaft I, Tübingen, 1930, 186-187.

2. INTERPRETERS OF ATHANASIUS

2.1 The Modern Critics

In the last one hundred years the character and, therefore, the reliability of Athanasius as a witness and recorder of the theological disputes and ecclesiastical events of the fourth century have come under considerable scrutiny and, often, a high degree of criticism. In the course of these critiques a number of charges of misconduct or blatant self-interest have been made against the bishop of Alexandria. We wish to examine here those charges which are of special importance to our study.

The accusations may be listed under three general categories:

1. the deliberate forging of documents, which Athanasius later included in his historical records as genuine;

2. the strong possibility that the consecration of Athanasius as bishop of Alexandria was irregular, if not invalid; and

3. the use of intentional and often brutal violence by Athanasius in the suppression of the Meletian schism in Egypt.

Of these charges, which are very much interrelated, the last two deal directly with Athanasius's ecclesiology and specifically with his view of synods and canon law. The first charge of forgery, however, is also important because the writings of Athanasius provide us with a large portion of the primary source materials used in the investigation of fourth-century church controversies.

This charge of forgery, however, first made by Otto Seeck in 1896,[3] is no longer considered credible, having been well refuted by scholars such as S. Rogala, N. H. Baynes, and R. Seiler.[4] It now seems to be generally recognized that many of Seeck's charges arose out of his own basic, and often antagonistic, attitude toward what he perceived as the political expediency of the church. In the mind of Seeck, the church often sacrificed the pursuit of truth to the end of political conciliation or advantage.[5] It is interesting to note that although Seeck's charges of forgery have now been set aside, his

---

[3]O. Seeck, *loc. cit.* Prior to making these charges, Seeck had been involved in research on the *Dossier* of Optatus with reference to the Council of Arles, AD 314, in which he found a number of what he considered to be forged documents which had been attributed to Constantine. Following this investigation Seeck turned his attention to the materials which surrounded the Council of Nicaea and then leveled his charges of forgery against Athanasius. Again, the charges of forgery were concerned with letters which were purported to have come from the hand of Constantine.

[4]Cf. S. Rogala, *Die Anfänge des arianischen Streits,* Forschungen zur christlichen Literatur und Dogmengeschichte, vol. 7, 1, Paderborn, 1907; N.H. Baynes, "Athanasiana," *JEA* 2 (1925): 61-65; R. Seiler, *Athanasius' Apologia contra Arianos: Ihre Entstehung und Datierung* (Diss., Tübingen), Düsseldorf, 1932, 39-40.

[5]O. Seeck, *Geschichte des Untergangs der antiken Welt* III, Stuttgart, 1920-1923, 208ff. and 442; *cf.* O. Seeck, "Untersuchungen," 33-34.

basic antagonism toward Athanasius was subsequently taken up by a number of other prominent scholars who succeeded him. Not the least among these was Eduard Schwartz.

The contribution of Schwartz to modern Athanasian studies has been enormous. Trained as a classical philologist, the "papers contributed by Eduard Schwartz to the *Nachrichten* of the Göttingen Academy between 1904 and 1911 are admitted on all sides to mark the beginning of a new era" in Athanasian studies.[6] It is important to note, however, that Schwartz, by his editors' admission, approached Athanasius with "undisguised dislike" and distaste.[7] The editors of Schwartz's *Gesammelte Schriften* sought to soften this position slightly by indicating that Schwartz's attacks were directed more against the halo or aureole of holiness surrounding Athanasius's image than against his personal greatness.[8] Nevertheless, it must be admitted that Schwartz's depiction of Athanasius is that of an unscrupulous and power-hungry oriental prelate, motivated by "der Wille zur Macht," who would make use of any means to insure his domination of the church in Egypt and, if possible, the domination of the other ancient sees as well.[9] The attitude of Schwartz concerning Athanasius has been summarized well by Norman H. Baynes: "To Schwartz Athanasius was always and in all circumstances the unbending hierarch; ambition, a ruthless will, and a passion for power are his constant characteristics."[10]

Schwartz, therefore, although not inclined to accept the charges of forgery made against Athanasius, did, for instance, dismiss the whole of Athanasius's historical and apologetical works as "mere propaganda."[11] This negative view of these works has subsequently been taken up by scholars such as E. Caspar, K.M. Setton, and, most importantly, by Hans-Georg Opitz, a student of Schwartz, who has provided us with the critical edition of most of Athanasius's historico-apologetical writings.[12]

Lecturing in 1944, F.L. Cross spoke of the contribution of Opitz to Athanasian studies: "Arising out of the discussions which Schwartz stimulated, and perhaps hardly second in influence, has been the new edition of Athanasius entrusted by the Prussian Academy to Dr. Opitz and the re-

---

[6]F.L. Cross, *The Study of Athanasius*, Oxford, 1945, 10.

[7]E. Schwartz, *Zur Geschichte des Athanasius, GS* III, Berlin, 1959, vi; *cf.* 209.

[8]W. Eltester and H.D. Altendorf, in their preface to the *Gesammelte Schriften* of Schwartz, *op. cit.,* vi.

[9]Schwartz, *op. cit.,* 192.

[10]N. H. Baynes, *Byzantine Studies and Other Essays*, London, 1955, 367.

[11]Schwartz, *GS* III, 188.

[12]For the views of Caspar and Setton, see E. Caspar, *Geschichte des Papsttums* I, 182; and K.M. Setton, *Christian Attitude toward the Emperor in the Fourth Century, Especially as Shown in Addresses to the Emperor*, New York, 1941 (reprint, New York, 1967), 78.

searches to which it has given rise."[13] Even the events of the Second World War and the hostile state of relations between Great Britain and Germany could not prevent Professor Cross from paying "tribute to the highly rewarding labour which Dr. Opitz has expended upon" the critical edition, not to mention "the indebtedness in which all future students of the text will stand to his comprehensive survey of the manuscript evidence."[14] It is important to note, however, that the attitude of Opitz concerning the personality, reliability, and basic driving force of Athanasius differed very little from that of Seeck and Schwartz. According to Opitz, Athanasius was "through and through a power-hungry personality."[15]

Although Opitz's successor in the editing of the critical edition, W. Schneemelcher, has deviated from the approach of his mentor in many areas, he has nonetheless accepted and continued to expound the harsh judgment of Athanasius promoted by the predominantly German critical school. Schneemelcher also sees the bishop of Alexandria as one primarily involved in a struggle for ecclesiastical and political power. Schneemelcher states "that the documents, even the apologetic works, plainly present a picture of the driven nature of Athanasius, of his continual intrigues and his striving for power."[16] One must admit, however, that Schneemelcher gives Athanasius the "benefit of the doubt" by ascribing his motivation not simply to blatant self-interest alone but also to a basic misunderstanding on the part of the bishop concerning the true nature of the church. According to Schneemelcher, Athanasius erred by setting aside the "Pauline concept" of a community of faith in favor of a view which saw the church as "a refuge" or sanctuary "in which salvation is supervised, and is no longer the community of the justified, the Body of Christ raised up by the Spirit."[17]

The assumptions of Schwartz, Opitz, and Schneemelcher concerning the ruthlessness of Athanasius's character and his willingness to misrepresent persons and events have largely echoed those of Seeck and have continued to exert a strong influence on current Athanasian studies. This is despite the fact that the so-called forgeries of Seeck have long since been recognized as genuine[18] and that Schwartz himself has since been proved to have been in error on "several important points."[19] These charges of propagandizing, holding power at any cost, deception, and ruthlessness have, however, contributed and lent credence to very particular accusations of Athanasius in other areas.

---

[13]Cross, *The Study of Athanasius*, 10.

[14]*Ibid.*

[15]Opitz, 138-139, fn. 30f.

[16]W. Schneemelcher, "Athanasius von Alexandrien als Theologe und als Kirchenpolitiker," *ZNW* 43 (1950/51): 251.

[17]Schneemelcher, *op. cit.*, 253.

[18]*Cf.* fn. 4.

[19]Cross, *loc. cit.*

Before moving on to such specific accusations, however, it might be helpful to review the assessments of Athanasius's character and reliability which were made by certain nineteenth-century theologians who wrote previous to the assertions of Seeck and the more recent critical school of thought. There is a marked contrast.

2.2 Nineteenth-century Comparisons

Writing in 1844, J.A. Moehler, the German Roman Catholic biographer of Athanasius, could speak in glowing hagiographical terms of the bishop as "an ascetic during the time of his youth,"[20] accepting as historically factual Athanasius's own testimony of an early friendship with Antony. Beyond this, Moehler, in marked contrast to later German scholarship, saw ardent loyalty and open compassion as the keystones of the character of Athanasius. Far from painting a picture of a ruthless, deceiving, or power-hungry prelate, Moehler states that

> all those who had the occasion to know Athanasius well loved him, and those to whom he was pastor had a touching attachment to him. He knew how to recognize the worth of others, and he highly proclaimed that worth. He showed much indulgence for human weakness, even in the case of that weakness exercising an influence on faith; he preferred to highlight the truth which had been mixed in with falsehood, and he knew very well how to discover true interior faith contained within an exterior of error. When he had completely understood a person's character and recognized that the person was inwardly sound, he defended that person against all slander. Each time that he was forced to write against men to whom he was loyal, he fought their false principles, but refused to give their names.[21]

Having given this assessment of Athanasius's perceptiveness and collegial character, Moehler goes on to write that Athanasius was "not a man who confused dead formulas with living faith."[22]

According to Moehler, Athanasius's anger was reserved primarily for those "within the church who had become infected by decay and who served the church with malevolent purposes." Further, he was "an angry saint toward those who were the enemies of souls, bought by the blood of Jesus Christ."[23] Concerning the accusations made against Athanasius at Tyre in

---

[20]J.A. Moehler, *Athanase le Grand et l'eglise de son temps en lutte avec l'arianisme* (trans. by Zickwolff and Jean Cohen), Paris, 1849, I, 108.

[21]*Ibid.*

[22]*Ibid.*

[23]Moehler, *op. cit.*, I, 109.

AD 335, Moehler merely states that in all the confused and sordid affairs of the synod, Athanasius was the real victim.[24]

Moehler was joined in this positive appraisal of Athanasius by John Henry Cardinal Newman. F.L. Cross commented that "there was perhaps no one in any country who, in the first half of the nineteenth century, had a greater knowledge of Athanasius than Newman."[25] Newman, in fact, freely admitted that his own religious pilgrimage both started and finished with study of Athanasius.[26]

To Newman, the bishop of Alexandria is "the great theologian,"[27] "the courageous heart,"[28] and "the champion of truth."[29] He is "the royal hearted Athanase / with Paul's own mantle blessed."[30] In Newman's writings Athanasius is the church Catholic's exemplar *par excellence*. Describing the bishop's talent as a writer, Newman states that Athanasius is "simple in diction, clear, unstudied, direct, vigorous, elastic, and above all, filled with character."[31] As a theologian, the bishop of Alexandria is commended for being rooted firmly in both Scripture and Christian tradition.[32] According to Newman, Athanasius is the universal Christian, for when the persecuted bishop is "driven from his Church," he "makes all Christendom his home, from Trèves to Ethiopia."[33] Extravagant in its praise of Athanasius, perhaps Newman's early verse in honor of the bishop of Alexandria from the *Lyra Apostolica* best sums up the impressions of a young and somewhat infatuated Oxford don:

> When shall our northern Church her champion see,
> > raised by divine decree,
> to shield the ancient Truth at his own harm?. . .
> > like him who stayed the arm,

---

[24]Moehler, *op. cit.*, II, 12-17.

[25]Cross, *loc. cit.*; Also see an extended essay on this subject by G. D. Dragas, "Conscience and Tradition: Newman and Athanasius in the Orthodox Church," *Internationale Cardinal Newman Studien*, elfte folge, Nürnberg, 1980 (reprinted in *Athanasiana, Essays in the Theology of St. Athanasius*, London, 1980, 175-186).

[26]Cf. preface to *Select Treatises of St. Athanasius in Controversy with the Arians*, London, 1881, I, viii.

[27]*Select Treatises* II, vi.

[28]*Catholic Sermons of Cardinal Newman*, London, 1957, 121.

[29]J.H. Newman, *Apologia Pro Vita Sua: Being a History of His Religious Opinions*, London, 1890, 26.

[30]J.H. Newman, *Lyra Apostolica* (14th edition), London, 1867, 117.

[31]*Select Treatises, loc. cit.*

[32]*Select Treatises* II, 250.

[33]J.H. Newman, *An Essay on the Development of Christian Doctrine*, London, 1974, 290.

of tyrannous power, and learning's sophist-tone,
  keen-visioned Seer, alone.

The many crouched before an idol-priest,
  Lord of the world's rank feast.
In the dark night, mid the saint's trial sore,
  He stood, then bowed before,
the Holy Mysteries,—he their meetest sign,
  weak vessel, yet divine![34]

A close contemporary of Newman, John Mason Neale, hymnodist and poet, is of primary importance in the present context for his minutely documented history of the patriarchates of the Eastern church which, tragically, was left uncompleted at his death. In writing his chronicle of the patriarchate of Alexandria, Neale took account of, and had access to, most of the standard fourth- and fifth-century church historians (including the synopsis of Philostorgius) as well as the major Coptic and Syriac histories.[35] In fact, Neale was able to make use of almost all the sources available to the modern church historian apart from the more recent critical editions (excepting H.I. Bell's *London Papyri 1913-1914,* which was unavailable until the 1920s). As a result of working with such materials, Neale finds the various ancient and the emerging modern accusations against Athanasius to be without foundation in the available evidence. Instead, Athanasius is pictured as a "holy confessor,"[36] who has "justly" claimed "the most illustrious place among the Confessors, and" is "known in his Church by the title of the Apostolic Patriarch."[37] As regards to any negative critique of the bishop of Alexandria, Neale is only willing to state in his chronicle of events that we "may suspect that Athanasius was not a man of much physical courage." According to Neale, however, this should only lead us "to admire the grace which enabled him to give so long and so arduous a proof of moral constancy."[38]

Almost a generation later, Henry Melvill Gwatkin wrote what was to become the standard text for many years concerning the Arian controversy. Although it is not without its critics, as in the recent work of Gregg and Groh,[39] *Studies of Arianism,* first published in 1882 (with a second revised

---

[34]J.H. Newman, *Lyra Apostolica,* 121.

[35]J.M. Neale, *A History of the Holy Eastern Church: The Patriarchate of Alexandria,* London, 1847, I, vi-xiii. That Neale does, in fact, take account of the Photian *Epitome* of Philostorgius can be seen in a number of references, such as those found on 128, 145, 192.

[36]Neale, *op. cit.,* 200.

[37]*Ibid.*

[38]Neale, *op. cit.,* 186.

[39]A recent criticism of the work of Gwatkin (as well as criticisms of a number of other nineteenth- and twentieth-century scholars) can be found in the

edition in 1900), still remains a highly respected volume of late nineteenth-century critical research into the events of the fourth century. Gwatkin, as can be seen by consulting the preface of the second edition, took into account what must be considered as the best research of his day. Unlike Moehler, Gwatkin is unable to regard Athanasius "as a genuine ascetic."[40] But when it comes to an assessment of the overall character and reliability of the bishop of Alexandria, Gwatkin, on the basis of his evaluation of the sources,[41] arrives at the following conclusion:

> Athanasius was before all things a man whose whole life was con-secrated to a single purpose. If it was spent in controversy, he was no mere controversialist. And if he listened too easily to the stories told him of the Arian misdeeds, his language is at worst excused by their atrocious treachery. As for the charge of persecution, we must in fairness set against the Meletians who speak through Epiphanius the explicit denial of the Egyptian bishops. And if we take into account his own pleas for toleration and the comprehensive charity of his *de Synodis* and of the council of Alexandria, we must pronounce the charge unproved. If we could forget the violence of his friends at Tyre, we might say more.[42]

When considering the many contemporary accusations against Athanasius, Gwatkin simply states that "the pertinacious hatred of a few was balanced by the enthusiastic admiration of many."[43]

---

monograph by R.C. Gregg and D.E. Groh, *Early Arianism—A View of Salvation,* London and Philadelphia, 1981. Gregg and Groh speak of "the need to penetrate the mist of battle between orthodoxy and heresy to uncover the scriptural hermeneutic of each party before making judgements" (8). The authors contend that this is a difficult process because "the mass of literature on Arianism" is "weighted against precisely such a venture" (8). It is in this "mass of literature" that Gregg and Groh place H.M. Gwatkin, along with J.H. Newman, J.N.D. Kelly, etc., as part of a "mistaken consensus of scholarship" (33, fn. 38). Notwithstanding such criticisms, in a recent bibliographic survey of English language books on the Arian controversy, Frances Young places Gwatkin's *Studies of Arianism* alongside *Early Arianism* as the only two entries in the category (*cf.* F.M. Young, *From Nicaea to Chalcedon,* London, 1983, 339). Admittedly, Gwatkin's chronology, as well as certain conclusions, stand in dire need of revision, some of which has been provided in R.P.C. Hanson's *The Search for the Christian Doctrine of God,* Edinburgh, 1988.

[40]H.M. Gwatkin, *Studies of Arianism* (second edition), London, 1900, 72, fn. 1.

[41]For a listing of Gwatkin's primary and secondary sources, *cf.* Gwatkin, *op. cit.,* xii-xvi.

[42]Gwatkin, *op. cit.,* 74.

[43]Gwatkin, *op. cit.,* 75.

Yet another late nineteenth-century estimate of the character of Athanasius was made by Archibald Robertson, bishop of Exeter and former master of Hatfield College, Durham, in the introduction to the writings of the bishop of Alexandria for the *Select Library of Nicene and Post-Nicene Fathers of the Christian Church.* First published in 1891, Robertson's comments stand in complete contradiction to those of Seeck published some five years later.[44] According to Robertson, Athanasius

> had the not too common gift of seeing the proportions of things. A great crisis was fully appreciated by him; he always saw at once where principles separated or united men, where the bond or the divergence was merely accidental. With Arius and Arianism no compromise was to be thought of; but he did not fail to distinguish men really at one with him on essentials, even where their conduct toward himself had been indefensible. So long as the cause was advanced, personal questions were insignificant. So far Athanasius was a partisan. It may be admitted that he saw little good in his opponents; but unless the evidence is singularly misleading there was little good to see. The leaders of the Arian interest were unscrupulous men, either bitter and unreasoning fanatics like Secundus and Maris, or more often political theologians, like Eusebius of Nicomedia, Valens, Acacius, who lacked religious earnestness. It may be admitted that he refused to admit error in his friends. His long alliance with Marcellus, his unvarying refusal to utter a syllable of condemnation of him by name; his refusal to name even Photinus, while yet exposing the error associated with his name; his suppression of the name of Apollinarius, even when writing directly against him; all this was inconsistent with strict impartiality, and, no doubt, placed his adversaries partly in the right. But it was the partiality of a generous and loyal spirit, and he could be generous to personal enemies if he saw in them an approximation to himself in principle.
>
> The Arian controversy was to [Athanasius] no battle for ecclesiastical power, nor for theological triumph. It was a religious crisis involving the reality of revelation and redemption.[45]

Further, Robertson argues that "in the whole of our minute knowledge of his life," Athanasius, far from seeking the establishment of his own power in the church, showed "a total lack of self-interest. The glory of God and the welfare of the Church absorbed him fully at all times."[46] The portrait of

---

[44]*Cf.* fn. 2, O. Seeck.

[45]A. Robertson, prolegomena to his edition of *Select Writings of Athanasius, Bishop of Alexandria,* LNPF, second series, vol. 4, 1891, lxvii.

[46]*Ibid.* This is a remarkable description by Robertson, especially when it is compared to the characterization provided by J. Ceska in "Die politischen Hintergründe der Homoousioslehre des Athanasius," *Die Kirche angesichts der*

Athanasius painted by Robertson bears little, if any, resemblance to that of his contemporary Seeck, although, again, both were making use of the same sources.[47]

Similar views concerning the character of Athanasius and a dismissal of the many accusations made against him can be found in the writings of any number of other nineteenth-century Athanasian scholars. One would only have to consult, in addition to those sources named above, the works of Neander, Kaye, Dorner, or Bright.[48] Or again, a similar outlook can also be found in the biographical studies of Fialon, Reynolds, Bush, or the extensive monographs on the life of Athanasius by Stanley in the mid-nineteenth century or Farrar at the end of the century.[49] In the last decade of the nineteenth century even Harnack pays tribute to Athanasius by comparing him to the "hero" of the Reformation, Martin Luther, stating that "Athanasius joined hands with Luther across the centuries."[50] Moreover, an amazing turn of argument is suggested in Harnack's *Lehrbuch der Dogmengeschichte* in which he indicates that Athanasius was far from being a political opportunist; it was solely due to the bishop's integrity that the church was saved from the snares of political power and became once again an "institute of salvation, with the preaching of Christ as its primary pur-

---

konstantinischen Wende (ed. by G. Ruhbach), Darmstadt, 1976, 307-308, in which Athanasius is described as always placing personal advantage over the doctrinal and ecclesiastical issues of his time.

[47]For an abbreviated list of Robertson's sources, see Robertson, *op. cit.*, xi-xiii. Again, it is important to note that neither Robertson nor Seeck had access to H.I. Bell's London Papyrus 1914. One must, therefore, assume a certain degree of subjectivity on the part of both writers for them to have arrived at such varying conclusions concerning the character of Athanasius.

[48]*Cf.* A. Neander, *General History of the Christian Religion and Church* (trans. by J. Torrey), Edinburgh, 1859, vol. 2, 50ff; J. Kaye, *Works of John Kaye*, London, 1876, 73ff; I.A. Dorner, *History of the Development of the Doctrine of the Person of Christ* (trans. by P. Simon), Edinburgh, 1897, vol. 2, 1, 292-306, 339-346, 350-351; and three particular pieces written by W. Bright, "Athanasius," *Dictionary of Christian Biography*, London, 1877, vol. 1, 179-203; his introduction to *St. Athanasius' Orations against the Arians*, Oxford, 1884, i-ci; and *Lessons from the Lives of Three Great Fathers*, London, 1891, 1-47.

[49]*Cf.* F. Fialon, *Saint Athanase*, Paris, 1877, 104-110; H.R. Reynolds, *Athanasius: His Life and Work*, London, 1889, 39-52, 180-188; R.W. Bush, *St. Athanasius: His Life and Times*, The Fathers for English Readers, London, 1888, 89-108, 215-226; A.P. Stanley, *Lectures on the History of the Eastern Church*, London, 1861, 263-301; and F.W. Farrar, *Lives of the Fathers, Sketches of Church History in Biography*, Edinburgh, 1889, vol. I, 445-571.

[50]A. Harnack, *Lehrbuch der Dogmengeschichte*, Freiburg, 1890-94, vol. 3, 814.

pose."[51] Similar positive assessments of Athanasius were carried into the early part of the twentieth century in the biographical studies by Lauchert and Bardy.[52]

Robertson's final comments on the character of Athanasius admirably sum up the attitude of the majority of scholars previous to the emergence of the critical tradition which followed Seeck, and Bell's publication of the London Papyrus 1914 in 1924. Robertson says of the character of Athanasius that it

> has won the respect and admiration even of those who do not feel that they owe to him the vindication of all that is sacred and precious. Not only a Gregory or an Epiphanius, an Augustine or a Cyril, a Luther or a Hooker, not only Montfaucon and Tillemont, Newman and Stanley pay tribute to him as a Christian hero. Secular as well as Church historians fall under the spell of his personality, and even Gibbon lays aside his "solemn sneer" to do homage to Athanasius the Great.[53]

At this point, one may wonder what has caused, or actually stands behind, the change in attitude which has taken place as regards the character of Athanasius in the twentieth century. A simple explanation might be that just as the nineteenth-century writers were captive to the somewhat romantic religious and literary tone of their day, those who have followed Seeck have been captive to the equally transitory critical spirit of theirs. Although this would explain the motivations behind the two sets of writers, it does not fully take into account the emergence of new historical sources and/or new methods used in the interpretation of such extant or standard materials.

Interpretations, however, by their very nature tend to be subjective rather than objective in their attempted perceptions. In the case of Athanasius, this has resulted in two assessments/interpretations which now stand side by side. One is the standard history of Athanasius which views him, in the main, as a hagiographical figure. The other is an almost hypercritical view of Athanasius which tends to deprecate both his character and contribution. Both, however, claim certain source materials as evidence for their respective positions.

2.3 Current Views

In the last two decades these two opposing views of the character and reliability of Athanasius have been joined by a third, and somewhat more central, stream of thought. Scholars such as Leslie W. Barnard, Frances Young, and G. Christopher Stead have come to a renewed appreciation of

---

[51]A. Harnack, *Lehrbuch der Dogmengeschichte*, Freiburg, 1900-10, vol. 2, 224.

[52]*Cf.* F. Lauchert, *Leben des heiligen Athanasius des Grossen*, Cologne, 1911, 25-134; and G. Bardy, *Saint Athanase*, Paris, 1925, 22-50, 202-207.

[53]A. Robertson, *op. cit.*, lxviii.

Athanasius in spite of what they see as his many faults and foibles as a theologian, bishop, and historian.[54] Another example of this centrist school of
Athanasian studies is the German scholar Martin Tetz. In his recent "Zur
Biographie des Athanasius von Alexandrien,"[55] Tetz calls for a rather radical
revision of the critical view of Athanasius which has been built up over the
last century. He concludes that Athanasius was more deeply concerned with
the *imitatio sanctorum* than many modern scholars have cared to admit, and
that Scripture, not personal or political intrigues, must be seen as the one
overall normative factor in Athanasius's career.[56]

Even more conservative rehabilitations of Athanasius's career and
writings have been taken up by others. In 1962 the American theologian
Jaroslav Pelikan wrote of "the great moral character of Athanasius" in his
monograph *The Light of the World* and stated that from the available evidence "even historians and theologians unsympathetic to orthodox beliefs are
really obliged to concede the same."[57] Pelikan has been joined in this very
positive assessment of Athanasius by a number of historians and theologians, among whom one could cite G. Florovsky, T. Torrance, G.D. Dragas,
E.D. Moutsoulas, V. Twomey, and R. Person.[58]

---

[54]*Cf.* L.W. Barnard, "Some Notes on the Meletian Schism in Egypt," *Studia
Patristica XII* (TU 115), Berlin, 1975, 399-405; "Athanasius and the Roman
State," *Latomus* 36 (1977): 422-437, see especially the comment of Barnard on
Athanasius's contribution, 437; "Athanasius and the Meletian Schism in Egypt,"
JEA 59 (1975): 183-189; and "Two Notes on Athanasius. 1. Athanasius'
Election as Archbishop of Alexandria. 2. The Circumstances Surrounding the
Encylical Letter of the Egyptian Bishops (*Apologia contra Arianos* 3, 1-19, 5),"
OrChrP 41 (1975): 344-356. Also *cf.* F. Young, *op. cit.*, 65-68, and especially
her concluding evaluation of Athanasius, 82-83; and *cf.* G. Christopher Stead,
"Atanasio," *Dizionario patristico e di antichità cristiane* (ed. A. Di Berardino), I
(1983): 423-432; "The Thalia of Arius and the Testimony of Athanasius," *JThS*,
NS 29 (1978): 20-52, see especially his remarks on Athanasius, 38; *cf.* Stead's
critique of Athanasius's method of argumentation in "Rhetorical Method in
Athanasius," *VC* 30 (1976): 121-137; "Freedom of the Will and the Arian
Controversy," *Platonismus und Christentum (Festschrift für Heinrich Dörrie)*,
Münster, 1983, 245-257, see especially Stead's comments on Athanasius's
polemical writing, 254 ff.

[55]*ZKG* 90 (1979): 304-338.

[56]*Op cit.*, 337, 338; also *cf.* "Über nikäische Orthodoxie: Der sog. Tomus
ad Antiochenos des Athanasios von Alexandrien," *ZNW* 66 (1975): 194-222;
"Athanasius von Alexandrien," *Theologische Realenzyklopädie*, Berlin (1977):
II, 333-349; and "Athanasius und die Einheit der Kirche. Zur ökumenischen
Bedeutung eines Kirchenvaters," *ZThK* 81 (1984): Heft 2, 196-219.

[57]J. Pelikan, *The Light of the World: A Basic Image in Early Christian
Thought*, New York, 1962, 77.

[58]*Cf., e.g.*, G. Florovsky, *Bible, Church, Tradition: An Eastern Orthodox
View*, New York, 1968, 80-83; *The Eastern Fathers of the Fourth Century*, Paris,
1931; "The Concept of Creation in Saint Athanasius," *Studia Patristica VI* (TU

One must admit, however, that the critical tradition which started in Athanasian studies with Otto Seeck is still very much an active force, albeit with varying degrees of severity. Timothy Barnes, for example, accepts without question the view of Athanasius as "violent" to the extent of portraying the bishop as "a gangster."[59] While maintaining an otherwise high regard for the bishop of Alexandria and following the literary tradition of Bardy and Duchesne, Charles Kannengiesser has, nonetheless, recently called into question the Athanasian authorship of *Contra Arianos* III.[60] William Rusch has cited the somewhat suspect historical narratives of Philostorgius as preferable to parallel historical accounts in Athanasius;[61] K.M. Girardet has expressed his suspicion concerning the so-called one-sided orthodox materials of the fourth century;[62] Jean-Marie Leroux has cast doubts upon the actual influence of Athanasius within the Eastern churches during his lifetime;[63]

---

115) (1962): 36-57; T. F. Torrance, "Athanasius: A Study in the Foundations of Classical Theology," *Theology in Reconciliation*, London and Grand Rapids, 1975, 215-266; "Spiritus Creator: A Consideration of the Teaching of St. Athanasius and St. Basil," *Theology in Reconstruction*, London, 1965, 209-228; "The Hermeneutics of St. Athanasius,"*Ἐκκλησιαστικὸς φάρος* 52 (1970): no. 1-4, 446-468, 89-106, 237-249, vol. 53 (1971): no. 1, 133-149; G.D. Dragas, "Holy Spirit and Tradition," *Sobornost*, NS 1 (1979): 51-72 (contained, along with several other essays, in G.D. Dragas, *Athanasiana: Essays in the Theology of St. Athanasius*, I, London, 1980); *St. Athanasius Contra Apollinarem, Church and Theology* VI, Athens, 1985, especially cf. 11; E.D. Moutsoulas, *'Ο Μέγας 'Αθανάσιος*, Athens, 1974; V. Twomey, *Apostolikos Thronos: The Primacy of Rome as Reflected in the Church History of Eusebius and the Historico-apologetic Writings of Saint Athanasius the Great*, Münsterische Beiträge zur Theologie 49, Münster, 1982, 231ff.; and R.E. Person, *The Mode of Theological Decision at the Early Councils*, Basle, 1978.

[59]T.D. Barnes, *Constantine and Eusebius*, London and Cambridge, Mass., 1981, 230.

[60]C. Kannengiesser, *Athanase d'Alexandrie évêque et écrivain*, Paris, 1983; "Athanasius of Alexandria—Three Orations against the Arians: A Reappraisal," *Studia Patristica* XVIII (1982): 981-995; also of importance and interest is Kannengiesser's recent review of Athanasian literature, "The Athanasian Decade 1974-84: A Bibliographical Report," *ThSt*, 46 (1985): 524-541. In this report Kannengiesser seems to show approval towards the efforts of M. Tetz in reexamining Athanasius's view of the episcopal office (527, 528) and W. Schneemelcher's more considered view of Athanasius's political and clerical ambitions (531, 532).

[61]W. G. Rusch, "A la recherche de l'Athanase historique," *Politique et théologie chez Athanase d'Alexandrie* (ed. C. Kannengiesser), Paris, 1974, 161-180.

[62]G. K. Girardet, *Kaisergericht und Bischofsgericht: Studien zu den Anfängen des Donatistenstreites (313-315) und zum Prozeß des Athanasius von Alexandrien (328-346)*, Bonn, 1975, 54.

[63]J.M. Leroux, "Athanase et la seconde phase de la crise arienne (345-373)," *Politique et théologie*, 145-156.

William Schneemelcher, although maintaining a cautious tone, continues to see political motivations and subsequent deceptions in many of the Athanasian writings;[64] and Annik Martin has reopened the issue of the Meletian schism and its possible strength and popularity as it affected Athanasius's authority (or lack of it) within the Egyptian church.[65]

Much more could be said concerning all of the above authors, and several others as well, but as there will be frequent references to such recent scholarship throughout this study, it is perhaps best to turn our attention to those issues and main areas of contention regarding the character of Athanasius which have received such renewed interest.

---

[64]W. Schneemelcher in his *Athanasius von Alexandrien als Theologe und als Kirchenpolitiker*, Gesammelte Aufsätze, Thessaloniki, 1974, has moved away from the position of Schwartz and is more willing to allow Athanasius to stand as a theological and ecclesiastical figure whose life was not *always* driven by ambitious motives. Schneemelcher does remain, however, in this author's opinion, a product of the critical school as compared with the other authors named above.

[65]A. Martin, "Athanase et les Méletiens (325-335)," *Politique et théologie*, 31-62.

3. ISSUES IN DISPUTE

3.1 An Identification of the Issues

A recent overview of the life and writings of Athanasius by Frances Young has outlined current attitudes towards the bishop of Alexandria and has indicated those materials which stand behind certain of the more negative assessments of his character. Young states that "there seems to have been a pitiless streak in" Athanasius's "character—that he resorted to violence to achieve his own ends is implied by a good deal of evidence."[66] It is further indicated that in his concern with the Meletian schism in Egypt, Athanasius "did not scruple to use force in his dealings with this group."[67] Finally, the assertion is made that Athanasius's "deposition at Tyre was based, not on doctrinal considerations, but upon his misconduct in Egypt. Rusch is certainly right in suggesting that the hostile reports of Philostorgius, the evidence of the papyri, and the criticisms that Gregory Nazianzen felt he had to answer in his panegyric, must be admitted in the search for the historical Athanasius."[68]

Young here refers to a recent study by William Rusch in which he examines materials which he thinks must be consulted in the construction of a true historical picture of Athanasius.[69] The three particular items which Rusch sees as being of importance, alongside the other narrative sources for such a history, are these:

1.   the reports of the fifth-century church historian Philostorgius, of which we possess only fragments incorporated in the ninth-century *Epitome* of Photius;[70]
2.   London Papyrus 1914, a fourth-century Egyptian letter which came to light in the early twentieth century and was edited, annotated, and published by H.I. Bell in 1924;[71]
3.   a festival oration of Gregory Nazianzen in which the life and theological activities of Athanasius are eulogized and defended.[72]

---

[66]F. Young, *op. cit.*, 67.

[67]*Ibid.*

[68]*Ibid.*

[69]W. Rusch, *op. cit.*, 161-177.

[70]The standard English translation of this text is by E. Walford, *The Ecclesiastical History of Philostorgius*, London, 1855, 425ff. The standard critical edition was prepared by J. Bidez, *Philostorgius Kirchengeschichte* (revised edition), Berlin, 1981.

[71]In H.I. Bell, *Jews and Christians in Egypt*, London, 1924, 53-71.

[72]Gregory Nazianzen, *Oration* 21, in LNPF, second series, vol. 7, Oxford, 1894, 269-280 (standard English translation). The Greek text is preserved in PG 35, col. 1081-1128 and a critical edition of the text in SC 270 (ed. J. Mossay), Paris, 1980, 86-193.

Together, these three sources are those which for the most part have contributed to recent critical revisionist accounts of the life and character of Athanasius. When linked to the often hostile opinions of the German critical school and the accusations initiated by Seeck, it is well within the realm of possibility to see the bishop of Alexandria as someone very different from the traditional hagiographical image of Athanasius the Great. If, however, such a radical reversal in opinion is to be truly warranted, a careful and un-prejudiced examination of each of these three sources must be made.

3.2 Philostorgius and the Consecration Controversy

It is claimed by Rusch that the *Ecclesiastical History* of Philostorgius, contained in the *Epitome* of Photius, ninth-century patriarch of Constantinople, has preserved a genuine historical tradition concerning Athanasius, albeit of a nonorthodox kind.[73] He has been joined in this assessment by F. Young and L.W. Barnard, with tacit agreement to this proposition indicated by W.H.C. Frend.[74] In fact, owing in part to the in-fluence of Seeck and Schwartz, many modern historians have tended to dis-trust the so-called orthodox sources for the history of this period. K.M. Girardet has characterized such orthodox sources as promoting a "one-sided pro-Athanasian" point of view.[75] This has resulted in nonorthodox sources receiving a greater deal of credence than they might possible deserve on the basis of both internal and external evidence. L.W. Barnard goes so far as to suggest that the tradition that Philostorgius was essentially an Arian apologist is incorrect, although the passages cited from the *Ecclesiastical History* by Barnard to prove this point seem, in this author's opinion, more likely to have been the interpolations of Photius.[76]

Philostorgius's history, written between AD 425 and AD 433, has long been recognized as "a late apology for the extreme Arianism of

---

[73]Rusch, *op. cit.*, 161, 162.

[74]*Cf.* F. Young, *loc. cit.*; L.W. Barnard, "Two Notes on Athanasius," *OrChrP* 41 (1975): 348, 349; and W.H.C. Frend, "Athanasius as an Egyptian Leader in the Fourth Century," *New College Bulletin* 8 (1974): 24. Frend has continued this tacit acceptance of Philostorgian accounts, although they are not credited as such, in his description of Athanasius's career in *The Rise of Christianity*, Philadelphia, 1984, 523ff.

[75]K.M. Girardet, *op. cit.*, 54.

[76]L.W. Barnard, *loc. cit.* The three examples given by Barnard to show that Philostorgius was not "an out and out Arian sympathizer" (Bk. 1,3; 1,9; 2,3) do appear, in this author's opinion, from a study of Bidez's text to be interpolations by Photius. In any case, one may, at the very least, assume along with F. Young that the chief purpose of Philostorgius in the *Ecclesiastical History* was the defense of Eunomius and that, therefore, the attacks of Philostorgius are directed towards "all who oppose Eunomius ... whether homoousian or homoiousian, (or) even Arians!" (F. Young, *op. cit.*, 30).

Eunomius."[77] Photius himself describes Philostorgius in the following terms:

> Read the so-called *Ecclesiastical History* by Philostorgius the Arian, the spirit of which is different from that of nearly all other ecclesiastical historians. He extols all Arians, but abuses and insults all the orthodox, so that this work is not so much a history as a panegyric of the heretics, and nothing but a barefaced attack upon the orthodox. His style is elegant, his diction often poetical, though not to such an extent as to be tedious or disagreeable. His figurative use of words is very expressive and makes the work both pleasant and agreeable to read; sometimes, however, these figures are overbold and far-fetched, and create an impression of being frigid and ill-timed. The language is variously embellished even to excess, so that the reader imperceptibly finds himself involved in a disagreeable obscurity. In many instances the author introduces appropriate moral reflections of his own. He starts from the devotion of Arius to the heresy and its first beginnings, and ends with the recall of the impious Aetius. This Aetius was removed from his office by his brother heretics, since he outdid them in wickedness, as Philostorgius himself unwillingly confesses. He was recalled and welcomed by the impious Julian. The history, in one volume and six books, goes down to this period. The author is a liar and the narrative often fictitious.[78]

Although Philostorgius may, in fact, have had access to some Arian sources now lost to us, it must be admitted that the fragments which remain are not only biased, but, in many places, patently inaccurate as well.[79] This is especially true of those portions in Philostorgius which concern Athanasius.

In the fragments of Philostorgius's *Ecclesiastical History* preserved by Photius in the *Epitome*, only two passages make direct reference to Athanasius.[80] The first of these passages claims to be an account of the consecration of Athanasius following the death of Alexander. The second passage recounts the events which led to the return of Athanasius to Alexandria following his first exile. Of these two portions of Philostorgius, the former passage has received the greater attention in the search for the historical Athanasius, for it calls into question the events which surrounded the elevation of Athanasius to the throne of St. Mark. It also calls into question

---

[77] J. Quasten, *Patrology,* Antwerp, 1975, III, 531.

[78] *Ibid.*

[79] J. Quasten *op. cit.,* III, 532, speaks of Philostorgius's "bias and inaccuracy." That Quasten appears to be correct in this assessment may be seen in the examples given in the text.

[80] *Cf.* fn. 70.

the veracity of Athanasius in his account of both his consecration and his later defense at Tyre in AD 335.[81]

Philostorgius's account of the events surrounding the consecration of Athanasius is epitomized by Photius as follows:

> The impious contriver of lies [*i.e.*, Philostorgius] asserts, that after the death of Alexander, bishop of Alexandria, the votes of the prelates were not unanimous, and that there was a diversity of sentiment, and after a considerable amount of time had been spent in altercation, the divine Athanasius (τὸν θεῖον 'Αθανάσιον) suddenly appeared one evening in the church called after Dionysius, and finding there two Egyptian bishops, firmly closed the doors with the assistance of some of his followers, and so was ordained (χειροτονίαν) by them, though strongly against the will of the ordainers. For a power from above fell upon them, and so constrained their will and powers that what Athanasius wished was done at once. Philostorgius adds, that the remainder of the bishops then present anathematized Athanasius on account of this transaction; and that the latter, having first thoroughly strengthened his cause, addressed to the emperor certain letters relating to his ordination, in the name of the entire state; and that the emperor, thinking that the letters in question were written by the assembly of the Alexandrians, ratified (κατοχὴν) the election with his approval. Afterwards, however, upon being informed of the details of the transaction, he sent Athanasius to Tyre, a city of Phoenicia, to give an account of the matter before a synod which was assembled there.[82]

According to Photius, Philostorgius goes on to describe the events which took place at the Synod of Tyre, where, again according to Philostorgius, Athanasius is said to have been accused of fraud, immorality, illegal ordination, and the oft-reported violence against the so-called Meletian priest Ischyras. Philostorgius goes on to assert that "Athanasius, who had hoped to escape trial altogether, went away after having been convicted of a double crime, not merely an illegal ordination (οὐκ εὐαγοῦ χειροτονίας), but also a foul calumny; and so, by the common consent of all, a sentence of deposition was passed against him."[83]

Philostorgius further states that for these reasons Athanasius was excommunicated by a second sitting of the synod and that it was at this time (*i.e.*, AD 335) that Gregory the Cappadocian was consecrated and sent to Alexandria to take Athanasius's place.[84] The latter event did not, in fact,

---

[81]*Cf. Apol.* 3-20.
[82]Philostorgius, *HE*, II, 11 (Bidez, *op. cit.*, 22-23).
[83]*Ibid.*
[84]*Ibid.*

take place until AD 341, and then it was at the behest of the Synod of Antioch.[85]

How then are we to evaluate the accusations of Philostorgius concerning the election and ordination of Athanasius? First, we must note that the account of Philostorgius was written, along with the other histories of Socrates and Sozomen, a full hundred years after the events under discussion and was based upon uncertain and, we may assume, biased Arian sources.[86] Second, we must acknowledge that the consecration account of Philostorgius is only one among many such Arian, Eusebian, and Meletian accounts which seem to have been widely circulated following the death of Athanasius and which called into question the validity of Athanasius's election and consecration as bishop of Alexandria. As we shall see, however, none of these nonorthodox accounts agree, either as concerning a general outline of events or in their specific details.

The church historian Socrates, using, it would appear, mainly Athanasian materials as his source,[87] writes in his *Ecclesiastical History* that a short time after their return from exile (*i.e.,* following Nicaea), the Eusebians

> objected to the ordination of Athanasius, partly as a person unworthy (ἀναξίου) of the prelacy, and partly because he had been elected by disqualified persons (μὴ ὡς ὑπὸ ἀξιοπίστων). But when Athanasius had shown himself superior to this calumny (for having assumed control [ἐγκρατὴς] of the church of Alexandria, he ardently contended for the Nicene Creed), then Eusebius exerted himself to the utmost insidiously to cause the removal of Athanasius and to bring Arius back to Alexandria.[88]

Yet another version of the election and ordination of Athanasius is found in Sozomen's *Ecclesiastical History*.[89] In his account of the events surrounding the elevation of Athanasius, Sozomen tells of how Athanasius sought to "avoid this honor by flight, but that he, although being unwilling, was afterwards constrained by Alexander to accept the bishopric."[90] After confirming the above statement with the testimony of one "Apollinarius the

---

[85]Sozomen, *HE*, III, 5; Socrates, *HE*, II, 10; Theodoret, *HE*, II, 3.

[86]*Cf.* Quasten, *op. cit.*, III, 531.

[87]Socrates most likely made use of the *Synodal Letter of the Egyptian Bishops of AD 338, cf. Apol.* 6, 5-6 (Opitz 90, 41-93, 14).

[88]Socrates *HE*, I, 23 (PG 67, 139, C9-141, 10); English trans., LNPF, second series, vol. 2, 26.

[89]Sozomen, *HE*, II, 17 (J. Bidez, SC 306, Paris, 1983, 296, 70-73); English trans., E. Walford, *op. cit.* (see fn. 70), 74, speaks of the vote "directed by Divine will" to Athanasius.

[90]*Ibid.*

Syrian," Sozomen provides us with an alternative Arian account of the election:

> The Arians assert that after the death of Alexander, the respective followers of that bishop and of Meletius held communion together, and fifty-four bishops from Thebes, and other parts of Egypt, assembled together, and agreed by oath to choose by a common vote, the man who could advantageously administer the Church of Alexandria; but that seven of the bishops, in violation of their oath, and contrary to the opinion of all, secretly ordained Athanasius; and that on this account many of the people and many of the Egyptian clergy seceded from communion with him.[91]

Sozomen, however, seems to dismiss the validity of this Arian account. He states: "For my part, I am convinced that it was by Divine appointment (οὐκ ἀθεεὶ παρελθεῖν) that Athanasius succeeded to the high-priesthood (ἀρχιερωσύνην)"[92] and proceeds to extol the virtues of Athanasius. Sozomen ends his narrative of events by relating the apocryphal[93] story of Athanasius's "boy baptism," his subsequent service in the household of Bishop Alexander, and his friendship with St. Antony.[94]

Two further accounts of the election of Athanasius as bishop of Alexandria are provided by Epiphanius of Salamis in the *Panarion*.[95] Most likely completed in AD 377,[96] the *Panarion* gives two somewhat conflicting narratives concerning the elevation of Athanasius to the throne of St. Mark. The first of these is related in a discussion of the Meletian schism in Egypt and is concerned with what appears to have been an attempted Meletian usurpation of the see of Alexandria at the time of Alexander's death. The passage states that

> Alexander of Alexandria drew near to death soon after the synod which had taken place in Nicaea. But Athanasius was not present at the death of Alexander, for at that time he was Alexander's deacon and had been sent to a meeting (κομητάτον). Alexander had ordered that no one should be appointed to succeed him but Athanasius alone; to this arrangement Alexander, many clergy, and the whole church had borne witness. Taking this opportunity [*i.e.*, of Alexander's death], however, the Meletians installed a bishop of Egypt, owing to there now being

---

[91]Walford, *op. cit.*, 75.

[92]*Ibid.* (Bidez, *op. cit.*, 298, 73-74).

[93]Walford, *op. cit.*, 75, 76; *cf.* Rufinus, *HE*, I, 14; and Socrates, *HE*, I, 15.

[94]Walford, *loc. cit.*

[95]For the critical text, *cf.* K. Holl, *Epiphanius, Panarion Haer.* 65-80, GCS, Leipzig, 1933. The English translations are my own.

[96]Quasten, *op. cit.*, III, 388.

no bishop of Alexandria (because Alexandria never had two bishops as other cities have); they, therefore, instead of obeying the will of Alexander, installed a bishop of Egypt named Theonas, who after being in office three months died. Athanasius then returned, not long after the death of Theonas, and from all the region round about a synod of the orthodox gathered which installed him [Athanasius] and gave him the throne as the one worthy ($\tau\hat{\omega}$ $\dot{\alpha}\xi\dot{\iota}\omega$), who had already been prepared by God's will ($\tau\dot{\eta}\nu$ $\theta\epsilon o\hat{\upsilon}$ $\beta o\dot{\upsilon}\lambda\eta\sigma\iota\nu$) . . . , and the witness and command of blessed Alexander.[97]

The second account of the election found in the *Panarion* seems, from all outward appearances and internal evidence, to be based upon Arian sources.[98] It is provided in connection with Epiphanius's history of the Arians in Egypt. That it is based upon an historical account different from the passage cited above is evident from the contradictory nature of the two narratives. Further, the claim made in this second account of Epiphanius, that a certain Achillas was elected as bishop of Alexandria, either by the Arians alone or by the whole of the Egyptian clergy (excluding the Meletians),[99] is, according to L.W. Barnard, "unsupported and is [also] open

---

[97]*Haer.* 68, 7 (Holl, *op. cit.*, 147, 4-17). Two intriguing points are raised by Epiphanius in this passage. First is his terminology for the clergy, οἱ τοῦ κανόνος. Second is his editorial comment that part of the reason for the electoral crisis was that "Alexandria never had two bishops as other cities have." It is unclear exactly what Epiphanius means by this comment, as even within the patriarchal sees there was not a system of suffragans. It also seems unlikely that he was making reference to the sad case of the divided church in Antioch with what Epiphanius would, it seems sure, have considered a schismatic bishop or rival bishop. In any case, this would not have been true of Alexandria, for it is probable that the Meletian schism arose out of Meletius's usurping of Bishop Peter's authority in consecrations and ordinations (*cf.* K. Baus, "Meletius of Lycopolis," *LThK*, vol. 7; W. Telfer, "Meletius of Lycopolis and Episcopal Succession in Egypt," *HTR* 48 [1955]: 227-237; and L.W. Barnard, "Some Notes on the Meletian Schism in Egypt," *Studia Patristica* 12 [TU 115], Berlin, 1975, 399-405). The concept of one bishop in one city, following the pattern of Cyprian, with presbyters taking on additional responsibilities for the area surrounding the city seems to have been followed in Alexandria and is attested to by Eusebius (*HE* 8, 13, 7; *Epist. episc. Aegypt.*, PG 10, C1566). Perhaps Epiphanius is referring to the problem of there being no other local bishop close at hand to assist in the consecration of a successor.

[98] According to L.W. Barnard, "Two Notes," *op. cit.*, 350, this election account indicates "that the Arians elected a certain Achillas as bishop."

[99] Despite Barnard's assertions (*cf.* fn. 98 above), the text is unclear as to the doctrinal persuasion of the Alexandrian electors. That the Meletians would have been excluded from the electoral process is, it would seem, certain, as the Council of Nicaea appears to have excluded from such a process all persons who had been found to have been in a schismatic state. Girardet, *Kaisergericht und Bischofsgericht, op. cit.*, 54, assumes that those Meletians who had been ordained

to the insuperable objection that Achillas was bishop of Alexandria before, and not after, Alexander."[100] In any case, the account is as follows:

> As soon as Arius had been anathematized the following events took place in this manner. In the same year that Alexander went to his rest he was succeeded by Achillas (and Theonas was installed by the Meletians). Then Achillas, who became bishop for three months, was succeeded by the blessed Athanasius who had been Alexander's deacon and had, at that time, been sent by him to a meeting (κομητᾶτον); to whom, Alexander, when he was about to die, had ordered that the bishopric should be given. It was, however, the custom in Alexandria not to delay the installation of bishops after the death of the previous bishop, but to have this done immediately for the sake of peace and to avoid friction (παρατριβᾶς) among the people, because some would want this one and others that one. So out of necessity, because of Athanasius's absence, they installed Achillas. But the throne and priesthood (ἱερωσύνη) had been prepared for the one [i.e., Athanasius] who had been called by God (τῷ ἐκ θεοῦ κεκλημένῳ) and had been appointed by the blessed Alexander. Because Athanasius then came and was installed, and because he was zealous for the faith and in the defense of the church, many schismatic gatherings began to take place of the so-called Meletians (the reasonings of Meletius we have already stated); but Athanasius, for the reasons, stated above, desired the unity of the divided church.[101]

Before turning to Athanasius's own account of his election and ordination as bishop of Alexandria, there are yet two other sources describing this event which are of interest and importance.

The first of these two sources is Gregory Nazianzen's oration in honor of Athanasius. Commonly referred to as *Oration* 21,[102] this panegyric was delivered at Constantinople by Gregory at some point between AD 379 and 381.[103] Although *Oration* 21 contains a disputed passage concerning

---

by persons other than Meletius could have participated in the election of the bishop of Alexandria. That this view is much broader than the one which this author believes would have actually been taken by the participants is very clearly put forward by A. Martin in "Athanase et les Méletiens," *Politique et théologie*, 40-44, where the argument is put forward that it is reasonable to assume that Athanasius, as well as many of the other Egyptian clergy, would have interpreted the canonical strictures of Nicaea in accordance with their most literal sense.

[100]L.W. Barnard, "Two Notes," *op. cit.*, 350.

[101]*Haer.* 69, 11 (Holl, *op. cit.*, 161, 6-23).

[102]For the critical text, see J. Mossay, SC 270, Paris, 1980, 86-193. English trans., LPNF, second series, vol. 7, 269-280.

[103]*Cf.* Mossay, *op. cit.*, 99-103, for the arguments concerning the exact dating of *Oration* 21. Mossay concludes that the oration cannot be dated beyond

charges made against Athanasius at the Synod of Tyre (which charges will be examined in another context), it is of greater importance at this point in our study to examine that portion of the panegyric which describes the election and consecration of Athanasius as bishop of Alexandria. Gregory first says of Athanasius's ordination to the priesthood (and to the episcopate) that he was "deemed worthy of the holy office and rank, and after passing through the entire series of orders (πᾶσαν τὴν τῶν βαθμῶν ἀκολουθίαν διεξελθών) he was (to make my story short) entrusted with the chief rule (προεδρίαν) over the people."[104] Gregory then goes on to speak specifically and directly of Athanasius's election to, and installation in, the throne of St. Mark. Possibly basing his account on the *Synodal Letter of the Egyptian Bishops of AD 338,*[105] Gregory states that

> by the vote of the whole people (ψήφῳ τοῦ λαοῦ παντός), not in the evil fashion which has since prevailed, nor by means of bloodshed and oppression (οὐδὲ φονικῶς τε καὶ τυραννικῶς) but in an apostolic and spiritual manner, he is led up to the throne of Saint Mark, to succeed him in piety, no less than in office; in the latter indeed at a great distance from him, in the former, which is true of succession, following him closely. For unity in doctrine deserves unity in office; and a rival teacher sets up a rival throne (ἀντίθρονον); the one is the successor in reality, the other but in name. For it is not the intruder, but he whose rights are intruded upon, who is the successor, not the law breaker, but the lawfully appointed (ὁ προβληθεὶς ἐννόμως), not the man of contrary opinions, but the man of the same faith; if this is not what we mean by successor, he succeeds in the same sense as disease to health, darkness to light, storm to calm, and frenzy to sound sense.[106]

The second of these two sources has its basis in a Coptic oral tradition which has found its way into patristic literature in the *Apophthegmata Patrum 78.*[107] Although the exact origin and date of the narrative in question is more difficult to trace than certain of the other texts which have been cited above, both the context and subject matter point to its being a record of an incident which took place in Egypt during the episcopate of Athanasius. Some scholars, as V. Twomey, have sought to set a date slightly after the death of Athanasius (AD 373) for this text, although this is by no means cer-

---

saying that it was composed "en 379, 380 ou 381, pour une fête solonnelle d'Athanase d'Alexandrie" (103).

[104]*Oration* 21, 7 (Mossay, *op. cit.,* 122, 7, 7-10); English trans., LNPF, second series, vol. 7, 271.

[105]*Apol.* 6, 5-6 (Opitz, 92, 20-93, 5).

[106]*Oration* 21, 8 (Mossay, *op. cit.,* 124, 8, 1-14); English trans., LNPF, *loc cit.*

[107]PG 65, 341, B9-15; the English trans. is my own.

tain.[108] This particular narrative was, however, placed in a more definitive textual tradition with its inclusion in the late fifth-century compilation of the *Apophthegmata Patrum*. Two versions of the text are extant; the shorter recension is in Greek, the longer in Syriac.[109] The Greek text reads: "At this time certain heretics came to Abba Poemen, and they began to speak against the archbishop of Alexandria, for they claimed that he had received ordination from presbyters (πρεσβυτέρων ἔχει τὴν χειροτονίαν)."[110] In E.A.W. Budge's translation of the same passage from the Syriac text, the point concerning presbyterial ordination is made in an even stronger way and seems, from the limited evidence of the text, to be directed against the whole episcopal structure of Alexandria. Budge translates the passage in the following manner: "Certain heretics came on one occasion to Abba Poemen, and they began to caluminate the Archbishop of Alexandria, and to speak evil things concerning him, and they sought to prove that as they [the archbishops] had received consecration from the priests, they were consecrated like [other] priests."[111]

Finally, in any assessment of the historical veracity of Philostorgius's account, as well as the accuracy of the other historians and writers cited above, we must turn to not only the earliest, but also to the most complete, record of those events which surrounded the selection, ordination, and consecration of Athanasius as bishop of Alexandria. This is to be found in the aforementioned *Synodal Letter of the Egyptian Bishops of AD 338* which is included by Athanasius in the *Apologia secunda*.[112] That Athanasius himself speaks through the letter in defending himself against a number of charges is without doubt. One must also admit, however, that the *Synodal Letter of AD 338* claims to be the testimony of the entire "holy synod assembled at Alexandria, out of Egypt, the Thebais, Libya, and Pentapolis."[113] Further, the synod sought to confirm the truthfulness of their account by stating that "of all this [*i.e.*, the election procedure] we are witnesses, and so is the whole city, and the province too."[114] We must also note that those gathered at this synod were well acquainted with the charges

---

[108]V. Twomey, *Apostolikos Thronos, op. cit.*, 556. Although Twomey dates this passage at AD 375, the contrary opinions of Turner, Gore, and Telfer are very well epitomized by E.W. Kemp, "Bishops and Presbyters at Alexandria," *JEH* 6 (1955): 136, 137.

[109]For a listing of the various editions, *cf.* Quasten, *op. cit.*, III, 187, 188.

[110]PG 65, 341, B9-15; the English trans. is my own.

[111]E.A.W. Budge, *The Paradise of the Holy Fathers*, London, 1907, 64 (sec. 284).

[112]*Apol.* 6, 5-6 (Opitz, 92, 20-93, 5). I refer to this document as the *Letter of AD 338* following the designation of Opitz, *Schreiben der Synode von Alexandrien 338*, Opitz, 89.

[113]*Apol.* 3, 1 (Opitz, 89, 1-2).

[114]*Apol.* 6, 5 (Opitz, 92, 24-25).

which had been made by the Eusebian-Meletian alliance against Athanasius concerning his election and ordination and were, therefore, very much prepared to give as full an account of the events as possible. Their statement is as follows:

> They [*i.e.*, the Eusebians] prejudiced the Emperor against him [*i.e.*, Athanasius]; they frequently threatened him with Councils; and at last assembled at Tyre; and to this day they cease not to write against him, and are so implacable that they even find fault with his appointment to the Episcopate, taking every means of shewing their enmity and hatred towards him, and spreading false reports for the sole purpose of thereby vilifying his character.
>
> However, the very misrepresentations which they now are making do but convict their former statements of being falsehoods, and a mere conspiracy against him. For they say, that "after the death of Bishop Alexander, a certain few having mentioned the name of Athanasius, six or seven Bishops elected him clandestinely in a secret place:" and this is what they wrote to the Emperors, having no scruple about asserting the greatest falsehoods. Now that the whole multitude and all the people of the Catholic Church (ὁ λαὸς τῆς καθολικῆς ἐκκλησίας) assembled together as with one mind and body and cried, shouted, that Athanasius should be Bishop of their Church, made this the subject of their public prayers to Christ, and conjured us to grant it for many days and nights, neither departing themselves from the Church, nor suffering us to do so; of all this we are witnesses, and so is the whole city, and the province too. Not a word did they speak against him, as these persons represented, but gave him the most excellent titles they could devise, calling him good, pious, Christian, an ascetic, a genuine Bishop. And that he was elected by a majority (πλείονες) of our body in the sight and with acclamations of all the people, we who elected him also testify, who are surely more credible witnesses than those who were not present, and now spread these false accounts.[115]

The only further reference we have concerning objections to the election and consecration of Athanasius as bishop of Alexandria comes from the *Chronicon Athanasianum*[116] and may well be supported by a remark in the letter of Constantine which is quoted by Athanasius in the *Apologia secunda*. In the *Chronicon* III the compiler of the festal letters states that in AD 330-331 Athanasius

> went to the Imperial Court to the Emperor Constantine the Great, having been summoned before him, on account of an accusation his

---

[115]*Apol.* 6, 3-6 (Opitz, 92, 11-29). English trans., LNPF second series, vol. 4, 103.

[116]LNPF, *op. cit.*, 503.

enemies made, that he had been appointed when too young. He appeared [before Constantine], was thought worthy of favour and honor, and returned when the [quadragesimal] fast was half finished.[117]

It is possible that it was this incident which Constantine had in mind when writing to the people of Alexandria in AD 331-332.[118] Constantine states that Athanasius's enemies appeared before him, complaining that "such an one is too old; *such an one is a mere boy;* the office belongs to me; it is due to me, since it is taken away from him. I will gain over all men to my side, and then I will endeavor with my power to ruin him."[119] Constantine's response to these charges was one of scorn and derision and a dismissal of the accusers, stating that "theirs [Athanasius's enemies'] is the mere force of envy, supported by those baneful influences which naturally belong to it."[120]

If we are to discover, with any degree of certainty, what actually took place in Alexandria concerning those events which surrounded the elevation of Athanasius to the throne of St. Mark in AD 328, a critical, careful, and impartial evaluation of all of the above materials must be undertaken. This is of even greater importance, if, as we have stated before, we wish to call into question the use of Philostorgius as a reliable witness in the search for the historical Athanasius. That the central portion of Philostorgius's account of Athanasius is concerned with a so-called contested election and consecration is a matter which leads to yet further difficult questions concerning (1) pre-Athanasian consecration practices in the church of Alexandria, (2) proper and improper methods of consecration and canonical revision and clari-

---

[117]*Ibid.*

[118]*Apol.* 61-62, the earlier dating of AD 332 seems preferable for this letter; *cf.* Opitz, 141, notes 2 and 4. This is, however, an admittedly earlier dating than AD 334, which is suggested by P.R. Coleman-Norton, *Roman State and Christian Church*, London, 1966, I, 198.

[119]*Apol.* 62, 3 (Opitz, 142, 4-6); English trans., LNPF, *op. cit.*, 133; emphasis added. The age of Athanasius at the time of his consecration has continued to be the focus of controversy. A. Martin raised the point that Athanasius may indeed have been younger than the canonical age of thirty (with reference to the synod of Neocaesarea 318/320 and its imposition of that age for the episcopate) in "Athanase et les Mélitiens," *op. cit.*, 32-61; *cf.* "Aux origines de l'eglise copte: L'Implantation et le développement du christianisme en Egypte (Ie-IVe siècles)," *Revue des études anciennes* 88 (1981): 35-56, also by A. Martin. Also of interest on this point of Athanasius's age at the time of his consecration is G.F. Hernández, "El cisma meleciano en la iglesia egipcia," *Gerión* 2 (1984): 168. From the evidence of the *Historia acephala* and the Index of Athanasius's festal letters (both contained in a new critical edition, SC 317, 1985, ed. M. Albert) it seems that Athanasius may have been either thirty years of age or very slightly younger in the summer of AD 328.

[120]*Apol.* 62, 4 (Opitz 142, 10-11); English trans., LNPF, *op. cit.*, 133.

fication at the Council of Nicaea, and (3) Meletian involvement in the Alexandrian episcopal election of AD 328.

3.2.1 Pre-Athanasian Consecration Practices in the Church of Alexandria.

That this question impinges upon the so-called contested election of Athanasius is clear. Writing in 1952, W. Telfer argued on the basis of texts from Jerome, Epiphanius, Ambrosiaster, and Eutychius,[121] among others, that the system whereby the bishop of Alexandria was elected and consecrated by the Alexandrian presbyters was set aside only "when Athanasius, deacon to Alexander, succeeded him in the throne" of St. Mark.[122] According to Telfer it was only as a result of the fourth canon of the Council of Nicaea[123] that this change came about at all and that, therefore, "the probability is that the old custom was undisturbed until Nicaea, that Alexander was the last Alexandrine pope to take office without the imposition of living episcopal hands, and that a new order came in with Athanasius."[124] Writing in a similar context in 1955, Telfer again states that, "until Nicaea, Egyptian ideas on episcopal succession were peculiar" and that "after Nicaea there is no reason to doubt that orthodox Egypt superimposed the requirements of the Nicene Canon upon the traditional Egyptian pattern in these matters."[125]

Telfer's view has been accepted and echoed by H. Nordberg, who, in a monograph published in 1963, stated that "when Bishop Alexander died, he had already made arrangements in two respects for the election of his successor. Firstly, he had the election procedure changed, so that the Archbishop was no longer to be chosen by and within the presbyter's collegium in Alexandria, but jointly by the Bishops of all the ecclesiastical provinces."[126] Nordberg is of the opinion that this change was made "mainly in view of the Meletians," whom he believes were set to assume a

---

[121]*I.e.,* Eutychius, Melchite patriarch of Alexandria, AD 933-943.

[122]W. Telfer, "Episcopal Succession in Egypt," *JEH* 3 (1952): 10.

[123]The fourth canon of the Council of Nicaea states: "The Bishop shall be appointed by all (the bishops) of the eparchy (province); if that is not possible on account of pressing necessity, or on account of the length of journeys, three (bishops) at the least shall meet, and proceed to the imposition of hands (consecration) with the permission of those absent in writing. The confirmation of what has been done belongs by right, in each eparchy, to the metropolitan." C.J. Hefele, *A History of the Christian Councils* (trans. by W.R. Clark) Edinburgh, 1871, vol. 1, 381. A more complete examination of the significance of this canon, as regards the church of Alexandria, will be undertaken in the text below.

[124]Telfer, "Episcopal Succession," *op. cit.,* 10,11.

[125]Telfer, "Meletius of Lycopolis," *op. cit.,* 236, 237.

[126]H. Nordberg, *Athanasius and the Emperor,* Commentationes Humanarum Litterarum XXX, 3, Helsinki-Helsingfors, 1963, 17.

more powerful role in the affairs of the Egyptian church.[127] Nordberg adds that second, "Bishop Alexander had openly expressed the wish that Athanasius should be his successor."[128] In considering the length of time between the death of Bishop Alexander (which he wrongly places as "shortly before Easter")[129] and the election of Athanasius on 8 June 328, Nordberg states that "it is apparent that the election, besides the adoption of a new election procedure, took place under exceptional conditions."[130] It is important to note that Nordberg rejects the early testimony of the synodal letter of the Egyptian bishops and, following the later Arian accounts contained in Sozomen[131] and Philostorgius,[132] states that "the election itself [*i.e.*, of Athanasius] was unobtrusively effected by an insignificant number of bishops—seven or two."[133] According to Nordberg, it was for these reasons that Athanasius sought confirmation of his election from the emperor Constantine and then made an extensive tour of his archepiscopal see in order to gain the approval of those bishops not present in Alexandria at the time of his consecration.[134]

L.W. Barnard, writing in 1975, is more careful in his handling of the available evidence.[135] He rightly rejects the overburdened theory of Telfer

---

[127]Nordberg, *op. cit.*, 17, 18. This is, of course, very much in keeping with Nordberg's major thesis in this monograph, namely that the Meletians are at the very heart of Egyptian church policy decisions made during the first four decades of the fourth century.

[128]Nordberg, *op. cit.*, 18.

[129]Nordberg, *op. cit.*, 18. Alexander of Alexandria died on 22 Pharmuthi (17 April) in the forty-fourth year of Diocletian (AD 328). From the *Festal Letters Index* we know that Easter for this year was celebrated on 19 Pharmuthi (14 April). From the available evidence, it appears that Athanasius was enthroned in Alexandria on 14 Pauni (8 June) in this same year. *Cf. Festal Index*, LPNF second series, vol. 4, 502, 503.

[130]Nordberg, *loc. cit.*

[131]Sozomen, *HE*, II, 17.

[132]Philostorgius, *HE*, II, 11.

[133]Nordberg, *loc. cit.*

[134]Nordberg's assumption concerning Athanasius's seeking confirmation of his election from Constantine does seem very much open to question. To place this practice at the time of Athanasius is possibly archaic, and the documentary evidence summoned by Nordberg to support his contention may not be what it seems. The primary text for this confirmation procedure from the hand of Constantine, also alluded to by Girardet (*Kaisergericht, op. cit.*, 56), is a letter of doubtful provenance contained in Philostorgius (Bidez, *op. cit.*, 23, 31ff.). This letter, as the editor Bidez points out (*op. cit.*, xci), is most likely the product of an Arian historian who is unknown to us. We may not, therefore, give unqualified assent to the information contained in the text of the letter, which may well be an *ex parte* statement.

[135]L.W. Barnard, "Two Notes," *op. cit.*, 344-356.

that a Meletian bishop named John Archaph had prospective rights to the see of Alexandria following the death of Alexander under the terms of an agreement made with Constantine about the time of Nicaea.[136] Barnard states that "Telfer's ingenious reconstruction will not bear critical investigation resting, as it does, mainly on conjecture rather than contemporary evidence."[137] Barnard does, however, seem to follow Telfer and Nordberg on a number of other points, including that of the so-called new election procedure which was supposed to have come into effect at the death of Alexander. Barnard contends that "Alexander, before he died, made arrangements for Athanasius's election and for the changing of the [election] procedure."[138] Making use of arguments similar to those of Nordberg, Barnard, although more cautious in his overall evaluation of the Alexandrian context, does comment a priori that "it seems certain that the election" of Athanasius "was disputed."[139]

Both Barnard and Nordberg seem to have been either unaware of, or to have set aside, the important critique of Telfer's position concerning the pre-Athanasian consecration practices of the church of Alexandria made by E.W. Kemp in 1955.[140] Following an examination of how Telfer makes use of various texts, with special attention being given to a disputed passage from Jerome on the Alexandrian method of consecration,[141] Kemp rightly points to the fact that Telfer "places more weight on the evidence than it will properly bear."[142] Furthermore, commenting on the use of Epiphanius as an independent witness of the ancient practices of the church of Alexandria viz-à-viz episcopal consecration in general, and that of Athanasius in particular, Kemp remarks that "as a general historian" Epiphanius "is not very reliable and this particular statement" concerning Athanasius's election and Alexandrian consecration customs "is not strengthened by the context in which it appears."[143] After showing the many inaccuracies contained in Epiphanius's "second Arian" account[144] of the election of Athanasius and

---

[136]Cf. Telfer, "Meletius of Lycopolis," op. cit., 235; and L.W. Barnard, "Two Notes," op. cit., 350, 351.

[137]Barnard, loc. cit.

[138]Barnard, "Two Notes," op. cit., 345.

[139]Barnard, "Two Notes," op. cit., 346.

[140]E.W. Kemp, "Bishops and Presbyters at Alexandria," JEH 6 (1955): 125-142.

[141]Cf. Kemp, op. cit., 127-129; and Telfer, "Episcopal Succession," op. cit., 4,5.

[142]Kemp, op. cit., 129.

[143]Kemp, op. cit., 132.

[144]Epiphanius, Haer. 69, 11 (Holl, op. cit., 161).

the supposed custom of immediate succession,[145] Kemp rightly argues that this passage "cannot be accepted without independent support."[146]

In Telfer's argument that a change in consecration practices took place at the time of Alexander's death, Kemp seeks to confirm disputed passages, such as those in Epiphanius, by the use of much later writers.[147] Special reference is made to the work of Eutychius, the Melkite patriarch of Alexandria (AD 933-943), also known as Sa'id ibn Batrik. In his *Annals* Eutychius made the following claim:

> This custom of the twelve presbyters of Alexandria appointing the patriarch out of themselves continued till the time of the patriarch Alexander, who was of the three hundred and eighteen; he forbade the presbyters henceforth to appoint the patriarch, and ordered that when the patriarch was dead the bishops should assemble and ordain a patriarch. He ordained, moreover, that at a vacancy they should elect some outstanding and upright man from any part of the land, whether he were one of the twelve city presbyters or not and make him patriarch. Thus ceased the ancient custom of the presbyters appointing the patriarch, and there took its place the rule of the patriarch being made by the bishops.[148]

Kemp, however, has pointed out that "it is generally agreed that Eutychius was an ignorant and blundering writer, and evidence which appears for the first time in his annals cannot be relied upon with any degree of certainty."[149]

Kemp makes similar statements in regard to Telfer's handling of other material as well, such as the *Vita Petri*[150] and the writings of Severus of El Eschmouein[151] and Severus of Antioch.[152] Many of Telfer's arguments are

---

[145]The supposed custom of succession in Alexandria being that no time was to intervene between the death of one bishop and the enthronement of his successor. This is according to Epiphanius, *loc. cit.*

[146]Kemp, *loc. cit.*

[147]*Ibid.; cf.* Telfer, "Episcopal Succession," *op. cit.,* 6,7.

[148]Quoted by Kemp, *op. cit.,* 137-138; Eutychius, *Annals,* PG 111, col. 982.

[149]Kemp, *op. cit.,* 138.

[150]Quasten styles the *Vita Petri* as "a late falsification" which is not attributable to Alexander in any way (Quasten, *op. cit.,* III, 17). Telfer, however, speaks of this panegyric as having been "pronounced by Alexander" ("Episcopal Succession," *op. cit.,* 7). *Cf.* Kemp, *op. cit.,* 134.

[151]Telfer, "Episcopal Succession," *op. cit.,* 6,7; Kemp, *op. cit.,* 132-134.

[152]Telfer ("Episcopal Succession," *op. cit.,* 1) here draws on the work of E.W. Brooks, "The Ordination of the Early Bishops of Alexandria," *JThS* 2

considered by Kemp to be "pure conjecture."[153] None of the constructions presented by Telfer appear to justify his conclusion that "there is no longer room for doubt that early popes of Alexandria took office without the intervention of bishops of other sees."[154]

Telfer's insistence on the historicity of a macabre ceremony in which it is implied that consecration actually took place through the imposition of the hands of the dead bishop upon the person of his successor is, as Telfer himself admits, "conjectural."[155] Telfer, however, builds upon this assumption and maintains that both this ceremony, and the practice of presbyterial consecration, were retained until the time of Alexander: "The probability is that the old custom was undisturbed until Nicaea, that Alexander was the last Alexandrine pope to take office without the imposition of living episcopal hands, and that a new order came in with Athanasius."[156] In reply to such an extraordinary claim based upon such dubious sources, Kemp merely comments, "The reader will, perhaps, consider that here conjecture has run far beyond the limits of reliable evidence."[157] Kemp, on the weight of the available evidence, rightly rejects Telfer's theory and indicates that if such unusual customs had actually been in force, they had most likely ceased following the episcopate of Heraclas of Alexandria (AD 233-49).[158] Further, "In view of the place which Alexandria occupies in the fourth century it is very remarkable that no contemporary or near contemporary reference should have survived if the change was made as late as the time of Nicaea and with the election of Athanasius."[159]

It is clear that apart from one disputed passage in Jerome, the only other clear statement we have on the exact time and circumstances of such a change is "to be found in an inaccurate writer of the tenth century," *i.e.*, in the *Annals* of Eutychius.[160] Although Kemp allows the possibility that there is "evidence of the survival at Alexandria to a later date than elsewhere of a presbyterial college with episcopal powers," the overall thrust of his argument is that such a collegium was no longer empowered to consecrate a bishop in the early decades of the fourth century.[161] It would, in fact, be reasonable to state that the use of such a collegium had probably ceased to

---

(1901): 612, 613. It is clear, however, that Telfer has drawn more extensive conclusions from the extract from Severus than even Brooks allowed in his study of the material. *Cf.* Kemp, *op. cit.*, 137.

[153]Kemp, *op. cit.*, 134.

[154]*Ibid.*

[155]Telfer, "Episcopal Succession," *op. cit.*, 10.

[156]*Ibid.*

[157]Kemp, *op. cit.*, 136.

[158]Kemp, *op. cit.*, 128, 129.

[159]Kemp, *op. cit.*, 139.

[160]*Ibid.*

[161]Kemp, *op. cit.*, 140.

perform this function by the middle of the third century.[162] Kemp, considering the citations from Jerome, Eutychius, and Severus of Antioch, concludes: "It is possible to argue with some plausibility as do Gore and Turner that we have in these writers merely traces of what was originally an Arian calumny about Athanasius."[163]

---

[162]The recent study of Arius by Rowan Williams has also considered the evidence concerning the unusual situation of the bishops of Alexandria in the early fourth century. In the debate between Kemp and Telfer as to whether or not Athanasius represented part of the "old" tradition of "presbyterial consecration" or the more "current" Nicene model, Williams has sought middle ground. The following excerpt from Williams's study is representative:

> The bishop of Alexandria occupied at this date what may seem a highly paradoxical position in the Egyptian church: on the one hand—as our evidence has already hinted—he more closely resembled an archbishop or even a patriarch than any other prelate in Christendom. The letter of the four imprisoned bishops to Meletius speaks of Peter as something more than a mere senior confrere: the plain implication of the text is that he has the right to appoint "commissaries" in vacant sees; and there is a fair amount of evidence that he normally consecrated other Egyptian bishops, and perhaps even nominated them. At least from the time of Dionysius, he was addressed as *papa*, and other bishops in Egypt refer to him as their "father." On the other hand, within Alexandria itself the bishop was surrounded by powerful and independent presbyters, supervising their own congregations: there is already something like a "parochial" system, with the bishop as president of a college of near equals. Dionysius still writes to his "fellow presbyters" in the mid third century. A rather confused tradition long survived that, until the accession of Athanasius in 328, the bishop was consecrated by the Alexandrian presbyterial college and not by any other bishop; and although the evidence is unclear, such a practice would by no means be surprising. Despite his unique powers in the rest of Egypt, the Alexandrian pope remained, in his own city, a *primus inter pares*. (*Arius: Heresy and Tradition,* London, 1987, 42.)

Although we would agree with Williams concerning the unique powers enjoyed by the bishop of Alexandria, it does seem, from the evidence presented, that the practice of "presbyterial consecration" in Alexandria did not, as we have indicated in the text, survive beyond the mid-third century. It should be stated, however, that Williams's collecting of materials, both with regard to this issue and the emergence of Alexandria's parochial system (with commentary on Epiphanius's "Mendidion"), is a valuable contribution to the study of early fourth-century Alexandria (*op. cit.,* 42). The consideration of such documents gains even greater importance given Williams's conclusion in setting the background for the emergence of Arius in Alexandria, that "the presbyters—as has been noted—were not docile diocesan clergy but members of a collegiate body. It is not entirely surprising that we should come across disputes between bishop and presbyters over the respective limits of their authority" (*ibid.,* 44).

[163]Kemp, *op. cit.,* 139, 140.

Kemp is followed in this particular judgment by J. Lecuyer,[164] who applies this argument to the Alexandrian consecration calumny found in the *Apophthegmata Patrum 78* and cited in the text above.[165] In examining this Arian accusation, we must reject C.H. Turner's theory that the archbishop being accused is Theophilus[166] and follow the argument of Gore that Poemen was already a well-established anchorite by about AD 375.[167] The subject of the accusation would, therefore, most likely be either Athanasius of his immediate successor, Peter. From the silence of Poemen in answering the accusation, Telfer assumes some degree of truth in the statement that the archbishop "had received ordination from presbyters."[168] This view, however, does not take into account the Syriac version of the story which speaks of the archbishops of Alexandria in the plural[169] and clearly characterizes the entire exchange as an heretical exercise in slander.[170] If we accept Gore's date of AD 375 for this story, it seems even more likely that the purpose of the slander was twofold. First, it may have been meant to cast aspersions on the memory of Athanasius, who had only recently died in AD 373, and second, it may have sought to call into question the validity of orders conferred by Athanasius which were still operative in orthodox Egypt. Although the story may have had its origins in the more distant past concerning the ancient method of appointing bishops of Alexandria, it appears from the evidence that there was no basis in fact to apply such a slur to the memory of Athanasius.

From all of the above we may come to certain reasonable conclusions concerning the question of the pre-Athanasian consecration practices of the church of Alexandria. The first conclusion is that Telfer's ingenious reconstructions are unable to be maintained under Kemp's careful scrutiny, being based upon either unreliable writers far removed in time from the events being considered or upon very selective and highly disputed passages from more contemporary sources. Second, we may find fault with the state-

---

[164]J. Lécuyer, "Le Problèm des consécrations épiscopales," *Bulletin de littérature ecclésiastique* 65 (1964): 256, 257.

[165]PG 65, col. 341, B9-15.

[166]*Cf.* the appended note of C.H. Turner in Brooks, *op. cit.*, 613.

[167]C. Gore, "On the Ordination of the Early Bishops of Alexandria," *JThS* 3 (1902): 279, 280.

[168]Telfer, "Episcopal Succession," *op. cit.*, 11.

[169]In Budge's translation (*Paradise of the Holy Fathers, op. cit.*, 64) the "heretics" accuse "the Archbishop of Alexandria" in the singular, but then state that "they (i.e. the Archbishops of Alexandria as a group) were consecrated like other priests."

[170]In the Greek version the "heretics" simply "speak against" (καταλαλεῖν) the archbishop, whereas in the longer Syriac recension they (according to Budge) "calumniate" the archbishop and "speak evil things concerning him." *Cf.* PG 65, col. 341, B9-15; and Budge, *loc. cit.*

ments of both Nordberg and Barnard that a new method of consecration came about only after the death of Alexander and during the subsequent election of Athanasius.

Finally, comment needs to be made concerning two of the texts mentioned above, which seem to give support to Philostorgius's narrative concerning the so-called disputed election of Athanasius. First, we note that the "second Arian" account of Athanasius's election given by Epiphanius finds no support in the evidence examined.[171] His remarks are not only confused historically (*e.g.*, the fact of Achillas having been bishop before, and not after, Alexander), but it is also apparent from his twisting of the facts to fit his own preconceptions that Epiphanius, in reality, had no firsthand knowledge of either the actual customs of the Alexandrian church or the sequence of events surrounding the election of Athanasius. Similarly, we may set the accusation found in the *Apophthegmata Patrum 78* in its proper context—that of a late Arian slander which perhaps drew upon ancient folklore but had as its motive a calling into question of the validity of orthodox Alexandrian orders which had their source in the episcopacy of Athanasius. We may, therefore, conclude that any dispute which may have surrounded the elevation of Athanasius to the throne of St. Mark had nothing whatsoever to do with a change in Alexandrian consecration practices, if, in fact, such a dispute took place at all.

3.2.2 Proper and Improper Methods of Consecration and Canonical Revision and Clarification at the Council of Nicaea. This issue follows, and is connected with, the question of the pre-Athanasian consecration practices of the church of Alexandria set out above. This point is also directly related to the account of Athanasius's election and ordination provided by Philostorgius in his *Ecclesiastical History.*[172]

In the letters of Severus of Antioch, a sixth-century Monophysite bishop of that see, a passage has come to light which implies that presbyterial consecration continued in Alexandria until the time of the Council of Nicaea. In the course of an argument that old customs may not be retained following later synodal decrees, Severus says,

> The bishop also of the city, renowned for its orthodox faith, of the Alexandrines was in old times appointed by presbyters: but in modern times in accordance with the canon which has prevailed everywhere, the solemn institution of their bishop is performed by bishops, and no one makes light of the accurate practice that prevails in the holy churches

---

[171]*Haer.* 69, 11.
[172]Philostorgius, *HE* II, 11.

and recurs to the earlier condition of things, which has given way to the later clear and accurate, deliberate and spiritual injunctions.[173]

Telfer makes use of this passage to reinforce his argument concerning the late date of a change in Alexandrian consecration practices.[174] Kemp, however, points out that "the Syriac version of Severus may very well be rendering the Greek χειροτονεῖν which is itself an ambiguous word and can mean either appoint or consecrate or both."[175] In any case, the force of Severus's statement "implies that such a change was made as a result of the fourth canon of Nicaea."[176] Kemp finds this use of the fourth canon unusual, as "the wording of the canon shows that it was framed for quite another purpose than to bring such a change as is suggested to have happened at Alexandria."[177] Apart from this suggested use of the canon, Severus tells us little else of interest concerning the election of Athanasius to the see of Alexandria. It is, nevertheless, Severus's use of the fourth canon which is taken up by Telfer as support for his general thesis. He goes so far as to say that "orthodox Egypt superimposed the requirements of the Nicene canon upon the traditional Egyptian pattern"[178] in matters of episcopal consecration. Elsewhere, Telfer states that the fourth canon "appears as something new" in the Egyptian church.[179] One would perhaps be wise, however, to regard these last statements more as expressions of Telfer's own theological outlook than as statements of fact.[180]

---

[173]E.W. Brooks, *The Sixth Book of the Select Letters of Severus Patriarch of Antioch in the Syrian Version of Athanasius of Nisibis*, London, 1903, vol. 2, 213 (II, 3).

[174]Telfer, "Episcopal Succession,"*op. cit.*, 6.

[175]Kemp, *op. cit.*, 138.

[176]Kemp, *op. cit.*, 139.

[177]*Ibid.*

[178]Telfer, "Meletius of Lycopolis," *op. cit.*, 237.

[179]Telfer, "Episcopal Succession," *op. cit.*, 12.

[180]In pressing his argument concerning the late date of a change from presbyterial to episcopal election and consecration in Alexandria (*i.e.*, after the time of Nicaea and beginning with the consecration of Athanasius), Telfer is seeking to uphold his own theological position, which rejected the necessity of an unbroken chain of the laying on of hands by bishops as what constitutes apostolic succession. This is made clear in the course of a report of the committee appointed by the archbishop of Canterbury in 1951 to negotiate with the churches of Norway, Denmark, and Iceland, in which we read: "Professor Molland also referred to the fact that the Alexandrian Church did not have the Apostolic Succession up to the Council of Nicaea. ... *Dr. Telfer agreed with this last point,* but said that after the Fourth Canon of Nicaea, Athanasius was consecrated by the Egyptian bishops, and the great Church of Egypt came into line with the rest of Christendom" (*The Church of England and the Churches of Norway, Denmark, and Iceland*, London, 1952, 30; emphasis added.) In his own article, Telfer was to add

It is clear that a closer examination of both the content and the intent of fourth canon is required. The fourth canon of Nicaea is as follows:

A bishop should most certainly be chosen (καθίστασθαι) by all the other [bishops] of the province (ἐπαρχίᾳ). But if this poses a difficulty, because of an urgent need, or because of the length of the journey, then at least three [bishops] shall meet in one place, and with the votes of those absent having been communicated in writing, they shall proceed to the consecration (χειροτονίαν). The confirmation of what has been done, however, belongs in each province to the metropolitan (μητροπολίτῃ).[181]

That this canon is not concerned primarily with either the future or present procedures for the election of a bishop of Alexandria as of AD 325 is evident in its very form and language. Had it wished to intimate a change in a well-known custom of an ancient see, we may safely assume that the canon would have been framed by the council in a way similar to canons 6 and 7, in which such sees are specifically named.[182] As to Telfer's assumption that this canon has introduced an innovation, it might be more accurate to say that the council, by the use of this canon, sought to clarify and codify a widespread practice which had already been in effect for sometime.[183]

In terms of early church law, the fourth canon of Nicaea had a precedent in the twentieth canon of the Synod of Arles (AD 314), "ut sine tribus episcopis nullus episcopus ordinetur,"[184] which may well have drawn on yet

---

that in the days of Nicaea "there was no general belief that valid episcopal succession was inseparable from an unbroken chain of consecrations by laying on of hands. . . . The tyranny of legalism was still at bay" (Telfer, "Episcopal Succession,"*op. cit.,* 12).

[181]The Greek text is found in Hefele, *op. cit.,* vol. 1, 328. The translation is that of the author.

[182]*Cf.* Hefele, *op. cit.,* vol. 1, 388 (canon 6) and 404 (canon 7). In canon 6 the jurisdiction of the churches of Alexandria, Antioch, and Rome are spoken of in a specific manner. Similarly, the ancient rights of the bishop of Aelia (Jerusalem) are confirmed by name in canon 7.

[183]The real change in procedure concerning the election and consecration of bishops which was effected at Nicaea seems to have consisted mainly in a change of emphasis from the joint suffrage of *plebs*, presbyters, and bishops, to the wishes of the "bishops of the province" (canon 4). One must admit, however, that the joint suffrage of the three groups named above continued for some time after Nicaea, especially in the West. For a more complete discussion of this point, see H. Hess, *The Canons of the Council of Sardica AD 343: A Landmark in the Early Development of Canon Law,* Oxford, 1958, 90-94, and in the text below.

[184]"De his qui usurpant sibi quod soli debeant episcopos ordinare, placuit ut nullus hoc sibi praesumat nisi assumptis secum aliis septem episcopos. Si tamen non potuerit septem infra tres non audeat ordinare" (Hefele, *op. cit.,* 195).

earlier collections of canonical prescriptions.[185] As Hefele recounts, this fourth canon of Nicaea "was afterwards in its turn reproduced and renewed by many councils—by that of Laodicea (c. 12), of Antioch (c. 19), by the fourth Synod of Toledo (c. 19), the second of Nicaea (c. 13): it is also reproduced in the *Codex Ecclesiae Afric.* (c. 13)."[186] That there may have been fourth-century exceptions to this rule, as claimed by Telfer, only serves to prove that the provisions of this canon were, for the most part, observed with great regularity both immediately before and following Nicaea.[187]

At this point in our discussion, it would be prudent to look again at the so-called historical account of the election and ordination of Athanasius provided by Philostorgius.[188] In our present context, one item in the narrative is of particular interest. Philostorgius reports that there was a lack of unanimity among the assembled bishops as to who should succeed Alexander and that following "a considerable amount of time" spent in argument, Athanasius took matters into his own hands. According to Philostorgius, Athanasius "suddenly appeared one evening in the church called after Dionysius, and finding there *two Egyptian bishops*, firmly closed the doors with the assistance of some of his followers, and so was ordained by them, though strongly against the will of the ordainers."[189] It is interesting to note that although both Telfer and Barnard hold to a "disputed consecration" interpretation of the events of AD 328 in Alexandria, they both indicate that this particular portion of Philostorgius's narrative seems to be little more than an exercise in slander, made in light of the provisions of the fourth canon of Nicaea.[190] Barnard, however, suggests that Philostorgius was, nonetheless, attempting to emphasize "the uncanonical nature of the election" of Athanasius.[191] If we follow the argument of A. Martin that Athanasius would have been scrupulous in his observance of the synodal decrees of

---

[185]*Cf., e.g.,* the statement of Hippolytus that a bishop should be chosen by all the people (ὑπὸ παντός τοῦ λαοῦ) and that the choice made by the people should then be approved by all the presbyters and bishops who have assembled (*The Apostolic Tradition,* I, ii, 1-2, ed. G. Dix, London, 1968, 2, 3). The material in Hippolytus may be of even greater importance in the present discussion if one accepts the argument for its early circulation in the churches of Syria and Egypt (*op. cit.,* xlvi). In any case, we may accept Dix's dating of the collection to *c.* AD 215 (*op. cit.,* xxxvii) a date which is early enough for the *Apostolic Tradition* to have been formative for other and later collections of canonical prescriptions concerning the election and consecration of bishops.

[186]Hefele, *op. cit.,* 385.

[187]Telfer, "Meletius of Lycopolis," *op. cit.,* 237.

[188]Philostorgius, *HE* II, 11.

[189]*Ibid.* (Walford, *op. cit.,* 439; Bidez, *op. cit.,* 22, 23); emphasis added.

[190]Telfer, "Episcopal Succession," *op. cit.,* 10; Barnard, "Two Notes," *op. cit.,* 349.

[191]Barnard, *loc. cit.;* cf. Nordberg's acceptance of the possibility that Athanasius was consecrated by as few as two bishops, *op. cit.,* 18.

Nicaea concerning the qualifications of episcopal electors,[192] it seems incredible to imagine that he would knowingly violate the fourth canon.[193]

Although this singular report of the "two bishops" represents a central problem of credibility in the narrative of Philostorgius, it is by no means the only difficulty one finds in this confused and interpolated text. Even his citing of the Church of Dionysius as the location for Athanasius's ordination, for example, may not be accepted without reservation. It is, in fact, possible that the name of this church was taken by Philostorgius from the listing of the churches of Alexandria by Epiphanius.[194] The Church of Dionysius seems to have only later been definitely used as an episcopal residence, and then it was in AD 357 when it was occupied by George, the Arian intruder.[195]   Furthermore, Philostorgius's assertion that "the remainder of the bishops then present anathematized Athanasius on account of this transaction," i.e., the forced ordination,[196] finds no support in any other account and makes Athanasius's subsequent tour of Egypt seem very unlikely, if not impossible.[197] The further claim that the election was later confirmed by Constantine, an opinion followed to various degrees by Barnard, Girardet, and Nordberg on the strength of Philostorgius, seems to have its basis in a very unreliable and possibly forged Arian document of a somewhat later date.[198]   The entire account if further complicated by Philostorgius's complete lack of historical accuracy in recounting the events surrounding the Synod of Tyre and his confusion concerning the subsequent intrusion of George the Cappadocian into the see of Alexandria.[199]

We may, therefore, conclude with some degree of certainty that if the election and ordination of Athanasius was in any way influenced by the fourth canon of Nicaea, it would have been to cause even greater care and attention in the following of the instructions contained in the pronouncement.

---

[192]Cf. the discussion of this point in fn. 99.

[193]If, as Hefele states, "Meletius was probably the occasion of this canon" (op. cit., I, 384), it seems almost unbelievable that Athanasius would hold to a synodal decree by which he set aside the Meletians as electors, and then immediately open himself to charges of uncanonical consecration under that very same canon which had been intended for use against the Meletians!

[194]Haer. 69, 2 (Holl, op. cit., 153).

[195]Historia Acephala V (LNPF second series, vol. 4, 497). For further discussion of this point, cf. "Les Premiers siècles du christianisme à Alexandrie," Revue des etudes augustiniennes 30 (1984): 212, 213. In the text of this article one should especially consider the comment of A. Calderini (212, n. 7) on how Epiphanius made use of the listing of churches.

[196]Philostorgius, loc. cit.

[197]Epiphanius, Haer. 68, 6.

[198]Nordberg, op. cit., 18; Girardet, op. cit., 56; and Barnard, "Two Notes," op. cit., 346. Also cf. the discussion in footnote 134.

[199]Philostorgius, loc. cit.

It is important to note that, apart from Philostorgius, no other extant writer either intimates or outrightly accuses Athanasius of violating this particular canon. We may be sure that had there been a basis in fact for such an accusation, there would have been many of those opposed to Athanasius who would not have been hesitant in the least to make such a charge.

In dealing with the disciplinary purpose of the fourth canon of Nicaea, it would seem reasonable to follow the judgment of Hefele that "Meletius was probably the occasion of this canon."[200] It is to this Meletian involvement in the so-called contested election of Athanasius that we must now turn our attention as a third difficulty in interpretating the events of the summer of AD 328.

3.2.3 Meletian Involvement in the Alexandrian Episcopal Election of AD 328. The Meletian schism in Egypt arose out of a dispute which broke upon the scene during the Diocletian persecution. This most lengthy and serious persecution which the Christian church had endured was initiated by Diocletian in February, AD 303. It was most severe in Africa and the eastern portion of the empire. In the western portion of the empire, under Maximian and Constantius (the father of Constantine), very little was done to promulgate the persecution or, indeed, other decrees issued by Diocletian.[201] In Egypt, however, the persecution was intense and martyrdom was common. Upon Diocletian's retirement in AD 305 the situation became markedly worse with the accession of Galerius and his appointment of Maximin as Caesar over the civil diocese of Oriens which included Egypt and the Palestinian and Syrian littoral. The severity of the persecution in Egypt continued unabated under Maximin apart from a brief interruption in the spring of AD 311 as Galerius himself was dying. Maximin, however, resumed his efforts against the churches in the east by the autumn of that same year.[202] The persecution in Egypt finally came to an end in AD 313 after Licinius seized control of the empire in the east.

In the course of these events, most likely during the latter portion of AD 305 or early in AD 306, certain of the bishops who were being held as prisoners wrote a letter to complain about the actions of Meletius of Lycopolis, a newly appointed bishop who had replaced Apollonius of Lycopolis who had apostacized.[203] The four prisoner bishops, Hesychius, Pachomius,

---

[200]Hefele, *loc. cit.*

[201]*Cf.* T.D. Barnes, *Constantine and Eusebius,* London, 1981, 11, for other examples of decrees not being promulgated in the West despite Diocletian's issuance of such decrees "in the name of all the emperors" and his speaking "as if legislating for the whole empire."

[202]Galerius seems to have issued, if not an edict of toleration, at least a monition in the spring of AD 311. For a Greek translation, see Eusebius, *HE* 8. 17, 1-10; the Latin text is preserved in Lactantius, *De Mort.,* 34.

[203]Codex Verona LX, the critical text in F.H. Kettler, "Der melitianische Streit in Ägypten," *ZNTW* 35 (1936): 155-193. For a discussion of Apollonius

Theodorus, and Phileas, directed this letter to Meletius himself and argued that he had taken liberties in ordaining priests in their dioceses during their absence contrary to the canons and customs.[204] They further stated that they had made adequate provision for the people of their dioceses during their time of imprisonment through a system of "visitors."[205]

Although the language of the letter was strong, the bishops did address Meletius as "dilecto et comministro in Domino" and it does not appear that they had any intention of breaking relations with him.[206] The letter would seem to be better understood as a warning which had arisen out of troubled times.

During this period we are uncertain as to the exact location of Peter, the bishop of Alexandria. Rowan Williams is inclined to place the bishop somewhere within Egypt on the basis of Codex Verona LX and further argues that Meletius continued his schismatic ordination of presbyters, including one named Isidore and another named Arius, not during imprisonment (the consensus view), but during a "visitation" of Alexandria where he also excommunicated certain presbyters loyal to Peter who were in hiding.[207] When Peter was informed of this action, he wrote a letter to his flock instructing them to hold Meletius excommunicate. For Williams, therefore, the cause of the schism has to do with a struggle over pastoral care and administration of the church in lower Egypt during the time in which a void had been created owing to the arrest of a large number of bishops and the tentative hold of Peter upon Alexandria. In such an interpretation of events, Meletius could be seen as simply one who responded to a need arising out of persecution and whose motives were ultimately misunderstood.

Williams's reconstruction does seem plausible given the evidence which is presented, although it directly contradicts the sequence of events and circumstances given by Epiphanius, who most likely derived his material directly from Meletian sources.[208] According to Epiphanius, the initial rela-

---

and the accession of Meletius, see R. Williams, *Arius: Heresy and Tradition,* London, 1987, 259 (fn. 40).

[204]The names of these four bishops are given in Codex Verona LX, cited above in fn. 203.

[205]The exact nature of these "visitors" remains disputed. For a discussion of E. Schwartz's contention that these "visitors" were not, in fact, presbyters, see R. Williams, *op. cit.,* 259 (fn. 39).

[206]Kettler, *op. cit.,* 160.

[207]Williams, *op. cit.,* 37. For an example of the consensus that these ordinations did take place during the imprisonment of either Meletius or those who were ordained, see C. Schmidt, *Fragmente einer Schrift des Märtyrbischofs Petrus von Alexandrien* (TU 5, NS), Leipzig, 1901.

[208]Epiphanius, *Haer.* 68, 140ff; *cf.* H. Achelis, "Meletius von Lycopolis," *PRE* (third ed.), vol. 12, 558-562, concerning Epiphanius's possible use of Meletian documents by means of a Meletian convert to the catholic side of the schism.

tionship between Peter and Meletius was much closer, more like a bishop and coadjutor, and the schism arose over Peter's canons concerning those who had lapsed under persecution. In this scenario the quarrel between Peter and Meletius on the question of the lapsed began while both were in prison, or at least during a time when neither was at liberty. When they were both released, late in AD 305 or early in AD 306, Meletius entered the dioceses of the four Egyptian bishops (who were still in prison) and attempted to secure a following by undertaking the ordination of those who agreed with his more rigorous stance in regard to the lapsed. Meletius's subsequent foray into Alexandria and ultimate excommunication followed within the year. Still later, according to this account, Meletius and a number of his followers were arrested and banished to the mines where the schism remained and even grew among the Christian prisoners until the ultimate release of Meletius under the temporary edict of toleration promulgated by Galerius in AD 311.[209]

There are, without doubt, a number of difficulties with the circumstantial account of Epiphanius, which Williams has pointed out with great clarity. It is questionable, however, that we have sufficient documentation to support Williams's contention that "we can be confident that" the issue of the lapsed "was not the main cause of the schism, since it is perfectly clear that Meletius was active before the spring of 306."[210] The location of Peter during this time, the exact meaning of certain portions of the letter of the four bishops to Meletius, the later designation of Meletians as "the church of the Martyrs," and the notorious inaccuracies of Epiphanius would seem to prevent such a dogmatic assertion, although it seems clear that Williams has developed another way in which we might view this turbulent period in Egyptian church history.

In any case, following the renewal of the persecution by Maximin and the martyrdom of Bishop Peter on 25 November AD 311, disorder reigned in lower Egypt and there appears to have been a vacancy, of disputed length, before the accession of Achillas as bishop of Alexandria.[211] If we give weight to the later reports of Athanasius, the Meletians maintained an active opposition to Achillas during his short episcopate and continued to develop a separate organization throughout Egypt.[212] Their subsequent relations with Alexander after his accession to the see of Alexandria are also problematic as we have only the accounts of Epiphanius and Athanasius to depend upon for information relative to this period.[213] The actions of the Council of Nicaea concerning the Meletians, and the death of Alexander shortly following the

---

[209]*Cf. supra* fn. 202.

[210]Williams, *op. cit.*, 35.

[211]The length of the vacancy is disputed. For an interesting, although dated, discussion see, J.M. Neale, *op. cit.*, 113 (fn. 1).

[212]*Ad epp. Aeg. et Lib.* 23 (PG 25, 592 B).

[213]*Ibid.*; *Apol.* 59 (Opitz, 139, 1-18); Epiphanius, *Haer.* 68, 140ff.

council, lead us to the question of Meletian involvement in the Alexandrian election of Athanasius in AD 328.

It is, however, difficult to establish an exact chronology of events or even a general outline of circumstances for the period between the Council of Nicaea in AD 325 and the election of Athanasius as bishop of Alexandria in AD 328 with any certainty, for the documents and records which might be of assistance are unclear and often contradictory. This difficulty is especially evident as we attempt to discover the exact extent of Meletian involvement in the election itself. In examining this particular difficulty two points must be discussed. The first point, mentioned in passing above, is the contention of W. Telfer that after the death of Bishop Alexander, Meletius himself had an effective claim to become bishop of Alexandria, a claim which was later taken up by John Archaph, once the Meletian bishop of Memphis.[214] A second point, also previously touched upon, is the thesis of A. Martin that the so-called contested election of Athanasius arose owing to Meletian anger over being disenfranchised from their part in the Alexandrian election procedures of AD 328.[215] Although the two arguments are based upon different assumptions, their conclusion is the same—the Meletians, in reaction to the election of Athanasius, again went into schism and formed an important opposition party in Egypt during his early episcopate.

A large part of Telfer's argument is based upon his insistence that Athanasius's elevation to the throne of St. Mark was an innovative affair as regards the traditions of the church of Alexandria. This is a claim which, from the evidence cited above, appears suspect. Telfer states that "the succession of Athanasius to the bishopric of Alexandria involved . . . a breach alike of tradition and of existing agreements. Athanasius was not an Alexandrine presbyter, he did not as pope bury his predecessor, and his elevation set aside the consideration of any claims a Meletian candidate might have."[216] According to Telfer, there were "such claims awaiting consideration," for Constantine had contrived to assure the Meletians that, following the death of Alexander, one John of Memphis, "acknowledged leader of the Meletian interest after Meletius himself," would have "prospective rights not in regard to the see of Memphis but to that of Alexandria" itself.[217]

Telfer partially bases this reconstruction of events upon the enigmatic phrase found in Athanasius's transcription of the schedule of Meletian bishops presented to Alexander sometime after Nicaea, that John of Memphis was the one "whom the emperor ordered to be with the archbishop."[218] This John of Memphis is considered by Telfer to be, in all probability, the same

---

[214]Telfer, "Meletius of Lycopolis," *op. cit.,* 232-237.

[215]Martin, "Athanase et les Méletiens," *op. cit.,* 40-44.

[216]Telfer, "Meletius of Lycopolis,"*op. cit.,* 235.

[217]*Ibid.*

[218]*Apol.* 71 (Opitz, 150, 34).

person who reappears during the period of the Synod of Tyre as John Archaph, the added name being an allusion to his role in the Meletian church as "Arch-apa," or "supreme father."[219] Finally, Telfer suggests that Constantine in his later letter to John Archaph hinted "at some great reward to follow upon his reconciliation with Athanasius."[220] Such an interpretation, however, does not entirely fit the pattern of his argument that this would have involved an elevation within the Alexandrian church, for Athanasius was already in possession of the see at this time and would have had to agree to any such proposal.

Once again, we must agree with L.W. Barnard that Telfer's "ingenious reconstruction will not bear critical investigation resting, as it does, mainly on conjecture rather than contemporary evidence."[221] For Telfer, the "rights" of John of Memphis are inextricably linked with those of Meletius. When, therefore, the first argument fails under the pressure of evidence, so likewise does the second. It may also be noted that the phrase which follows the name of John of Memphis in the *Breviarium Melitii* is by no means conclusive. To be designated "$\kappa\epsilon\lambda\epsilon\upsilon\sigma\theta\epsilon\grave{\iota}\varsigma$ $\pi\alpha\rho\grave{\alpha}$ $\tauο\hat{υ}$ $\beta\alpha\sigma\iota\lambda\acute{\epsilon}\omega\varsigma$ $\epsilon\hat{\iota}\nu\alpha\iota$ $\mu\epsilon\tau\grave{\alpha}$ $\tauο\hat{υ}$ $\dot{\alpha}\rho\chi\iota\epsilon\pi\iota\sigma\kappa\acute{ο}\piο\upsilon$" is very ambiguous at best.[222] Robertson's comment, following Newman, is that the "archbishop" referred to here is Meletius (in the sense that he was the "first" in preeminence among the Meletian bishops) and that as this "is the first occurrence of the word" $\dot{\alpha}\rho\chi\iota\epsilon\pi\iota\sigma\kappa\acute{ο}\piο\upsilon$, it does not carry its later "fixed sense."[223] He further

---

[219]Telfer, "Meletius of Lycopolis," *op. cit.*, 236. We may note that Athanasius considers "Archaph" to be a native name (*Apol.* 70), while the church historian Socrates turns this appellation into the ill-fated scriptural name of Achab (*HE* I, 30). H.I. Bell identifies John Archaph with the $\dot{\alpha}\pi\alpha$ '$I\omega\acute{\alpha}\nu\nu\eta\nu$ who is mentioned in London Papyrus 1914. Although there is convincing evidence that the designation of $\dot{\alpha}\pi\alpha$ does correspond to that of $\dot{\alpha}\beta\beta\hat{\alpha}$ in Coptic usage, Bell does not present any evidence that positively links the personage in LP 1914 with John Archaph and certainly not with the John of Memphis who is found in the schedule. The common use of the name '$I\omega\acute{\alpha}\nu\nu\eta\nu$, which may be seen in Preisigke's *Namenbuch* (Heidelberg, 1922), and the uncertain nature and use of titles for clergy during this period makes any positive identification of a person from circumstances alone very risky (*cf. Jews and Christians in Egypt*, London, 1924, 67, fn. 34).

[220]Telfer, *loc. cit., cf. Apol.* 70 (Opitz, 148, 13ff).

[221]Barnard, "Two Notes," *op. cit.*, 350, 351.

[222]*Apol.* 1 (Opitz, 150, 34).

[223]Robertson, LNPF, second series, vol. 4, 137, fn. 6. Epiphanius also refers to the fact that Meletius was considered to be $\dot{\alpha}\rho\chi\iota\epsilon\pi\iota\sigma\kappa\acute{ο}\piο\varsigma$ of the province of Thebaïs (*Haer.* 69, 3). Although Epiphanius does not seem to be using the term in its later specific sense, its use may be used as a support to Robertson's identification of Meletius as the person who is the subject of this reference.

states, "the historical allusion is obscure."[224]   Although Nordberg understands the "archbishop" in the above passage to refer to Alexander, he confesses that it was a "vague stipulation" which would have been variously interpreted by the two parties in the dispute.[225] The ultimate and certain fate of John of Memphis is also obscure. John of Memphis, so called, disappears from the documents of the day and John Archaph is indicated as the leader of the Meletians by AD 333/34. Barnard states that Archaph "is probably to be identified with the John, Bishop of Memphis" listed in schedule.[226] He cites Nordberg and Telfer but indicates that Telfer's understanding of the name Archaph as a party title, and which, therefore, links him to John of Memphis, is "uncertain as it is bound up with Telfer's theory that this John had prospective rights to the see of Alexandria."[227] As to the role of Constantine in this affair, Barnard rightly argues against Telfer that

> there is no evidence that he wished to give John Archaph prospective rights to the Alexandrian see. His one concern was to reconcile Catholics and Meletians so that peace might reign in the Empire. The Emperor was little concerned with the ecclesiastical rights of John or the Meletians, although he was concerned that they should not be subject to oppression.[228]

It is impossible, on the basis of the extant evidence, to give full credence to the theories of Telfer as to the prospective rights of the Meletians to episcopal leadership in the see of Alexandria. A more plausible explanation for the reentry into schism of the Meletians following the election of Athanasius has been put forward by Annik Martin.

Martin contends that the reason for Meletian anger and accusations following the election of Athanasius was owing to their disenfranchisement and inability to participate in the process. After a brief review of the evidence for the "contested election" of Athanasius, Martin puts forward a key question: "Did the Meletian bishops, under the terms of the accords of Nicaea, have the right to participate in this election?"[229] From the evidence of Sozomen, who, according to Martin, "knew very well the content of the" later Meletian "accusations," there is little doubt that the "Meletians wanted

---

[224]Robertson, *loc. cit.*

[225]Nordberg, *Athanasius and the Emperor*, 13.

[226]Barnard, "Some Notes," *op. cit.*, 401. Opitz also indicates that the John listed in the schedule is John Archaph, the leader of the Meletians, but gives no evidence for such a claim beyond referring the reader to Athanasius's statement in *Apol.* 70, which does not bring any additional clarity or help in the process of identification (Opitz, 150, fn. to line 34).

[227]Barnard, *loc. cit.*

[228]Barnard, "Two Notes," *op. cit.*, 351.

[229]Martin, "Athanase et les Méletiens," *op. cit.*, 41.

to participate in the election" and most likely went into schism once again when they were excluded.[230] Again, however, Martin asks the question, "Did they have the right?"[231]

> The synod of Nicaea specified that they did not have the power to elect or to propose the name of a candidate in their diocese, the catholic bishop of the place retaining the sole prerogative. One can easily assume that when two bishops occupied the same see, the Meletian would be excluded as well from the right to participate in the election of the bishop of Alexandria; when he was the sole title holder he held it against contrary forces. Would not the Meletians have looked for the recognition by their catholic colleagues of the totality of their ancient episcopal rights, especially at the occasion of the succession to Alexander? This is what is signified in the allusion cited by Sozomen above. The catholic bishops who had a Meletian for a colleague would have, without doubt, shown themselves hostile to such a solution.[232]

Martin further comments that Athanasius "could scarcely have accepted the participation at his election of disputing bishops and he, therefore, would have held to the strict application of the agreements made at Nicaea."[233] According to Martin, it was this inability to stand and participate as equals with the catholic bishops which drove the Meletians back into schism.

Martin has correctly singled out the crucial issue. Did the Meletians have any right to participate in the election of the successor to Alexander? Furthermore, would they have been allowed to participate in the election by the catholic bishops? To answer the former query, we must turn our attention to the synodal letter sent from Nicaea to the Egyptian and neighboring churches concerning the admission of the Meletians into the fellowship of the catholic community in Egypt which was under the episcopal rule of Alexander. The letter is as follows:

> Since the synod was disposed to act kindly, for in strict justice he was not worthy of leniency, it was decreed that Meletius should remain in his own city and that he would have no authority to make appointments ($\pi\rho o\chi\epsilon\iota\rho\iota\zeta\epsilon\sigma\theta a\iota$) or to lay on hands ($\chi\epsilon\iota\rho o\theta\epsilon\tau\epsilon\hat{\iota}\nu$) or to appear in any city or village for such a purpose, but should possess only the title of his rank, bishop. Those who have already been appointed by him, after they have been confirmed by a more sacred ordination ($\mu\upsilon\sigma\tau\iota\kappa\acute{\omega}\tau\epsilon\rho a \chi\epsilon\iota\rho o\tau o\nu\acute{\iota}a$) may on meeting this condition be admitted to fellowship and have their rank and the ability to

---

[230]*Ibid.;* cf. Sozomen, *HE*, II, 17 (J. Bidez, SC 306, Paris, 1983, 296).

[231]Martin, *loc. cit.*

[232]Martin, "Athanase et les Méletiens," *op. cit.,* 43.

[233]*Ibid.*

officiate, but they shall be under the rule of those enrolled in each parish and church who have been appointed by our most honorable colleague Alexander. These have no authority to make appointments (προχειρίζεσθαι) of persons pleasing to them or to propose names or to do anything without the permission of the bishop of the catholic and apostolic church serving under Alexander. . . . If it should come to pass that any at that time in the church die, then those who have been recently received are to succeed to the office of the deceased, but only if they appear worthy, and the people choose them, with the catholic bishop of Alexandria concurring in the election and ratifying it.[234]

I have followed Everett Ferguson in rendering the word προχειρίζεσθαι—"make appointments."[235] The clear intent of the letter is twofold. First, it seems clear that Ferguson is correct in stating that the "passage must mean that the Meletian clergy are to receive a new ordination."[236] We may also note that any further elevations to the episcopate among the Meletians are not a prescribed right, for the candidate must receive the approval of the bishop of Alexandria, the assent of the people, and be considered "worthy" (ἄξιος). In other words, they would be involved in the same pattern of events which would hold true for any episcopal candidate. Second, the Meletians are restrained from making lower appointments within their own spheres of influence, or even making nominations, without the explicit permission of the catholic bishop of the place.

In light of such restrictions on a local basis, it seems almost incomprehensible to suggest that the Meletians had a "prospective right" to the throne of St. Mark or even the expectation of being allowed to participate in the election of Alexander's successor. Martin is certainly correct, contrary to Telfer and Girardet, that the accords reached at Nicaea would have been interpreted by Athanasius and his followers in the most literal sense.[237] We may

---

[234]The text of the letter is preserved in Socrates, *HE* I, 9; Theodoret, *HE* ix, 7ff.; and Gelasius, *HE* II, 33. This translation is based upon the text in Theodoret, *HE* ix. 7ff. (GCS, edited by L. Parmentier and F. Scheidweiler, second edition, Berlin, 1954, 39-41).

[235]E. Ferguson, "Attitudes to Schism at the Council of Nicaea," *Schism, Heresy, and Religious Protest* (ed. Derek Baker), Cambridge, 1972, 58.

[236]*Ibid.*

[237]Martin, *op. cit.*, 43. This conclusion may be compared not only to Telfer's "prospective rights" argument ("Meletius of Lycopolis," *op. cit.*, 235) but also to the legalistic interpretation of Girardet that Nicaea was concerned only with those bishops who had actually been ordained by Meletius and not with those who had followed him into schism or supported him (*Kaisergericht und Bischofsgericht*, 54). Clearly the intent of the synodal letter of Nicaea was to deal with all of those in schism. We agree with Martin that Athanasius and his followers would have been unwilling to allow disputing bishops who had recently been schismatic to participate in the election.

conclude, therefore, that it is extremely unlikely that the Meletians were considered to have the right to be involved in any substantial manner in the Alexandrian episcopal election of AD 328. It is altogether possible, however, that it was their exclusion from that process which may have then prompted them to enter into schism once again and eventually to seek an alliance with the Arians against Athanasius. When considered against such a background of events, the later accusations of the Meletians and the Arians against Athanasius as regards the irregular nature of his election and consecration take on a somewhat different meaning.

There is one further scenario which some have suggested might have influenced the Meletian involvement (or noninvolvement) in the election of the successor to Alexander. This is the possibility that there was a second session of the Council of Nicaea which dealt with the continuing problems of schisms and theological divisions which were confronting the church, with special attention being given to the Egyptian situation. Many, on the basis of the evidence presented by Schwartz, Seeck, and Opitz, regard this second session as an historical fact.[238] Others, however, such as Robertson, Telfer, and, more recently, Jan-M. Szymusiak, have followed the more traditional understanding of Montfaucon that the time between Nicaea and the final presentation of the *Breviarium Melitii* to Alexander was protracted by the Meletians and did not take place until AD 327 with no other substantial synodal sessions in the intervening period.[239] Much of the speculation concerning a second session of Nicaea has arisen owing to the remark by

---

[238]Space does not permit a full discussion of the "second session" debate concerning the Council of Nicaea. It is sufficient to say that the hypothesis was first put forward by Seeck ("Untersuchungen," *op. cit.*, 69ff.) and taken up in turn by Schwartz (*GS* III, 205ff.) and Opitz ("Das syrische Corpus Athanasianum," *ZNW* 33 [1934]: 156-158). According to this hypothesis the second session of the council of Nicaea was summoned by Constantine in order to reconcile the Arians who had refused to subscribe to the decisions of the council, such as Eusebius of Nicomedia and Theognis of Nicaea. This reconstruction of events has gained wide acceptance by a large number of respected scholars such as H. Lietzmann (*Geschichte* III, 111, 112), Nordberg (*Athanasius and the Emperor*, 13), and Girardet (*Kaisergericht und Bischofsgericht*, 53, 54). The document on which this hypothesis is partly based however, has been doubted as to its authenticity even though Opitz included it in his *Urkundensammlung* (Opitz III, Urkunde 31, 65) as being genuine. For the dissenting opinions concerning this document, see Rogala, *Anfänge des arianischen Streites*, 78-85; and Baynes, "Athanasiana," *JEA* 2 (1925): 58.

[239]The initial argument of Montfaucon (PG 25, lvii) has been followed by Robertson (LNPF, second series, vol. 4, xxi) and in more recent times by Telfer ("Meletius of Lycopolis," *op. cit.*, 234). More complete arguments against the "second session" hypothesis have been advanced by J.-M. Szymusiak in Appendice I, "A propos d'une deuxième session du concile de nicée," in *Apologie a l'empereur Constance: Apologie pour sa fuite*, SC 56, Paris, 1958, 169-173; and C. Luibhéid, "The Alleged Second Session of the Council of Nicaea," *JEH* 34, no. 2 (April 1983): 165-174.

Athanasius that when his predecessor Alexander died, five months had not passed from the time of the Meletian reconciliation.[240] Although Athanasius does not indicate that Alexander died five months after the Council of Nicaea, some, like Theodoret, placed that meaning upon the statement.[241] Gelasius suggested that the Council of Nicaea actually lasted three years (strengthening Theodoret's misunderstanding of the statement by Athanasius), but it is known that the main sessions of the council were held and completed in a relatively short time in the summer of AD 325.[242]

In all probability the reconciliation of the Meletians which prompted the final presentation of the *Breviarium* took place at a special gathering which had been summoned by Constantine to deal exclusively with the schism within the Egyptian church. This argument has been advanced as a distinct possibility by Colm Luibhéid. Such a scenario does appear to reconcile the remarks of Eusebius of Caesarea, concerning a second meeting which took place following Nicaea, with the brief period of peace between the catholic and Meletian parties in Egypt which occurred immediately before the time of Alexander's death in April of AD 328.[243] The need for further mediation by Constantine may well have been occasioned by a Meletian refusal to accept the accords which had been decided upon at Nicaea and which effectively limited their power in the "newly constituted" episcopate of Alexandria. Given the tone of Athanasius's later remarks concerning the admission of Meletius into communion ("would that he would never have been admitted") it seems to have been a disagreeable proposition for both sides from the beginning and was certainly made worse by Athanasius's subsequent election and the Meletians' nonparticipation in the process.[244]

By making use of the wide variety of sources which are at our disposal, a plausible reconstruction of the pivotal events under discussion could be as follows. At the Council of Nicaea several decisions were reached which would have a profound impact upon the ecclesiastical structure of the Egyptian church quite apart from the theological pronouncements which had been set forth concerning Arius. First, the council sought to give legislative approval to the traditional territorial authority of the bishop of Alexandria, which under canon six was understood to include "Egypt, . . . Libya, and . . . Pentapolis," that is, the whole of the Nile valley and all of that region which stretched across Pentapolis.[245] Although the exact extent of his control over the four civil provinces of Egypt, Libya, Pentapolis, and Thebais would be debated in the years to come, the Nicene fathers sought to indicate

---

[240]*Apol.* 59 (Opitz, 139, 15-18).

[241]Theodoret, *HE* I, 26.

[242]Gelasius, *HE* 2, 37, 38; *cf.* Philostorgius, *HE* 2, 7.

[243]Luibhéid, "Alleged Second Session," *op. cit.,* 172; and Eusebius, *VC* 3, 21.

[244]*Apol.* 71 (Opitz, 149, 13,14).

[245]Hefele, *History of the Councils,* I, 388.

the special position and prestige of the bishop of Alexandria by means of this canon. This unique range of authority was further emphasized by a comparison with the similar status of the bishops of Rome.[246] Second, the fourth and fifth canons determined and regularized the proper procedure for the election and ordination of bishops as well as the initial authority of a provincial synod.[247] As Hefele indicates, "Meletius was the probable occasion" of the fourth canon, not a particular concern on the part of the council with the Alexandrian model of episcopal consecration.[248] Finally, the council dispatched a synodal letter to the Egyptian and neighboring churches which indicated the exact provisions for the reinstatement of the Meletian clergy.[249] It may be easily appreciated that these provisions, taken together, gave Alexander a very strong hand with which to deal with the question of the Meletian difficulties in Egypt upon his return from the council during the latter portion of AD 325.[250]

The majority of the Meletian party in Egypt would not have been overly pleased with the results of the council concerning their particular position. Telfer describes well the post-Nicene situation of the Meletians:

> It is evident that Meletius was himself willing to be reconciled. But that being so, it fell to him to communicate the terms of the Synodal letter to each of his suffragans and persuade them to accept. We need not be surprised that it was into the third year before he was able to present to Alexander the whole company of persons to be reconciled and to benefit under the terms of the Synodal letter.[251]

---

[246]*Ibid.*

[247]Hefele, *op. cit.*, 381, 386.

[248]Hefele, *op. cit.*, 384.

[249]*Vide supra*, fn. 220.

[250]T.D. Barnes, drawing upon the *Chronicle of Jerome,* states that the final event of the Council of Nicaea was the celebration on 25 July AD 325 of the emperor's *vicennalia,* after which "he summoned them once again for a farewell discourse" before the bishops departed (*Constantine and Eusebius,* 219). This agrees with Eusebius's account in *VC* 3, 15ff. The Coptic calendar, however, celebrates the 318 Fathers on 5 November, keeping alive the tradition that Alexander and Athanasius did not return until that time and only then were the synodal letters published. That the decisions of Nicaea strengthened the hand of Alexander upon his return from the council, we may refer to the comment by R. Williams that "Nicaea dealt not only with the Meletian problem and the case of Arius, but also with the regularization of episcopal succession and jurisdiction in Egypt; and it is not fanciful to see behind this conjunction some sense of interrelatedness of these issues" ("Arius and the Meletian Schism," *JThS,* NS 37, 1 [April 1986]: 52).

[251]Telfer, "Meletius of Lycopolis," *op. cit.*, 234.

It would appear that this process created so many difficulties and such a disturbance that the issue once again threatened the peace of the Egyptian church. Eusebius is very clear that the difficulties which attracted the attention of Constantine after the end of the Council of Nicaea were specifically Egyptian in their origin.[252] The hypothesis that this involved a full second session of the Council of Nicaea, as Luibhéid has pointed out, presents many more problems than it solves.[253] On the other hand, to view Eusebius's "synod" simply as a meeting of the Egyptian clergy, along with perhaps other church leaders, at which Constantine brought his influence to bear upon the participants and "gave his sanction to the decrees of the council" would help to explain the somewhat tardy and strained admission of the Meletians into the ranks of the Egyptian clergy.[254] This meeting and final submission does appear to have taken place in the context of, or immediately after, some large meeting of the clergy, for Athanasius states that those individuals listed in the *Breviarium Melitii*—twenty-eight bishops, four presbyters, and three deacons—were actually presented in person to Alexander by Meletius.[255] Although each side may have been persuaded by Constantine to accept the accords reached at Nicaea, neither party seems to have been pleased with the arrangement which appears to have been concluded during the last few months of AD 327.[256] Within less than five months of the conclusion of this settlement, Alexander was dead and Meletius had also disappeared from the scene, probably dying within a short time as well.[257]

Alexander of Alexandria died on 17 April AD 328, just three days after Easter.[258] Ephiphanius informs us that Alexander had chosen Athanasius as his successor, a report which would be congruous with Alexandrian tradition

---

[252]Eusebius, *VC* 3, 23.

[253]Luibhéid, *op. cit.*, 174.

[254]Eusebius, *loc. cit.*

[255]*Apol.* 72 (Opitz, 151, 10).

[256]As we know that Alexander of Alexandria died on 17 April AD 328 from the evidence of the *Festal Index* (Robertson, LNPF, second series, vol. 4, 503; and Larsow, *Fest-Briefe, op. cit.*, 26, 27), we may approximate the time of the short-lived reconciliation by counting back five months to the latter portion of AD 327.

[257]*Apol.* 59 (Opitz, 139, 15,16). The statement of Epiphanius that Meletius had died before the Council of Nicaea (*Haer.* 68, 3) may certainly be discounted on the strength of the statement by Athanasius that he presented his bishops to Alexander in person (*Apol.* 72). The exact date of Meletius's death is unknown, although during the next phase of the controversy—those events which led directly to the Synod of Tyre—John Archaph is the recognized leader of the Meletians. Neale reports the conflicting claims as to whether or not Meletius himself died in schism (Neale, *Patriarchate of Alexandria*, 150, fn. 2). In any case, it seems clear that Meletius was removed from the controversy at about the same time as Alexander of Alexandria died.

[258]*Festal Index, op. cit., (cf. supra, fn. 256).*

in such matters.[259] Athanasius was not in Alexandria at the time of Alexander's death. Some accounts place him at court on church business, while others indicate that he was attempting to flee the honor.[260] In either case, there appears to have been an attempt at usurpation in his absence. While inaccurate as regards detail, Epiphanius does appear to preserve a Meletian tradition concerning an attempt to place one of their own on the throne of St. Mark.[261] Such an attempt, however, would have been regarded by the catholic clergy as completely irregular according to the synodal letter of Nicaea and the recent submission of the Meletian clergy to Alexander and, therefore, immediately rejected. Perhaps the Meletians hoped to take advantage of what Barnard calls "Egyptian psychology . . . for there was a long tradition in Egypt that the King's successor had to be enthroned immediately on his death in order to avert cosmic and political chaos."[262] Epiphanius does indicate that it was an Alexandrian custom for a bishop's successor to be appointed immediately to ensure the peace and stability of the church.[263] Within a short time, however, Athanasius returned to Alexandria where a good number of bishops had already assembled and, we are told, were being entreated by the people to elect Athanasius, calling him "good, pious, Christian, an ascetic, a genuine bishop."[264] Either owing to their failed (or short-lived) attempt to elect their own candidate, or because of the strict interpretation of the decisions contained within the synodal letter (and possibly its subsequent enforcement by Constantine), the Meletian bishops were apparently excluded completely from any further part in the election. By the week following the feast of Pentecost (1 June AD 328) all of the bishops who were competent to take part in the election could have made their way to Alexandria, having completed the full cycle of Easter celebrations in their own churches where they would have been presiding. During that week Athanasius was elected by a majority ($\pi\lambda\epsilon\ell o\nu\epsilon s$) of the bishops present (indicating that there may have been some dissent), received the acclamation of the *plebs*, and on 8 June AD 328, seven and one-half weeks after the death of Alexander, "having passed through the entire series of orders," he was ordained by the gathered bishops in accordance with the fourth canon of

---

[259]*Haer.* 68, 7 (Holl, *op. cit.*, 147, 4-17) (*cf. supra*, fn. 97).

[260]*Ibid.*; Sozomen, *HE* II, 17; Theodoret, *HE* II, 26.

[261]*Haer.*, *loc. cit.*; it is difficult to agree fully with the statement of T.D. Barnes that after Theonas died, "the Meletians clearly replaced him, since the accidental find of a papyrus shows that a Meletian bishop of Alexandria existed in 334" (*Constantine and Eusebius*, 230). Barnes is making reference to London Papyrus 1914, which only comments concerning $\dot{\epsilon}\pi\iota\sigma\kappa\dot{o}\pi o\upsilon$ $\dot{\epsilon}\nu$ $\tau\hat{\eta}$ $\pi\alpha\rho\epsilon\mu\beta o\lambda\hat{\eta}$ near to Alexandria, but in no sense does this indicate that the person in question was the "Meletian bishop of Alexandria" (London Papyrus 1914, 1.7ff.).

[262]Barnard, "Two Notes," *op. cit.*, 352.

[263]*Haer.* 69, 11 (Holl, *op. cit.*, 161).

[264]*Apol.* 6 (Opitz, 91, 17, 18).

Nicaea.[265] It is, however, possible that as he mounted the throne of St. Mark in the sight of the people, he had yet to attain the full canonical age of thirty years.[266] Not surprisingly, as Nordberg has pointed out, the first challenge that awaited the new bishop was a renewed schism on the part of the Meletians which threatened the unity and stability of the Egyptian church.[267]

When compared with other contemporary sources, the account of the consecration and election of Athanasius given by Philostorgius is undoubtedly defective both in the details which are offered and in its general reporting of events and personalities. It appears very probable that Philostorgius only repeated a random assortment of fraudulent Arian and Meletian calumnies against Athanasius which have been compressed into a single narrative that has little basis in fact. That there was a separate tradition concerning Athanasius preserved by Philostorgius, there can be little doubt. That it was, in the words of Rusch, a "genuine historical tradition" seems to be an unacceptable evaluation of the evidence presented. Of all the sources available which purport to give an account of the election of Athanasius, the one presented by Philostorgius appears to be the most contrived and the most removed from other documentary evidence, whether Arian, Meletian, or orthodox.

By way of contrast, the material contained within the synodal letter of the Egyptian bishops, written in AD 338/39, only a decade after the event, while admittedly defending an orthodox position, does appear to be a more reliable report of what actually took place.[268] The other accounts which are contained in Epiphanius, Sozomen, Socrates, and Gregory Nazianzen do acknowledge the circulation of Arian and Meletian versions of the election, but they are, for the most part, discounted, and the general outline of events can be reconciled with the report and witness of the Egyptian bishops. For this reason we cannot agree with Rusch's contention that Philostorgius is a vital help to the modern researcher who is involved in the task of constructing a true historical picture of Athanasius. On the contrary, Philostorgius apparently so distorts the image of Athanasius that it is difficult to find any kind of true historical representation of the bishop of Alexandria in his entire ac-

---

[265]Cf. Barnard, "Two Notes," op. cit., 349.

[266]Festal Index, loc. cit.; Also on the question of the age of Athanasius and its relationship to the question of his election and consecration, cf. Martin, op. cit., 32-61. Charles Kannengiesser has shown considerable concern about the effect of the date of Athanasius's birth on the dating of his "earliest writings" and tends to agree that Athanasius was slightly younger (perhaps only by months) than the age set by the synod (cf. "La Date de l'apologie d'Athanase 'Contre les païens' et 'Sur l'incarnation,'" RSR 58 (1970): 383-428). (Cf. supra, fn. 119 for further references on this issue).

[267]Nordberg, op. cit., 19.

[268]Apol. 6 (Opitz, 91-93).

count, unless one is seeking the variety and manner with which Athanasius was assailed by those who opposed him.

3.3 The Meletians and London Papyrus 1914

There is little doubt that Athanasius faced following his enthronement in the summer of AD 328 an unenviable situation in Egypt. Although, as stated above, it appears that Athanasius was elected with the support of the majority of the clergy and people gathered in Alexandria, the church in Egypt as a whole seems to have been beset by continuing divisions. As John Griffiths has stated, "The lack of unity in the earlier years of the rule of Athanasius is plain enough. The Meletians, the Arians, and the Manichees were all attracting support in a divisive sense; and there was always the danger that the monastic movement . . . would fail to support the spiritual leadership of Alexandria."[269] The pattern of schisms and divided loyalties within the Egyptian church at this time is difficult either to trace or fully comprehend. It is obvious, from both the extant materials and subsequent events, that a large number of Meletians entered into schism once again following the election of Athanasius. There were, however, a number of Meletian bishops, presbyters, and deacons who appear to have transferred their full support to Athanasius in the very early years of his episcopate. For example, the presbyter Macarius, who is later implicated in the Ischyras incident, appears to be the same man of that name who is listed in the *Breviarium Melitii*.[270] A Meletian bishop, Theon of Nilopolis, also listed in the schedule, is later mentioned by Athanasius as having died in possession of an orthodox bishopric.[271] Henric Nordberg argues convincingly that Athanasius brought several former Meletian bishops and presbyters with him to Tyre, stating that "out of 47 Egyptian clericals at Tyre" accompanying Athanasius "probably at least 17 had been earlier sup- porters of the Meletian church."[272] From the evidence presented, it seems clear that Nordberg is fully justified in claiming that in Athanasius's first few years as bishop he "succeeded in winning for his cause a number of schis- matic leaders."[273]

During the time between Athanasius's election in AD 328 and the synod of Tyre in AD 335, similar attempts to win over the disaffected Meletians were being conducted by the Arian party headed by Eusebius of

---

[269]John Gwyn Griffiths, "Egyptian Influences on Athanasius," *Studien zu Sprache und Religion Ägyptens (Festschrift W. Westendorf)*, vol. 2, Göttingen, 1984, 1023.

[270]Μακάριος πρεσβύτερος τῆς Παρεμβολῆς, *Apol.* 71 (Opitz, 151, 9, no. 42 in the schedule). Nordberg is convinced of this identification (*cf.* Nordberg, *op. cit.*, 22). Opitz, however, is more cautious in his note on the matter (Opitz, 140, fn. to 1. 15ff.).

[271]Robertson, LNPF, second series, vol. 4, xxi, fn. 6.

[272]Nordberg, *op. cit.*, 29.

[273]*Ibid.*

Nicomedia. With the reinstatements of the exiled Eusebius and Theognis of Nicaea in AD 328, the Arian controversy entered upon a new chapter.[274] Eusebius, soon after his own restoration, began to forge a political alliance with many of those Meletians who had rejected the leadership of Athanasius. Thomas Kopecek has described the ends toward which the Eusebians were moving at this time: "Those bishops who had supported Arian theology turned their attention to realizing two practical goals, namely, the reinstatement of Arius to the Alexandrian priesthood and the deposition—on non-theological grounds—of Nicaea's defenders."[275]

The origin of this tactical alliance between the Eusebians and the Meletians is shrouded in mystery. The claim by Sozomen that Arius had once been a follower of Meletius has been accepted by many scholars, reinforced as it is by a note contained within the Codex Verona LX.[276] Rowan Williams, however, has put forward the view that the Arius mentioned in these two sources as a companion of Meletius is most likely not to be identified with the heresiarch.[277] For, in the controversy which followed, not only did Alexander fail to mention the background of Arius in this regard, but, as Williams has pointed out, Athanasius also refrained from making any reference to such information. This portion of Williams's argument is stated as follows:

> Even stranger [than the silence of Alexander] is the silence of Athanasius—never an overscrupulous controversialist (as we have seen, he had no qualms about accusing Meletius of apostasy). If anyone was in a position to know what was recorded of the younger Arius in the chancery files of Alexandria, he was. Yet he can describe the Meletian origins, and the later tactical alliance of Arians and Meletians, without

---

[274]The return from exile of Eusebius and Theognis at about AD 328 on the basis of their appeal to Constantine (Opitz III, Urkunde 31) is verified by both Sozomen (*HE* 2, 16) and the less reliable Philostorgius (*HE* 2, 7). T. Kopecek sees in their return to Nicomedia and Nicaea and their acceptance, at least verbally, of the Constantinian settlement, the end of "the initial stage of the Arian controversy" (*A History of Neo-Arianism*, vol. 1, Philadelphia, 1979, 59).

[275]Kopecek, *op. cit.*, 76.

[276]Concerning the importance of this document and its history and contents, *vide* W. Telfer, "The Codex Verona LX (58)," *HTR* 36 (1943): 169-246. The portion which deals with the question of the identity of Arius may be found on p. 184. A critical text of those portions of the codex which deal with the Meletian schism may be consulted in F.H. Kettler, "Der melitianische Streit in Ägypten," *ZNW* 35 (1936): 159-163.

[277]R. D. Williams, "Arius and the Meletian Schism," *JThS*, NS 37, 1 (1986): 50. His argument is in opposition to that of Kopecek that "Arius had backed the Meletian schism in the first decade of the fourth century" and only broke with Meletius after about AD 322, when Arius "articulated a theological position which Meletius found to be totally unacceptable" (Kopecek *op. cit.*, 3, 4).

ever exploiting what would surely have been a heaven-sent opportunity for blackening the names of both groups of adversaries at once. He uses predictably—the familiar trope of the dog returning to its vomit against the Meletians; why not against Arius reverting to his past mode of disruptive behavior?[278]

In any case, it seems unlikely that an Arian-Meletian alliance would have grown out of Arius's earlier association with Meletius; for those same sources which invite such speculation also indicate that this was but a brief episode in the life of the heresiarch which ended in an atmosphere of mutual antagonism.[279]

It seems clear, therefore, that the Arian-Meletian alliance postdates Athanasius's election and the subsequent elevation of John Archaph to the leadership of the Meletians. Yet a vexing question remains: When did Athanasius become aware of the conspiracy which was being formulated against him? From his own testimony in *Apol.* 59, Athanasius indicates that in the early stages of the alliance the Meletians had Eusebius as their "secret friend" ($\kappa\rho\dot\upsilon\phi\alpha$ $\phi\dot\iota\lambda o\varsigma$).[280] This might suggest Athanasius's own lack of awareness concerning the situation at this time. In his *Festal Letters* we may witness his progress in perception as to the reality of the alliance. In his *Festal Letter* for AD 332, Athanasius states that he is at court, having been summoned by Constantine, at the instigation of "the Meletians, who were present there," seeking his "ruin before the Emperor."[281] In his *Festal Letter* for AD 333, Athanasius makes several references to the "schismatics" (*i.e.*, the Meletians), but it is not until the *Festal Letter* for AD 338 that he speaks of all "those who dispute with Christ," *i.e.*, the Arians, "but also ... the schismatics; for they are united together, as men of kindred feelings."[282] Athanasius's conviction that the Meletians had made common

---

[278]Williams, *op. cit.*, 46.

[279]Epiphanius, *Haer.* 68, 6 (Holl, *op. cit.*, 144, 1-5). In this account the story is preserved of Meletius's first instigating the accusation of heresy against Arius. We may note, however, that Epiphanius does not indicate any earlier association even though he "has quite a bit to say about the Arian-Meletian alliance and the role of Eusebius of Nicomedia in organizing and cementing it" (Williams, *op. cit.*, 46).

[280]*Apol.* 59 (Opitz, 139, 20).

[281]LNPF, *op. cit.*, 517 (Larsow, *Fest-Briefe*, 88).

[282]LNPF, *op. cit.*, 531. I have here followed the chronology for the *Festal Letters* which has been put forward by R. Lorenz, *Der zehnte Osterfestbrief des Athanasius von Alexandrien*, Berlin and New York, 1986, 30-31. Lorenz is convincing in redating the AD 334 letter to AD 345 and placing the fragment assigned to the later date within the earlier year. Lorenz has also put forward a forceful argument for placing the tenth letter in the year AD 338 upon the assumption that it was in this year that Antony the Hermit visited Alexandria. Within this context (81) Lorenz also observes that the tenth letter contains the

cause against him with Eusebius of Nicomedia appears to have been the result of a gradual process which found its final culmination near to the time of the calling of the synod of Caesarea in AD 334. By the time of the Synod of Tyre in July AD 335, any reservations he might have had concerning the reality or the predatory nature of the alliance would have been completely dispelled.[283] After this time, Athanasius is consistent in his identification of the Meletians in Egypt as an extension of the Arian party under Eusebius.[284]

---

first open attack on Arianism. This contention appears to agree with the case which I have put forward in the present study that Athanasius was far more concerned with the Meletian threat and only later became aware of their links with the Eusebian or pro-Arian party. This restating of the Schwartzian chronology is, therefore, most helpful.

[283]The question concerning the relative strength of the Arians in Egypt before the emergence of their alliance with the Meletians has yet to be answered in a satisfactory manner. Nordberg is convinced that the major threat in Egypt in the early years of Athanasius's episcopate was the Meletian schism. Recent scholarship, for a variety of reasons, has tended to support this view (cf. Barnes, op. cit., 230; W.H.C. Frend, The Rise of Christianity, Philadelphia, 1984, 525). The more controversial aspect of Nordberg's claim, however, is that the fragment of a letter from Constantine to Athanasius, preserved in Apol. 59 (Opitz, 140 and Opitz III, Urkunde 45), is a command from the emperor to readmit the Meletians to the fellowship of the church. Most scholars have accepted that this letter concerns Arius rather than the Meletians (cf. Frend, loc. cit.; Lietzmann, op. cit., 3, 129-132; Barnes, op. cit., 231; L.W. Barnard, "Athanasius and the Roman State," Latomus 36 (1977): 425, to name but a few). Even the dating of the letter has been the subject of some controversy (cf. N. Baynes, "Athanasiana," JEA 2, 58ff.), although a date between AD 328 and AD 330 seems probable (cf. Dörries, op. cit., 95; H. Kraft, Kaiser Konstantins religiöse Entwicklung: Beiträge zur historischen Theologie 20, Tübingen, 1955, 352ff.; and Barnes, op. cit., 231). The fragment of this letter preserved by Athanasius is as follows: "As you now have knowledge of my will, which is that all who wish to enter the church may freely do so, you must not forbid entrance to any. For if I should learn that you have hindered or excluded any who have been willing to be admitted to the communion of the church, I will immediately send and depose you by my decree, and will send you from your place" (Opitz, 140, 7-10). Athanasius's reply to this order was to inform the emperor that "communion between an anti-Christian heresy and the catholic Church could not exist" (μηδεμίαν εἶναι κοινωνίαν τῇ χριστομάχῳ αἱρέσει πρὸς τὴν καθολικὴν ἐκκλησίαν) (Apol. 60, Opitz, 140, 11, 12). This statement seems to refer to Arius (cf. Barnard, "Athanasius and the Roman State," op. cit., 425), although, depending upon the dating of the letter, Athanasius could be referring to the Meletians in terms of their alliance with Eusebius of Nicomedia. Nevertheless, such a conclusion would require an almost complete reordering of the evidence as well as a very early knowledge by Athanasius as to the existence of the alliance. Such does not appear to be the case from Athanasius's Festal Letters from the period under consideration.

[284]Cf. Apol. 59ff.

We may conclude that by AD 335 the Meletians in Egypt had fragmented. A sizable segment had given their loyalty to Athanasius—according
to Nordberg, almost half of those listed in the *Breviarium Melitii*.[285]
Another large party, under the leadership of John Archaph, entered into an alliance of convenience with Eusebius of Nicomedia. Yet another group, similar to those described by Barnard as "semi-Coptic Meletian monks" who "in a
rural *milieu*, would have retained something of the indigenous, puritanical
outlook of the 'Church of the Martyrs,'" seem not to have given their alle-

---

[285]Of the forty-two Meletian clerics listed in the *Breviarium Melitii (Apol.
71*, Opitz, 149-151), Nordberg identifies "at least seventeen" individuals who
later supported Athanasius at the synod of Tyre in July AD 335 (Nordberg, *op. cit.,*
29). In reviewing Nordberg's evidence, the process of identification falls into two
categories. Twelve of the individuals listed in the *Breviarium Melitii* may be
identified with a very high degree of probability owing to their unusual names, to
a particular association (as in the case of the Meletian presbyters who are grouped
together in the schedule, or Timotheus of Diospolis, who appears to have
remained with his bishop, Ammonius when they reappear at Tyre), or to other
references in various church histories (as the identification of the Meletians who
accompanied John Archaph to Tyre by Sozomen in *HE* 2, 25, as well as the
position of Macarius as a follower of Athanasius). Another five of Nordberg's
identifications appear to be based almost exclusively either on name and
approximate location in AD 335 or on the mention of their death in possession of
an orthodox bishopric in later years by Athanasius in a *Festal Letter* (as in the case
of Theodoros of Kopto and Pelagius of Oxyrhynchus in *Festal Letter* 19 for the
year AD 347). The following list indicates those Meletians from the *Breviarium
Melitii* who appear to have accompanied Athanasius to Tyre. The first twelve
names give the more secure identifications while the last five are more doubtful.
The first column of numbers corresponds to those in Opitz for the *Breviarium
Melitii, BM* (149-151), and the second column corresponds to the brief presented
by Athanasius's supporters at Tyre (159).

	Name	BM	Tyre
1.	Ἀμμώνιος ἐν Διοσπόλει	5	5
2.	Πελάγιος ἐν Ὀξυρύγχῳ	12	27
3.	Πέτρος ἐν Ἡρακλέους	13	4
4.	Ἁρποκρατίων ἐν Βουβάστῳ	23	10
5.	Μωσῆς ἐν Φακουσαῖς	24	11
6.	Κρόνιος ἐν Μετήλι	32	41
7.	Ἀγαθάμμων (Ἀλεχανδρέων)	33	22
8.	Ἀπολλώνιος πρεσβύτερος	35	15
9.	Διόσκορος πρεσβύτερος	37	37
10.	Τύραννος πρεσβύτερος	38	6
11.	Τιμόθεος διάκονος	39	38
12.	Μακάριος πρεσβύτερος	42	39
13.	Θεόδωρος ἐν Κόπτῳ	9	21 or 32
14.	Θέων ἐν Νειλουπόλει	14	28
15.	Ἡρακλείδης ἐν Νικίους	16	20 or 48
16.	Πινινούθης ἐν Φθενεγύ	31	29
17.	Εἰρηναῖος πρεσβύτερος	36	33

giance either to Athanasius or John Archaph, but only to their own cenobitic *ἀπα*.[286] On the basis of the available evidence it is difficult, if not impossible, to envision the Meletian community in Egypt by the year AD 335 as a single, well-ordered, or homogeneous movement.

There also seem to have been in addition to the fragmented Meletian party in Egypt a number of other smaller schismatic and/or heretical groups who were involved in the ecclesiastical politics of the Alexandrian see during this period. Unlike the Meletians, however, it is difficult to determine fully the political or popular influence which any of these parties exercised. W.H.C. Frend contends that there were, at the time of Athanasius's election, only "three problems besetting the Church in Egypt—Arius's supporters, the Manichees, and the Meletians," but that Athanasius considered the Meletians to be "the most pressing problem" of the three.[287] Nordberg asserts that during this period "the Arians were a diminishing minority within the church; the Meletians a rather important one."[288] Charles W. Griggs agrees with Nordberg, yet indicates that it was the Meletian intrusion into the Egyptian monastic communities which most concerned Athanasius.[289]

There was, however, an additional break-away group in Egypt. It seems clear from the case of Ischyras that a number of those who had been involved in the Colluthian schism had chosen not to make peace with either Alexander or his successor, Athanasius. Some of these, like Ischyras himself, eventually ended up allied with the Eusebians and the Meletians.[290]

---

[286]Barnard, "Some Notes," *op. cit.*, 400; London Papyrus 1917 does indicate a theology which is somewhat removed from what is usually associated with the Arians of the time, although Barnard perhaps grants more attention to the matter of language in this document than is appropriate. The papyrus does, however, indicate the independent state which these monastic communities appear to have enjoyed (*cf.* London Papyrus 1917 in H.I. Bell, *Jews and Christians in Egypt*, London, 1924, 80-86). Further questions as to the exact monastic structure which was employed by these monks have been raised by E.A. Judge in his review of the London papyri which make up the collection from the archive of Apa Paieous in "The Earliest Use of *Monachos* for 'Monk' and the Origins of Monasticism," *Jahrbuch für Antike und Christintum* 20, Münster, 1977, 84, 85.

[287]W.H.C. Frend, "Athanasius as an Egyptian Christian Leader in the Fourth Century," *Religion Popular and Unpopular in the Early Christian Centuries*, London, 1976, 30.

[288]Nordberg, *op. cit.*, 16.

[289]C. W. Griggs, *History of Christianity in Egypt to AD 451*, Ph.D. thesis, University of California, 1979 (University Microfilms International, 80/360), 107ff.

[290]A study which contends that the Colluthian schism was linked to Arius in the ante-Nicene period has been written by Vlasios Feidas, *Τὸ Κολλούθιαν ἐχίεμα καὶ αἱ ἀρχαὶ τοῦ Ἀρειανισμοῦ*, Athens, 1973, esp. 28ff. Although one is unable to accept all of Feidas's conclusions, the study does point to the exceptional power of Alexandrian presbyters during the time of Alexander's

The petition of Athanasius's supporters at the Synod of Tyre confirms that part of the evidence against Athanasius had resulted from the fact that "Eusebius and his fellows contrived that a letter be presented, as coming from the Colluthians, the Meletians, and Arians, and directed against us."[291] Although the original Colluthian schism had been confined to Alexandria itself, and Colluthus himself appears to have been reconciled to Alexander at a synod of Egyptian bishops held in AD 324/25 (with Ossius of Cordova in attendance), some, as Ischyras, remained separated from the main body of the church in Egypt.[292] Although we cannot ascertain from the available materials how large a group the post-Nicene Colluthians constituted, the Egyptian bishops at Tyre considered them enough of a threat to list them alongside the Meletians and Arians.

We are also uncertain as to the exact strength of the Arian party (or parties) in Egypt during the period before the Synod of Tyre in AD 335. Edward R. Hardy states that "in the first stage, the forces against Athanasius were a combination of the crypto-Arians, headed by Eusebius of Nicomedia, outside Egypt, and the Meletians inside."[293] Kopecek claims that, following Nicaea, Theognis and Eusebius had been "conspiring with Alexandrian Arians," but he gives no indication or evidence as to who these persons were or what positions they held.[294] We have no reason to believe that Arius ever returned to Alexandria following Nicaea, as most sources indicate that he remained in exile until his death in AD 336.[295] Further, some scholars, such as Rowan Williams, have speculated that Arius's theological position may have resulted in "the relative isolation of Arius himself within a movement called by his name."[296] In Egypt, it seems probably that the movement was less than monolithic and included in it both those who strictly adhered to Arius's views (disciples) as well as those who only sympathized

---

episcopate. Concerning the connection of Ischyras with the Colluthians, cf. *Apol.* 12 (Opitz, 97, 8ff.).

[291]*Apol.* 77 (Opitz, 157, 9-11). This is just one of several references which link the activities of the Arians, Meletians, and Colluthians in *Apol.* 77 and 78. In both of their letters of petition, to the bishops gathered in Tyre (*Apol.* 77) and to Count Flavius Dionysius (*Apol.* 78), the connection between these three groups is perceived by the Athanasians to be a συσκευὴν ἄδηλον (Opitz, 156, 24 and 158, 3).

[292]*Apol.* 74 (Opitz, 153 and 154). Concerning Colluthus himself, cf. Epiphanius, *Haer.* 69; Theodoret, *HE* 1, 3; and Augustine, *Haer.* 65.

[293]Edward R. Hardy, *Christian Egypt: Church and People*, Oxford, 1962, 57.

[294]Kopecek, *op. cit.*, I, 58.

[295]Rufinus, *HE* 10, 11ff.; Socrates, *HE* 1, 37; Sozomen, *HE* 2, 29.

[296]R. D. Williams, "The Quest of the Historical *Thalia*," *Arianism, Historical and Theological Reassessments: Papers from the Ninth International Conference on Patristic Studies* (ed. R. C. Gregg), Philadelphia, 1985, 25.

with Arius's ecclesiastical/political situation (allies).[297] Although we are uncertain as to the danger which this group initially posed to the power of Athanasius, it appears, from subsequent and repeated references in the *Festal Letters*, that the threat increased with each passing year from the time of his election through the Synod of Tyre.[298]

Apart from those parties and movements which had their genesis within the church, consideration must also be given to others which existed on the fringes of the Egyptian ecclesiastical community. Griffiths has suggested the following scenario: "Intellectually, of course, Alexandria itself represented an amalgam, the fused elements being Greek, Egyptian, Jewish, Iranian, and Babylonian—to mention only the most prominent."[299] P.M. Fraser has commented on the fact that Persian influences became much more pervasive in Alexandrian society throughout the Roman era, especially through Manichaeism and Mithraism.[300] Further afield, the more native Coptic communities were also affected. The appeal of the Manichaeans to the widely spread monastic communities in Egypt was real enough that when Athanasius wrote his *Life of Antony* a special point was made to include the Manichaeans with the Arians and the Meletians: "In things having to do with faith, he," Antony, "was truly wonderful and orthodox. Perceiving their wickedness and apostasy from the beginning, he never had communion with the Meletian schismatics. And neither toward the Manichaeans nor toward

---

[297]*Ibid.* Williams notes that Arius's disciples (*i.e.*, those who accepted his view of "the Son's limited knowledge") were more likely to reside in Egypt than elsewhere, and were Arius's "less prominent and powerful supporters." Given our limited knowledge of the Arian party in Egypt following Nicaea, however, it seems reasonable to assume that there was some diversity of opinion even among his earliest followers in Alexandria and the region which lay round about.

[298]In Athanasius's *Festal Letter* for AD 329, the Arians are not mentioned. Even the Meletians, who may have been creating disturbances during this period, are not given a single word. The letter for AD 330, however, speaks of heresy in general terms and is linked with exhortations to "hold to the tradition" (5, 6) and to recognize that "there is no fellowship whatever between the words of the saints and the fancies of human invention" (7). The third *Festal Letter* for AD 331, misplaced by an ancient editor as letter fourteen for AD 342 (*cf.* Lorenz, *Der zehnte Osterfestbrief*, 30-31), only states that the bishop has "confidence in your wisdom and doctrinal care" and "such points as these have often been touched upon by us and in various letters" (2). In his fourth letter for AD 332, he makes plain references to the Meletians and his political problems, but again with no mention of the Arians. In the letter for AD 333, Athanasius only condemns the schismatics who "rend the coat of Christ" (4). The *Festal Letters* of AD 334-337 are lost (apart from a fragment for AD 334), and it is not until AD 338 and the tenth letter that Athanasius fully attacks the Arians (Lorenz, *op. cit.*, 81). This all points to a gradual realization concerning the Meletian-Arian alliance and the minority status of the Arians in Egypt at least until Tyre in AD 335.

[299]Griffiths, *op. cit.*, 1029, 1030.

[300]P.M. Fraser, *Ptolemaic Alexandria* I, Oxford, 1972, 138.

any other heretics did he profess friendship. . . . So in the same manner did he abhor the heresy of the Arians."[301] Even if we accept the judgment of Schwartz that Athanasius "used" Antony for his own political and theological purposes, his grouping of the Manichaeans with those other parties which had threatened the Alexandrian see is suggestive of their relative influence.[302]

We may safely indicate, therefore, that the state of affairs in Egypt during the first years of Athanasius's episcopate appears to have been somewhat unstable in regard to the life of the church. The Meletian community had fragmented. Remnants of the Colluthian schism continued to create difficulties, with some of its adherents entering into the Eusebian-Meletian alliance. The Arians in Egypt and Alexandria proper consisted of individuals of varying theological perceptions without, it would appear, a single guiding force. The Egyptian monastic community had yet to become a cohesive movement loyal to the bishop of Alexandria and was also subject to various influences.[303] In addition to the difficulties he faced in Egypt, Athanasius had also by AD 335 been stripped of many of his allies elsewhere, such as Eustathius of Antioch, Asclepas of Gaza, and a host of the other main defenders of Nicaea.[304] This then was the context in which Athanasius began his episcopate and attempted to unify the Egyptian church, facing the double challenge of external distrust and internal dissension.[305] The question facing the modern researcher is How did Athanasius respond to these circumstances?

---

[301]*Vita Ant.* 68 (PG 26, 940B).

[302]Schwartz, *Zur Geschichte des Athanasius,* 286.

[303]The struggle for the support of the monastic communities appears to have been a prolonged process for Athanasius. Gregg and Groh are certainly correct in speaking of early monastic communities (AD 330s) "who viewed the orthodox leadership in Alexandria with suspicion or enmity" (*Early Arianism,* 135). Athanasius's eventual success in winning over the majority of the monks through the years is clear. As Frend has commented, "Athanasius was the true archbishop" for the monks of Egypt and appears to have won them over by his "many-sided" personality and strength of will; in later years, the monks of Egypt became "the eyes and ears of the archbishopric" ("Athanasius as an Egyptian Christian Leader," *op. cit.,* 32, 33).

[304]*Hist. Arian.* 5 (Opitz, 185); *cf.* R.P.C. Hanson, "The Fate of Eustathius of Antioch," *ZKG* 95 (1984): 2, 171-179, who presents a convincing argument that "Eustathius was deposed, not in 326 but in 328 or 329" (179); the reasons presented for his deposition perhaps skirt the "intricate movements of ecclesiastical politics" and do not provide a wholly satisfactory conclusion (*ibid.*). It still appears as though his deposition had to do with his opposition to the Arians of his see rather than with immorality (Socrates *HE* 1, 21) as Hanson allows.

[305]Writing about the whole of Athanasius's episcopate, Colin Walters has commented how the initial fragmented condition of the Egyptian church was transformed, writing that "it is in this period that one detects the emergence of a unified Egyptian Church, with the Alexandrian and Egyptian elements coming

In 1924, Sir Harold Idris Bell announced the acquisition by the British Museum of a group of ten papyri which promised to be "new lights on Saint Athanasius."[306] In describing this collection of papyri, Bell made the following initial evaluation:

> These letters (for all but one are letters) despite their Byzantine fluffiness, which veils a little meaning in a monstrous jumble of words, are of exceptional interest for the light they throw on the life of a Christian community in the reign of Constantine the Great. But it is by virtue of two only of the papyri that the collection boasts its special importance. One of these, the only contract in the series, fixes at last the disputed date of the Synod of Caesarea ... the other and more interesting, a long letter from an Alexandrian Meletian, gives a vivid picture of the sufferings to which the sectaries were exposed at the hands of Athanasius and his adherents.[307]

After a brief description of the content of the letter, which Bell claimed exposed Athanasius's "official persecution" of the Meletians during the period before the Synod of Tyre, he concluded by making this comment:

> The new letter places the proceeding at Tyre in a new light. It is, of course, like Athanasius' own narrative, a partisan statement, but it shows, what was suspected before, that there was more justification for the attack on Athanasius than the Catholic tradition allows to appear, *and it may rank among the most precious documents of fourth-century ecclesiastical history.*[308]

The publication later that year of the ten papyri as part of a volume entitled *Jews and Christians in Egypt* provided the opportunity for a more detailed examination of the document referred to above which was catalogued as London Papyrus 1914, or LP 1914.[309] (My transcription of the document appears below, in the appendix.)

From internal evidence, Bell dates LP 1914 as having been written sometime in May or June of AD 335.[310] His argument for this particular dating of the letter may be summarized as follows:

---

together to present a solid front to the common enemy" (*Monastic Archaeology in Egypt,* Warminster, 1974, 5).

[306] H.I. Bell, "New Lights on Saint Athanasius," *The Adelphi* (1924): 1006.

[307] *Ibid.*, 1008.

[308] *Ibid.*, 1009, emphasis added.

[309] H.I. Bell, *Jews and Christians in Egypt,* London, 1924; London Papyrus 1914, 53-71.

[310] Bell, *Jews and Christians, op. cit.,* 57.

1.   It was written during the time that Athanasius was in actual possession of the see of Alexandria, that is, after June AD 328.
2.   It describes the actions of Athanasius during a time when, although he was able to instigate measures against the Meletians, he was far from secure himself. Bell asserts that "there is no trace in our tradition of such insecurity during the early years of his episcopate, and indeed it is very unlikely that till their alliance with the Eusebian party the Meletians were strong enough to constitute a real menace."[311] Furthermore, "this alliance was probably not formed till late in 330."[312] The extreme limits according to Bell are, therefore, late AD 330 and Easter AD 340 (the beginning of the second exile of Athanasius).
3.   Within the limits of this decade, Bell has then eliminated those periods when Athanasius was absent from Egypt. Athanasius was at court facing the accusations of the Meletians in late AD 331, not returning to Alexandria until Easter of AD 332.[313] He left Alexandria again on 11 July AD 335 to attend the synod at Tyre and was subsequently banished, not returning to Alexandria until 23 November AD 337. Bell, moreover, discounts any possibility that the letter may date from after the first exile of Athanasius, leaving the possible years of authorship as AD 331-AD 335, with those certain exceptions named above.
4.   The Egyptian month of Pachon is mentioned three times in LP 1914 (11.6, 45, 47). As the letter appears to have been written soon after the events described, Bell places it within May-June of one of the four years cited above.
5.   Although the text is not exact as to the identity of the personages reported upon, Bell considers the ἄπα 'Ιωάννην of the letter to be the Meletian leader John Archaph, who is either at, or going to, Antioch (1.34). The letter states that as Athanasius was preparing to go on a journey (1.39ff.), a certain Archelaus (whom Bell identifies as a confederate of Athanasius) was arrested at the orders of Apa John (1.35ff.). This follows the earlier arrest of Macarius (1.30, 31). With the actions against the Meletians and the events above in mind, Bell states that "the situation strongly

---

[311]*Ibid.*, 55.

[312]*Ibid.*

[313]*Ibid.*; Bell here disputes the traditional dating by Robertson (that Athanasius left for court in late AD 330). Bell argues rightly that the evidence of the texts of the *Festal Letters* for this period should have been given a greater weight than the often mistaken *Acephala (cf.* Robertson, LNPF, *op. cit.*, xxxviii; and Bell, *Jews and Christians, op. cit.*, 55, fn. 2). For further discussion on Athanasius's movements during this period, *vide* Nordberg, *op. cit.*, 22-30.

suggests the time immediately preceding the Synod of Tyre in 335."[314]

6. Setting aside the year AD 332 as being a time when Athanasius "cannot have contemplated going abroad" so soon after his return from court, Bell also excludes AD 331, as Athanasius's departure would have been too late in the year to allow for a May-June dating.[315] It would seem that AD 334 is another possibility in view of the calling of the Synod of Caesarea, but Bell points out that the summons from the emperor came in February or early March, and, in any case, Athanasius finally refused to attend. Although such hesitation on Athanasius's part is seen in LP 1914 (1.38ff.), Bell considers the subsequent period of two months (until May-June) to be "rather a long time after the summons" still to be undecided and, therefore, disallows AD 334.[316]

7. Finally, Bell cites the use of names in LP 1914 which may be related to personalities who are known to have been involved with those events which surrounded the Synod of Tyre. He admits, however, that the only persons mentioned in the letter who can be identified with any degree of certainty are Athanasius himself; Isaac, Bishop of Letopolis; and Athanasius, son of Capito.[317] The further identification of Apa John as John Archaph, as well as that of Archelaus and Macarius as those known supporters of Athanasius involved with the Synod of Tyre, is less certain. The use of this information, however, as concerns the dating of LP 1914, is, as Bell says, "no doubt, extremely dubious" and without weight or substance in such a determination.[318]

It is then, the result of this process of elimination which allows Bell to state his conviction that it is "highly probable that 1914 is to be dated May-June, 335."[319]

From the text of the letter itself we know its author to be a person named Callistus (11.1, 63). Bell identifies him as "doubtless a Meletian monk or cleric" and, from the style of the letter, as "a Copt" who was "not wholly at home in Greek."[320] The letter was being sent to Apa Paiêou and Patabeit who were priests (1.1). Bell states that the purpose of the letter is to give a "circumstantial account of the sufferings of his fellow Meletians at

---

[314]Bell, *Jews and Christians, op. cit.,* 56.

[315]*Ibid.*

[316]*Ibid.; cf.* London Papyrus 1913; Bell, *op. cit.,* 45-53.

[317]Bell, *Jews and Christians, op. cit.,* 57.

[318]*Ibid.*

[319]*Ibid.*

[320]*Ibid.,* 53.

the hands of Athanasius's adherents and of Athanasius himself."[321] The standard interpretation of LP 1914, first presented by Bell in 1924, may be summarized as follows:

On the evening of 24 Pachon (19 May) AD 335, slightly less than two months before Athanasius's departure for Tyre, an attack took place at Nicopolis, a suburb of Alexandria known as a stronghold of the Meletians, and continued in the military camp which adjoined the community.[322] The attack had begun at the house of Heraclius the Recorder the previous day (11.3, 4). On the day in question, however, Isaac of Letopolis after seeing Heraiscus at Alexandria had come to dine with his host or another unknown bishop "in the camp" (11.6-8). According to Bell's translation, "the adherents of Athanasius" heard about the visit and with the assistance of the soldiers of the camp, attempted to kidnap Isaac (11.8, 9).

Callistus informed his readers that the attackers were intoxicated as the attack began, but they still managed to break into the military camp in pursuit of Isaac (1.10). By this time, however, Isaac and the other bishop had been hidden by some sympathetic soldiers. Their quarry having escaped, the attackers turned on four other "brethren" who were coming into the camp and beat them (1.14). Finally, the attackers made their way to a hostel near the west gate of the city of Alexandria (some distance outside the camp) and seized the keeper asking him, "Why do you admit Meletian monks to the hostel?" (11.20, 21). Others who had entertained the visitors received similar rough treatment. The following day the *praepositus* of the soldiers is described as being ashamed of his drunken behavior the night before and, "although a Gentile," he presented an offering (ἀγάπην) as a sign of penance (1.28).

According to Bell, the remainder of the letter describes the concurrent attitudes and actions of Athanasius and his followers immediately before the Synod of Tyre. Athanasius is described as being "very despondent" and "causing distress" owing to events which involved the emperor and the possible arrest of Macarius (11.30, 31). The following lines are mutilated (1.31ff.) and are, therefore, of little help in further explaining the circumstances which follow. Athanasius, according to Bell, sent Archelaus and Athanasius, the son of Capito, to attempt to ἀποσπάσαι Macarius, but were themselves detained by "Apa John at (in) Antioch" (11.35-36). Owing to this apparent reversal, Athanasius is reported as being hesitant to leave the country (11.38, 39).

---

[321]*Ibid.*

[322]An unusual feature of LP 1914 is the setting of Nicopolis as the scene of this encounter. From the evidence of the *Breviarium Melitii,* the areas of Meletian strength seemed to be, without exception, outside the immediate vicinity of Alexandria (*cf.* Barnard, "Some Notes," *op. cit.,* 400).

A further break in the text occurs at line 41, but Bell assumes that the subject of the remainder of the letter continues to be Athanasius.[323] The letter tells of his "carrying off a bishop of the Lower Country" who was then confined in a meat market (1.42) and of a priest and deacon who were also imprisoned (11.43, 44). Heraiscus, who appears to have been taken in the original attack, remained in the camp and was, according to Callistus, scourged through the course of four days (11.45, 46). On 27 Pachon (22 May) a further seven bishops were exiled, including Emês and Peter (11.47, 48). Bell identifies this Peter with the person of the same name in the *Breviarium Militii.*[324]

The final portion of the letter is taken up with the distribution of bread within the community and assorted greetings to those who lived in the same area as the recipients.

As a result of the information contained within this letter, Bell came to several conclusions which have gained wide acceptance. It must be stated, however, that the central thrust of these conclusions is the result of Bell's particular interpretation of the text; his insistence on dating the letter to just prior to the Synod of Tyre; and his preferred translation of certain obscure passages. This being said, it must be admitted that Bell does attempt to present a careful and balanced view of Athanasius within the limits imposed by his understanding of LP 1914. Bell asserts that Athanasius, while answering the charges made against him at Tyre concerning the chalice incident and the murder of Arsenius said nothing about the other accusations made against him in regard to charges of violence and oppression towards the Meletians.[325] According to Bell,

> The reason is now clear: these charges were in part true. That he was himself responsible for the violence of the soldiery on the evening of Pachon 24 Callistus does not state, *and it is not probable*; but we may doubt whether he took much trouble to prevent such outrages, and he is definitely charged with imprisoning the schismatics and with other high-handed measures. Very important too is what Callistus tells us of the attempt to carry off Macarius. He does not indeed allege that the three would-be kidnappers were commissioned by Athanasius, but he does state that Athanasius was very despondent when he heard of Archelaus's arrest, and it is hardly conceivable that the confederates can have acted without at least his tacit consent. We must conclude that there was a germ of truth in the picture given of Athanasius by his

---

[323]Bell, *Jews and Christians, op. cit.,* 68, fn. 42.
[324]*Ibid.,* 69, fn. 48.
[325]*Ibid.,* 57.

enemies as a self-willed, unruly man, apt to treat even the Imperial authority with contempt.[326]

In his final comments concerning Athanasius and the charges made against him, which appear to have been confirmed in LP 1914, Bell is cautious in his judgment of the bishop of Alexandria and gives this evaluation: "Yet it must not be forgotten that the letter of Callistus also is an *ex parte* statement. The facts he relates can hardly be doubted, but they may have had a justification which he does not allow to appear. And in any case it would be unfair to found on these and similar facts a general condemnation of Athanasius, though we admit faults in his character and errors in his conduct."[327] Bell further states that the leaders of both sides in this conflict were lacking in Christian charity towards their opponents, and while each complained of persecution, each was more than willing to make use of forceful methods of persuasion against the other.[328] Yet, according to Bell, "A fair and critical judgement between Athanasius and his opponents must rest on a consideration, not of such details, but of total personality and of the main issue at stake."[329]

Writing one year later in 1925, Bell indicates, however, that LP 1914 only assisted in proving what could already be assumed was the case—that is, that Athanasius was actively involved in the persecution of the Meletians. Bell comments that the "young Athanasius" who had succeeded Alexander in the episcopal throne of St. Mark "was of a masterful temperament, with all the intolerance and all the impatience of youth *and even without* the evidence of the document [*i.e.,* LP 1914] to be quoted presently, one need feel little hesitation in accepting as a least partially true the accusation of his enemies that he persecuted the Meletians."[330] The question must then be asked, What evidence, apart from LP 1914, gave rise to this prior assumption by Bell of the guilt of Athanasius?

In his introduction to the Meletian papyri collection, Bell cites only two other sources which deal with Athanasius's "violent conduct" towards the Meletians. The first of these is the reference of Sozomen to earlier charges of violence and oppression towards the Meletian party, along with similar, but more detailed, accusations which were supposedly found by the church historian in the minutes of the Synod of Tyre, which, unfortunately, are no longer extant.[331] The second source is the material contained within the letter of the Oriental Council of Sardica which was written in AD 343. The narrative

---

[326]*Ibid.*; emphasis added.

[327]*Ibid.*, 58.

[328]*Ibid.*

[329]*Ibid.*

[330]H.I. Bell, "Athanasius: A Chapter in Church History," *The Congregational Quarterly*, 3, no. 2 (April, 1925): 164; emphasis added.

[331]Sozomen, *HE* II, 22, 25; Bell, *Jews and Christians*, 47.

in the letter is both graphic and specific in describing the charges which were made against Athanasius:

> Accusatus praeterea est de iniuriis, violentia, caeda, atque ipsa episcoporum internicione [*i.e.*, Arsenius]. Quique etiam diebus sacratissimis paschae tyrannico more saeviens ducibus atque comitibus iunctus, quique propter ipsum aliquos in custodiam recludebant, aliquos vero verberibus flagellisque vexabant, ceteros diversis tormentis ad communionem eius sacrilegam adigebant.[332]

We may note that although Bell appears to accept the general meaning of the letter, he is less than committed to all the particular details to which it alludes. For example, he comments that the stories concerning Macarius and the chalice incident "grew in the course of time. In the letter of the Oriental Council of Sardica Athanasius is accused of having *personally* broken the chalice, smashed the altar, overturned the priest's chair, and demolished the church!"[333] That the stories of Athanasius's supposed misdeeds had been greatly embellished by his enemies in a relatively short period of time there can be little doubt. Furthermore, we must acknowledge that both the Synod of Tyre and the Oriental Council of Sardica, from which the records of such misdeeds are drawn, were actively hostile towards Athanasius and were filled with those who sought his destruction.

The impact of LP 1914 upon subsequent evaluations of Athanasius and his character has been profound. Although Bell did not agree with the opinions about Athanasius which had been expressed by Seeck and Schwartz, the interpretation of LP 1914 which was presented in *Jews and Christians in Egypt* did seem to lend support to their view of Athanasius as an unscrupulous and ruthless man who would make use of any means to achieve his own ends.[334] Bell, however, was only willing to admit that Athanasius often showed "perhaps more of the wisdom of a serpent than the harmlessness of the dove," and that "altogether one discerns in his career the hard, somewhat unamiable outline of the ecclesiastical statesman rather than the figure of the saint or scholar."[335]

That the standard interpretation of LP 1914, first offered by Bell in 1924, has been accepted and expanded upon by a large number of Athanasian scholars is clearly evident. In recent studies, LP 1914 is often the only source

---

[332]Hilary of Poitiers, IV (CSEL 65, Feder 48, 9-67, 20).

[333]Bell, *Jews and Christians, op. cit.*, 46.

[334]Concerning Seeck, Bell states: "I do not think Seeck is successful in his attempt to prove" Athanasius "a downright liar and forger" (Bell, "Athanasius," *op. cit.*, 175). Of Schwartz, Bell asserts that regarding the popularity Athanasius achieved in later years, "the enthusiastic devotion of the Alexandrians, pagans as well as Christians, would be incredible had he been the cold, selfish, unscrupulous schemer portrayed by Schwartz" (*ibid.*, 176).

[335]*Ibid.*, 175.

which is cited when reference is made to the "violence of Athanasius." For example, Nordberg makes use of LP 1914 in describing the political and religious situation in Egypt which led Athanasius to "take drastic measures against the most extreme Meletians."[336] The letter is also the basis for A.H.M. Jones's comment concerning "Athanasius's bullies" and L.W. Barnard's claim that "the charges that Athanasius had engaged in violence, oppression, and reprisals against the Meletians were not without foundation."[337] Barnard does, however, in another place, qualify this statement by making the observation that Athanasius had adopted such methods against the Meletians "who themselves had shown much violence and persecution towards the orthodox."[338] Timothy Barnes accepts the entire contents and interpretation of LP 1914 without reservation as an indication of the state of the church in Egypt immediately before the Synod of Tyre.[339] Although W.H.C. Frend is more cautious than many and does not charge Athanasius himself with direct persecution of the Meletians, he nonetheless accepts the report of the papyrus as proof of a violent extension of Athanasius's "propaganda" campaign.[340] Gregg and Groh speak of LP 1914 as evidence of "how military officials could be pressed into service against the Meletians (and innocent villagers who had dealings with them) by the partisans of Athanasius."[341] Many more examples could be given of the influence of LP 1914 on current Athanasian studies. It is perhaps sufficient to say that this one document has provided great support for the negative evaluation of the character of Athanasius first put forward by Seeck and Schwartz.

A good deal of attention has also been given to the letter of Callistus by those who have been mainly interested, as was Bell, in papyriological evidence of life and letters in Ptolemaic and Roman Egypt. As a result, LP 1914 has figured prominently in many such studies which have been undertaken in the course of time since 1924.[342] Certain scholars, such as

---

[336]Nordberg, op. cit., 27.

[337]A.H.M. Jones, The Later Roman Empire, Oxford, 1964, 827; L.W. Barnard, "Some Notes," op. cit., 402.

[338]Barnard, "Athanasius and the Roman State," op. cit., 426.

[339]Barnes, op. cit., 235, 236.

[340]Frend, "Athanasius as an Egyptian Christian Leader," op. cit., 32; cf. Frend, The Rise of Christianity, 526.

[341]R.C. Gregg and D.E. Groh, Early Arianism, 191, fn. 131.

[342]Some of the more important studies include: J. Van Haelst, "Les Sources papyrologiques concernant l'eglise en Egypte à l'époque de Constantin," Proceedings of the Twelfth International Congress of Papyrology, Toronto, 1970, 499 (nos. 29-35); J.G. Winter, Life and Letters in Papyri, Ann Arbor, Michigan, 1933, 175ff.; O. Montevecchi, La Papirologia, Torino, 1973, 258 (no. 70); Hans Hauben, "On the Melitians in P. London VI (P. Jews) 1914: The Problem of Papas Heraiscus," Proceedings of the XVI International Congress of Papyrology, Chicago, 1981, 447-456; E.A. Judge, "The Earliest Use of Monachos for 'Monk' (P. Coll. Youtie 77) and the Origins of Monasticism," Jahrbuch für Antike und

E.A. Judge, have attempted to place LP 1914 within the wider context of other papyri finds of the same period.[343] As a result, questions have been raised concerning LP 1914 which were left unanswered by Bell. Some of these concerns will be considered in our discussion below. Yet, apart from these more specialized interests, most of these studies have, in an *a priori* manner, accepted the general interpretation of LP 1914 which Bell first put forward.

There are, however, a number of difficulties with Bell's interpretation of those events which are described in LP 1914. The first of these is that Bell's interpretation is based upon a somewhat simplistic concept of the religious situation which existed in Egypt during the decade following Athanasius's consecration as bishop of Alexandria in AD 328. Bell appears to assume that there were only two predominant parties involved in the ecclesiastical politics of Alexandria during this period—the Athanasian party and the Meletian party. In the Gregynog Lectures for 1946, which two years later were published under the title *Egypt from Alexander the Great to the Arab Conquest: A Study in the Diffusion and Decay of Hellenism*, Bell could write a history of the entire period with no reference to the Manichaeans and only a passing mention of Mithras.[344] In the Forwood Lectures for 1952, published one year later as *Cults and Creeds in Graeco-Roman Egypt*, Bell again appears to disregard the importance of these groups which existed on the fringes of the Christian community, although he at least mentions the influence of the Manichaeans upon monastic communities in Middle Egypt and the Nile Valley.[345]

Perhaps even more important than these outright omissions is Bell's insistence upon viewing the Meletian schism and the emerging factions within the Alexandrian church in a manner which disregards the obvious confusion and intricacies of the period in question. For example, while Bell comments in several places on the importance of the Meletian-Eusebian alliance which caused the Meletians to be "strong enough to constitute a real menace" to Athanasius, only a passing reference is made to those many

---

Christentum, 20 (1977): 72-89; and E.A. Judge and S.R. Pickering, "Papyrus Documentation of Church and Community in Egypt to the Mid-Fourth Century," *Jahrbuch für Antike und Christentum* 20 (1977): 47-71.

[343] Judge and Pickering make a number of very helpful comments in their "Papyrus Documentation of Church and Community," *op. cit.,* concerning the changes in social structure which were taking place during this time (66-71). That the soldier commanding the attackers in LP 1914 returns the next day to offer a personal apology is seen to "make clear where the social precedence now lies" (71). Such an observation also adds to the complexity of this text. Could the Meletians, living in a suburb of Alexandria, enjoy such a privileged position while Athanasius was constantly attacking them with the aid of the military— even with the aid of Meletian sympathizers among the soldiers?

[344] H.I. Bell, *Egypt from Alexander the Great to the Arab Conquest: A Study in the Diffusion and Decay of Hellenism*, Oxford, 1948.

[345] H.I. Bell, *Cults and Creeds in Graeco-Roman Egypt*, London, 1953, 96.

Meletians who allied themselves with Athanasius—and Bell indicates that this only took place in the period *after* Tyre![346] Bell also makes no differentiation between the Meletians who had allied themselves with the Eusebians and those in the monastic communities (as in LP 1917) who appear to have had little to do with either the Eusebians or Athanasius.[347] In fact, Bell consistently indicates that the Meletians presented a somewhat solid party of opposition against Athanasius, disallowing even the suggestion that an individual listed in the *Breviarium Melitii*, such as Πέτρος ἐν Ἡρακλέους, could possibly have sided with Athanasius by the time of Tyre.[348] For Bell, there is only the one Meletian party under the leadership of John Archaph which, owing to defections and exiles after the Synod of Tyre, receded into obscurity. From the arguments which have been presented above, however, this does not appear to have been the probable situation in Egypt during this time. Moreover, apart from the mention of Arius as an original adherent of Meletius, Bell makes no further mention of the Arian party in Egypt or their activities within this period, only commenting (following Sozomen) that, "in course of time the Arians were popularly called Meletians in Egypt."[349] Furthermore, the adherents of Colluthus are not referred to at all in any of Bell's written work concerning this era.[350]

Certainly there is very little evidence to support such a simplistic view of the situation in Egypt in the ten years which followed the elevation of Athanasius to the throne of St. Mark, and there is much evidence against it. As has been discussed above, Athanasius himself was concerned in his writings with the Manichaeans, the Meletians, the Arians, and the Colluthians. Nordberg's research has indicated that it is highly probable that a large number of Meletians had given their support to Athanasius *before* the Synod of Tyre and were actively engaged in opposing and discrediting their former brethren. Certain papyri, such as LP 1917, point to other, largely independent, communities of Meletians who, while certainly not Arian (or Eusebian) in their theological outlook also expressed little or no loyalty towards the ecclesiastical establishment in Alexandria. Finally, the Meletian-Eusebian alliance which existed both inside and outside of Egypt during the time under consideration and attracted many supporters is well attested to in a wide variety of sources.

In addition to the mere fact that these various groups actually existed and exerted influence during this turbulent period in Egypt, there is every reason to imagine that all of these parties, and the individuals within them,

---

[346]Bell, *Jews and Christians*, 41.

[347]*Cf.* LP 1917, *op. cit.*, 80-86.

[348]Bell, *Jews and Christians, op. cit.*, 69, fn. 48.

[349]*Ibid.*, 41.

[350]A complete bibliography of H.I. Bell's published works may be consulted in *JEA* 40 (1954): 3-6, with additions and corrections in *JEA* 53 (1967): 139, 140.

formed a pattern of shifting alliances and mixed loyalties. In the case of Ischyras, for example, we apparently see a man "ordained" by Colluthus who chose to remain in schism after his leader's reinstatement in the Alexandrian church.[351] After some years in isolation, serving only his family as a priest, it appears that he joined himself to the Meletians (probably after the submission of Meletius, for his name does not appear on the schedule which was submitted to Alexander).[352] Still later, he is brought to the Synod of Tyre as an accuser of Athanasius, under the protection of Eusebius of Nicomedia and John Archaph.[353] Ischyras was eventually persuaded by his relatives to retract his charges against Athanasius and was reconciled to the bishop, although placed under censure.[354] This situation, however, was soon reversed when Ischyras again broke with Athanasius, renewed his charges, and was "given the name of bishop" by the Eusebians.[355] Although the case of Ischyras is far from typical, it does illustrate the point that the ecclesiastical situation in Egypt was far from stable and cannot be reduced to the somewhat simplistic scenario which is assumed by Bell.[356] As Bell himself has said, "the historian, however eminent, is a bold man who seeks to interpret the history of the fourth century on the lines of modern rationalism."[357] While his reference in this quotation is to Constantine, it could well apply to any attempted interpretation of the ecclesiastical politics of post-Nicene Egypt.

The religious and political situation described above takes on even greater importance when an attempt is made to understand and evaluate the events which are described in LP 1914. As Bell himself admits, the circumstances in which the letter was written proved a key to its interpretation:

> The style of the letter is unfortunately awkward and at times obscure; and moreover a private letter, the writer of which, referring to matters familiar to his correspondent, does not need to be as definite as an historian, is always apt to be a little difficult of comprehension. Hence

---

[351]*Apol.* 12 (Opitz, 97).

[352]*Apol.* 71 (Opitz, 49-151).

[353]*Apol.* 12 (Opitz, 97).

[354]*Apol.* 64 (Opitz, 143).

[355]*Apol.* 37 (Opitz, 116, 22, 23).

[356]We may note that the supposed object of an Athanasian "murder," Arsenius of Hypsele, was also reconciled to Athanasius and in AD 346/347 succeeded to the sole episcopate of that place according to the Nicene settlement—even though he had not been listed in the *Breviarium Melitii (cf. Festal Letter* for AD 347, LNPF, *op. cit.,* 548). This is another example of a Meletian, with strong monastic connections, who after being allied with the Eusebians returned once again to the side of Athanasius. His case might also be considered as an example of either Athanasius's reasonable nature or his political astuteness, or both.

[357]Bell, *Egypt, op. cit.,* 105.

it is not surprising that parts of our letter are by no means clear and admit of more than one interpretation.[358]

A clear example of the need to understand the circumstances under which this letter was written is provided in lines 8-9 of the text of LP 1914. Those who attempted, with the aid of the soldiers, to kidnap Isaac of Letopolis and his host are referred to in the text as οἱ διαφέροντες (11.8, 9). This has been translated by Bell as "the adherents of Athanasius."[359] But, is this the actual meaning which the writer intended? In an essay on "The Problem of Translation," Bell made the following observation:

> Only a minority of words, chiefly substantives expressing some concrete object or specific notion, have but one definite meaning. Most have various senses, passing one into another by almost imperceptible gradations; and it is only rarely that the corresponding word in another language will show that particular range of meanings. Thus a single word may in translation have to be rendered, on various occasions, by any one of several different words.[360]

It might be suggested that this is especially true when dealing with a phrase such as that given above, for there are, in its root and use as a participle, two possible translations which carry opposite meanings. Is the text speaking of "those who are kinsfolk or adherents of Athanasius," or is it informing us of the actions of "those who differ from Athanasius"? It is possible, given the meaning of the root διαφέρω to even speak of "those who are in competition with Athanasius," although this would likely stretch the meaning of the phrase beyond that which was intended by the writer. We must note that Lampe, in assigning the concept of adherence to this phrase is only able to provide this solitary example out of LP 1914, while the milder meaning of "kinsfolk" and the root meaning of "difference" is attested to in a wide variety of sources.[361]

In considering such questions we must return to certain initial observations and impressions concerning LP 1914. From a detailed examination of the papyrus itself, there can be no doubt at all that the reading of the words οἱ διαφέροντες is absolutely correct. It is clear, however, that Callistus, the writer of the letter, has difficulty writing in Greek and that the intricacies of the language and the shades of meaning which the syntax and

---

[358]Bell, *Jews and Christians, op. cit.,* 53.

[359]*Ibid.,* 61.

[360]H.I. Bell, "The Problem of Translation," *Literature and Life, Addresses to the English Association,* London, 1948, 14.

[361]*A Patristic Greek Lexicon,* ed. G. Lampe, Oxford, 1961, 362, 363. No cognate references are listed in *Lexicon Athanasianum,* ed. G. Müller, Berlin, 1952. Within the Athanasian corpus διαφέρω is used exclusively in the sense of "difference" (*cf.* Müller, *Lexicon Athanasianum,* col. 328).

structure of language provided were beyond his literary abilities. Although there are a good many features of his grammar and style which are familiar within his period and geographical setting, we must still note that his repetitious use of words and phrases without connecting particles or conjunctions (ll. 9, 10), his omission of connecting words (l. 38), and his use of supplementary clauses without conjunctions (ll. 24, 48) all show a basic difficulty with handling the language. The exact meaning, therefore, of the phrase which Bell has translated as "the adherents of Athanasius" could very possibly carry another meaning. Certainly, it is possible to suggest from contemporary usage of the root word διαφέρω that the translation rendered by Bell may not, in fact, be wholly satisfactory. This particular phrase illustrates Bell's comment that "a translator is an interpreter, and unless he is faithful to his original his interpretation may be entirely misleading."[362] This, of course, is not to suggest that Bell was intending to render anything other than a faithful translation of the text. It is possible, however, that his translation of this particular phrase was overly influenced by his understanding of the letter's context and, therefore, reflected his own bias. For Bell there were only two parties involved—the Athanasians and the Meletians. The translation, therefore, had to fit within this scheme of things. As some of those who were being attacked are identified as Meletians, the attackers had to be Athanasians.

Given our present understanding of the numerous groups who were competing for power in the Egyptian church during this period, it is possible to see things differently. The attackers may have indeed been the "adherents of Athanasius," but more in the literal sense of those who were "close kinfolk"—such as those Meletians who had given him their allegiance. This seems very likely. Conversely, the attackers might have been those who were actually "in competition" with Athanasius and the events recorded in LP 1914 could be the result of some internecine struggle of which we are unaware. Although we may only speculate at this point, there were a large number of groups active in Egypt who could very aptly be described as being "in competition with Athanasius." Were the attackers Meletians who had gone over to Athanasius? Were they Colluthians, who had no great love for the Meletians before the time of Nicaea and may have reemerged in this turbulent period? The text is unclear, but both the context and the language permit the consideration of a number of possibilities.

Clearly, there is much contained within this letter which remains unexplained, both in terms of context and personalities. E.A. Judge has commented concerning the question as to exactly what sort of monks in this period, Meletian or otherwise, had their center of activity located between an army camp and the largest city in Egypt. As Judge writes, we may "wonder what kind of 'solitaries' they were—certainly not ones in full retreat from society."[363] We are also left with the mystery of the exact role of πάπαν

---

[362]H.I. Bell, "The Problem of Translation," op. cit., 25.
[363]E.A. Judge, "The Earliest Use of Monachos," op. cit., 84.

'Ηραείσκον (1.25) within this community. He was, as Bell says, "apparently a person of some importance," and his title of πάπας would indicate that he was a priest, or bishop, or, perhaps, the leader of a monastic community.[364] There has even been speculation that he was "a sort of antipope, set up by the Meletians in opposition to Athanasius."[365] Yet, as Bell says, "it is a serious objection to this view that neither Athanasius nor any of the ecclesiastical historians should refer to him."[366]

Yet another difficulty in the text of LP 1914 occurs owing to a blemish in the papyrus following the first portion of line 41. Bell would later comment that "here a sacrilegious worm has eaten away much of the papyrus."[367] It is a most unfortunate difficulty, for the portion eaten away most likely indicates the subject of the remaining lines. Although Bell states that "evidently Athanasius is the subject," there is nothing which positively indicates that this is so.[368] Athanasius is clearly the subject of that portion of the text which comes before the break (11.29-41), but the context and change of scene indicated by Callistus following line 41 makes it possible that another person or party has been introduced into the account. Athanasius himself is not mentioned again by name after line 41. When the actual physical state of the papyrus itself is examined, it becomes clear that even the scant information provided in lines 41 and 42 must be viewed with a very critical eye. We cannot, therefore, automatically assume that

---

[364]Bell, *Jews and Christians, op. cit.*, 63, 64.

[365]Hans Hauben, "On the Meletians in P. London VI (P. Jews) 1914," *op. cit.*, 447-456, contends that Heraiscus was, in fact, the Meletian bishop of Alexandria (453). This assertion is based entirely upon the information contained within LP 1914 with no other contemporary external sources cited. Although the grammatical structure of LP 1914 could lead one to such a conclusion, the lack of external confirmation seems even more important in such an evaluation. It is difficult to believe that Athanasius would fail to mention such a person in the course of his polemics and that the Meletian leaders, John Archaph and Eusebius of Nicomedia, would fail to include such an individual in the events surrounding Tyre. Although such an identification solves some questions, such as the report of Theonas's succession by Epiphanius (*Haer.* 68, 7), it fails to deal adequately with the position of John Archaph, Achillas (*Haer.* 69, 11), and related issues. Hauben, however, may be right in identifying Heraiscus as the bishop of this particular group in LP 1914. If this is so, then Hauben is right in his suggestion that this indicates a new era in the schism in which a point of no return had been reached (456). Furthermore, it is possible that this confirms the scattered nature of the schism at this point in time, as well as the independence of the various Meletian communities. That the Meletian group in LP 1914 had contact with mainstream Meletians is clear from the visit of Isaac of Letopolis and the apparent mention of John Archaph in Antioch (only spoken of, however, as άπα 'Ιωάννην in 1. 34 of the text). We may only speculate on what sort of contact this constituted.

[366]Bell, *Jews and Christians, op. cit.*, 63, fn. 7.

[367]Bell, "Athanasius," *op. cit.*, 167, fn. 1.

[368]Bell, *Jews and Christians*, 63, fn. 42.

Athanasius is the individual who "carried off a bishop of the Lower Country and shut him up in a meat market" (11.42, 43), imprisoned the deacon (1.44), ordered Heraiscus scourged (1.46), or exiled the seven bishops (1.47). Those bishops who were exiled could, in fact, belong to any of those parties named above, including the Athanasian.[369]

Further doubts may be expressed concerning how Bell dated LP 1914. As we have seen, the date of May-June AD 335, immediately before the Synod of Tyre, was arrived at largely through a process of elimination. There are, however, several difficulties in the pattern of events which has been suggested by Bell. Although it may be agreed that LP 1914 was written after Athanasius became the bishop of Alexandria, that is, after AD 328, more recent scholarship would strongly disagree with Bell's contention that Athanasius spent his first years as bishop of Alexandria in relative security.[370] The Meletians were a menace in Egypt even before their alliance with the Eusebians, and Bell seems incorrect in his suggestion to the contrary.[371] Further, although we may eliminate those periods which Athanasius spent away from Egypt (at court, synods, or in exile), it does not seem improbable to suggest that the events in the Alexandrian see were such that there was continued instability even after Athanasius's return from his first exile on 23 November AD 337. These two concerns alone open up the possibilities for the dating of the letter from the middle portion of AD 328 (Athanasius's election) to Easter AD 340 (the beginning of Athanasius's second exile) with those certain exceptions which have been noted. The personages whom Bell notes within the text, especially Isaac of Letopolis (apart from Athanasius, the only positively identified person), were all active throughout the entire span of this twelve-year period.[372] Finally, the hesita-

---

[369]There are also other examples of difficulties in translation and interpretation in LP 1914. For example, in line 29 we read the following: Ἀθανάσιος δὲ μεγάλως ἀθυμῖ καὶ αὐτὸς παρέχι ἡμῖν κάματον διὰ τὰ γραφώμενα. It is obvious from this portion of the text that Athanasius is "very despondent," but it is less than clear how or why his writings are causing distress among the colleagues of Callistus. A suggestion might even be made that the distress caused is from sympathy rather than antipathy, although this would not seem to be in keeping with the remainder of the letter.

[370]Cf. Bell, *Jews and Christians, op. cit.,* 55, and Nordberg, *op. cit.,* 18, 19, for very different impressions of Athanasius's position after his enthronement.

[371]Bell, *loc. cit.*

[372]We know, for example, that Isaac of Letopolis was prominent in the actions against Athanasius which took place in Tyre, for later Ischyras places some of the blame for his false accusations on his influence (*Apol* 64; Opitz, 143, 11. 18-20). Sozomen recounts that Isaac was one of those who also accused Athanasius of violent conduct (*HE* 2, 25). Later he was one of the signatories at the Oriental Council of Sardica (Hilary of Poitiers, IV, 77). John Archaph was exiled following the Synod of Tyre (Sozomen *HE* 2, 31), but we may assume that

tion which Athanasius is said within the text to have experienced (i.38ff.) could have taken place at many times during this period, most especially in early AD 334 when he refused the summons of Constantine to attend the Synod of Caesarea. If the summons had been received in late March, as suggested in LP 1913, and Callistus's letter reporting his hesitation was written in mid-May, this would not appear to be the terribly protracted period which concerned Bell.[373] Given, therefore, the possibilities of a different context from that envisioned by Bell, and a different approach to dating, the entire thrust of LP 1914 and its subsequent interpretation is radically changed. We must admit that as an item of evidence, LP 1914 is unable to uphold its own intrinsic set of described circumstances and self-proclaimed message of persecution.

Much more could be said concerning LP 1914 and other, perhaps novel, interpretations of the letter could be put forward, but this would take us beyond the scope of our present study. Bell often admitted that he was "not a theologian" and only interested in the history which his study of papyri revealed.[374] The intricate questions which made the Meletian schism a fascinating area of historical research obviously intrigued Bell. It is also clear that he had an attachment to the study of Athanasius which went beyond the study of papyri. For example, Bell's desire to identify LP 1929 as a genuine autograph letter of Athanasius is indicative of his fascination with the bishop of Alexandria.[375] Bell's work is to be much commended for its attention to detail and his careful and, usually, balanced considerations, but clearly any single papyrus or collection of papyri is unable to reveal all the facts of a particular situation. They are merely indicators and guides within a wider circle of historical investigation. As Bell himself wrote, "there is a danger of exaggerating the darker side. Such evidence as that of the papyri may easily mislead; for it is abuses, difficulties and irregularities, rather than the normal working of the system which such documents record."[376]

---

he remained active in the strongholds of Eusebian power, one of which was Antioch.

[373]Bell, *Jews and Christians, op. cit.*, 56, 57.

[374]*Cf.* Bell, "Athanasius," *op. cit.*, 160; *HTR* 42 (1949): 53.

[375]Bell, *Jews and Christians*, 115-120. Bell's enthusiasm for the identification of LP 1929 as an authentic letter of Athanasius may be appreciated from the following: "The most we can say is that there is at least a reasonable probability that we have in the present document a specimen of the hand of the great champion of orthodoxy, and the mere possibility gives to our letter an interest which, in its sadly mutilated state, it would not otherwise possess." (118). In his article one year later, "Athanasius," *op. cit.*, Bell states that, "several considerations suggest that this" letter "may be" from "St. Athanasius himself" (171).

[376]*Cambridge Ancient History* (ed. S.A. Cook, F.E. Adcock, and M.P. Charlesworth), Cambridge, 1954 (second edition), I, 655.

It is enough to say that, although all of the alternatives described above do not eliminate the possibility that Bell's initial interpretation and translation of LP 1914 is absolutely correct, they must at least insert a note of doubt and caution in the use of the document as proof positive of the violent nature of Athanasius's character. As with any piece of written historical evidence we must continue to ask certain questions: Is this piece of writing genuine? Is its message trustworthy? How are we to be certain? What is the relationship between the author and the event (or events) recorded? How does it compare with other contemporary statements? In other words, we must make use of an informed historical common sense and not be distracted or led astray by our own preconceptions or prejudices.

In considering the evidence of LP 1914, which, whatever its ecclesiastical or political source, is clearly an *ex parte* record of events, we should also consider Athanasius's own remarks on the subject of the use of violence to further a religious cause. Clearly, there are those who would accuse Athanasius of duplicity, but his writings need to be considered as at least a public expression of his own concerns. Although it is not impossible that he used violence, we may question whether Athanasius would employ a method of systematic persecution against opponents which he would later describe at length as "an instrument of the devil."[377] He further commented that "the truth is not preached with swords or with darts nor by means of soldiers; but by persuasion and counsel . . . what counsel is there when he who withstands them receives at the end banishment and death?"[378] In Athanasius's later writings he would condemn those who "turn to violence, and in the place of fair reasoning seek to injure" their opponents.[379] This view was part of his conviction that "it is not the part of true godliness to compel, but to persuade."[380] Moreover, Athanasius saw violent intimidation in the following terms:

> It is in this manner that the devil, when he has no truth on his side, attacks and breaks down with axes and hammers the doors of them that admit him. But our Saviour is so gentle that he teaches in this way, "if any man wills to come after me," and "whoever wills to be my disciple"; and coming to each person he does not force them, but knocks at the door.[381]

It must be admitted that in these passages Athanasius was writing against those who had persecuted *his* followers. We must ask ourselves, however, Would he be willing to expose himself to the charge of duplicity in

---

[377]*Hist. Arian.* 33 (Opitz, 201, 1. 15ff).

[378]*Ibid.* (Opitz, 201, 11. 20-23).

[379]*Apol.* 2 (Opitz, 88, 11. 16, 17).

[380]*Hist. Arian.* 67 (Opitz, 219, 1. 39-220, 1. 1).

[381]*Hist. Arian.* 33 (Opitz, 201, 11. 15-19).

such an open manner if he was known to be guilty of such crimes? Some, such as Bell, have claimed that there must have been some measure of truth in the accusations of violence towards the Meletians which were made against Athanasius, owing to his silence in answering such charges at Tyre.[382] Yet the silence of Athanasius at Tyre on this smaller question (when compared to the cases of Ischyras and Arsenius) should be viewed in context. He may not have answered because the absurdity of the charges did not call for a refutation in the same manner as the more serious accusations. It is important to note that this is basically the position which was taken by the Alexandrian synod in AD 338/39 as they categorically rejected the charges made against Athanasius at Tyre.[383]

A more immediate and contemporary impression of Athanasius's view of persecution may be gained from an examination of his tenth *Festal Letter*, which was composed in AD 338 either while enroute from his exile in Trier or while in Alexandria.[384] Here Athanasius encourages his church to look upon their persecutors as friends, to imitate the "forgiveness of David," the "meekness of Jacob," and the "pity of Joseph" towards those who have "inflicted evil" upon them.[385] Above all, they are exhorted to "imitate the example of our Saviour, who grieved for those who did such things."[386] Again, Athanasius may have been guilty of duplicity. But would he have done so in a letter to the very persons who would have witnessed his earlier excesses? For one who is acknowledged by all to have been a master politician, it would seem a very imprudent course to have followed.

Exiled five times, with friends and colleagues subjected to persecution, torture, and death, Athanasius was more often sinned against than sinning, or so it would appear when it comes to the question of violence. We must, of course, give proper regard to the other interpretations of LP 1914 and, indeed, to the other charges which have been made against Athanasius. Yet, on the whole, it is possible that Hermann-Josef Vogt was correct when he commented that "Athanasius never gave way to a blind party spirit, and never lost sight of the issues which lay behind and beyond the disputed formulations."[387]

---

[382]Bell, *Jews and Christians*, 57; *cf.* Barnard, "Some Notes," *op. cit.*, 402.

[383]We may also note that the Alexandrian synod of AD 338 was very specific in stating that οὐ πρεσβύτερος, οὐ διάκονος ἀνῃρέθη παρὰ Ἀθανασίου · οὐ φόνον, οὐκ ἐξοριστίαν ἔδρασεν ὁ ἄνθρωπος (*Apol.* 5, Opitz, 91, 11. 8, 9).

[384]*Cf. Festal Letter X*, LNPF, second series, vol. 4, 527-532, the Oxford translation revised by Payne-Smith, *cf.* note 282 above.

[385]*Festal Letter* 10, 4-5 (LNPF, *op. cit.*, 529).

[386]*Ibid.*

[387]H.J. Vogt, "Parties in the History of the Church" (trans. by F. McDonagh), *Concilium* 1973-1979, pt. 1, 49.

If this is true concerning the great theological issues of his time, can we imagine that Athanasius was any less concerned with the unity of the Egyptian church and the ways in which that unity might be achieved? Clearly, the employment of persecution by Athanasius against his opponents would have been counterproductive in the long term. Moreover, it is difficult to imagine that he would have had such success in attracting Meletian converts had he personally directed a campaign of violence and intimidation against them in the early years of his episcopate. We must also keep in mind that it was during these early years in particular that a number of Meletians appear to have become ardent supporters of the young bishop of Alexandria, apparently without coercion, for many of their colleagues lapsed into opposition without any immediate consequences.

In the final analysis, we must consider what is likely to have taken place in this troubled situation given all of the available information. Although many possible scenarios may be constructed, most do not, in fact, appear probable. Some build only upon an argument of silence, preferring to view Athanasius as a shadowy figure whose true actions are unknown owing to the secrecy of the conspiracies in which he was involved. Yet, what of the evidence? Athanasius's vindication by the synod of Egyptian bishops, his support by large numbers of former Meletians, his acceptance by the rigorous monastic communities of the Egyptian desert, his own written legacy concerning persecution, and his later vast popularity in Egypt all argue against the standard interpretation of LP 1914 as *prima facie* evidence of Athanasius's violent conduct towards his theological and political opponents. The internal questions, therefore, which have been raised in LP 1914 are by no means completely settled and have yet to be fully reconciled with external evidence and placed within their proper historical setting.

3.4 The Oration of Gregory Nazianzen

The final, and most surprising, source that is listed by Frances Young and William Rusch in their reassessments of the character of Athanasius is the festival oration (*Oration* 21) of Gregory Nazianzen in which the life and theological activities of Athanasius are eulogized and remembered.[388] Their recourse to this document as an aid in the reassessment of Athanasius is, of course, an unusual use of a panegyric as evidence, for the work has as its avowed intention the exaltation of the memory of the bishop of Alexandria; as Gregory says, "In praising Athanasius, I shall be praising virtue. To speak of him and to praise virtue are one in the same, because he had, or to speak more correctly, has embraced virtue in its entirety in himself."[389] Young and Rusch, however, perceive in Gregory's overt and intense praise a

---

[388]The critical text of *Oration* 21 is contained in J. Mossay, *Grégoire de Nazianze, Discours 20-23*, SC 270, Paris, 1980, 110-193. Mossay has also provided an introduction to the text, *op. cit.*, 86-109. The Benedictine edition of the text may be found in PG 35, cols. 1081-1128.

[389]*Oration* 21, section 1; Mossay, *op. cit.*, 111, 11. 1-2.

more subtle motivation and object—the defense of the memory of Athanasius against the critical, and often hostile, nonorthodox reports concerning his actions and character which were still in circulation when Gregory delivered this address sometime between AD 379 and AD 381.[390] Drawing upon the research of Rusch, Young simply states that there were "criticisms that Gregory Nazianzen felt he had to answer in his panegyric."[391]

The argument of Rusch which seems to give substance to this statement builds upon the premise that the accounts of Philostorgius and the traditional interpretation of LP 1914 must be included in the construction of a true historical picture of Athanasius. For Rusch, the festival oration of Gregory confirms that these critical nonorthodox accounts concerning the bishop of Alexandria, especially those recorded by Philostorgius, were still prevalent enough to cause concern and, therefore, shaped the address of Gregory, who was attempting to preserve the orthodox memory of Athanasius. Rusch states his case in the following manner:

> *Oration* 21 of Gregory Nazianzen [is] a sermon probably given in 380 at the feast of St. Athanasius, seventy [sic] years after his death. As we have said above, this sermon of Gregory presents Athanasius as a saint and pillar of the Church who defended her against the Arian menace. But certain passages of the text may tentatively be taken as an attempt to deny allegations from the non-orthodox tradition. The end of section 15 is a denial of the truth of the history of Arsenius which casts it aside as though it were common gossip and without substance as an established deed. Sections 8 and 9 relate to the election and general conduct of Athanasius. One finds no explicit mention of the kind of information provided by Philostorgius, but it is clear that these chapters tend to refute the Philostorgian presentation of Athanasius. The election of the latter is presented as unanimous. He appeared sublime in action, humble in spirit, amiable, sweet, reproving with the tenderness of a father, etc. (see section 9). Cannot the listing of these traits be seen as a record set against the other recollections of Athanasius which were still alive and more in accord with the non-orthodox tradition? In that case, Gregory's *Oration* 21 gives witness at

---

[390]The exact date of *Oration* 21 is uncertain. Mossay considers it to have been composed in Constantinople, in 379, 380, or 381 for the feast of Athanasius of Alexandria (Mossay, *op. cit.*, 103). As it seems to have been delivered in Constantinople on 17 January or 2 May (*cf.* Mossay, 99-102), it would appear that AD 380 is a preferable date owing to the later arrival of Gregory in Constantinople in AD 379. There is, however, the possibility that the oration was delivered after Gregory's installation in the Church of the Apostles, and that, therefore, the address was not delivered until AD 381 (*cf.* Mossay, 102, 103; Rosemary Ruether, *Gregory of Nazianzus: Rhetor and Philosopher*, Oxford, 1969, 43-46; and Kopecek, *A History of Neo-Arianism* II, 510ff.).

[391]Young, *Nicaea to Chalcedon*, 67.

the end of the fourth century to those elements of a non-orthodox tradition which continued to slur the memory of a canonized patriarch.[392]

While it seems certain, as has been stated earlier in this section, that there were a number of variant traditions concerning Athanasius still extant in the late fourth and early fifth centuries, the argument of Rusch concerning *Oration* 21 is less than satisfactory for a number of reasons. First, it does not seem to take into account the literary genre to which *Oration* 21 belongs.[393] The listing of Athanasius's virtues by Gregory in section 9, which Rusch refers to above, continues in section 10 with reference to the Pauline "model for future bishops."[394] These listings, however, need not be seen as an answer to contrary opinions but merely as a rhetorical device. Commenting on sections 9 and 10 in *Oration* 21, Rosemary Reuther has written that "in the panegyric this" approach to the listeners

> could also be given a hyperbolic turn by pretending that the virtues of the person being praised were so great that the orator was exhausted in trying adequately to describe them all, and he called upon his audience to help him out. Thus, after describing the early career of Athanasius, Gregory makes a fresh start with the words: "Come then to aid me in my panegyric; for I am labouring heavily, and though I desire to pass by point after point, they seize upon me one after the other, and I can find no surpassing excellence in a form which is in all respects well proportioned and beautiful, for each as it occurs to me seems fairer than the rest and so takes by storm my speech."[395]

Another common figure used by an orator such as Gregory was paraleipsis, in which the speaker "recounts some facts or events while declaring his intention to pass over them in silence." Again commenting on *Oration* 21, Reuther states, "Thus in the passage following the one quoted above, Gregory declares that he must pass over most of Athanasius' virtues in silence, since they could fill myriad discourses (having, of course, already enumerated all these virtues in considerable detail), and confine his account only to the most important points."[396] Far from designing his discourse to answer the particular charges of critics from outside the orthodox tradition, Gregory may much more reasonably be regarded as merely following in this address the literary style which he deemed appropriate for such an occasion.

---

[392]Rusch, "A la recherche de l'Athanase historique," *Politique et théologie*, 176.

[393]*Cf.* Mossay, *op. cit.*, 95-99.

[394]Mossay, *op. cit.*, 128, section 10, 11. 6, 7.

[395]Ruether, *op. cit.*, 77.

[396]*Ibid.*, 77, 78.

We need not, therefore, attach any special significance to Rusch's selected sections of this address beyond making allowance for Gregory's concern with a particular type of oratory.

Second, Rusch places great emphasis on what he perceives to be Gregory's singular intention in formulating this oration concerning Athanasius. Rusch suggests that Gregory is attempting to "deny allegations from the non-orthodox tradition" and is concerned with those "elements of a non-orthodox tradition which continued to slur the memory of a canonized patriarch."[397] For Young, there are "the criticisms that Gregory . . . felt he had to answer."[398]

Both of these views are contrary to the opinion of Justin Mossay, who, in his introduction to the critical text of *Oration* 21, considers the intent of Gregory to be threefold:

1.   to show Athanasius as a model of what it means to be a bishop;
2.   to explain the manner in which Athanasius was able to cooperate with the monastic communities in Egypt and reconcile active participation in the church with the ideal of solitude;
3.   to present Athanasius as a preeminent defender of trinitarian faith.[399]

Furthermore, Mossay considers the oration to go beyond simply an address in praise of Athanasius at that point in sections 34 and 35 where Gregory relates the particular issues that the bishop of Alexandria faced to the pressing issues of the universal church of his own day.[400] Certainly, it is not difficult to see *Oration* 21, with the themes set out above, as having a particular message for Gregory's Constantinopolitan congregation during the period surrounding Theodosius's reforms. It is, perhaps, not without significance that Gregory in section 35 portrays Athanasius primarily as a reconciler who "bound together" differing parties "in a unity of action."[401]

In Reuther's analysis of *Oration* 21 similar themes emerge, albeit with a greater emphasis on the use of particular rhetorical forms.[402] She notes that, following the introductory sections 1-9, "Gregory then uses the same technique that he used in the oration on Cyprian."[403] Following a recitation

---

[397]Rusch, *op. cit.*, 176.

[398]Young, *loc. cit.*

[399]Mossay, *op. cit.*, 92-95. The trinitarian concerns in the orations is also considered by E.P. Meijering, "The Doctrine of the Will and of the Trinity in the Orations of Gregory of Nazianzus," *NedThT* 27 (1973): 224-234.

[400]Mossay, *op. cit.*, 95.

[401]Mossay, *op. cit.*, 186, 11. 35, 36.

[402]Ruether, *op. cit.*, 111.

[403]*Ibid.*; Ruether also notes that "in the two orations on Cyprian and on Athanasius, both being models of powerful churchmen in times of upheaval, Gregory follows the *topoi* of the encomium somewhat more closely" than in his other orations on particular persons (*op. cit.*, 109, 110).

of Athanasius's virtues, however, Gregory passes on, Reuther indicates "to what is most important":

> In this case what is most important turns out to be the story of Athanasius' expulsion from Alexandria by the Arian bishop George of Cappadocia. In the process, Gregory gives us a specimen of his best invective style: "There was a monster from Cappadocia, born on our furthest confines, of low birth and lower mind."[404]

Considering the events in Constantinople from AD 379-AD 381, including the expulsion of the Arian bishop Demophilus and Gregory's move, with his orthodox congregation, from the Church of the Anastasis to the Church of the Apostles in AD 380, it is possible to view *Oration* 21 as having a very particular intention, but probably not the one suggested by Young and Rusch.[405]

It is, perhaps, better to consider *Oration* 21 in the light of Gregory's stated intention "to speak of and fully admire" Athanasius. In performing this service Gregory may have been drawing upon his own encounter with the bishop while a student in Alexandria in AD 350, although this is by no means certain.[406] It is apparent, however, that Gregory was very much alive

---

[404] *Ibid.*, 111.

[405] A useful summary of the events taking place during this period in Constantinople is provided by Kopecek, who relates

> the arrival of Theodosius in Constantinople in late November AD 380 and his subsequent support of the Nicene position. Already in February of the same year Theodosius had heralded his Nicene commitment in his famous edict *Conctos populos:* the theological positions of Damasus of Rome and Peter of Alexandria were set up as the touchstones of imperially-approved "Catholic" Christianity. Then, soon after he entered Constantinople in triumph the emperor summoned Demophilus, the official bishop of the capital. Theodosius gave the prelate a choice: assent to the Nicene Creed or surrender the city's churches. The bishop chose the latter and began to celebrate the Eucharist outside the city's walls. With Demophilus out of the way, Theodosius gave episcopal control of the capital's churches to the Neo-Nicene Gregory of Nazianzus. On January 10, AD 381 the emperor issued a law which widened his attack on Arianism and his support of Nicaea to include the entire eastern empire. (Kopecek, *op. cit.*, II, 510)

Although we cannot be certain as to Gregory's intentions, it would certainly seem reasonable to see a reflection of the events in Constantinople AD 379-AD 380 in the particular themes which Gregory chose to emphasize in *Oration* 21.

[406] Ruether, *op. cit.*, 19, fn. 4. Although Ruether states that "Gregory speaks of Athanasius with great affection" (*ibid.*), possibly as a result of meeting him in AD 350, Charles G. Browne and James E. Swallow wrote that *Oration 21* "lacks ... the charm of personal affection and intimate acquaintance with the inner life which is characteristic of the orations concerned with his own relatives and friends" (LNPF, second series, vol. 7, 269).

to the orthodox tradition concerning the life and career of Athanasius and presents it in a manner that is suited to his own particular purpose. If, in fact, the case of Arsenius is treated as "common gossip," Gregory's condemnation of Arius is no less succinct in section 13. His description of Nicaea likewise lacks a degree of historical accuracy but succeeds, rightly or wrongly, in placing Athanasius "in the first rank among the members of the Council, for preference was given to virtue equally with that of office."[407] In such a context, Gregory's slight reference to the Arsenius affair as "the hand which was produced by fraud against the saint, and the corpse of the living man," is neither out of place nor, more importantly, out of character considering the nature of the address.[408] There is little reason to see either in this comment or in the mention of Athanasius's election in section 8 veiled references to the Philostorgian accounts, or, indeed, to conclude that any other sections of the oration are in response to similar slurs on the memory of the bishop from outside the orthodox tradition.

The contention of Rusch, and by inference Young, is essentially an argument based upon silence. We have no certain way in which we can ascertain the true and absolute intention of Gregory in *Oration* 21. Upon considered reflection, however, the purposes outlined by Mossay and the rhetorical style elucidated by Reuther appear to be somewhat more persuasive indicators of Gregory's intention in the writing of the panegyric. Moreover, there would appear to be some degree of justification in relating *Oration* 21 to the immediate context of the controversy in Constantinople rather than to Gregory's entry into an historical debate concerning the character of Athanasius with sources which not only were suspect, but also are mixed accounts of which we have little certain knowledge. Although it is within the realm of possibility that another interpretation of Gregory's oration may, in fact, be correct, there is little, if any, evidence available to support the speculative assertions of Rusch and Young.

---

[407]*Oration* 21, section 14; Mossay, *op. cit.,* 138, 11. 5-7.
[408]*Ibid.,* section 15; Mossay, *op. cit.,* 140, section 15, 11. 7-9.

4. CONCLUDING CONSIDERATIONS

Within this first section, an attempt has been made to examine once again those sources which have contributed to more recent critical revisionist accounts of the life and character of Athanasius. In the examination of these sources special attention has been given to those particular reports which might give weight to the opinion of Frances Young that "there seems to have been a pitiless streak in" Athanasius's "character—that he resorted to violence to achieve his own ends is implied by a good deal of evidence."[409] An evaluation of the particular documents cited by William Rusch—the Philostorgian narratives, LP 1914, and *Oration* 21 of Gregory Nazianzen— has also been undertaken, along with reviews of certain important ancillary issues which arise out of these sources, such as the consecration of Athanasius in AD 328 and the role of the Meletians within the Egyptian church in the period between the Council of Nicaea in AD 325 and the Synod of Tyre in AD 335.[410]

From this study, certain preliminary conclusions may be stated. It should be noted, however, that these preliminary conclusions must remain tentative, rather than absolute, owing to the interpolations in the Philostorgian narratives and the continued uncertainty as to the actual context in which LP 1914 was written. It must also be acknowledged that both Young and Rusch admit that there are elements in "the good tradition" which "are certainly right," and that the historical Athanasius is likely to be found "in the middle ground."[411] Nevertheless, their insistence on accepting the evidence of Philostorgius, LP 1914, and Gregory Nazianzen is representative of the more recent revisionist accounts of Athanasius which we named in the first portion of this section.[412]

There can remain little doubt that Philostorgius is a valuable source of information with regard to a large number of random Arian and Meletian calumnies against Athanasius which are collected and preserved in Photius's *Epitome*. That these assorted slanders have little basis in fact, however, is also apparent when they are compared with other contemporary or near-con-

---

[409]Young, *op. cit.*, 67.

[410]Rusch, *op. cit.*, 161-177. There are other issues which arise in this decade concerning Athanasius's character. The vast majority of these accusations, however, are brought forward at Tyre in AD 335. Certain of these charges have already been discussed in the first section of the present work. Other accusations will be considered in the second section within the discussion on the Synod of Tyre.

[411]Young, *op. cit.*, 68; Rusch, *op. cit.*, 176, 177.

[412]*Vide supra*, fn. 54, for others who have taken a moderate position concerning the character of Athanasius while accepting many of the accusations made against him.

temporary accounts of the same events—even those contained in histories which are not wholly favorable to Athanasius.[413]

The Philostorgian account of the consecration of Athanasius remains a case in point.[414] In this particular narrative it is difficult, if not impossible, to separate the report of Philostorgius from the editorial comments of Photius. Furthermore, the figures who are named in the account, the details which are offered, and the general sequence of events which is provided are at such variance with the other histories and documents to which we have access as to be almost completely without credence in any attempt to provide a reasonable reconstruction of what actually took place. Certainly, Rusch is correct in writing that "the portrait of Athanasius" that is provided "by Philostorgius merits our attention, notwithstanding the hostile nature of the presentation."[415] To suggest, however, that Philostorgius has preserved a nonorthodox tradition concerning Athanasius that is of equal value to other contemporary accounts and that we may set aside only at our "risk and peril" seems to go beyond what the documentary evidence allows.[416]

The description of Athanasius in LP 1914 is somewhat more problematic.[417] As we have indicated in this study, the historical context in which LP 1914 was written is uncertain. The dating of the papyrus by H.I. Bell is completely circumstantial and by no means definitive.[418] The various factions and parties mentioned in the letter are not identified with any degree of certainty, and Bell's translation owes much to his own understanding of those events as he assumed they surrounded its writing. Bell, as has been shown, tended to ignore the complexities of the religious situation in Egypt and, by means of his introduction and annotation of the papyrus, gave greater weight to this document than it might otherwise have merited.

LP 1914 remains an intriguing item of historical interest, but with certain shortcomings. The genuineness of the document both in regard to its dating and context is uncertain. The type of monastic community which is described in LP 1914 as being near to the city and hard by the military camp is difficult to reconcile with other evidence from the period.[419] The message of the papyrus, as Bell himself admits, is to some extent unclear owing to the personal nature of the correspondence.[420] The reader of LP 1914 may

---

[413]*Cf.* Sozomen, *HE*, II, 17 (J. Bidez, SC 306, Paris, 1983, 296); Socrates, *HE*, I, 23 (PG 67, 139, C9-141); and Philostorgius, *HE*, II, 11 (J. Bidez, *Philostorgius Kirchengeschichte* [revised edition], GSC, 22-23).

[414]Philostorgius, *HE*, II, 11 (Bidez, *loc. cit.*).

[415]Rusch, *op. cit.*, 162.

[416]*Ibid.*, 177.

[417]H.I. Bell, *Jews and Christians, op. cit.*, 53-71 (esp. LP 1914, 11. 8, 9; 29-47).

[418]Bell, *Jews and Christians, op. cit.*, 54-57.

[419]LP 1914, 11. 5-15.

[420]Bell, *Jews and Christians, op. cit.*, 53.

only speculate upon the relationship between the author, Callistus, and the events which he claims to be reporting. Finally, although Athanasius's treatment of the Meletians was brought into question at the Synod of Tyre in AD 335, the events described to the assembled bishops and the emperor's representative are not those which are related in LP 1914 except in the most general sense possible.[421]

All of the above comments do not, of course, diminish the relative importance of LP 1914. They do, however, call into question its use as absolute evidence of Athanasius's guilt. This is most especially true if Athanasius's own writings concerning the subject of persecution are taken into account, along with the very different concerns which are mentioned in the *Festal Letters* from the first decade of his episcopate. Furthermore, corollary accounts contained within the histories of the period provide little substantiation for the circumstances which are described in LP 1914. In any case, current references to LP 1914 show clearly that few pieces of evidence can be used for historiography in the state in which they are found; they are necessarily subjected to the actions and subtle reasonings of the researcher and interpreter.[422] Those who would seek to make use of LP 1914 as proof of Athanasius's violent character have yet to show the papyrus to be decisive evidence; *i.e.*, evidence which confirms only one view and excludes its rivals. Clearly, LP 1914 is not such a piece of evidence in its current state and, barring further corroborating materials, is likely to remain so in the future.

Gregory Nazianzen's *Oration* 21 concerning Athanasius fits into yet another category of evidence and argument. Rusch has contended that Gregory's oration was, at least in certain sections, motivated by his desire to dispel rumors concerning the bishop's character which had arisen from

---

[421]It may be noted here that in addition to the accusation concerning the murder of Arsenius, Athanasius was also charged with the arrest and imprisonment of a number of Meletian church dignitaries, including Ischyras, Callinicus (bishop of Pelusium), and others who were not named (Sozomen, *HE*, II, 25, 3ff. [Bidez, SC 306, 301ff]; *cf.* Schwartz, *GS* III, 248ff.). Although the charges are similar to the actions described in LP 1914, 11. 41-47, the names given are different and no further information is provided to connect this incident and the accusations at Tyre, if, indeed, there is any connection to be made.

[422]An example of this may be seen in K. Holl, *Gesammelte Aufsätze* 2 (1928), 286, in which it is claimed that Bell did "not recognize the reference to Tyre" in LP 1914, 11. 31, which would secure the dating of the papyrus. Although the papyrus contains a break followed by υρω, it it impossible, either from the papyrus itself or the context, to insist upon this reading to the exclusion of others. Holl, however, was convinced by Bell's circumstantial evidence for the dating of the letter and carried this assumption in his examination of LP 1914. In Bell's writings, however, this author has yet to find his acknowledgment of Holl's reading. Holl's reading has, however, been taken up by T.D. Barnes, who provides a colorful, if not wholly factual, rendering of the events described in LP 1914 (T.D. Barnes, *Constantine and Eusebius*, 235, 336; 387 fns. 100, 101).

nonorthodox sources.[423]   By putting forward this argument Rusch is
attempting to look beyond and behind the oration itself to its possible
motivations. The search for causation and motivation, however, is, by its
very nature, subjective. In the case of Gregory's oration such an approach is
further complicated in that we must set aside Gregory's own stated intention
in the address, as well as his adherence to particular conventional rhetorical
devices which are evidenced elsewhere, in order to accept Rusch's argument.
After careful consideration of the insights provided by Rosemary Reuther and
Justin Mossay into the themes and structure of *Oration* 21, such an approach
as is outlined by Rusch would seem to be unacceptable.[424]   Moreover,
many other circumstances more closely related to the context and style of the
address would appear to have equal or greater claims to causation or
motivation than those which have been advanced by Rusch and Young.[425]

To assert an absolute or certain historical knowledge concerning the
character of Athanasius is, of course, difficult, if not impossible. It is possible, however, to arrive at certain reasonable conclusions on the basis of a
critical examination of the documentary evidence at hand in order to assess
the probability of the truthfulness of the accounts contained within such materials. Admittedly, our comprehension of the events which took place between AD 325 and AD 335 is imperfect, yet the only historical understanding
we will ever arrive at concerning those crucial years is one that is based upon
the extant evidence, opinions, and reports. An argument which is based upon
silence or upon our inability to ascertain the truth of a situation is, in reality,
an argument without substance. This would appear to be the case with many
of those more modern accusations of violence which have been advanced
against Athanasius.[426]   Furthermore, it should be acknowledged that the
burden of proof is on the advocates of these fresh hypotheses which represent
a radical break from the more moderate views of earlier scholars within the

---

[423]Rusch, *op. cit.*, 176.

[424]Ruether, *op. cit.*, 77, 78; Mossay, *op. cit.*, 95-99.

[425]*Vide supra*, fn. 389.

[426]T.D. Barnes states that "in Alexandria itself" Athanasius "maintained
the popular support which he enjoyed from the outset and buttressed his position
by organizing an ecclesiastical mafia." Furthermore, Barnes comments that
Athanasius was "like a modern gangster" and "evoked widespread mistrust,
proclaimed total innocence—and usually succeeded in evading conviction on
specific charges" (Barnes, *op. cit.*, 230). In using such words as *mafia* and
gangster, Barnes is, of course, intimating that much of what Athanasius did was in
secret and was protected by an extended organization which the modern scholar is,
for the most part, unable to penetrate. Such an argument, however, is one that is
based upon silence and surmise rather than documentary evidence. Moreover, the
reasoning in such an approach must of necessity be circular: *i.e.*, there is little
documentation because of the secret method of operation; therefore, we must
assume a secret method of operation because there is little documentation. Such a
contention, however, does not take into account much of the documentation which
we do possess and tends to read such documents within a set pattern of bias.

field. Such proof must not only be sustained from within a particular documentary source, such as those we have examined, but must also be shown to be consonant with the surrounding body of knowledge and materials. Finally, the rule governing our response to these materials must be that of probability rather than an attempt to establish some notion of an absolute view of the events and persons in question. If this rigorous standard of judgment is applied, it must be admitted that the more vituperative critics of Athanasius have failed to provide clear and convincing evidence for a revisionist portrait of the bishop of Alexandria.

From the documents and issues which have been examined thus far, it is clear that any view of the early career of Athanasius must take into account his relationship with the larger structures of the church of his day, specifically the ecumenical and provincial synods. Although Nicaea gained greater importance in his theological thought with the passing years, the provincial synod which took place at Tyre in AD 335 had an even more immediate, direct, and dramatic impact on him, resulting in his exile from Alexandria at the conclusion of the meeting and later objections to his eventual reinstatement.[427] It is also within the records of this synod that we find the first definitive accusations made against Athanasius by his contemporaries within an ecclesiastical setting.[428] In the second section of the present work, therefore, an attempt will be made to reconstruct an historical narrative and chronology of those events which led to the Synod of Tyre, as well as an examination of the process by which the synod arrived at its judgments concerning the bishop of Alexandria which affected him so greatly during the first two decades of his episcopate.

---

[427]Cf. Colm Luibhéid, *The Council of Nicaea,* Galway, 1982, 136-143; J.N.D. Kelly, *Early Christian Creeds,* third edition, London, 1972, 254-262; and Leo Davis, *The First Seven Ecumenical Councils (325-787): Their History and Theology,* Wilmington, Delaware, 1987, 90.

[428]*Vide supra,* fn. 405, for a discussion of the majority of these accusations in connection with contemporary scholarship in the field.

SECTION II

ATHANASIUS AND THE SYNOD OF TYRE

SECTION II
ATHANASIUS AND THE SYNOD OF TYRE

1. THE BACKGROUND OF THE SYNOD OF TYRE

By the time of his third exile, AD 356-AD 362, Athanasius had formulated a particular view concerning the authority, structure, and validity of ecclesiastical synods. His views were largely based upon his own experience of condemnation and vindication by a variety of synods in the thirty years which separated his third exile from the decrees of the Council of Nicaea in AD 325. The questions of context and character which have been examined in the first section of this present study, especially in regard to those events which surrounded the Synod of Tyre in AD 335, were an ever-present source of concern for the bishop of Alexandria. The sentence of banishment imposed by Constantine following the Synod of Tyre provided Athanasius's enemies with an opportunity for continual attacks throughout this period and, as has been noted above, gave rise to lingering doubts concerning the character and motivation of the bishop of Alexandria. It is, then, to the Synod of Tyre that we must give our full attention in any attempt to understand Athanasius's early episcopal career and the manner in which this synod affected his later actions and writings.

Frances Young states that Athanasius's "deposition at Tyre was based, not on doctrinal considerations, but upon his misconduct in Egypt."[1] There can be little doubt, however, that the series of events which reached their peak at Tyre began with Athanasius's refusal to readmit either Arius or the Meletians to the communion of the church of Alexandria in accordance with the command of Constantine.[2]

Following the return of Eusebius, bishop of Nicomedia, to his see, a campaign had been set into motion which had as its primary objective the

---

[1]F. M. Young, *From Nicaea to Chalcedon*, London, 1983, 67.
[2]*Vide supra*, Section I, fn. 283.

readmission of Arius to the church in Alexandria along with a secondary demand for a greater Meletian presence and role in the affairs of the Egyptian church. Rowan Williams appears to be correct in tracing the genesis of this movement to the Bithynian synod of late AD 328 which met under the chairmanship of Eusebius and issued a "renewed appeal to Alexandria for Arius's restoration" (as well as for the settling of the Meletian schism by their reception).[3] In spite of the fact that the request had been approved and sanctioned by the emperor, it was refused outright by Athanasius.[4] Although ultimately threatened with deposition and exile by the emperor, Athanasius remained intransigent.[5] In reply to the imperial demands, the bishop of Alexandria "wrote and sought to convince the emperor, that an anti-Christian heresy had no fellowship with the Church Catholic."[6] This sentiment is echoed in Athanasius's *Festal Letter* for Easter AD 330 in which he states that "there is no communion at all between the words of the saints and the fanciful thoughts of human invention."[7]

1.1 Athanasius at Psamathia, AD 331/332

The Arian-Meletian alliance appears to have been arranged by Eusebius of Nicomedia during the period which immediately followed the Synod of Bithynia, that is, *ca.* AD 329-AD 331.[8] According to Athanasius, Eusebius persuaded the Meletians "to produce some pretext, such as they had done against Peter, Achillas, and Alexander, in order" that they might "invent and spread reports against us as well."[9] Epiphanius places the beginning of the alliance in a slightly different context by indicating that when a delegation of Meletian bishops arrived at court to present a petition to the emperor which requested protection for their churches from repeated catholic intrusions, the emperor's attendants refused to grant them access to Constantine. Remaining in the region of Constantinople and Nicomedia, they turned to Eusebius of Nicomedia for assistance in bringing their case before the emperor. Eusebius granted their request, but only with the condition that they would accept Arius into fellowship.[10]

Once again, however, Epiphanius appears muddled in regard to dating and context, indicating that this interview took place while Alexander was

---

[3]R. Williams, *Arius. Heresy and Tradition,* 76; *cf.* Socrates, *HE* I, 27 (PG 67, 152B), and Sozomen *HE* II, 18 (Bidez, 74, 9-14).

[4]Sozomen, *HE* II, 22 (Bidez, 79, 5-15).

[5]*Cf. Apol.* 59, 4-5 (Opitz, 139, 20-140, 10).

[6]*Apol.* 60, 1 (Opitz, 140, 11-12); *vide supra,* section I, fn. 283.

[7]*Festal Letter* II, 7 (Robertson, LNPF, second series, vol. 4, 510).

[8]Sozomen, *HE* II, 21 (Bidez, 77, 6ff.); *cf.* Epiphanius, *Haer* 68, 6ff. (Holl, 145, 27ff.).

[9]*Apol.* 60, 1 (Opitz, 140, 13-15).

[10]Epiphanius, *Haer.* 68, 6ff. (Holl, 145, 27ff.).

still alive, that is, before the spring of AD 328. Timothy Barnes has indicated that such a scenario is impossible, for "even Athanasius concedes that the Meletians caused no trouble in the winter of 327/8, and Constantine left Nicomedia in the spring of 328, not returning for fully two years."[11] By connecting the presentation of charges to Constantine through the "good offices" of Eusebius of Nicomedia, however, Epiphanius may be relating from Meletian sources the substance of an account of the beginning of the Arian-Meletian alliance which should, in reality, be set in the summer of AD 330, following Constantine's return to the East and the dedication of Constantinople.[12] As Eusebius had failed to enjoin enforcement of Constantine's earlier letter to Athanasius, the Meletians would have presented a new opportunity for attacking the bishop of Alexandria. It is possible, therefore, that the account of Epiphanius and the first set of accusations made against Athanasius before the emperor in Nicomedia are related and may signal the beginning of their alliance against the bishop of Alexandria.

In Athanasius's own account of the beginning of the alliance, written almost thirty years after the events in question, he relates that three members of the Meletian clergy, Ision of Athribis, Eudaemon of Tanis, and Callinicus of Pelusium, with the advice of Eusebius, put forward the initial accusation that as bishop Athanasius had imposed an unlawful tax in kind upon the Egyptians, possibly taking over the prerogative which by civil decree and custom had formerly belonged to the hierarchy of the pagan temples and, therefore, violating the rights of the local Roman administration.[13] The exact nature of the tax is uncertain, apart from its being related to a local levy on linen tunics which, so the delegation claimed, had been first imposed upon the Meletians themselves.[14] The location of this first accusation was most probably Constantinople, where Constantine was in residence from 16 July AD 330 to 30 June AD 331.[15] It is possible, however, that Constantine visited Nicomedia during this period as well, although Epiphanius's account of the matter is unclear.[16]

The exact location of Athanasius at this time also remains uncertain. The *Index* to the *Festal Letters* indicates that he visited the Thebaid during the winter of AD 330/331 and from that location issued his Easter letter of AD

---

[11]T. Barnes, *Constantine and Eusebius*, 231.

[12]*Ibid.*

[13]*Apol.* 60, 2 (Opitz, 140, 15-18).

[14]στιχάρια, *ibid.; cf.* E. Schwartz, *GS* III, 193, fn. 2, and K.M. Girardet, *Kaisergericht und Bischofsgericht*, 57, 58.

[15]T. Barnes, *The New Empire of Diocletian and Constantine*, London, 1982, 78.

[16]*Ibid.*, 78, fn. 132; Epiphanius, *Haer.* 68, 5-6 (Holl, 145, 4ff.); *cf.* Socrates, *HE* I, 27, 8 (PG 67, 152B).

331.[17] E. Schwartz, however, argued that this letter, traditionally ascribed to AD 331, should, in fact, be redated in favor of AD 342.[18] In reply, L.T. Lefort constructed a convincing argument for maintaining the traditional dating of the letter, which would, therefore, place Athanasius in the Thebaid during the period in question and at a good distance from Alexandria and more direct communication with either Constantinople or Nicomedia.[19]

This first accusation concerning illegal taxation, therefore, was not answered directly by Athanasius but, rather, by two Alexandrian presbyters, Apis and Macarius, who were at court.[20] Henric Nordberg comments that "this detail alone is interesting as it reveals how Athanasius kept up a continuous contact with Constantine. Already during Alexander's time the presbyter, Apis, was his envoy to Constantine, which proves that the Archbishop had an established embassy or in any case a stationary envoy at the court."[21] According to Athanasius, the result of their advocacy on his behalf was the condemnation of the Meletian envoys, in particular Ision, and his own acquittal on the charge.[22] This was very possibly owing to the presence of Macarius, who appears to be identical with the presbyter of the same name listed in the *Breviarium Melitii* from the village of Parembole on the Mareotic lake.[23] The combination of the ex-Meletian, Macarius, and the presbyter, Apis, who had been an envoy at Constantine's court since the time of Alexander, would have been especially effective in confronting and turning aside the accusation of the Meletian delegation.[24] Notwithstanding his

---

[17]*Histoire "Acephale" et Index Syriaque des Lettres Festales d'Athanase d'Alexandrie* (A. Martin with M. Albert, eds.), SC 317, Paris, 1985, 229.

[18]Schwartz, *GS* IV, 7; *cf.* V. Peri, "La cronologia delle lettere festali di Sant' Atanasio e la quaresima," *Aevum* 35 (1961): 45ff.

[19]L.T. Lefort, "Les Lettres festales de Saint Athanase," *Bulletin de la classe des lettres de l'Académie royale de Belgique* 39 (1953): 646ff.; an unexplained reference by Athanasius in *Festal Letter* III, 1, remains. Athanasius comments that he is "under restraint," that is, not at full liberty to write all that he might wish (Robertson, *op. cit.,* 512). We know from the existing chronology that Athanasius was not appearing before the emperor at this time (*cf.* Barnes, *The New Empire,* 78) and that this letter was written from the Thebaid (*Histoire* [A. Martin], 229). It is possible that he was under a sense of restraint from writing at length owing to the delicacy of dealing with Meletian intrusions within the monastic communities where he was engaged in an episcopal visitation (H. Nordberg, *Athanasius and the Emperor,* 22). Without further documentary evidence, however, it is impossible to give an exact explanation of the context, and we may only speculate as to the meaning of this oblique reference.

[20]*Apol.* 60, 3 (Opitz, 140, 19-20).

[21]Nordberg, *Athanasius and the Emperor,* 22.

[22]*Apol.* 60, 3 (Opitz, 140, 19-21).

[23]*Apol.* 71, 6 (Opitz, 151, 9).

[24]For a more complete treatment of the extent to which Athanasius made use of a large number of ex-Meletians, *vide supra,* section I, fn. 285.

condemnation of the Meletians, however, Constantine ordered Athanasius to appear before him.[25] The reason for the summons is not given by Athanasius, and the letters of Constantine which he quotes are no longer extant within the text of *Apologia contra Arianos*.

Athanasius, according to custom, would have returned to Alexandria from the Thebaid, to be present for the Easter celebrations which took place during the second week of April AD 331. The *Festal Letter Index* III, appears to be misplaced in the chronological sequence, as its description of events obviously belongs to *Festal Letter* IV.[26] The summons from Constantine does not seem to have been urgent, if one judges from Athanasius's lack of timely compliance with the emperor's request. The bishop finally arrived at the imperial residence of Psamathia, on the outskirts of Nicomedia, to appear before Constantine in the late autumn of AD 331 and remained there through the greater portion of the winter (*ca.* November AD 331 to January AD 332).[27] He was still at court when he sent his Easter letter to the church of Alexandria for AD 332 during the early portion of that same year.[28]

It appears that upon learning that Athanasius had been summoned to appear before the emperor, Eusebius convinced the Meletian delegation to remain in the area of Nicomedia with the intent of presenting the emperor with a series of accusations against Athanasius. The three members of the Meletian delegation (Ision, Eudaemon, and Callinicus) were joined by a fourth person whom Athanasius describes as "the ridiculous Hiercammon, who being ashamed of his name, calls himself Eulogius."[29] Of the four, Hiercammon is the only member of the delegation who is not listed in the schedule of Meletian clergy which had been presented to Alexander approximately four or five years earlier.

The initial civil charge of illegal taxation which had originally been brought forward by the Meletians would be joined to three further accusations—two of an ecclesiastical nature and one additional civil indictment. When Athanasius appeared before Constantine at Psamathia the four charges he had to answer were these:

1. The original accusation of illegal taxation of the Egyptian populace, and the Meletians in particular, in regard to the linen tunics mentioned above, was reiterated. Such a method of taxation in kind would not have been unusual in Egypt during the Roman period but, as has been indicated above, would have usurped the authority of the Egyptian civil administration unless

---

[25]*Apol.* 60, 3 (Opitz, 140, 20-21).

[26]*Histoire* (A. Martin), 229.

[27]Barnes, *The New Empire*, 78.

[28]*Festal Letter* IV (Robertson, *op. cit.*, 517).

[29]*Ibid.*

it had been confined to the church as a form of voluntary offerings.[30]

2. The second accusation, not mentioned by Athanasius but indicated in the *Festal Letter Index*, was that he had been "appointed" as bishop "while too young."[31] Although this brief reference to Athanasius's age at the time of his election appears to refer directly to canon 11 of the ante-Nicene Synod of Neocaesarea, it may be reflective of a more general consecration controversy which surrounded his elevation to the throne of St. Mark in AD 328.[32]

3. The third accusation was that Macarius, the ex-Meletian priest who defended Athanasius when the Meletian delegation first arrived, acting upon the instructions of Athanasius and under his responsibility, had earlier been sent to the region of Mareotis to summon Ischyras, a schismatic priest, to Alexandria. In the course of this "pastoral visitation" Macarius is said to have been involved in an altercation during which he broke a chalice belonging to the church of Ischyras.[33]

4. The fourth, and most serious, accusation appears to have been put forward by what Socrates refers to as "the Eusebian party," that is, Eusebius of Nicomedia, Theognis of Nicaea, Maris of Chalcedon, Ursacius of Singidnum in Upper Moesia, and Valens of Mursa in Upper Pannonia.[34] Athanasius was charged with treasonable conspiracy in that he was alleged to have provided Philumenus, a former master of the offices accused of having plotted to assassinate Constantine, with a casket of gold.[35] Although Hans Lietzmann, among others, suggests that this was only a question of "the bribery of a king's messenger," it is clear from Athanasius's own account that the charge was treason, that is, being the "enemy of the emperor."[36]

---

[30]A. K. Bowman, *Egypt After the Pharaohs: 332BC-AD642, from Alexander to the Arab Conquest,* Oxford, 1986, 93, 183; Socrates, *HE* I, 27, 9 (PG 67, 153A).

[31]*Histoire* (A. Martin), *loc. cit.*

[32]J. Hefele, *History of the Councils of the Church* I, 228; for a more complete treatment of this aspect of the accusations against Athanasius, *vide supra,* section I, subsection 3.2 and following.

[33]*Apol.* 60, 4 (Opitz, 140, 22-23).

[34]Socrates, *HE* I, 27, 9 (PG 67, 153A).

[35]*Cf.* Barnes, *Constantine and Eusebius,* 386, n. 69.

[36]The phrase κατὰ βασιλέως γενόμενος which is used by Athanasius leaves little doubt as to his understanding of the implications contained within the charge made against him (*Apol.* 60, 4; Opitz, 141, 1). Several writers, however, have interpreted the accusation as an Athanasian attempt to bribe an official who

Clearly, the intent of the Meletians and Eusebians in presenting these charges against Athanasius before Constantine was to secure his deposition from the see of Alexandria. The odd catalogue of civil and ecclesiastical misdeeds which are set out above appear to have no common link apart from this desired end. It is probable that the Eusebians had already learned that such a mixture of innuendo, scandal, and theological or canonical improprieties could be an effective method in their campaign to remove the more vocal proponents of the Nicene definition. That Athanasius had become the primary object of this campaign was most likely owing to his rejection of Arius and his relative lack of support at this time among the eastern bishops.

An earlier target of such a campaign had been Eustathius of Antioch. Although R.P.C. Hanson has put forward the case that Eustathius was deposed, in AD 328 or 329, primarily for Sabellianist views and at the instigation of the Eusebians (in this case, however, Eusebius of Caesarea), there were certainly other charges which were brought against him.[37] Furthermore, although Eusebius of Caesarea may have taken the lead in the proceedings, it is difficult not to place Eusebius of Nicomedia and Theognis of Nicaea as coconspirators in the actions taken against Eustathius. The accusations made against the bishop of Antioch were similar in character and number to those which were leveled against Athanasius only a few years later.

The eastern bishops at Sardica hint that the bishop of Antioch was deposed not for doctrinal reasons but because of his evil manner of life.[38] Athanasius, writing thirty years after the event, states that Eustathius, "a confessor and a man of sound faith," was deposed owing to "invented accusations" against him, including the charge that he had "insulted" Constantine's mother.[39] Had Eustathius been deposed on a charge of Sabellianism alone, one would not expect such a characterization by Athanasius given the theological climate in which he was writing. Barnes summarizes the case made against Eustathius as follows:

---

was in disgrace; *cf.* H. Lietzmann, *From Constantine to Julian*, London, 1961, 129; A.H.M. Jones, *Constantine and the Conversion of Europe*, London, (second edition), 1972, 178; and W.H.C. Frend, *The Rise of Christianity*, London, 1984, 526. A troubling aspect of this view is what reasoning might stand behind the bribing of an official in disgrace. Certainly, it is difficult to see what advantage might be gained by such an action on the part of Athanasius. If, as Barnes suggests (Barnes, *loc. cit.*), Philumenus was involved in a plot to kill Constantine, there would be far greater reason for Athanasius to fear the charge, understanding it as κατὰ βασιλέως γενόμενος.

[37]R.P.C. Hanson, "The Fate of Eustathius of Antioch," *ZKG* 95 (1984): 2, 179.

[38]Hilary, *Collectio Antiariana* (Feder, CSEL 65), IV, 27, 66.

[39]*Hist. Arian.* 4, 1 (Opitz, 184, 31-185, 3).

His opponents believed him guilty of Sabellianism and included this among the counts against him. Yet that was not the main charge. Eustathius was deposed for moral delinquencies; he dishonored the priesthood, he lived in a disorderly fashion, he kept a mistress, and he had spoken disrespectfully of the emperor's mother while she was in the East. The charges may have been exaggerated or partly invented. But the council [of Antioch, *ca.* AD 328] sustained them, and Constantine, who reviewed the case and examined Eustathius in person, raised no objection to the verdict of the council.[40]

There can be little doubt that the Eusebians, with the help and assistance of the Meletian delegation, believed that such a strategy would also be effective in removing Athanasius from Alexandria. The absence of a theological issue in the case of Athanasius is of little surprise. The primary Eusebian objective in removing Athanasius from Alexandria remained the reinstatement of Arius. The raising of a theological point in regard to Athanasius over against Arius would only have provided the bishop of Alexandria with an opportunity to resort to the Nicene definition and anathemas to which Constantine had already given his assent. Alexandria's unique position as the focus and starting-point of the Arian controversy would have added to the danger of such a course of action. In contrast, the removal of Athanasius on civil or, more precisely, canonical grounds would accomplish the same purpose without an immediate reexamination of the Nicene formulations.

It is important to note, therefore, that although certain of the charges against Athanasius were of a civil nature, the desired end remained his canonical deposition from Alexandria. This could be accomplished only by the decision of a synodal assembly and the assent of the emperor, unless, of course, Athanasius was found to be guilty of a treasonable act of a purely political or civil nature. In such circumstances the Eusebians might be assured of a summary judgment on the part of Constantine, such as a sentence of exile, or the immediate calling of a synodal assembly which could pass a sentence of deposition. If, however, other, less dramatic, civil charges could be proved, such as the tax relating to linen tunics, canonical deposition remained possible. The second canon of Nicaea stated that clergy who, upon the proof of two or three witness, were found guilty of a "grave" or "capital offense" would be subject to immediate deposition.[41] Hefele's paraphrase of this section of the canon, "the rule is that they shall be deposed if they commit a serious offence," contains the meaning and intent of this particular canonical prescription of the council.[42]   The civil charges of

---

[40]Barnes, *Constantine and Eusebius,* 228.

[41]The phrase ψυχικὸν τι ἁμάρτημα used within the canon does not appear to have reference only to moral transgressions but to capital offenses in the civil realm as well (Hefele, *op. cit.,* I, 379).

[42]*Ibid.,* I, 379.

illegal taxation and treasonable conspiracy would both fall under the jurisdiction of this canon, as would the ecclesiastical accusation concerning Macarius's breaking of the chalice.

The numerous accusations concerning irregularities in regard to Athanasius's election and consecration as bishop of Alexandria have been considered in greater detail in the first section of the present work and require little further comment. It is important to note, however, that, without exception, all of the charges surrounding Athanasius's elevation to the throne of St. Mark are connected to canonical prescriptions, whether of age, the number of consecrating bishops, or the exclusion of Meletian involvement in the election itself.[43] Yet, as has been pointed out by A.H.M. Jones in numerous examples, there remained a lack of consistency during this period concerning the manner in which bishops were elected and the age which was required for consecration.[44] It is, therefore, unlikely that Constantine would have considered this charge to have been substantial, and, as will be seen, his response to this accusation was derisory. In any case, as has been noted, Constantine had given his approval to the election and consecration of Athanasius almost immediately after the actual event and would have been loathe to rescind such a decision given the present circumstances.

Some have attempted to interpret the charges which were placed against Athanasius as being primarily of a civil, with only the accusation concerning the breaking of the chalice being ecclesiastical.[45] Such a view, however, appears to ignore the motivation which stood behind the charges on the part of the Meletians and the Eusebians, namely, the reinstatement of Arius. Owing to Athanasius's intransigence concerning Arius's return to Alexandria, the only possibility which remained appeared to be the deposition of the bishop of Alexandria by any means possible. In the case of Eustathius, little attention was given to whether the charges were civil or ecclesiastical by the Synod of Antioch or, apparently, by Constantine, who reviewed the case afterwards. Clearly, the only point at issue for the Eusebians was the removal of Eustathius by any means possible. Under the second canon of Nicaea, all that was necessary for a bishop's deposition was his conviction of an offense of a suitably serious nature—whether civil or ecclesiastical. The multiplicity of charges made against both Eustathius and Athanasius, civil and ecclesiastical, were merely meant to provide sufficient cause for such a deposition or, at the least, to provide for an embarrassing judicial inquiry by a synodal assembly. During the course of such an inquiry, further allegations might be raised and, in a carefully selected assembly, the final verdict would be a foregone conclusion.

When Athanasius arrived at Psamathia in November of AD 331, he appears to have been unaware of the forces which were arrayed against him.

---

[43]*Vide supra*, section I, subsection 3.2.

[44]A.H.M. Jones, *The Late Roman Empire 284-602*, Oxford, 1964, Vol. 2, 914-920.

[45]V. Twomey, *Apostolikos Thronos*, 348, 349.

Throughout the interview with Constantine concerning the charges which had been raised, Athanasius seems to have been under the impression that the Meletians were the primary source of the accusations. Even the charge concerning the gold sent to Philumenus appears to have been brought to Constantine's attention through the representations of the Meletian delegation.[46] Although Athanasius would later indicate that Eusebius of Nicomedia was the "secret friend" of the Meletians, his awareness of this fact was limited at the time.[47] The process of the interviews with Constantine and the investigation into the various charges took place over a period of approximately four months, from *ca.* November AD 331 to *ca.* February AD 332. During these months which constituted an inclement winter, Athanasius was afflicted with a severe illness, possibly as a result of the "lengthy journey" he had undertaken from Alexandria to Nicomedia.[48]

As a result of Constantine's investigation and his interviews with Athanasius during these months, the bishop of Alexandria was apparently acquitted of all the charges which had been brought against him. Unfortunately, no record remains as to the exact disposition of the various accusations, although Athanasius indicates that the emperor rejected the charge concerning Ischyras as a part of the "falsehood" of the Meletians.[49] Concerning the remainder of the charges, Athanasius was apparently able to convince the emperor of his complete innocence.

Athanasius celebrated his triumph, writing in his Easter letter for AD 332, "I am at the Court, having been summoned by the emperor Constantine to see him. But the Meletians, who were present there, being envious, sought our ruin before the emperor. But they were put to shame and driven away as slanderers, being confuted by many things."[50] Athanasius had apologized earlier in the letter for being late in writing and, therefore, unable to give proper notice of the beginning of the Lenten fast.[51] This may indicate that the entire case was not decided until late January or early February AD 332. As it was, the Easter letter had to be sent by a special messenger under the command of one of Athanasius's friends at court, Flavius Ablavius, who served as a praetorian prefect under Constantine.[52] Although the letter was sent later than usual, Athanasius considers it to be "well timed, since our enemies having been put to shame and reproved by the

---

[46]For further details concerning this charge, cf. Girardet, op. cit., 58-60.

[47]*Apol.* 59, 3 (Opitz, 139, 20).

[48]*Festal Letter* IV, 1 (Robertson, op. cit., 515).

[49]*Apol.* 65, 1 (Opitz, 144, 3-6).

[50]*Festal Letter* IV, 5 (Robertson, op. cit., 517).

[51]*Ibid.* IV, 1 (Robertson, op. cit., 516).

[52]*Ibid.* (Robertson, op. cit., 517); cf. Barnes, *The New Empire*, 104. Flavius Ablavius was the father of the unfortunate Olympias who was betrothed to Constans and was later betrayed by Constanius, cf. *Hist. Arian.* 69, 1 (Opitz, 221, 4).

Church, because they persecuted us without a cause, we may now sing a festal song of praise, uttering the triumphant hymn against Pharaoh; 'We will sing unto the Lord, for he is to be gloriously praised; the horse and his rider he has cast into the sea.'"[53]

In the passages given above, Athanasius writes of his enemies being "put to shame" before Constantine and "reproved by the Church." It is possible that Athanasius writes of "reproof by the Church" in only general terms and for an intended effect upon the Alexandrian and Egyptian faithful. It is also possible, however, that Athanasius, and perhaps others, viewed the investigation which had taken place under Constantine's oversight as a joint civil/ecclesiastical inquiry. It is not unlikely that the Meletian delegation which had first appeared before Constantine had violated the eleventh canon of the Synod of Antioch, held very shortly before, which forbade bishops or priests to go to court without the prior consent of their metropolitan and the approval of their provincial synod.[54]

Although it is doubtful that Athanasius would have upheld the authority of the synod which had deposed Eustathius and perhaps many others, this violation may, in fact, have been the reason why Constantine did not meet with the Meletian delegation after their first arrival at court and his subsequent recourse to the Alexandrian presbyters, Macarius and Apis. Such a scenario may also explain Athanasius's summons to court and the merely peripheral actions of Eusebius of Nicomedia at this stage of the controversy. It is, therefore, possible that Constantine called for Athanasius not only to question him concerning the accusations which had been made against him but to inquire more fully into the actions of the Meletian delegation who were then "put to shame and driven away as slanderers." If the crux of the issue was the resolution of the Meletian issue rather than the catalogue of accusations which had been presented, Athanasius would have been correct in viewing the proceedings as essentially ecclesiastical in nature. Admittedly, such involvement in canonical concerns would not, of course, have been unusual for Constantine. As A.H.M. Jones has commented, "Constantine's conviction that he was God's servant impelled him to intervene in ecclesiastical disputes with conviction and energy."[55] Furthermore,

---

[53]*Festal Letter* IV, 1 (Robertson, *op. cit.,* 516).

[54]J.D. Mansi, *Sacrorum Conciliorum Nova et Amplissima Collectio,* Florence, 1760, vol. 2, 1308-1320. These canons, which are often ascribed to the Synod of Antioch Encaenia, were, more likely, enacted by the Synod of Antioch which was held *ca.* AD 328-AD 329, (*cf.* Jones, *Late Roman Empire, op. cit.,* II, 1084, n. 41). For the date of this earlier Synod of Antioch, *cf.* T.D. Barnes, "Emperor and Bishops, AD 324-344: Some Problems," *American Journal of Ancient History* 3 (1978): 53-56. In opposition to the view of Jones and for a traditional dating of the canons, *cf.* Hefele, *op. cit.,* II, 64-66. In favor of Jones, *cf.* H. Hess, *op. cit.,* Appendix II, 145-150.

[55]Jones, *Late Roman Empire, op. cit.,* I, 96.

Constantine held to the general principle "that it was the right and duty of the imperial government to suppress heresy and schism."[56]

That Athanasius did not wholeheartedly share this conviction is evident from his earlier refusal to obey Constantine in regard to both Arius and the Meletians. That he did allow for the authority of the emperor in select issues touching ecclesiastical matters throughout his career is also clear, although after the death of Constantine in AD 337 Athanasius is also willing to denounce those decisions made by emperors which were at variance with his own position.[57] At this stage in his relationship with Constantine, however,

> Athanasius accepted imperial jurisdiction in civil matters and did not even contradict the power of the Emperor to repudiate and banish bishops if the civil power acted according to canonical principles. The case was however very different in matters which touched the essence of the Christian faith. Here Athanasius was uncompromising. He held that the Church was a sacramental body with a mystical character with which the Emperor could have nothing to do. . . . His ideal was probably cooperation between the Church and State with the bishops

---

[56]*Ibid.*

[57]Concerning Athanasius's relations with imperial authority, K.M. Setton has stated that the bishop of Alexandria's "ideal . . . was an independent Church protected by the God-given Emperor" (*Christian Attitude toward the Emperor in the Fourth Century*, New York, 1941, 54). For Athanasius's relationships with hostile imperial authorities, *cf.* Setton, *op. cit.*, 78ff., and Nordberg, *Athanasius and the Emperor*, 43ff. A valuable contribution to this area of study has been made by S. Papadopoulos, Ἀθανάσιος ὁ Μέγας καὶ ἡ θεολογία τῆς οἰκομενικῆς συνόδου, Athens, 1975. Papadopoulos indicates that Athanasius's flexibility as to "the placement of the political power in the work of the synod" is central to his view of imperial power (*op. cit.*, 183). This is important although "the judgment of the bishops and the emperor may differ" (*op. cit.*, 187). In the view of Papadopoulos, the Athanasian ideal is not to "mix the empire and the church" in matters of faith and ecclesiastical order (*op. cit.*, 194), but he recognized that varying approaches must be used with each differing emperor in turn. L.W. Barnard echoes this conclusion in stating that, "it is then not surprising that Athanasius's attitude towards the Roman State has to be inferred from scattered and incidental references in his writings. He was dealing with the transition of the Empire from paganism to Christianity, not with an established Christian State. There was not one imperial policy with which he had to deal, but the religious policies of several emperors" (L.W. Barnard, "Athanasius and the Roman State," *Latomus* 36 [1977]: 423). That Athanasius changed his policy, at least to some extent with the differing regimes, is certainly apparent. Barnard, however, has stated the key issue of Athanasius's policy as follows: "Athanasius claimed the right of the Church to manage its own affairs without imperial interference— indeed the sum total of his (later) charges against Constantius derive from the one premise that the Emperor had infringed, ecclesiastical order and mingled Roman sovereignty and the constitution of the Church" (*ibid.*, 435).

having the freedom to decide Church matters in their own gatherings and the Emperor having the right to maintain the peace of the Church and to defend its faith.[58]

During the years which immediately followed the Council of Nicaea through to the aftermath of the Synod of Tyre in AD 335, Athanasius very likely held to a view of imperial authority that was not substantially different from Eusebius of Caesarea, although Athanasius never attempted to formulate a theology of the emperor.[59] Nevertheless, he appears to have accepted willingly the post-Nicene action of Constantine toward the Egyptians when he "confirmed and sanctioned the decrees of the council."[60] Given this background and considering that no doctrinal issues appear to have been brought forward at this time, one can easily accede to the possibility that Athanasius viewed the whole affair at Psamathia as a quasi-ecclesiastical event and attempted to present it as such to the Egyptian church. In any case, given the content of the Easter letter of AD 332, it is difficult to imagine that Athanasius regarded what had taken place as merely being a successful civil judicial hearing.

Athanasius was dismissed in peace from the emperor's presence and returned in triumph to Alexandria, arriving in late March of AD 332.[61] Constantine appears to have departed from Psamathia during the late winter to take command of the last stages of the campaign against the Goths. By 12 April AD 332 he was resident in Marcianopolis, later to be the headquarters of Valens in the Gothic war of AD 367, and of Lupicinus in AD 376.[62] On 20 April AD 332, the Goths surrendered to Constantine, having been decimated by cold and starvation.[63] Before taking leave for his campaign, however, Constantine had dispatched a letter "to the people of the catholic church at Alexandria" in which he castigated those who had brought the charges against their bishop and praised Athanasius.[64]

Certain aspects of this letter from Constantine to the catholic Christians of Alexandria merit special attention. In his address, Constantine

---

[58]*Ibid.*, 436, 437; *cf.* Frend, *The Rise of Christianity*, 526.

[59]*Cf.* Barnard, *op. cit.*, 429.

[60]τὰ τῆς συνόδου δόγματα κυρῶν ἐπεσφραγίζετο; Eusebius, *Vita Constant.*, III, 23 (Heikel, GCS 7, 88, 89).

[61]*Festal Letter Index* III, *Histoire* (A. Martin), 229; The reference to Athanasius's appearance before Constantine and his return to Alexandria is misplaced in the *Index* and ought to have been placed under *Index* IV which relates to the *Festal Letter* for AD 332.

[62]*Cf.* Barnes, *The New Empire*, 79; H.M. Gwatkin, *Studies of Arianism*, 87, fn. 4.

[63]*Cf.*, Barnes, *loc. cit.*, and T.D. Barnes, "The Victories of Constantine," *Zeitschrift für Papyrologie und Epigraphik* 20 (1976): 151ff.

[64]*Apol.* 61, 1 (Opitz, 141, 4-5).

makes no mention of the accusations concerning the tax on the linen tunics, Philumenus, or the case of Ischyras. He does, however, intimate that the root cause of the present problems have to do with the envy of Athanasius's enemies concerning his election as bishop of Alexandria. Although they are not mentioned by name, the enemies which Constantine appears to have in mind are the Meletians. In the letter they are described "quarrelsome men" who have left the "haven of brotherly love."[65] Moreover, the emperor states that the confusion and trouble which has been stirred up in Alexandria is owing to the "envy" and the "defects of ungrateful men."[66] In reference to the multitude of accusations which were placed before him by the Meletians, Constantine writes that these "foolish men carry their maliciousness at the tips of their tongues."[67] The primary motivation for the wide variety of charges which have been brought against Athanasius is described by Constantine as follows:[68]

> ... their very turning aside makes them disgruntled, while they unwisely put themselves forward to places of preeminence, although they are unworthy.[69] What wickedness this is! They say, "this one is old and this one is young;[70] the honor[71] belongs to me, it is owed to me; this must be taken away from him, I will win over others to my side, and by my power I will seek to put him to the test."[72]

Constantine describes the manner in which Athanasius was to be put to the test as having arisen out of "their outrageous gatherings and assemblies of election."[73] The emperor assures the Alexandrians, however, that "those wicked persons"[74] have no power against their bishop, Athanasius, whom Constantine is convinced is a "man of God."[75]

From this letter, certain conclusions made be made. First, although they were assisted by Eusebius of Nicomedia, the Meletians were the primary

---

[65]τῶν ἐρεσχηλούντων, Apol. 61, 1 (Opitz, 141, 10-11).

[66]φθόνου, Apol. 61, 2 (Opitz, 141, 12); τῶν ἀχαρίστων ἐλαττώματα, Apol. 61, 2 (Opitz, 141, 15).

[67]οἱ γὰρ μωροὶ ἐπὶ τῆς γλώττης κειμένην ἔχουσι τὴν κακίαν, Apol. 62, 1 (Opitz, 141, 29).

[68]Apol. 62, 3 (Opitz, 142, 3-6).

[69]ἀναξίους, ibid., (Opitz, 142, 4).

[70]ἐκεῖνος πρεσβύτερός ἐστι καὶ ἐκεῖνος παῖς, ibid. (Opitz, 142, 4-5).

[71]ἡ τιμή, ibid.

[72]πειράσομαι, ibid. (Opitz, 142, 6).

[73]ἀρχιαιρεσίαν, ibid. (Opitz, 142, 7).

[74]οἱ πονηροί, Apol. 62, 5 (Opitz, 142, 12).

[75]Apol. 62, 6 (Opitz, 142, 18).

accusers of Athanasius at Psamathia.[76] Second, their central concern appears to have been to discredit the election of Athanasius either on the basis of his age, an irregularity in the election itself, or some unknown prior understanding that they would have certain rights in the election of the successor of Alexander, although, as has already been stated, this seems unlikely.[77] Third, it would appear that Constantine did not regard the other charges which were brought against Athanasius to have any substance or merit and seems to have set them aside without any further consideration. It may be noted that the accusation concerning the illegal taxation of the linen tunics is never repeated in subsequent actions against Athanasius. The same is also true of the more serious charge of treasonable conspiracy in regard to the case of Philumenus. Such silence in regard to the latter must once and for all set aside the suggestion that Athanasius supported a rebellion in Alexandria as a protest against Constantine's choice of Byzantium as the site of the new capital of the empire.[78] Finally, the altercation which involved Macarius and Ischyras is not mentioned specifically, although the charge would be expanded and would reappear in the near future. It may be assumed, however, that with the presence of Macarius at court to defend himself and to give personal testimony concerning the matter, Constantine was satisfied as to his innocence and gave no further attention to the matter.

For Constantine, the central issue at hand appears to have been the validity of Athanasius's election which was being contested owing to the envy of the Meletians. It is almost certain, as has been stated above, that Athanasius was not yet thirty years of age when elected as bishop of Alexandria, although the shortfall is more likely to be measured in months, rather than years.[79] That this issue in itself would raise no real impediment to his election and consecration is clear from the widespread disregard of the eleventh canon of Neocaesarea within the church throughout the fourth to sixth centuries.[80] It must also be allowed that the language of Constantine's letter suggests that youth may not have been the central issue, but simply the passing of the office from the elder Alexander to the younger Athanasius as a matter of course and in spite of Meletian protests at the time.[81]

---

[76]*Cf.* Opitz, 142, fn. 1. 12.

[77]*Vide supra*, section I, fn. 237.

[78]J.G. Milne, *A History of Egypt Under Roman Rule*, London, 1898. Milne suggests that "this slight upon Alexandria did not tend to improve the feeling of the inhabitants towards the emperor; and one Philmenos attempted to raise a rebellion in Egypt, with the assistance, as it is said, of Athanasius; but his plans were discovered and crushed before any serious rising could occur" (*op. cit.*, 90). It may be noted that no documentary evidence has been put forward to support this claim.

[79]*Vide supra*, fn. 70.

[80]Hefele, *op. cit.*, I, 228; *cf.* Jones, *Late Roman Empire, op. cit.*, II, 914.

[81]*Cf. supra*, fn. 70.

Constantine, however, considered the Meletians to be "ungrateful"; for having received generous treatment as a result of the provisions agreed upon at Nicaea, they continued to put themselves forward for positions of honor and were filled with envy and malice when they were passed over.[82] With all of this in mind, and surely with some understanding of the liturgical significance of the term, Constantine wrote that they did not receive places of honor because, in fact, they were "unworthy" of such positions.[83]

It is clear throughout the letter that Constantine envisioned himself as being involved in a matter that was primarily ecclesiastical in nature. Although he did not hesitate in making use of his civil authority in such cases, his judgment at Psamathia appears to have referred back to his role in confirming and sanctioning the decrees of Nicaea, especially in regard to the Meletians.[84] That Constantine did not consider the proceedings at Psamathia to be of a civil nature, at least in regard to the final judgment which he delivered, may be seen in the fact that two years later he threatened the Meletians with punishment under civil law (something not yet done) if they persisted in their disruptive behavior.[85] It seems possible that Eusebius of Nicomedia recognized Constantine's turn to precedent and, following the dismissal of the other accusations, separated himself from the Meletians, at least in the public eye, while remaining their "secret friend."[86] This would explain Constantine's almost total absorption with the Meletians in his letter, as well as Athanasius's lack of suspicion concerning any conspiratorial alliance between the Eusebians and the Meletians at this particular time.[87]

1.2 The Concern over Libya, AD 332-AD 333

With Constantine's public declaration concerning the proceedings at Psamathia in the hands of the catholic community in Alexandria, Athanasius celebrated the paschal feast with his church on 2 April AD 332, having completely triumphed over his adversaries. During the course of the year he undertook pastoral visitations throughout the regions of the Pentapolis and

---

[82]Cf. supra, fn. 66, and Hefele, op. cit., I, 384, fn. 220.

[83]αναξίους, Apol. 62, 3 (Opitz, 142, 4).

[84]Eusebius, Vita Constant., IV, 24 (Heikel, GCS 7, 126).

[85]Cf. Apol. 68, 7, (Opitz, 147, 3-4). The contention by some, such as V. Twomey, that this case and subsequent judgments by Constantine were primarily civil in nature is certainly not correct in regard to the judgment under discussion and appears to be based upon a false distinction. It remains somewhat obvious, however, that Athanasius's adversaries hoped for his conviction upon a crime against the state which would result in a capital sentence, or subsequent deposition from his see, or both, (cf. V. Twomey, op. cit., 348, 349).

[86]κρύφα φίλος, Apol. 59, 4 (Opitz, 139, 20).

[87]Festal Letter IV, 5 (Robertson, op. cit., 517) mentions only the Meletians as adversaries at court.

Ammoniaca (Libya Superior and Libya Inferior).[88] It appears as though Athanasius's visit to the Pentapolis was relatively brief, while his stay in the area of Ammoniaca (the oasis of Ammon, close by the Qattara depression) was longer.[89] Although some have sought to characterize these travels as part of a "policy of visiting troubled areas under his jurisdiction," such journeys, as to the Thebaid in the winter of AD 330/331 and to Libya in AD 332, may only have been the normal routine of a somewhat newly elected metropolitan.[90]

It has also been suggested that Athanasius may have visited Libya during this time in order "to intervene in Libyan episcopal elections" over against renewed Arian activities in the area.[91] Although such an explanation may seem plausible, there is little exact information available concerning the situation in Libya during this period. During the time immediately preceding the Council of Nicaea, Arianism appears to have had its greatest degree of support within Libya. In the *Thesaurus* of Nicetas Choniates, which is preserved by Philostorgius, the Libyan bishops who supported Arius are named first and the list includes the major sees of the Pentapolis, as well as certain smaller towns: "From Libya Superior: Sentianos of Boreion, Dachios of Berenice, Secundus of Teuchera, Zopyrus of Barka, Secundus of Ptolemais, Theonas of Marmarica."[92] At Nicaea, Dachios of Berenice, Secundus of Teuchera, and Zopyrus of Barka all appear to have signed in support of the definition, but the name of Sentianos does not appear.[93] Secundus of Ptolemais and Theonas of Marmarica, who had already been excommunicated by Alexander in AD 324, however, proved intransigent at the council and, along with Arius, were banished by Constantine, although no replacements appear to have been named.[94] If Philostorgius is to be believed, Secundus and Theonas left Nicaea harboring a sense of betrayal and

---

[88]*Festal Letter Index* IV, *Histoire* (A. Martin), 231.

[89]*Ibid.*

[90]Williams, *Arius, op. cit.*, 76.

[91]Barnes, *Constantine and Eusebius*, 232.

[92]Nicetas, *Thesaurus*, 5, 7 (PG 139, 1368).

[93]*Cf.* the collection of the lists of signatories printed in Mansi, *op. cit.*, II, 692ff. That these lists are incomplete may be seen by simple comparison. The fact, therefore, that Sentianos of Boreion is not listed may only mean that he is among the missing signatories, although his presence at Nicaea is uncertain. For further information concerning the lists of the bishops who were present at Nicaea with regard to those from Libya, *cf.* the following fundamental studies of E. Honigmann: "Recherches sur les listes des pères de Nicée et de Constantinople," *Byz* 11 (1936): 429-449; "Sur les listes des évêques participant au concile de Nicée," *Byz* 12 (1937): 323-347; "La Liste originale des pères de Nicée," *Byz* 14 (1939): 17-76; "The original lists of the members of the Council of Nicaea," *Byz* 16 (1942/1943): 20-28; "Une liste inédite des pères de Nicée," *Byz* 20 (1950): 63-71.

[94]*De Decretis* 35, 6 (Opitz, 32, 18-19); *ibid.* 36, 5 (Opitz, 35, 5-6).

ill will towards those who had been less firm in their convictions, especially Eusebius of Nicomedia.[95] Their unwillingness to "sign and explain later" concerning their theological position, as was the case with the Eusebians, remains a mystery. Some, as Otto Seeck, have contended that their "intimate friendship" with Arius, rather than any doctrinal concern, made them unable to part company from him at Nicaea.[96]

It is uncertain whether or not Secundus and Theonas had been restored to their sees by the time of Athanasius's journey to Libya in AD 332. Although Rowan Williams states that "Athanasius often speaks as if their restoration had been part of the great Eusebian campaign of the years after 328," the only clear references to the post-Nicene activities of Secundus we have from the bishop of Alexandria date from the time of his third exile, that is, after AD 356.[97] Henry Chadwick, however, also indicates that "probability favors the view that their return was quite soon, perhaps 327-328. It was certainly earlier than the Jerusalem dedication of September when the inferior clergy of Alexandria, once associated with Arius, were reconciled."[98] Although Chadwick considers the provisions of the Jerusalem encyclical as applying specifically to "presbyters," it seems probable that the mention of "Arius and his fellows" most likely indicates the inclusion of deposed bishops, such as Secundus and Theonas.[99] Such an interpretation would, therefore, stand in opposition to Chadwick and suggest that Secundus and Theonas were fully restored, to both their sees and imperial favor, along with Arius, as a result of the Synod of Jerusalem in September AD 335 rather than at an earlier date. Philostorgius only indicates that Secundus and those with him were restored by Constantine but does not record either the date or circumstances of the recall.[100] Only during Athanasius's first exile following the Synod of Tyre does the evidence show Secundus becoming active once again in the area, even attempting to supplant the absent bishop of Alexandria with Pistus, a candidate of his own choice, during the summer of AD 337.[101]

---

[95]Philostorgius, *HE* 1, 10.

[96]O. Seeck, *Geschichte des Untergangs der antiken Welt,* III (second edition), Stuttgart, 1921, 401.

[97]*Cf. Hist. Arian.* 65, 3 (Opitz, 219, 3-6); *ibid.,* 71, 4 (Opitz, 222, 17); *De Syn.* 12, 3 (Opitz, 239, 20); *Ad epis. Aeg. et Lib.* 19 (PG 25, 584B). That Secundus was eventually received by the Eusebians is attested to by Athanasius, but with no hint as to the date or context; *cf. Ad epis. Aeg. et Lib.* 7 (PG 25, 553A).

[98]H. Chadwick, "Faith and Order at the Council of Nicaea: A Note on the Background of the Sixth Canon," *HTR* 53 (1960): 192.

[99]*Ibid.,* fn. 69; *cf. De Syn.* 21, 3 (Opitz, 248, 1) along with Opitz's note on the question of what persons were received (*ibid.,* line 1, fn.).

[100]Philostorgius, *HE* 2, 1, 1b.

[101]*Apol.* 24, 1-2 (Opitz, 105, 9-15).

On balance, the evidence would tend to support the conclusion that Secundus and Theonas had not yet been restored to their sees at the time of Athanasius's journey through the Pentapolis, although they may, along with Arius, have been in the region.[102] Their presence, and the independence of the Libyan churches, which the sixth canon of Nicaea probably sought to restrain, may have provided Athanasius with adequate incentives to take matters personally in hand in the region, although, again, this is by no means certain.[103] The evidence, however, does not suggest that episcopal elections were taking place in the region, or that any other single issue impelled Athanasius to engage upon this course of visitations. It is, perhaps, only a matter of coincidence that the next issue which occupied both Constantine and the faithful in Alexandria was to arise out of Libya as a result of Arius's frustration with Athanasius's refusal to allow the heresiarch's restoration within the Alexandrian church.

By the latter portion of AD 332, almost thirteen years had passed since Alexander's expulsion of Arius from his home church in Alexandria. Condemned by the Council of Nicaea in AD 325 and subsequently rehabilitated by Constantine and the Bithynian synod in late AD 328, Arius had, nonetheless, lived in virtual exile during these years.[104] Although Constantine, in AD 328, had attempted to effect Arius's readmission to the Alexandrian church, Athanasius remained obstinate in his refusal to allow such an action to take place. For almost five years afterwards, Arius wandered from place to place seeking to enlist support for his readmission to the Alexandrian church. H.M. Gwatkin has suggested that some of this time may have been spent in Illyricum, where Ursacius and Valens became his "personal disciples."[105] R. Williams is of the opinion that "Constantine's letter inviting Arius to court promises him the chance to return to his 'native land' if all goes well; and it is likely enough that he was in Libya for some years."[106]

Writing from the Thebaid early in AD 331, Athanasius indicates that "the time is one of tribulation which the heretics excite against us."[107] During this time Athanasius labels the Meletians only as "schismatics" and, therefore, may be referring to a resurgence of Arian activity in either Egypt or, more probably, Libya.[108] If Arius had returned to Libya in AD 330/331 in an attempt to garner support for his position, such a move may well have been in conjunction with the efforts which were being made on his behalf at court by Eusebius of Nicomedia. Athanasius's subsequent appearance and

---

[102]Williams, *op. cit.,* 76.

[103]*Cf.* Chadwick, *op. cit.,* 189-192.

[104]*Cf.* Williams, *op. cit.,* 75, 76.

[105]Gwatkin, *Studies of Arianism, op. cit.,* 90, fn. 2.

[106]Williams, *op. cit.,* 76.

[107]*Festal Letter* III, 5 (Robertson, *op. cit.,* 514).

[108]*Ibid.* V, 4 (Robertson, *op. cit.,* 519).

vindication at Psamathia and his tour of the Pentapolis in AD 332, bearing
with him the emperor's testimony and approval as a "man of God," may have
forced Arius's hand and impelled him to present his case to Constantine in a
more strident manner.[109]

Late in AD 332, or early in AD 333, Arius wrote, most likely from
Libya, what appears to have been an indignant letter of protest to the
emperor.[110] It has been suggested plausibly that "the surviving fragments
of this letter suggest a man at the end of his tether."[111] In his appeal to
Constantine, Arius gravitated between pleading for the emperor's assistance
over against the uncompromising attitude of those who will not receive him
into communion and threatening the possibility of schism if the matter is
not resolved to his satisfaction.[112] Arius appears to have indicated that he
retained a sufficient base of support within Libya, where many had received
him, that he could, in fact, organize and remain within a body of churches
which would be independent of Alexandria's metropolitical authority.[113]

Such an arrangement, of course, would have been in direct violation of
the sixth canon of Nicaea, and one can be sure that Athanasius would have
protested such an infringement of his rights, especially in regard to the
ordination of bishops within the region.[114] It is probably correct, however,
that it is "an anachronism to think of anything like a self-consciously 'Arian'
church in Libya emerging or being envisaged at this date"; but there can be
little doubt that Arius was suggesting an arrangement which would have
effectively separated the actions of those Libyan churches which had received
him from the authority of Alexandria.[115] Perhaps with the Donatists in
mind or, more likely, with the recent Meletian troubles in view,
Constantine's reply to Arius was to be unyielding and severe in the extreme.

Constantine immediately dispatched two documents to Alexandria
which arrived, most probably, in early AD 333, and which were carried by
the *agentes in rebus* Syncletius and Gaudentius.[116] The first of the two
documents is an imperial edict which is addressed to the bishops and the laity
and was read by the prefect Paterius in an open forum in the governor's
palace.[117] In this edict Constantine compares Arius to the pagan Porphyry,

---

[109]ὡς ἄνθρωπον ... θεοῦ, *Apol.* 62, 6 (Opitz, 142, 18).

[110]That Arius was in Libya may be inferred by the references in
Constantine's reply (*cf.* Opitz III, U34, 20; 72, 1-2) and by the fact that the letter
was addressed to those in Alexandria, the metropolitan see of the region under
canon six of the Council of Nicaea.

[111]Williams, *op. cit.*, 77.

[112]*Cf.* Opitz III, U34, 11 (70, 18-19); U34, 20 (72, 2); U34, 39 (74, 16ff.).

[113]*Cf.* Opitz III, U34, 20 (72, 2).

[114]Hefele, *op. cit.*, I, 388.

[115]Williams, *op. cit.*, 77.

[116]Opitz III, U34, 43 (75, 6); *cf. Apol.* 59, 6 (Opitz, 140, 5).

[117]Opitz III, U33 (66-68).

"that enemy of piety," whose written works against the church were destroyed.[118] Likewise, Arius and those who follow him, whom the emperor designates as "Porphyrians," should also have their works destroyed.[119] The treatises of Arius are to be "consigned to the flames," and those who attempt to conceal any writing of Arius are threatened with immediate execution upon conviction.[120]

An open letter addressed to Arius and his followers, the second document has rightly been characterized as being "long, rambling, and abusive, the work of a man who feels angry and affronted."[121] The contrast between Athanasius, Constantine's "man of God," and Arius, who is described as "an evil interpreter" who "in reality is the image and representation of the devil," is striking.[122] The emperor calls Arius "Ares," a god of war who is only interested in creating an atmosphere of violence and ill will.[123] The theology of Arius, which appears to have been presented to Constantine in yet another profession of faith, is denounced and ridiculed. The contention of Arius that the Son is an "alien hypostasis" from the Father is contrasted with the Nicene definition that the Father and the Son are of "one essence" (οὐσία).[124] Constantine refers to the Sibylline Oracles concerning the judgment from heaven that will come upon the Libyans because of their sins and misdeeds and castigates Arius concerning his supposed support in that

---

[118]*Ibid.*, U33, 1 (67, 1-3).

[119]*Ibid.*, U33, 1-2 (67, 5 - 68, 1).

[120]*Ibid.*, U33, 2 (68, 3-6).

[121]Opitz III, U34 (69-75); Barnes, *Constantine and Eusebius, op. cit.*, 233. It is important to note that some have questioned the authenticity and/or the dating of portions of this document. J.-M. Sansterre considers only the closing portion of the letter (Opitz III, U34, 42) to be genuine, placing a date of *ca.* AD 325-AD 327 upon the material ("Eusèbe de Césarée et la naissance de la théorie 'Césaropapiste,'" *Byz* 42 [1972]: 159-161). H. Kraft, however, considers the greater portion of U34 to be authentic, although he remains uncertain as to the exact dating of the document (*Kaiser Konstantins religiöse Entwicklung*, Tübingen, 1955, 239-242). R. Williams and T.D. Barnes both accept the letter's authenticity and date the document to *ca.* AD 333, relying heavily upon the reference to the Egyptian prefect Paterius in U34, 43 (Opitz III, 75, 6) as a link to the *Festal Letter Index* V, for AD 333, which also lists Paterius as the prefect in Egypt (*cf. Histoire*, A. Martin, 231). This present study accepts the authenticity of U34 as a single document and, owing to the identification of Paterius and the other circumstantial evidence cited in the text, places its writing early in *ca.* AD 333, most probably before Athanasius's writing of his Easter letter for that year. Minor corrections to Opitz's text of U34 are suggested in H. Chadwick, "Athanasius, *De Decretis* XL.3," *JTS* 49 (1948): 168-169.

[122]Κακὸς ἑρμηνεὺς αὐτόχρημα εἰκών τε καὶ ἀνδρίας ἐστι τοῦ διαβόλου, U34, 1 (Opitz III, 69, 1).

[123]U34, 6 (Opitz III, 69, 26).

[124]U34, 14 (Opitz III, 71, 4-6).

region.[125] The result of Arius's continued lawlessness may clearly be seen in his own half-dead appearance.[126] For their continued separation from the catholic community Arius and his followers are threatened with penalties consisting of additional taxes and threats of conscription for public service.[127]

Within the conclusion of the letter, however, Constantine softens his tone by means of a personal appeal and extends an unexpected invitation to Arius: "Come to me, come I say, to the man of God. Be assured that I will search out the deepest parts of your heart with my questions. And if folly is found, I shall heal you in a glorious way by an appeal to the grace of God. If, however, you appear to be healthy in your soul, I will perceive in you the light of truth and, by God's grace, will rejoice with you over your piety."[128] Apparently having accepted the invitation to appear at court and having given a satisfactory account of his theology and intentions, Arius is next observed at the Synod of Jerusalem in AD 335 being received along with Euzoius by the bishops who had assembled for the celebrations on the occasion of the consecration of the Church of the Holy Sepulchre in September of that year.[129]

Despite Arius's ultimate acceptance by Constantine, it is important to place Athanasius's position in AD 333 in the proper perspective. It was, without doubt, a position of strength, regardless of a good number of continuing problems in the hinterlands of Egypt and Libya. Since his election and consecration in AD 328, Athanasius had managed to consolidate his base of support within Egypt to a considerable degree. Although what has been described as "the growth of a patriotic spirit among the Egyptian monks and an intensification of their loyalty to their bishop" probably still lay in the future, by AD 333 Athanasius had achieved much.[130] A process of winning converts from the Meletians still within Egypt appears to have progressed steadily during these years.[131] Athanasius had appeared before Constantine at Psamathia, had refuted completely the charges which had been made against him, and had returned to Alexandria bearing the emperor's own letter of commendation. The bishop's journeys to the Thebaid and the Pentapolis had, it appears, extended his support beyond Alexandria, and their success may have prompted the rash behavior of the Meletians and, in regard to the latter visitation, Arius. Finally, his earlier refusal to readmit Arius (and probably the Meletians) to the Alexandrian church on the orders of

---

[125]U34, 19-20 (Opitz III, 71, 23-72, 5).

[126]U34, 35 (Opitz III, 73, 33-74, 4).

[127]U34, 39 (Opitz III, 74, 16-20).

[128]U34, 42 (Opitz III, 74, 32-75, 4).

[129]Socrates, *HE* I, 33 (PG 67, 164C-165A).

[130]R.W. Thomson, ed., *Athanasius: Contra gentes and De incarnatione,* Oxford, 1971, xi.

[131]*Vide supra,* section I, fn. 285.

Constantine had been vindicated publicly by the response of the emperor to the machinations which he had now witnessed for himself.

Perhaps even more important for Athanasius during this period was the attitude of Constantine towards those issues, both theological and disciplinary, which had been decided upon at Nicaea. All of the issues which occupied Athanasius and, in consequence, Constantine, in regard to Egypt were intimately connected with Nicaea, as has been indicated above. It appears that Constantine viewed himself during this period as the protector of the Nicene decrees. A. Grillmeier has summarized the situation:

> In the document [sic] between 325 and 335 Constantine betrays a wish to regard himself as a fellow-servant of the bishops, but also to watch over the dogmatic and disciplinary decisions of the Council of Nicaea (and also of other synods). This still would not amount to an involvement in the formation of doctrinal decisions, but would rather be a guarantee of their validity, in their function for the unity of the Church. In this sense we may understand the saying coined by Eusebius for the emperor, that he is ... the inspector general, for the observance of the decrees of the council.[132]

Certainly, the provisions concerning the consecration of bishops (as Athanasius), the position of the Meletians in Egypt, and the attachment of Libya to the see of Alexandria would all fall under this category. If, in fact, this represents properly Constantine's attitude during this period, Athanasius's intransigence over these issues, as well his actions concerning Arius, becomes much more understandable.

Furthermore, it would seem as though Constantine had good cause to maintain a reasonable relationship with Alexandria and its metropolitan. With the founding of Constantinople on 8 November AD 324 and its ceremonial dedication on 11 May AD 330, a new demand for Egyptian grain was created. On 18 May AD 332, Constantine began the distribution of free grain within the city, and the "harvests of Egypt, formerly transported to Italy, were diverted eastward."[133] According to Socrates, the imperial city soon required a daily ration of eighty thousand *modii*, of which the greater portion was shipped through the port of Alexandria.[134] The keeping of the peace in Alexandria, therefore, was very much an economic and political priority as well as an ecclesiastical concern. The timing of Constantine's decree concerning the provision of grain for Constantinople also appears to have coincided with the numerous events concerning Athanasius which have

---

[132]A. Grillmeier, *Christ in Christian Tradition*, vol. 1: *From the Apostolic Age to Chalcedon (451)*, London (second edition), 1975, 260; *cf.* Eusebius, *Vita Constant.* I, 28 (Heikel, GCS 7, 28, 19-20), οἷά τις κοινὸς ἐπίσκοπος ἐκ θεοῦ καθεσταμένος.

[133]Barnes, *Constantine and Eusebius, op. cit.*, 223.

[134]Socrates, *HE* II, 13 (PG 67, 210A).

been outlined above as having taken place in AD 332/333. It would seem safe to conclude, therefore, that the continuing difficulties in Alexandria had, in some sense, become in Constantine's mind an increasingly important matter of imperial policy.

At this point in early AD 333, Athanasius appears to have enjoyed a brief respite, which may be seen in his Easter letter for that year. The theme of the letter is reflected in Athanasius's call for unity:

> This [feast] also leads us on from the cross through this world to that which is before us, and God produces even now from it the joy of glorious salvation, bringing us to the same assembly, and in every place uniting all of us in spirit; appointing us common prayers and a common grace proceeding from the feast. For this is the marvel of his lovingkindness, that he should gather together in the same place those who are at a distance; and make those who appear to be far off in the body, to be near together in unity of spirit.[135]

In contrast to the unity of the faithful which the feast proclaims, Athanasius comments that "the schismatics keep" the feast "in separate places and with vain imaginations."[136] Moreover, he exhorts his readers to keep the feast as a witness of their unity "to the schismatics": "in not rending the coat of Christ, but in one house, even in the Catholic Church, let us eat the Passover of the Lord."[137] Athanasius's repeated references in this letter to schismatics may indicate continuing difficulties within Egypt concerning the Meletians and, perhaps, the Colluthians. No mention is made, however, of "heretics" (*i.e.*, Arians), or of any other disturbances within the Egyptian church, such as had been the case in the Easter letters for the previous three years. The reality of the Arian-Meletian alliance appears to have remained hidden from Athanasius's sight during this period. Certainly, he must have been aware of the continuing activities of the Eusebians as well as the other competing sects in Egypt and Libya, but with the emperor's actions against Arius and the bishop's own vindication at Psamathia, Athanasius probably considered such groups to have become somewhat less of a threat than they had been at the outset of his episcopate.

1.3 The Arsenius Affair, AD 333-AD 334

There remains a good deal of confusion as to exactly when the next series of accusations were brought against Athanasius, but it appears that they must have been put forward shortly after the publication in Alexandria of Constantine's letters concerning Arius. With Arius at least temporarily in disgrace in Egypt and with no hope that Athanasius would allow his

---

[135]*Festal Letter* V, 2 (Robertson, *op. cit.,* 517, 518).

[136]*Ibid.* V, 4 (Robertson, *op. cit.,* 518).

[137]*Ibid.* V, 4 (Robertson, *op. cit.,* 519).

readmission into the Alexandrian church under any foreseeable circumstances, it once again became apparent to the Eusebians that their only recourse was the deposition of Athanasius. The Meletians in Egypt were also being seriously constrained by the continued presence and visitations of the bishop of Alexandria and would have found little encouragement in the fact that many of their former brethren were now active associates of Athanasius. Once again acting in concert, these two groups conspired together against the bishop of Alexandria, with the Meletians again taking the position of being the primary or sole accusers.

Athanasius indicates that after his first interview with Constantine at Psamathia, "the Meletians remained subdued for a short time, but after this they manifested their hostility once more."[138] Sozomen states simply that "after the failure of their first attempt, the Meletians secretly invented other written" accusations "against Athanasius."[139] Athanasius names the Meletian accuser, possibly at court, as "Archaph, who is also called John."[140] The two charges were these:

1. Athanasius had ordered Macarius to break the chalice of Ischyras. This was a repeat of an earlier charge which had been made at Psamathia. It is probable, however, that the Meletians added further elaborations to the initial accusation.

2. Athanasius had arranged the murder of Arsenius, a Meletian bishop of Hypsele in Upper Egypt. Furthermore, Athanasius had cut off the dead bishop's arm and had retained it for magical purposes. The arm, however, had fallen into the possession of the Meletians, who were able to produce it as irrefutable proof of Athanasius's guilt.[141]

The substance of the two charges were presented to Constantine by the Meletians in a written form.[142] Once again, the object of the charges appears to have been the deposition of Athanasius on the basis of the Nicene settlement concerning the Meletians and the second canon of the council concerning serious offenses committed by those in orders.

The additional item in the second indictment, that Athanasius had cut off Arsenius's arm for magical purposes, may be regarded as either simple embellishment or as an attempt by the Meletians to picture the bishop of Alexandria as one who continually engaged in such practices. There is reason to believe that the Meletians had already promulgated such a rumor about

---

[138]*Apol.* 63, 1 (Opitz, 142, 24-25).

[139]Sozomen, *HE* II, 23, 1 (Bidez, 80, 12-13).

[140]*Apol.* 65, 5 (Opitz, 144, 25).

[141]*Apol.* 63, 4 (Opitz, 143, 6-14); Sozomen, *HE* II, 23, 1 (Bidez, 80, 12-16).

[142]Μελιτιανοὶ δὲ τῆς προτέρας ἀποτυχόντες πείρας ἑτέρας ὕφαινον κατὰ 'Αθανασίου γραφάς..., Sozomen, *HE* II, 23, 1 (Bidez, 80, 12-13).

Athanasius in regard to his consecration as bishop. This assertion possibly survives in the account of Philostorgius, who reported that Athanasius possessed the power to compel his consecrators to ordain him although this was strongly contrary to their own desires.[143] The Arabic paraphrase of the ninth canon of Nicaea suggests that a bishop or presbyter convicted of making use of magic was subject to deposition.[144] That Constantine would have been sensitive to such an indictment is certain. There were several instances in which the emperor showed himself to be harsh and unyielding in his punishment of persons who were suspected of making use of magic, the most celebrated case being that of a sometime advisor of Constantine, Sopater, who being condemned for "fettering the winds" and preventing the grain ships from reaching Constantinople was ordered to be beheaded.[145] In evaluating Constantine's attitude towards such practices, the opponents of Athanasius may have hoped that by adding such an accusation to their written indictment of the bishop of Alexandria, the emperor would be spurred to a faster and more severe response than he had been in the past.

Constantine refused to reopen the case of Ischyras. Since the first appearance of this charge at Psamathia, Athanasius had presented the emperor with further information concerning this supposed sacrilege. It appears as though Ischyras had first been "ordained" by Colluthus and chose to remain in schism even after his leader's readmission into the Alexandrian church.[146] During the time in question, Ischyras lived in a small village in the Mareotis named Secontarurus.[147] Although, under the provisions which were attached to the readmission of Colluthus, the status of Ischyras was that of a lay person, he appears to have continued to perform the functions of a priest in the home of an orphan named Ision.[148] His church was only designated as a private house and his congregation seems to have consisted only of those in his immediate family.[149] A nearby catholic presbyter complained to Athanasius concerning this violation while the bishop of Alexandria was on one of his visitations of the region.[150]

Subsequently, apparently during the period before Macarius was at court, that is, sometime before AD 330, he was sent by Athanasius to summon Ischyras to Alexandria, presumably to be disciplined. When Macarius arrived in Secontarurus along with the local presbyter, Ischyras was ill, although a catechumen was found in the house along with the father of

---

[143]Philostorgius, *HE* II, 11.

[144]Hefele, *op. cit.*, I, 414, 415.

[145]Barnes, *Constantine and Eusebius, op. cit.*, 253; *cf. ibid.*, 219, 220.

[146]*Apol.* 12, 1 (Opitz, 97, 8-9).

[147]*Apol.* 85, 7 (Opitz, 164, 7).

[148]*Apol.* 76, 3 (Opitz, 156, 6-12).

[149]*Apol.* 74, 3 (Opitz, 153, 36-154, 2).

[150]*Apol.* 63, 3 (Opitz, 143, 1-6).

the schismatic priest.[151]   Macarius and his fellow presbyter informed the father of the consequences should his son continue to function as a priest, apparently received assurances from the family that they would encourage Ischyras to desist, and then departed.   When Ischyras recovered, however, he forsook the Colluthian cause and joined himself to the Meletians.[152]   As a consequence of this action, Ischyras appears to have been compelled by two Meletian presbyters, Isaac and Heraclides, and the Meletian bishop, Isaac of Letopolis, to fabricate the charge of sacrilege against Macarius and Athanasius.[153]   While at Psamathia the accusation had focused upon the destruction of the chalice, by the time of this second presentation of the indictment it appears to have included the overturning of an altar, the burning of liturgical books, and the smashing of the chalice during the very act of offering the oblation.[154]

The information which Athanasius had already presented to Constantine consisted of a written confession from Ischyras himself that the charges were fabricated.[155]   Athanasius may have been able to obtain this statement during his earlier encounter with Constantine at Psamathia, although he only indicates that the emperor had "earlier heard of the matter concerning the cup."[156]   It seems more likely, however, that this letter was obtained by Athanasius after his return to Alexandria, for he indicates that Ischyras had been pressured by his friends and family to present himself to the bishop for a personal interview.[157]   The letter of Ischyras confirms this sequence of events as follows:

> When I came to you, my lord bishop, desiring to be received into the church, you reproved me for what I had said at the first, as though I had gone to such extremes of my own choice; I therefore lay before you this my apology in writing, so that you may understand that violence was used toward me and I was beaten by Isaac and Heraclides, and Isaac of Letopolis, and by those who were with them.   And I take God as my witness in declaring that you are not guilty of any of those matters of which they have spoken.   For no breaking of a cup happened, no casting over of the holy table occurred, but they forced me by violence to bring this forward.   And this defense I bring to you in writing,

---

[151]*Ibid.*

[152]*Ibid.*

[153]*Apol.* 64, 1 (Opitz, 143, 19-20).

[154]*Apol.* 83, 1-2 (Opitz, 162, 1-11).

[155]Apol. 64, 1-3 (Opitz, 143, 15-144, 2).

[156]κἀκεῖνος περὶ μὲν τοῦ ποτηρίου φθάσας ἦν ἀκούσας αὐτός..., *Apol.* 65, 1 (Opitz, 144, 4-5).

[157]*Apol.* 63, 5 (Opitz, 143, 11-13).

desiring and requesting for myself to be placed within your congregation.[158]

That this confession and recantation on the part of Ischyras took place in or near Alexandria is further attested to by the witnessing of the document by five presbyters from the Mareotis: Ammonas of Dicella, Heraclius of Phascos, Boccon of Chenebri, Achillas of Myrsine, Didymus of Taphosiris, and Justus of Bomotheus.[159] Four deacons from the Mareotis, Ammonius, Pistus, Demetrius, and Gaius, also witnessed the document in addition to three deacons from Alexandria, Paul, Peter, and Olympius.[160] All of those who signed were senior clergy: those from the Mareotis had held their positions from the time of Alexander, and the Alexandrian deacons appear to have been attached to the bishop's household in Alexandria for some years.[161] It may be assumed that Athanasius's choice of local Mareotic clergy (who would have been fully acquainted with Ischyras) and senior Alexandrian deacons (who may have cared for the administration of the diocese) as witnesses was intended to leave little doubt in Constantine's mind that the charges were false. The letter was very probably sent to Constantine after the initial interview at Psamathia and may have been unknown to either the Meletians or Eusebius.[162] In any case, Constantine was sufficiently

---

[158]*Apol.* 64, 1-3 (Opitz, 143, 16-24).

[159]*Apol.* 64, 3 (Opitz, 143, 27-28).

[160]*Ibid.* (Opitz, 144, 1-2).

[161]All of the witnesses to the confession of Ischyras had been active during the episcopate of Alexander of Alexandria and are listed in his deposition of Arius, 'Ενὸς σώματος (Opitz III, U4b, 6-11) which Opitz dates at *ca.* AD 319, but which Rowan Williams places during January/February, AD 325. In either case, it is clear that the Mareotic presbyters and deacons (Boccon of Chenebri being listed as a deacon in U4b, but raised to the presbyterate by the year AD 331/332) were clergy of long standing within the diocese and had given their loyalty to Athanasius following the death of Alexander in AD 328 (for the listing, *cf.* Opitz III, U4b, 11, 15-35). The Alexandrian deacons listed as having witnessed the confession of Ischyras may have been permanent members of the archbishop's staff from the time of Alexander (*ibid.,* 10, 34-11, 11). Information concerning the unique parish system in Alexandria, however, is lacking, and an exact identification cannot be made.

[162]It seems unlikely that the Meletians or the Eusebians would have reasserted their accusation concerning Ischyras had they known of his letter, which Athanasius must have immediately sent to Constantine. That the charge was repeated at the Synod of Tyre seems to have been occasioned by Ischyras's realignment with the Meletians subsequent to his letter of confession to Athanasius but before the calling of the synod by Constantine. The inducement for his defection to the Meletians this second time seems to have been owing to Athanasius's censure and the promise of being accepted as a presbyter by the Meletians and Eusebians. There is also evidence presented by Athanasius that Ischyras had been given to understand that he would be rewarded for his defection

satisfied with the evidence at hand and refused to reopen the case concerning Ischyras on this second occasion.

Although Constantine declined to hear the case concerning Ischyras, the alleged murder of Arsenius and the charge that Athanasius was involved with magic remained unresolved. Rather than hearing the case himself, however, the emperor wrote to his half-brother Flavius Dalmatius, then resident in Antioch, and ordered him to initiate a judicial inquiry.[163] The son of Constantius and Theodora, Dalmatius had been recalled to court some years earlier (*ca.* AD 326) and had eventually received from Constantine the title of *censor*, perhaps during his time as consul in AD 333.[164] He was apparently given certain executive powers in this case, for Socrates states that he had both the ability to try the accused parties and to order the punishment of those convicted.[165]

Dalmatius sent word to Athanasius concerning the alleged murder of Arsenius and instructed him to prepare his defense.[166] It is probable that this letter was received by Athanasius sometime within the first few months of AD 333 and that this is the summons referred to by Sozomen as having taken place "thirty months" before the bishop of Alexandria's arrival at the Synod of Tyre in August AD 335.[167] Certainly, Athanasius's Easter letter

---

by an eventual elevation to the episcopate and the building of a church in his village, *cf. Apol.* 85, 4 (Opitz, 163, 26-28).

[163]*Apol.* 65, 1 (Opitz, 144, 6-7).

[164]*Cf.* Barnes, *The New Empire,* 105. The research of W. Ensslin, "Dalmatius censor, der Halbbruder Konstantines I," *Rheinisches Museum* 78 (1929): 199-212, shows conclusively that Socrates was mistaken in assigning the title of *censor* to Constantine's nephew, Caesar Dalmatius, who was actually the son of Flavius Dalmatius, the *censor* who was involved in this episode concerning Athanasius; *cf.* Socrates, *HE* I, 27 (PG 67, 157A).

[165]Socrates, *HE* I, 27 (PG 67, 157A).

[166]*Apol.* 65, 2 (Opitz, 144, 7-8).

[167]τριάκοντα μῆνας, Sozomen, *HE* II, 25 (Bidez, 84, 10). This follows the suggestion of H.I. Bell that the thirty months mentioned by Sozomen must either be a textual corruption (λ´ for κ´?) or may refer back to an earlier summons. If thirty months are indicated by the text, the Synod of Tyre having begun in August AD 335, the previous time period would be February AD 333. If the text has been corrupted and only twenty months are indicated, the date of the summons would be December AD 333. In the first instance, the date of Athanasius's arrival at Tyre in August AD 335 appears certain, as the *Festal Letter Index* VIII states that he left for Tyre from Egypt on 11 July of that year. The text of Sozomen is probably better understood as indicating a thirty-month period which would place the summons to Athanasius concerning Arsenius in February AD 333. The twenty-month period, however, designating December AD 333 would fall very close to the time of Constantine's calling of the Synod of Caesarea for March of AD 334. Surely the letters for this synod must have been sent a full three months before the event itself and, therefore, a twenty-month period is also a possibility, but only if the present text is incorrect (*cf.* Bell, *Jews and Christians,* 48; and *Histoire,* A.

for AD 333 betrays little anxiety concerning such an accusation having been brought against him, although, as will be seen below, his Easter letter for AD 334 is filled with denunciations of those who have "sworn deceitfully" to their neighbors.[168] It appears probable, therefore, that Athanasius received the letter from Antioch at some point after he had written the Easter letter for AD 333 but still somewhat early in the year, perhaps in February or March.

Although Athanasius may have sought to appear unconcerned in regard to this allegation of murder and magic, the letter from Dalmatius, and perhaps private information from his envoys at court, informed him that the emperor had become "troubled" over this particular charge.[169] The indictment had stated that a bishop within the jurisdiction of the Alexandrian church named Plusianus had, under orders from Athanasius, beaten Arsenius with leather thongs and had then burned him alive within his own house, although the bishop of Alexandria commented that he had not seen Arsenius in five or six years.[170] It is possible that Arsenius had earlier committed some offense and had fled to the Meletians in order to escape disciplinary action by Athanasius.[171] As Arsenius was already in hiding, the Meletians apparently had promised him continuing protection if he would agree to play a part by concealment in this latest intrigue against Athanasius.

Soon after receiving the note of inquiry from Dalmatius, Athanasius sent letters to the bishops in Egypt to ask their assistance in locating Arsenius and sent a deacon into the Thebaid where, apparently, he suspected "the murdered man" was in hiding.[172] That Arsenius was initially kept in this region points to the continuing strength of the Meletians, which Athanasius may have only begun to suspect through the course of events. Sozomen reports that the deacon learned where Arsenius was being kept in the Thebaid through the assistance of some monks in the region.[173] They indicated that Arsenius was being sheltered at the monastery of Ptermenkurkis, in the nome of Antepolis, by its Meletian presbyter,

---

Martin, 233, 244). The chronology of Schwartz concerning this period is hopelessly confused and contradictory owing to his placing of the Synod of Caesarea in AD 333, a full year before the gathering actually took place (cf. Schwartz, GS III, 246-247). On balance, it seems best to understand Sozomen as referring to the summons of Dalmatius and to place its date as February/March AD 333.

[168]Festal Letter IV, 11 (Robertson, op. cit., 522).

[169]ἐπειδὴ βασιλεὺς κεκίνητο, Apol. 65 (Opitz, 144, 9-10).

[170]Apol. 65, 2 (Opitz, 144, 11); Sozomen, HE II, 25, 12.

[171]Sozomen, HE II, 23, 1 (Bidez, 80, 15-16).

[172]Apol. 65, 2 (Opitz, 144, 10-11); Apol. 67, 2 (Opitz, 145, 20-21).

[173]Sozomen, HE II, 23, 4 (Bidez, 81, 10-11).

Pinnes.[174] The monks who had supplied the deacon with this intelligence, Pecysius (a presbyter), Silvanus, Tapenacerameus, and Paul, appear to have had an intimate knowledge of the affair and accompanied the deacon to Pinnes's monastery along with a number of other associates.[175] One of the monks, Paul, was from Hypsele and, therefore, would have been able to identify Arsenius.[176] Before their arrival at Ptermenkurkis, however, Pinnes had received word of their approach and had instructed a monk, Elias, to place Arsenius on a boat bound for the lower country.[177]

When Athanasius's deacon and his party arrived at the monastery, they found that their quarry had escaped. Pinnes and Elias, however, were taken to Alexandria for questioning before the *dux* of Egypt.[178] T.D. Barnes contends that the *dux* "tortured them separately, and they disclosed the truth," but Pinnes, in a letter written after the event, only stated that he "did not have the strength to deny" that Arsenius was still alive, and that the monk, Elias, made the same confession.[179] For Athanasius, it only remained to communicate these findings to Dalmatius and the emperor and then to find Arsenius, who remained in hiding among the Meletian communities in the lower country.

1.4 The Synod of Caesarea, March/April AD 334

While the search for Arsenius was taking place in Egypt, Athanasius's enemies remained active at court. Eusebius of Nicomedia, Theognis of Nicaea, and Theodorus of Perinthus pressed Constantine to convene a synod, presumably to consider the ecclesiastical ramifications of the judicial inquiry which had been undertaken by Dalmatius.[180] For some time, these leaders of the Eusebian party had been attempting to convince Constantine that

---

[174]Sozomen indicates that his name was Πρίνης although this is counter to the material contained in Athanasius (*HE* II, 23, 2 [Bidez, 80, 21]; *cf. Apol.* 67, 1 [Opitz, 145, 15-17]).

[175]*Apol.* 67, 2 (Opitz, 145, 21-22).

[176]*Ibid.*

[177]*Ibid.* (Opitz, 145, 23-24).

[178]*Apol.* 67, 3 (Opitz, 145, 27-29).

[179]Barnes, *Constantine and Eusebius,* 234. The text simply states that οὐκ ἴσχυσα ἀρνήσασθαι, *Apol.* 67, 3 (Opitz, 145, 28). It seems unlikely that Pinnes and Elias, having already been brought before the *dux* by those who had a somewhat complete knowledge of the affair, would then have been separately tortured to elicit this selfsame information. Certainly, the text does not give this indication. Furthermore, if, in fact, they were subjected to judicial torture by the *dux,* it seems very unlikely that they would have been given or allowed the liberty subsequently to communicate with John Archaph to provide him with a warning in the manner in which they did (*cf. Apol.* 67). Concerning the judicial use of torture in this period, *cf.* Jones, *Late Roman Empire, op. cit.,* I, 519, 520.

[180]Theodoret, *HE* I, 28, 2-4.

Athanasius and his bishops bore the primary responsibility for a supposed series of violent attacks upon other church parties in Egypt, as well as for the continuing divisions and schisms which had come to characterize the region over the last decade.[181]

At length, Constantine relented and called for a synod to meet at Caesarea in Palestine.[182] Although T.D. Barnes states that, "the *censor* Dalmatius was to be there, occupying a position analogous to that of the emperor at Nicaea," there is no documentary evidence to support this view.[183] It is equally possible that Eusebius of Caesarea was chosen to preside over this synod which was to meet in his see city.[184] Constantine most probably considered Eusebius as holding a centrist position in this controversy, and, at the earlier Synod of Antioch, he had presided over a similar inquiry concerning Eustathius of Antioch. Certainly, the *Festal Letter Index* VI indicates that part of Athanasius's refusal to attend this synod was based upon the location and, presumably, the leadership of the meeting.[185]

In early AD 334, "sacred imperial letters" were sent out "by the most pious emperor Constantine ordering certain persons from Egypt, both bishops and priests and many others ... to proceed to Caesarea in Palestinian Syria" for the synod.[186] Whether, in fact, Dalmatius or Eusebius had been instructed to preside over the workings of the assembly, it is clear that Constantine was responsible for calling the synod and that this was accomplished not through episcopal letters, but an imperial summons. One of those called to the Synod of Caesarea was a Meletian presbyter, Aurelius Pageus the son of Horus, the head of a monastic community at the village of Hipponon in the Heracleopite nome.[187] On 18 March AD 334, this native Egyptian priest wrote to leaders of the monastic community at Hathor in the Upper Cynopolite nome informing them that a deputy had been appointed to watch over Hipponon until his return from the synod.[188] It is puzzling why

---

[181]Sozomen, *HE* II, 22, 1-2 (Bidez, 78, 21-79, 1).

[182]Theodoret, *loc. cit.;* Sozomen, *HE* II, 25, 1 (Bidez, 84, 7-8).

[183]Barnes, *Constantine and Eusebius, op. cit.,* 234; Barnes also raises the question of the "court of the *censor*" in "Emperor and Bishops," *op. cit.,* 62, but provides little further documentation for his position apart from comparisons with the Synod of Tyre.

[184]*Cf.* Nordberg, *Athanasius and the Emperor,* 26.

[185]*Festal Letter Index* VI (*Histoire,* A. Martin, 231, 233).

[186]LP 1913, 1. 4-6 (Bell, *Jews and Christians,* 49).

[187]*Ibid.,* 1. 1-2.

[188]*Ibid.,* 1. 2-3. This text is also interesting in that it shows the manner in which secular administrative titles had, at this early date, found their way into the structure of the posts in the monastic community. Two particular instances are as follows: In line 14 of LP 1913, mention is made of the appointing of οἰκνομεῖν, a term borrowed from the officials who provided the financial administration of the

Pageus, a small village priest, would have been called to the synod. It is improbable that he was summoned to be a direct participant in the deliberations, but he may have been included as a witness. It seems clear from his invitation, however, that there was an attempt on the part of either Constantine or the Eusebians to include a number of "local" Meletian clerics in the proceedings.

Pageus apparently ascertained from the imperial summons that the Synod of Caesarea was being called "to come to a legal decision" or judgment "concerning the purification of the holy Christian people."[189] The force of the statement, as H.I. Bell admits, is that "the Synod of Caesarea was of the nature of a judicial assembly."[190] That the synod was to result in the purification of the church "seems to suit Constantine's conception of its functions very well."[191] The Synod of Caesarea, so far as the Eusebians were concerned, was intended to provide a legal vehicle, authorized by Constantine, which would secure the deposition of Athanasius under both an ecclesiastical and civil decree. The constitution of the synod, while similar to the assembly in Antioch which had deposed Eustathius, would enable Eusebius and his party to make use of the legal procedure for a criminal trial which had become set by this time: (1) establish jurisdiction, (2) issue the summons to the concerned parties, (3) the trial, (4) judgment by the presiding officer, and (5) execution of the sentence.[192] As the emperor remained competent to judge in all cases and following the principle that "jurisdiction goes with administration," the judgment and sentence of such a synod could

---

fifty nomes in Egypt. Their importance began to diminish during the Roman occupation and the title was subsequently taken up by the monastic establishments. The reader of LP 1913 is further informed that Pageus's deputy was empowered to προνοῆσαι καὶ διοικεῖν καὶ οἰκονομεῖν in line 13, which may be a possible reference to the διοικητής in the court, the financial administrator under the ruler. It seems probable that as these older terms relating to Ptolemaic Egypt slowly fell from public usage, they were taken up within the Egyptian monastic communities in order to designate officials and functions within the community.

[189] πρὸς διάκρισιν περὶ κ(α)θαρισμοῦ <τοῦ> ἁγίου Χρηστιανικοῦ (π)λήθους, LP 1913, 1. 6-7 (Bell, Jews and Christians, 49). As can be seen by the transcription of the text above, the reading of certain portions of this crucial passage remains somewhat unclear. Bell is correct, however, in pointing out that certain words, such as διάκρισιν and καθαρισμοῦ, although unexpected, do fit in with the sense of the passage (Bell, op. cit., 51, fn. 6f.). The reading of πλήθους, however, is very uncertain. From an examination of the papyrus, a better reading might be γένους, which has cognate usage in other literature of the period. Another possibility which fits the line with greater ease is κόσμου, but it suffers from the same lack of cognate usage in the period as πλήθους.

[190] Bell, loc. cit.

[191] Ibid.

[192] H.F. Jolowicz, Historical Introduction to the Study of Roman Law, Cambridge, 1954, 457-464.

be expected to receive almost immediate confirmation by Constantine.[193] There can be little doubt that the Eusebians and the Meletians envisaged Athanasius's condemnation as the probable outcome of the proceedings at Caesarea and believed that Constantine, as in the case of Eustathius, would confirm the sentence.

As the accused party, Athanasius also received the imperial summons to the Synod of Caesarea. His sources of information at court and throughout Egypt would certainly have informed him of the large number of invitations which were being extended to even minor Meletian clerics like Pageus. Having witnessed the expulsion of a number of pro-Nicene bishops over the previous several years by the Eusebians, Athanasius had few illusions as to what lay in wait for him at Caesarea. According to Theodoret, Athanasius was "well aware of the evil intentions of those who were to try him" and "refused to appear at the synod."[194] It was generally assumed that Athanasius was suspicious of those who had gathered at Caesarea owing to the power of its bishop, Eusebius.[195] Upon receiving word of Athanasius's refusal to appear at Caesarea, the bishops who were gathered in that place sent word to Constantine concerning Athanasius's "arrogance" and "contumacy."[196] This action of the bishop of Alexandria would later be used at the Synod of Tyre as an example of how Athanasius had "set aside the commands of the ruler."[197]

While the bishops were gathering at Caesarea, however, Athanasius had been busy in Egypt. Soon after the *dux* had released Pinnes and Elias from custody, the two Meletians attempted to warn John Archaph to desist in his accusations against Athanasius concerning Arsenius. Written from the monastery of Ptermenkurkis by the hand of a fellow monk, Paphnutius, Pinnes informed Archaph concerning the details of their capture and confession, ending the communication with this warning: "Thus, I inform you of these things, father, lest you should set yourself to accuse Athanasius; for I said" that Arsenius "was alive, and that he had been hidden with us. And all these things are known in Egypt and cannot be kept secret any longer."[198] Through the course of events, this letter from Pinnes to Archaph was intercepted by Athanasius's supporters and was given to the bishop who, subsequently, sent it on to Constantine. Meanwhile, Arsenius still remained at large, and Athanasius turned his full attention to apprehending the "murdered man."

---

[193]*Ibid.*, 441, 466.

[194]τὴν τῶν δικαζόντων δυσμένειαν ἐπιστάμενος, οὐχ ἧκεν εἰς τὸ συνέδριον, Theodoret, *HE* I, 26 (28), 2 (PG 82, 981B).

[195]τὸν Ἀθανάσιον ὑφορᾶσθαι τὴν Καισαρέων διὰ τὸν ἐκείνης ἡγούμενον, Theodoret, *HE* I, 26 (28), 4 (PG 82, 981C).

[196]Theodoret, *HE* I, 26 (28), 4 (PG 82, 981C).

[197]Sozomen, *HE* II, 25, 17 (Bidez, 86, 26-27).

[198]*Apol.* 67, 4 (Opitz, 145, 30-146, 1).

It seems likely that during the winter of AD 333/334 Athanasius went through the Lower Country of Egypt in search of Arsenius.[199] The search was made more difficult owing to Arsenius's ability to change his place of concealment constantly, probably with the assistance of the numerous Meletian sympathizers who had remained within the region.[200] At length, however, Arsenius was forced by the pressure of Athanasius's activities to quit Egypt and seek safety in Tyre. While there, however, he was discovered. Two servants of Archelaus, the governor of the province, overheard a conversation at an inn which suggested that Arsenius was alive and in hiding nearby. They reported this information to Archelaus, who thereupon seized Arsenius after discovering his place of concealment and immediately informed Athanasius. At first Arsenius would not admit to his own identity, but upon his appearance in an ecclesiastical court presided over by Paul, the bishop of Tyre, who was an old acquaintance, he could no longer maintain the fiction.[201] Thereupon, according to Tillemont, "he was convicted of being himself."[202]

It is unfortunate that in the midst of these activities, that is, in early AD 334, we have no fully extant Easter letter that might give us insight into Athanasius's state of mind.[203] The fragment which we do possess, mistakenly dated by an ancient editor to the year AD 345, informs us only concerning the day Easter is to be observed in Alexandria and the outlying districts.[204] This dating by R. Lorenz[205] solves the chronological enigma

---

[199]*Festal Letter Index* IV (*Histoire*, A. Martin, 231); T.D. Barnes believes this journey to have taken place almost a full year earlier, stating, "When he received Dalmatius's letter, Athanasius withdrew from Alexandria to make himself inaccessible" (*Constantine and Eusebius*, 234). The *Festal Letter Index* IV, however, appears to indicate the period immediately before the Synod of Caesarea, probably in the winter of AD 333/334 but sometime after Athanasius had received word of the inquiry at Antioch from Dalmatius the previous year. When the information contained in the *Index* is combined with the certainty that Athanasius had learned of Arsenius's flight into the region of the Lower Country from Pinnes and Elias, the stated reconstruction of events presented within the text seems likely.

[200]Socrates, *HE* I, 27 (PG 67, 157B).

[201]*Apol.* 65, 3 (Opitz, 144, 13-15); Socrates, *HE* I, 29, 2 (PG 67, 160C). From Athanasius's account it would appear as though Arsenius's apprehension took place early in AD 334 rather than shortly before the Synod of Tyre, as in the account of Socrates. In the letter of Constantine to Athanasius, Arsenius's prior arrest and exposure is certainly strongly suggested, *Apol.* 68, 2 (Opitz, 146, 14-16).

[202]L.S. Tillemont, *Histoire de saint Athanase*, vol. 8 of *Mémoires*, Paris, 1701, 27.

[203]Cf. Lorenz, *Der zehnte Osterfestbrief*, 30-31.

[204]*Op. cit.*, 16; *Festal Letter* XVII, in Robertson, *op. cit.*, 544.

[205]Lorenz, *loc. cit.*

observed by A. Roberston in his edition of the letters.[206] Such a revision of
the Schwartzian chronology leaves us, however, with little from the pen of
Athanasius for this critical year.[207]

As a consequence of the letters and reports which Constantine had
received from the *dux* of Egypt, Athanasius, and the governor Archelaus—all
of which affirmed the innocence of the bishop of Alexandria—the charges
against him were dismissed. Having further been reminded by Athanasius of
"what he had heard in Psamathia concerning Macarius the presbyter" two
years earlier (apparently referring to the letter of Ischyras), Constantine wrote
to Dalmatius and ordered the cessation of the judicial inquiry which had been
undertaken by the court of the *censor*, indicating that the charges against
Athanasius were false and fraudulent. The emperor then informed "Eusebius
and his fellows" that the synod being held at Caesarea was to be dissolved and
ordered them to return to their various cities.[208] From Athanasius's
language, it seems as though some of the bishops had not yet reached
Caesarea, although Sozomen indicates that the Eusebians later complained of
having been "kept waiting" at the synod owing to Athanasius's non-
attendance.[209]

Constantine then sent a letter to Athanasius in which he reviewed the
events whereby Arsenius, whom the Meletians claimed "had been killed with
the sword" was now seen to be alive.[210] The emperor also commented upon
the Meletian accusation concerning Macarius breaking the chalice of Ischyras,
which he concluded was simply a malicious plot fabricated against
Athanasius.[211] After rehearsing this catalogue of what Constantine calls
"false and pretended crimes," the emperor states that

> I desire this letter to be read frequently by your wisdom in public, in
> order that it may come to the knowledge of all men, and may especially
> be heard by those who have acted like this and have raised such
> disturbances; for my judgment is expressed justly and is confirmed by

---

[206]Robertson, *op. cit.*, 544, note 1.

[207]See Lorenz, *op. cit.*, 16-19, for this revising of Schwartz.

[208]Socrates, *HE* I, 27 (PG 67, 157B); *Apol.* 65, 4 (Opitz, 144, 17-21).
From Athanasius's statement it would appear as though the *censor*'s court
(probably held in Antioch) and the synod of Caesarea were separate events
requiring separate notification by the emperor: ... ἔπαυσε μὲν τὸ
δικαστήριον τοῦ κήνσωρος, ἔγραψε δὲ καταγινώσκων τὴν συκοφαντίαν
τῶν καθ᾽ ἡμῶν γενομένων καὶ τοὺς περὶ Εὐσέβιον ἐρχομένους εἰς τὴν
'Ανατολὴν καθ᾽ ἡμῶν ἐκέλευσεν ὑποστρέψαι, *Apol.* 65, 4 (Opitz, 144, 19-21).
Socrates, in his account of the matter, only makes mention of the suppression of
the court of the *censor*: Παύει δὲ ὁ βασιλεὺς τὸ ἐπὶ τοῦ κήνσορος
δικαστήριον ... , *HE* I, 27 (PG 67, 157B).

[209]*Vide supra*, fn. 208; Sozomen, *HE* II, 25, 17 (Bidez, 86, 24-26).

[210]*Apol.* 68, 2 (Opitz, 146, 12-13).

[211]*Apol.* 68, 3 (Opitz, 146, 16ff.).

the stated facts. Because we see in such conduct [of the Meletians] that there is great offense, let them understand that I have judged in this way and have come to this determination, that if they promote any further trouble of this sort, I will, in my own person, take notice of the matter, and [judge] not according to ecclesiastical, but according to public law.[212]

This latter provision for the prosecution by civil authorities of those ecclesiastical parties who continued to cause public disturbances would find its logical end in the proceedings of the Synod of Tyre which would be presided over by an imperial official, the *comes* Dionysius. It also indicates that the court of the *censor* and the Synod of Caesarea were, in all probability, two separate forums.

Athanasius's envoy at court in Constantinople, Macarius, quickly informed a number of influential bishops by letter of the sequence of events which had resulted in the vindication of his bishop in Alexandria.[213] As a result, Athanasius received a number of letters of congratulation from fellow bishops who were sympathetic to his cause.[214] Among the letters was one from Alexander of Thessalonica. Athanasius had earlier informed Alexander of the situation in Egypt by a letter which had been delivered in Thessalonica by Sarapion, the son of Sozon.[215] As Sozon had been known and esteemed by Alexander, Athanasius's use of Sarapion as a messenger may have been calculated to involve the elderly and well-respected bishop of Thessalonica more deeply in the controversy.[216] In his letter to Athanasius it is evident that Alexander had also received some contrary reports from John Archaph concerning the alleged murder of Arsenius. It seems likely, therefore, that a great deal of correspondence was taking place among those involved in order to gain wider support for their respective positions. For Alexander's part, his letter to Athanasius reports that he has been given "great pleasure" to hear that "the false accuser Archaph has met with disgrace" and hopes that he and his associates will receive the punishment "his crimes deserve" from "the righteous judge."[217]

---

[212]*Apol.* 68, 6-7 (Opitz, 146, 33-147, 4).

[213]That Macarius was in Constantinople during at least some portion of the time in question is confirmed in the letter to Athanasius which was written by Alexander of Thessalonica, *Apol.* 66, 3 (Opitz, 145, 9-10). It is possible, although by no means certain, that Macarius was entrusted by Athanasius with the letters and documents which were sent to Constantine to prove his innocence. It is equally possible that Macarius had remained at court during this period as Athanasius's permanent envoy to Constantine.

[214]*Apol.* 65, 5 (Opitz, 144, 21-33).

[215]*Apol.* 66, 1-2 (Opitz, 145, 3-8).

[216]*Ibid.*

[217]*Apol.* 66, 3 (Opitz, 145, 10-13).

As in the case of Ischyras, Athanasius also received a letter of submission from "Arsenius, [bishop of those who were under Meletius] in the city of Hypsele, along with the presbyters and deacons."[218]   As W.H.C. Frend has commented, this submission of Arsenius was "a tribute to" Athanasius's "powers of persuasion."[219]   Arsenius states in the letter that both he and his clergy "desire peace and union with the catholic church" and wish "to place ourselves under the canon of the church"; therefore, "according to ancient custom" they are writing their letter of submission to Athanasius as their "beloved father."[220]   As Arsenius and his clergy had refused to submit to Alexander in company with Meletius almost six years earlier,[221] he pledges no longer to hold communion with other schismatics, "whether bishops, presbyters, or deacons" and not to take part in any synods which such persons might call.[222]   Arsenius further promises that he and his clergy will not "send messages [i.e., letters] of peace to them or receive [messages] from them; neither without your consent [as] bishop of the metropolis will we set out any decision concerning bishops or on any other common church matter, but we will be obedient to all the canons which have before been set forward, following the good example of bishops Ammonian, Tyrannus, Plusianus, and the other bishops."[223]   Arsenius ends the letter by asking Athanasius first to answer them quickly and then to inform the other clergy in the various districts concerning his decision.[224]

The letter of Arsenius is an important piece of evidence concerning the situation in Egypt in ca. AD 334. It is evident that even though Athanasius had succeeded in attracting the support of a large number of the Meletian clergy who had made their submission to Alexander along with Meletius, there remained a substantial, albeit more hard-pressed, Meletian community scattered throughout Egypt. Along with the Colluthians and most probably certain Arians and other smaller sects, they appear to have established a variety of ecclesiastical structures of their own devising which existed in the shadows alongside those of the catholic community. From the events connected with the flight of Arsenius it is certain that the Meletians, at least, maintained a loose network of monastic establishments, but one that included communities with varying degrees of loyalty which were not immune to internal rivalries. In the letter of Arsenius to Athanasius it is also apparent that the Meletians, and perhaps the other schismatic groups as well,

---

[218]*Apol.* 69, 2 (Opitz, 147, 11-12); *cf.* Opitz's note on τῶν ποτε ὑπὸ Μελίτιον, *loc. cit.*

[219]Frend, *The Rise of Christianity,* 547, n. 3.

[220]*Apol.* 69, 2 (Opitz, 147, 14-15).

[221]Arsenius is not on the list presented by Meletius to Alexander; *cf. Apol.* 71, 6 (Opitz, 149, 20-151, 9).

[222]*Apol.* 69, 2 (Opitz, 147, 17-18).

[223]*Apol.* 69, 2 (Opitz, 147, 18-22).

[224]*Apol.* 69, 3 (Opitz, 147, 23-148, 3).

maintained communication through "letters of peace";[225] had a structured ministry of bishops, presbyters, and deacons; occasionally met in regional synods; and made determinations concerning the validity of episcopal incumbents and other common ecclesiastical matters. Arsenius further indicates that the acceptance of Athanasius's authority was a matter which was related to "obedience to all the canons," perhaps referring back to the Nicene accords concerning the absolute metropolitical rights of Alexandria or the letter which set forth the terms of the Meletian settlement.[226]

Arsenius appears to have kept his pledge of loyalty, for thirteen years later, in his Easter letter of AD 347, Athanasius informs his readers that Arsenius is in Hypsele, "having been reconciled with the Church."[227] The identity of the other bishops whose examples are mentioned by Arsenius is less certain. It is equally possible that they were Meletians (two names, Ammonian and Tyrannus, are listed in the brief presented to Alexander) who had lately been reconciled to Athanasius, or, although less likely, simply catholic bishops with whom Arsenius was acquainted.[228] In either case, Ammonian and Tyrannus are listed among the signers of the petition which was presented at Tyre on behalf of Athanasius,[229] and later, in AD 347, they are reported as having lost possession of their sees, perhaps through death.[230] The remaining bishop mentioned, Plusianus, would reemerge at Tyre, accused by the Meletians, surprisingly enough, of playing a major part in attempting to murder Arsenius at an earlier time.[231]

There was a final and intriguing sequel to the events surrounding the Synod of Caesarea. John Archaph, the Meletian bishop of Memphis and the chief accuser of Athanasius in the Arsenius affair, sent a letter to Constantine in which he confessed his part in the episode and "expressed his repentance."[232] Furthermore, it is implied that Archaph informed the emperor that he had joined the communion of the church and was at peace with Athanasius.[233] Finally, he requested permission to travel to court (probably from Antioch) to appear before Constantine.[234] The emperor immediately replied to Archaph's request. He was commended for "setting to the side all petty feelings" and instructed to make use of the *cursus publicus*

---

[225]γράμματα εἰρηνικά, Apol. 69, 2 (Opitz, 147, 18).

[226]... ἀλλ ' εἴκειν πᾶσι τοῖς προτετυπωμένοις κανόσι, Apol. 69, 2 (Opitz, 147, 20-21).

[227]Festal Letter XIX, 10 (Robertson, op. cit., 548).

[228]Cf. Opitz, 147, fn. 19.

[229]Apol. 78, 7 (Opitz, 159, 5, 6).

[230]Festal Letter XIX, loc. cit.

[231]Sozomen, HE II, 25, 12 (Bidez, 85, 26-29).

[232]Apol. 70, 1 (Opitz, 148, 9-12).

[233]Apol. 70, 2 (Opitz, 148, 15-17).

[234]Apol. 70, 2 (Opitz, 148, 19-20).

in order that there might be no delay in making his appearance at Constantine's "court of clemency."[235]

H. Nordberg was of the opinion that Archaph was encouraged by the Eusebians to make this approach to Constantine, believing that, as in the case of Arius, the emperor would be sympathetic to a repentant church leader and invite him to court.[236] The hope for a successful outcome as the result of such a personal interview was, according to Nordberg, based upon the Eusebians' judgment of how the emperor would react:

> They had many years of experience of Constantine's ways of handling church matters and knew that he was not sufficiently competent as a church politician to be able to judge independently a more complicated matter; his greatest ambition was to keep peace in the church. For this reason, almost every time one of the church leaders visited the Emperor personally, the result was one or several marks of favour on the Emperor's part. As a matter of fact, the same thing had recently happened to Athanasius himself.[237]

As John Archaph made his way to appear before the emperor, probably during second half of AD 334, Sozomen reports that the Meletians in Egypt, who had been alarmed by Constantine's threat of punishment under civil law, became more quiet for a time and that the churches throughout Egypt enjoyed peace and prospered.[238] Athanasius, however, seems to have recognized that the peace was artificial. He makes no mention of a reconciliation with John Archaph, and it is possible that none took place apart from Archaph stating his intention to do so in order to obtain an interview with Constantine. The bishop of Alexandria was certain that although the Meletians were, for the time being, "set back and covered with shame," the issue which remained central was the readmission of Arius to the Alexandrian church.[239] The primary concern of the Eusebians, therefore, remained Athanasius's deposition as bishop of Alexandria.

---

[235]*Apol.* 70, 2 (Opitz, 148, 15, 20-24).

[236]Nordberg, *Athanasius and the Emperor,* 25. It is important to note, however, that Nordberg mistakenly places this interview between John Archaph and Constantine in AD 333, before the Synod of Caesarea.

[237]*Ibid.,* 26.

[238]Sozomen, *HE* II, 23, 8 (Bidez, 81, 29-82, 2).

[239]*Apol.* 71, 1 (Opitz, 148, 25-28).

2. THE SYNOD OF TYRE

In his assessment concerning the importance of the Synod of Tyre, W.H.C. Frend made the following observation:

> For the future relationship between church and state in the East, the Council of Tyre was as important as that of Nicaea. It had been summoned by the emperor and organized like a court of justice but, unlike Arles (assembled to hear the Donatists' petition), it was presided over by an imperial official, the count Dionysius, a former consul. The emperor had intervened directly in a matter of church discipline and though sentence would be pronounced by the bishops, their proceedings would be supervised by a layman. This was to be the pattern for all the great councils of the patristic age.[240]

It is possible that Frend has overstated Tyre's significance as "the pattern for all the great councils of the patristic age," but his comments concerning the importance of the synod relative to Nicaea are essentially correct.[241] At Nicaea, however, the discussions were primarily concerned with doctrinal matters; issues of church order and discipline were of secondary importance. The deposition of Eustathius at the Synod of Antioch appears to have been the result of a combination of doctrinal and disciplinary or judicial concerns. At the Synod of Caesarea and the court of the *censor* at Antioch, two jurisdictions were employed, one ecclesiastical and one judicial, in an attempt to arrive at a decision concerning the accusations which had been brought against Athanasius. The Synod of Tyre would combine these two jurisdictions, although the ultimate sentence of the gathering would be pronounced by the bishops, not the count Dionysius, and would be forwarded to Constantine for his approval.[242]

2.1 The Calling of the Synod of Tyre, AD 335

John Archaph's interview with Constantine, probably during the latter portion of AD 334, resulted in yet another reexamination of the many charges which had been brought against Athanasius. Whether Nordberg is correct in his assertion that the Eusebians were the motivating force behind the visit of Archaph is uncertain, but documentation attests to their involvement in "contriving that a letter" directed against Athanasius "should be presented as though coming from the Colluthians, the Meletians, and the

---

[240]Frend, *The Rise of Christianity, op. cit.,* 527.

[241]Frend's assertion that "Athanasius, however, never questioned the rightness of the presence of the lay element there (*i.e.*, at an ecclesiastical synod), even when the case went against him," may be disputed, as will be seen in the text below (Frend, *loc. cit.*).

[242]*Cf.* Girardet, *Kaisergericht und Bischofsgericht, op. cit.,* 66ff.

Arians."[243] It is possible that Archaph transmitted this letter to Constantine in person at court. Having been presented once again with evidence of instability and division within the Egyptian church and being desirous of achieving unity before the offering of the gift of the Church of the Holy Sepulchre in Jerusalem in the autumn of AD 335, the emperor called for a synod to convene in Tyre. The purpose of the synod, as set forth by Constantine, was "to defend those in need of protection, to restore health to your brothers who are in danger, to bring back to unity of opinion those who are divided, to correct errors while there is still time; in order that you may restore harmony to many provinces."[244]

It was the emperor's avowed intention to resolve the Egyptian controversies which had troubled the peace of the church for almost half of his reign. To this end, Constantine agreed to send to Tyre the former governor of Syria, *comes* Flavius Dionysius, along with a military guard, for the purpose of supervision and maintaining "good order."[245] Constantine, however, clearly indicated that the judgment of the case would remain with the bishops who gathered at Tyre, as was consistent "with ecclesiastical and apostolic order."[246] Probably the emperor intended the synod to be a preliminary judicial assembly whose actions would merely prepare for the main business of church reunification, which would itself be completed later at his *Tricennalia* in Jerusalem. There, during the celebrations, a larger gathering would reinstate Arius and Euzoius and their followers and thus, so the emperor hoped, bring an end to the Egyptian schisms.

Perceiving that Constantine's patience with the Egyptian troubles was almost at an end, the Eusebians had set to the task of organizing the Synod of Tyre to their advantage. Flavius Dionysius, the presiding secular official, was, according to Athanasius, one of their own party.[247] Furthermore, the Eusebians persuaded Constantine to approve their own list of delegates to the synod (probably including a number of Meletian clerics) and to order the immediate arrest of Athanasius's envoy at court, Macarius, as one of the

---

[243]*Apol.* 77, 9 (Opitz, 157, 27-28); *cf. Apol.* 78, 5 (Opitz, 158, 23-25) and *Apol.* 80, 3 (Opitz, 160, 27-28) concerning the cooperation between the Arians, the Meletians, and the Colluthians.

[244]ἐπαμῦναι τοῖς χρῄζουσιν ἐπικουρίας, τοὺς ἀδελφοὺς ἰάσασθαι κινδυνεύοντας, εἰς ὁμόνοιαν ἐπαναγαγεῖν τὰ διεστῶτα τῶν μελῶν, διορθώσασθαι τὰ πλημμελούμενα, ἕως καιρὸς ἐπιτρέπει, ἵνα ταῖς τοσαύταις ἐπαρχίαις τὴν πρέπουσαν ἀποδῶτε συμφωνίαν ... ; Eusebius, *Vita Constant.*, IV, 42, 1 (Heikel, GCS 7, 134, 11-14).

[245]*Ibid.*, IV, 42, 3; *Apol.* 71, 2 (Opitz, 149, 2).

[246]... ὁμογνώμονι κρίσει, μήτε πρὸς ἀπέχθειαν μήτε πρὸς χάριν, ἀκολούθως δὲ τῷ ἐκκλησιαστικῷ καὶ ἀποστολικῷ κανόνι, τοῖς πλημμεληθεῖσιν ... ; Eusebius, *Vita Constant.*, IV, 42, 5 (Heikel, GCS 7, 135, 5-7).

[247]*Apol.* 72, 3 (Opitz, 151, 17-18).

material witnesses in the Ischyras episode, which was to be reexamined.[248] In order to ensure Athanasius's attendance, for the Eusebians may have feared a repetition of the debacle at Caesarea, Constantine wrote to the bishop of Alexandria and ordered him to make his way to Tyre.[249]   Although Athanasius was unwilling to make the journey, he eventually relented; perhaps Dionysius issued a threat of arrest, or, a distinct possibility, the bishop was "escorted" to Tyre by a military guard.[250]   If this latter suggestion is indeed true, and from Athanasius's language it does appear likely, then the alleged account of the bishop's hesitant departure for Tyre in LP 1914 would seem to be incorrect or an intentional fabrication on the part of the Meletians.[251] Athanasius departed for Tyre on 11 July AD 335.[252]

Before leaving for Tyre, however, Athanasius had begun to make provision for what he was about to face. It was apparent to all concerned that the Synod of Tyre was going to take the form of an ecclesiastical trial in which Athanasius would stand as the accused party. The principal accusers

---

[248]*Apol.* 71, 2 (Opitz, 149, 3).

[249]*Apol.* 71, 2 (Opitz, 149, 3-4).

[250]*Ibid.*; κόμης γὰρ ἦν ὁ ἀναγκάζων καὶ στρατιῶται εἷλκον ἡμᾶς; *Apol.* 72, 1 (Opitz, 151, 4).

[251]Bell, *Jews and Christians, op. cit.,* 60, 11. 38ff.; London Papyrus 1914 has been examined at length in section I.3.3 of the present work. It is perhaps sufficient to comment at this juncture that the supposed firsthand reporting of events just previous to the Synod of Tyre which LP 1914 is alleged to contain is far from certain. As has been stated in the text, the dating of the papyrus is entirely circumstantial and, as has been shown, raises considerable difficulties in any attempt to interpret the contents of the letter. Furthermore, as Athanasius was aware of John Archaph's petition to the emperor and his subsequent appearance at court, it seems unlikely that he would have engaged in a policy of wholesale violence against the Meletians in Egypt at exactly the same time. The reports of Athanasius's departure contained within the letter, as well as the disturbances within the Meletian community, seem more suited to the period before the Synod of Caesarea a year earlier. At that time there was a great deal of inter-Meletian rivalry, a frantic search was under way to discover the whereabouts of Arsenius, and Athanasius had, at some point during the year, traveled into the Meletian stronghold of the Lower Country, no doubt disturbing the regular routine of the Meletian monastic communities. There also remains the possibility that LP 1914 is, in fact, a fraudulent report designed to show that Athanasius was both engaged in violence (through his followers) and was unwilling to obey the imperial orders to make his way to the synod, whether at Caesarea or Tyre. Such a report, whether true or not, would have been welcomed and used by Athanasius's opponents at either synod. There is yet a further possibility that this letter relates events which are wholly unconnected with either the Synod of Tyre or the Synod of Caesarea and, as has been suggested above, is relating an incident of internecine rivalry between two competing schismatic groups in Egypt.

[252]*Festal Letter Index* VIII (*Histoire,* A. Martin, 233). This information is incorrectly placed under *Festal Letter Index* VIII, but refers to events in the year AD 335. Its proper placement, therefore, should be under *Festal Letter Index* VII.

would be the Meletians (led by John Archaph) and the Eusebians who, since the Synod of Caesarea, had become more open and public in their opposition to Athanasius. In order to provide himself with an adequate defense, the bishop of Alexandria undertook three separate measures.

First, Athanasius attempted to match the numerical strength of the Eusebians and Meletians at Tyre. During this period there were, according to Athanasius, between ninety and one hundred bishops in Egypt and Libya.[253] If the preface to *Apologia contra Arianos* 78 is correct, Athanasius selected forty-seven, or almost half, of those bishops resident in Egypt and Libya to accompany him to Tyre.[254] Of these forty-seven clerics, at least twelve (possibly as many as seventeen) had at one time been supporters of Meletius.[255] Certain of these former Meletians, such as Apollonius, Dioscorus, and Tyrannus, had been presbyters in the schismatic group and appear to have been raised to the episcopate by Athanasius along with the deacon, Timothy.[256] Others, such as Agathammon (in "the inland of Alexandria," *i.e.*, Mareotis), Harpocration of Bubastus, Moses of Phacusae, Peter of Heracleopolis, Pelagius of Oxyrhynchus, Ammonian of Diospolis, and Cronius of Metelis, had been raised to the episcopate by Meletius and, following their submission to the Alexandrian see, had retained their positions under Alexander and Athanasius.[257] It is possible that Athanasius also engaged the assistance of one Irenaeus, a former Meletian presbyter,[258] who, at an earlier time, had been an Arian deacon.[259] Athanasius was fully aware that the Meletian controversy would be one of the main issues under consideration at Tyre and, therefore, included a good number of ex-Meletians in the large company of clerics he had sent on to Tyre.

Second, Athanasius sought to ensure the availability of witnesses who would contradict the Meletian claims. Macarius had been taken into custody by the emperor and was already at Tyre. The former Meletian bishops who were included by Athanasius in his delegation would be able to supply firsthand knowledge of Meletian activities within Egypt and could testify as to how the Nicene accords had been put into effect under both Alexander and

---

[253]*Apol.* 71, 4 (Opitz, 149, 6-7); *cf. Ad Afros* 10 (PG 26, 1045C).

[254]*Apol.* 78, 1 (Opitz, 158, 1-2). Nordberg contends that the forty-seven persons mentioned as signing the letter to Dionysius were not all bishops, but he offers no positive proof for this assertion (*Athanasius and the Emperor*, 27). It is true that a person named Macarius is listed, but it is by no means certain that it is the former Meletian presbyter and court envoy of Athanasius. Opitz mistakenly lists forty-eight bishops (Opitz, 159, 1-48), but lines 2-3 are better read as Ἰσχυράμμων, who is listed in *Apol.* 49, 3 (Opitz, 128, 152).

[255]*Vide supra*, section I, fn. 286.

[256]*Ibid.*

[257]*Ibid.*

[258]*Apol.* 71, 6 (Opitz, 151, 36).

[259]Opitz III, U4a, 6, 9.

Athanasius. An essential witness, however, was the Meletian bishop Arsenius who, by his very presence at the synod, could disprove the accusations of murder and magic which had earlier been brought against the bishop of Alexandria. To this end, Athanasius arranged for Arsenius to remain in hiding outside of Tyre until the time of his presentation before the assembled bishops.[260]

Third, Athanasius brought with him to Tyre documentary evidence as to his innocence. The use of writing as being evidentiary (as in the older Roman system) had become accepted practice, and properly subscribed and witnessed documents were, in the fourth century, considered legally binding.[261] In the East, hellenistic influence helped to increase the value of written statements as binding upon the individual (or individuals) who subscribed to such briefs.[262] This approach was applied in an exacting way to those documents which contained confessions or described obligations.[263] If Athanasius intended to make use of the living Arsenius to disprove the charge of murder, he would present the synod with the schedule of clergy submitted by Meletius to Alexander to prove that Ischyras had never received valid ordination and was, therefore, outside of the Nicene accords concerning the Meletian settlement.[264] Presumably, Athanasius would also have been able to present the letter of Ischyras in which the schismatic priest confessed that no violence had taken place. It is certain that Athanasius entered this letter as evidence, along with the Meletian schedule and other documents, at the later Synod of Alexandria, AD 338/339, and the Synod of Rome, AD 340/341.[265]

Athanasius was well aware of the dangers which awaited him at Tyre, and if, as both Socrates and Sozomen suggest, he was apprehensive, there was good reason.[266] The Eusebians had failed in their attempt to convince the emperor to issue a summary judgment at Psamathia. At least one or, according to K. Girardet, two civil actions brought against Athanasius had also failed to secure his conviction.[267] Within the first few months of AD

---

[260]Sozomen, *HE* II, 25, 10 (Bidez, 85, 17-23).

[261]H.F. Jolowicz, *op. cit.*, 431.

[262]*Ibid.*

[263]*Ibid.*

[264]*Apol.* 72, 1 (Opitz, 151, 10-12); *Apol.* 28, 6 (Opitz, 108, 17-24).

[265]*Apol.* 17, 1 (Opitz, 99, 25-26); *Apol.* 28, 7 (Opitz, 108, 24-26).

[266]Socrates, *HE* I, 28 (PG 67, 160A); Sozomen, *HE* II, 25, 1 (Bidez, 84, 10-11).

[267]In addition to the civil action which was instituted under the jurisdiction of the court of the *censor* in Antioch in early AD 334, Girardet contends that an earlier action was proposed in Antioch following the initial accusations in Psamathia. According to Girardet, Eusebius of Nicomedia and Theognis were sent to act as the *consilium* (along with other unidentified bishops) of the *iudex delegatus* in Antioch who was to issue a judgment concerning those charges which

334 Paterius was replaced as the prefect of Egypt by Flavius Philagrius, an appointment which filled Athanasius with anxiety, for he recognized in the new authority one who was hostile to the church.[268] Finally, the Synod of Caesarea had been dissolved before any judgment of an ecclesiastical nature could be agreed upon or enacted, and the Eusebian and Meletian delegates had dispersed in frustration and anger.

Perhaps reflecting on these events, early in AD 335 Athanasius had written in his Easter letter, "Thus it is that sinners, and all those who are aliens from the catholic Church, heretics, and schismatics, since they are excluded from glorifying" God "with the saints, cannot properly even continue as observers of the feast."[269] Athanasius had probably come to realize the strength of the alliance which had been formed against him and had responded by insisting upon a clear demarcation the true nature of the church as well as a precise delineation of those who could legitimately participate in ecclesiastical affairs.

2.2 Procedure and Authority at the Synod of Tyre

It is difficult to ascertain with any degree of exactitude the procedure which was employed at the Synod of Tyre. P. Batiffol distinguished between Eastern and Western conciliar procedures. He considered the synods of the East to resemble the sort of open debate which was practiced in the schools; the West modeled church councils on the practices and procedures of the Roman senate.[270] N.H. Baynes, without making the distinction between East and West, simply states that "it has long been recognized that the procedure of the early Christian Councils was based upon that of the Roman senate."[271] This model, however, which involved a *relatio* in which the matter being discussed was read to the assembly, followed by a role call in which each delegate stated his *sententia*, after which a vote was taken, was not limited to the Roman senate but had been taken up by the municipalities as well.[272] In the case of the North African synods which indirectly followed this process, the resolution once voted upon would be placed in the

---

had been raised (Girardet, *op. cit.*, 63-65). Although such an action might have been possible, further documentary evidence would be needed to substantiate such a claim. Certainly, Athanasius makes no mention of the alleged proceedings.

[268]*Cf.* Schwartz, *GS* III, 246; *Epistola Encyclica*, 3 (PG 25, 228B).

[269]*Festal Letter* VII, 4 (Robertson, *op. cit.*, 525).

[270]The basic parameters of this argument are set forth in P. Batiffol, "Origines du règlement des conciles," *Études de liturgie et d'archéologie chrétienne*, Paris, 1919, 88-96.

[271]N.H. Baynes, *Constantine the Great and the Christian Church*, second edition, London, 1972, 88.

[272]*Cf.* P.R. Amidon, "The Procedure of St. Cyprian's Synods," *Vig. Chr.* 37 (1983): 328-339.

form of a letter which was then sent to all of the interested parties and placed in the archives of the church where the synod had been held.[273]

The appearance of the *relatio-sententia* sequence in synodal gatherings was, in all probability, owing to the widespread popularity of this format rather than being a direct copy of Roman senatorial practice.[274] As such, it is perhaps best to view the procedures employed by ecclesiastical gatherings in the fourth century as being hybrids which retained much that was familiar in civil affairs, but which also provided vehicles for the church to express itself in terms of limited juridical authority.[275] Although both F. Dvornik and H. Hess somewhat exaggerate the dependence of church synods upon the senatorial model and perhaps muddle the legislative distinctions between the magisterial and conciliar concerns of that body, there can be little doubt that there is a similar procedural tradition.[276] While it is beyond the scope of this study to comment fully upon the procedure which was used at the Council of Nicaea, it must be noted that the senatorial model of Baynes is substantiated only by the account of Eusebius, which may have placed Constantine in a more central position than is fully justified.[277]

---

[273]*Ibid.*, 329.

[274]*Ibid.*, 334.

[275]*Cf.* H. Hess, *The Canons of the Council of Sardica,* 38-39; Hess's conviction concerning the links between ecclesiastical synods and the model of Roman senatorial practice is clear in the following statement:

> It is reasonable to suppose that the adoption of particular types of civil records for ecclesiastical use was determined by the function which the records themselves customarily performed. By the time of Diocletian and Constantine the *senatus-consultum* was regarded simply as a counsel of advice. It is therefore not surprising that the synodical canon was patterned after the *senatus-consultum* before the conscious acceptance of an ecclesiastical rule of law; for a limited degree of authority, parallel to that of the *senatus-consultum,* seems to have been accorded to the canon until at least the late fourth century in the East and the late fifth century in the West. The emergence of the concept of the canon as an expression of juridical authority is closely associated with the later growth of an ecclesiastical corpus parallel in structure to the corpus of civil law. (Hess, *loc. cit.*)

Despite Hess's insistence on the advisory nature of the canons put forth by the Synod of Sardica, it seems probable that it was not the intent of the bishops either there, or at Nicaea, or Antioch, or, indeed, at Tyre merely to put forward suggestive proscriptions. If the church at large was hesitant to accept the decrees and canons of synods, it was probably owing to factors other than the jurisdictional intentions of the participants.

[276]*Ibid.;* cf. F. Dvornik, *Early Christian and Byzantine Political Philosophy,* Washington, 1966; and Amidon, *op. cit.,* 336.

[277]Baynes, *Constantine, op. cit.,* 88; *cf.* C. Luibhéid, *The Council of Nicaea,* 81.

E. Caspar, while allowing for certain differences between Nicaea and Tyre, contends that they were essentially similar, for as *Reichskonzilien* they combined ecclesiastical and civil jurisdiction and each met under the direct oversight of imperial authority;[278] an assumption is made that the procedure employed by each synod was also similar. K. Girardet has considered "the *Reichssynode* of Tyre" at somewhat greater length,[279] and, although giving little credence to the Athanasian accounts of Tyre, he clearly considers the synod to have been little more than an ecclesiastical trial which operated under the civil jurisdiction of the state: "The *iudex* in this process is Constantine" in the person of Dionysius, "the bishops being his *consiliarii*."[280] The sentence which such a synod would decide upon, therefore, would only be advisory in nature rather than an actual judgment, which would be left to Constantine.[281] V. Twomey suggests, however, that the Synod of Tyre possessed greater power than that of "an advisory *votum* of the imperial *consiliarii*" and expected to "pass sentence on Athanasius, a sentence which they," the Eusebians, "assumed had *automatically* the weight of a civil judgment and not simply an ecclesiastical one."[282] His conclusion is that "here Tyre and Nicaea must be considered as essentially different" in regard to authority and, presumably, procedure.[283]

A.H.M. Jones has summarized the conflicting attitudes towards, and evidence concerning, ecclesiastical synods during this period:

> The church had a great belief in the value of councils, but here again there were no accepted rules to determine who might summon them and what jurisdiction they possessed. The Council of Nicaea had, as we have seen, put provincial councils on a regular footing and defined their competence. In some areas larger councils were sanctioned by tradition. The bishops of Rome and Alexandria from time to time summoned councils from the Suburbicarian provinces and from Egypt, and the bishop of Antioch from all the diocese of Oriens. Councils of all the African provinces were regularly held under the presidency of the bishop of Carthage. But elsewhere there were no recognized authorities to convene larger councils.
>
> The imperial government often took the initiative. Only the emperor could summon a general council of the whole church: Constantine had established the precedent at Nicaea, and there was in any case no central ecclesiastical authority which could act. But the emperor also often summoned smaller councils to deal with some

---

278E. Caspar, *Geschichte des Papsttums* I, 141.
279K. Girardet, *op. cit.*, 66-75.
280*Ibid.*, 68.
281*Ibid.*, 71.
282V. Twomey, *Apostolikos Thronos*, *op. cit.*, 355, fn. 46.
283*Ibid.*

problem on which a provincial council was incompetent to decide: Constantine again set the precedent by calling the councils of Rome and Arles to deal with the Donatist controversy and those of Caesarea and Tyre to give judgement on Athanasius. Such *ad hoc* councils were also convoked by leading bishops, but whether they were summoned by imperial or episcopal initiative, their competence was disputable, and their verdict was frequently challenged by defeated parties who, often truly, alleged that they were packed.[284]

At the time of Tyre, synodal practice and procedure was still in the process of development. All may not have agreed concerning imperial participation, but, as S.L. Greenslade has observed, "the theory of councils was still so rudimentary that the practice often strengthened the authority of the emperor rather than the freedom of the Church."[285] Furthermore, it is often overlooked that both the Synod of Caesarea and the Synod of Tyre had a particular purpose, that of judging an eminent ecclesiastical figure who had been accused of particular violations of both civil and canon law. During the period surrounding the Synod of Caesarea, two separate forums were established to deal with such matters. We may assume that the bishops were to judge ecclesiastical concerns and that the court of the *censor* was to evaluate any civil ramifications. At Tyre these two functions were linked. Although the oversight of the Synod of Tyre was entrusted to an imperial official in a manner similar to Nicaea, the purpose was different, and the control of the emperor in a matter of discipline (as opposed to theology) was more far reaching.

Again, as A.H.M. Jones has commented, Constantine entrusted "the case of Athanasius to a hand-picked council presided over by an imperial commissioner. He himself pronounced on Athanasius's appeal from this council."[286] The result of "such a technique, whereby the emperor chose the bishops who were to make the decision, and through a lay president guided their discussions" was that the imperial government was given "a considerable *de facto* influence on ecclesiastical decisions."[287]

It seems proper, therefore, to regard the Synod of Tyre as primarily an ecclesiastical trial which operated under imperial authority in the person of Flavius Dionysius. It is possible that, as at Nicaea, there was also a presiding bishop who acted as the ecclesiastical counterpart to Dionysius, although the Egyptian bishops would latter complain that only "the *comes* spoke and all present remained silent or obeyed his instructions."[288]

---

[284]Jones, *Late Roman Empire, op. cit.*, II, 886-887.

[285]S.L. Greenslade, *Church and State from Constantine to Theodosius*, London, 1954, 20.

[286]Jones, *Late Roman Empire, op. cit.*, II, 936.

[287]*Ibid.*

[288]*Apol.* 8, 3 (Opitz, 94, 12-13).

Although the Egyptian bishops stated that Eusebius of Nicomedia controlled the proceedings of the synod through Dionysius,[289] it is more likely that Eusebius of Caesarea as the resident metropolitan, or possibly Flacillus of Antioch, would have been given the nominal role of presiding bishop.[290]

The Eusebians, however, believed the proceedings at Tyre to be primarily ecclesiastical in nature and assumed that their sentence would receive the approval and approbation of Dionysius and, by inference, Constantine.[291] Athanasius considered Tyre, at least upon reflection, as an *ex parte* trial which had no ecclesiastical authority and only the limited civil jurisdiction which had been allowed by the emperor.[292] As for Constantine himself, the emperor clearly considered it within his power to annul the decisions of the Synod of Tyre and to reexamine any disputed matters after the fact.[293] One may conclude, therefore, that the relative authority of the Synod of Tyre was, from the outset, regarded in a variety of ways by its differing participants.

The procedure which was followed by the Synod of Tyre appears to have included elements of a civil trial as well as the time-honored *relatio-sententia* ordering of the agenda. The synod began with a letter from Constantine to the assembled bishops in which he set forward the matter to be discussed (the *relatio*).[294] In this letter he also established the jurisdictional oversight of "Dionysius, a man of consular rank."[295] Furthermore, Constantine reiterated the summons which had been extended to all the interested parties and threatened banishment as a punishment for those who refused to attend.[296] This combining of the *relatio* with the question of jurisdiction and a repeat of the summons fits the hybrid nature of the Synod of Tyre. The procedure continued with the trial proper, in which the presiding officer called upon the interested parties to present their respective cases. The assembled bishops were then given an opportunity to state their opinions or to dispute evidence. Finally, each in turn would deliver his *sententia* or judgment of the matter, with the final verdict being placed in the form of a letter. This, in brief, appears to be roughly the process which was followed at Tyre.

---

[289]*Ibid.* (Opitz, 94, 15-16).

[290]Although Girardet claims that Eusebius of Caesarea was not present at the Synod of Tyre, the letter of the Egyptian bishops who were at Tyre, *Apol.* 77, 10 (Opitz, 157, 34), certainly implies his presence (*op. cit.,* 69, fn. 130); *cf. Apol.* 81, 1 (Opitz, 161, 6).

[291]Girardet, *op. cit.,* 71, fn. 151.

[292]*Apol.* 82, 1 (Opitz, 161, 17-19).

[293]*Apol.* 86, 2ff. (Opitz, 164, 16ff.).

[294]Eusebius, *Vita Constant.* IV, 42.

[295]*Ibid.*

[296]*Ibid.*

2.3 The Proceedings at the Synod of Tyre, July-October AD 335

Having left Egypt on 11 July AD 335, Athanasius probably arrived in Phoenicia later in the same month with the proceedings being initiated shortly thereafter. The total number of bishops who attended the synod remains uncertain. Socrates indicates that only 60 bishops were present.[297] Hefele accepts this number but notes that it probably does not include the Egyptian delegation.[298] H.M. Gwatkin estimates the number of bishops to have been about 150, inclusive of the Egyptian delegation.[299] It is probably correct to place the total number of bishops present at between 110 and 150. It is possible that the Egyptian bishops had not been officially summoned and that their names, therefore, did not appear on the list of judges to which Sozomen had access. Furthermore, many bishops were enroute to Jerusalem for the *Tricennalia* and may have arrived at this preparatory synod in Tyre after the proceedings had already begun.

Among the gathered bishops Athanasius would have found numerous enemies. John Archaph, one of "principal accusers" of Athanasius was present,[300] along with several other Meletian bishops, including Callinicus of Pelusium, Euplus, Pachomius, Isaac (of Letopolis?), Achilleus of Cusae, and Harmaeon of Cynopolis.[301] Among the other hostile bishops present were Eusebius of Nicomedia, Narcissus of Neronias, Maris of Chalcedon, Theognis of Nicaea, Patrophilus of Scythopolis, George of Laodicea, Theodore of Heraclea, Macedonius of Mopsuestia, Ursacius of Singidunum, and Valens of Mursa, all of whom favored Arius's reinstatement within the church of Alexandria.[302] Eusebius of Caesarea and Flacillus of Antioch have already been mentioned and were probably not any more well disposed towards Athanasius than those bishops listed above. In addition to his own bishops from Egypt, many of whom may have been excluded from the proceedings of the synod, the bishop of Alexandria was able to number a few friends, such as Maximus of Jerusalem, Marcellus of Ancyra, and the venerable bishop of Thessalonica, Alexander.[303] Despite these few supporters, it appears certain that Athanasius and those with him at Tyre were heavily outnumbered by their opponents.

Sozomen appears to have had access to some records or minutes of the proceedings of the Synod of Tyre and provides the most complete account of

---

[297]Socrates, *HE* I, 28 (PG 67, 160A).

[298]Hefele, *op. cit.*, II, 17.

[299]Gwatkin, *Studies in Arianism, op. cit.*, 89, fn. 2.

[300]Socrates, *HE* I, 30 (PG 67, 161C).

[301]Sozomen, *HE* II, 25, 3-4 (Bidez, 84, 18-25).

[302]*Cf. Apol.* 77, 1; 13, 2; 78, 1; and Sozomen, *HE* II, 25, 19.

[303]Sozomen, *HE* II, 25, 20 (Bidez, 87, 11-12); *Apol* . 80, 1 (Opitz, 160, 19).

what actually took place.[304] E. Schwartz contended that Sozomen's account made use of Meletian materials which had been gathered by Sabinus in his collection of synodal documents.[305] If this contention is correct, when such an account is combined both with the Athanasian documents which are contained in *Apologia contra Arianos* and with the other historians, it may be possible to arrive at a somewhat balanced view of the admittedly confused and hectic proceedings at Tyre.

As the bishops assembled, a letter from Constantine was read in which the purpose of the synod was set forward. The bishops were enjoined to heal the divisions of the church and to act with zeal and in a timely manner.[306] Having heard this exhortation from the emperor, the work of the synod began in earnest. From the outset, the Egyptian bishops who had been admitted to the proceedings protested against the leadership and intent of the gathering. Potammon of Heraclea attacked Eusebius of Caesarea as a leader of the opposition, saying, "How are you seated there, Eusebius, while the innocent Athanasius is judged by you . . . Were you not with me in prison during the time of persecution? I have lost an eye for the sake of the truth, but you have not suffered in any part of your body. How was it that you escaped from prison if not by deceitful promises or actual deeds?"[307] Another confessor, Paphnutius of Thebes, chided his friend and fellow confessor, Maximus of Jerusalem, for even keeping company with the opposition at Tyre.[308] It is possible that Eusebius of Nicomedia's standing within the synod was challenged owing to his earlier translation from Berytus to Nicomedia and his subsequent deposition from that see following Nicaea.[309] The Egyptians may well have claimed that Amphion was the true bishop of Nicomedia as was Chrestus in Nicaea, who replaced Theognis after his earlier deposition.[310] Any such challenges by the Egyptians, however, to the authority or membership of the synod were quickly set aside, and the accusations against Athanasius were brought forward.

The first set of charges involved the alleged violent repression of the Meletians in Egypt. The "presbyter" Ischyras had renounced his earlier pledge of loyalty to Athanasius and, possibly with the promise of being raised to the episcopate, joined himself to the alliance of Eusebians and Meletians.[311] Along with Meletian bishop Callinicus of Pelusiam, Ischyras

---

[304]Sozomen, *HE* II, 25, 1ff. (Bidez, 84-87).

[305]Schwartz, *GS* III, 248, 249.

[306]Eusebius, *Vita Constant.* IV, 42.

[307]Epiphanius, *Haer.* 68, 8, 3 (PG 42, 197A); *cf. Apol.* 8, 3 (Opitz, 94, 8-9).

[308]Rufinus, *HE* I, 17 (PL 21, 489B); Sozomen, *HE* II, 25, 20 (Bidez, 87, 10-11).

[309]*Apol.* 6, 6-7, 3 (Opitz, 92, 27-93, 26).

[310]*Apol.* 7, 1-2 (Opitz, 93, 16-21).

[311]*Cf. Apol.* 85, 7 (Opitz, 164, 5-11).

repeated the charge that Athanasius had ordered the breaking of the chalice and had overthrown an episcopal throne.[312] Furthermore, they alleged that Athanasius had arranged the earlier arrest and imprisonment of Ischyras, probably in AD 331/332, by Flavius Hyginus, the prefect of Egypt, on the false charge of desecrating images of the emperor.[313]

Callinicus, who had been with the Meletian delegation at Psamathia, complained that he had been deposed by Athanasius for reasons of conscience. The bishop of Pelusiam had been reconciled to the catholics under Alexander but had again taken up the Meletian cause sometime before the interview at Psamathia. He now claimed, however, that the reason for his deposition was that he had suspended communion with Athanasius until the bishop of Alexandria was cleared of charges related to the case of Ischyras. The result of this action, according to Callinicus, had been his arrest by the military followed by judicial torture while in custody. Athanasius meanwhile had replaced him in Pelusiam with Mark, who Callinicus claimed was a deposed priest.[314] Five other Meletian bishops, Euplus, Pachomius, Isaac, Achilleus, and Harmaeon, added to this indictment of violence and complained that they had been the objects of violent attacks by the Athanasians.[315]

During these initial proceedings, which centered upon the claims of Ischyras, the Meletian leader John Archaph remained silent, content to allow the Arian and Eusebian faction at the synod to press the Meletian case on his behalf.[316] Although Athanasius does not explicitly mention Archaph's status, the Egyptian bishops in AD 338/339 certainly imply that the Meletian leader's position in regard to the catholics had been regularized immediately before the time of Tyre.[317] Archaph's initial silence was perhaps owing to the consideration of a leadership role in the Egyptian church should Athanasius be deposed as a result of accusations which were being set forth.

---

[312]Sozomen, *HE* II, 25, 3 (Bidez, 84, 13-15).

[313]*Ibid.* (Bidez, 84, 16-17); *cf.* Barnes, *The New Empire,* 151, 152.

[314]Sozomen, *HE* II, 25, 4 (Bidez, 84, 18-23).

[315]Sozomen, *HE* II, 25, 5 (Bidez, 84, 23-25).

[316]*Apol.* 17, 3 (Opitz, 99, 31-100, 3).

[317]*Ibid.* There is, however, a seeming contradiction between the implication of the Egyptian bishops and the account of the Synod of Tyre given by Sozomen concerning the status of John Archaph. For although the *Letter of the Egyptian Bishops* AD 338/339 indicates that Archaph had been reconciled before the Synod of Tyre, Sozomen states that "John (Archaph) and his followers" were restored only at the conclusion of the synod, Sozomen, *HE* II, 25, 25 (Bidez, 86, 17-19). There appears to have been a policy, however, of recognizing such restorations in the public life of the church, as in a synod, although the restoration may have been effected at an earlier time. A similar case is presented in the persons of Arius and Euzoius at the Synod of Jerusalem which followed immediately after the main sessions of the Synod of Tyre.

Following this first recitation of alleged violence and intimidation, the Meletians put forward what they considered to be the primary cause for the past seven years of unrest in Egypt. Sozomen states, "They all agreed that" Athanasius "obtained the episcopate by means of the deceit of certain persons, it having been set forth that no one should receive ordination who could not clear himself of crimes brought against him."[318] Because they believed Athanasius to have been ordained illegally, the Meletians claimed that they separated from him and that the bishop of Alexandria had replied by means of violence and imprisonment.[319] Here again, it is clear that the Meletians were relying upon the canonical provisions of the Council of Nicaea in order to secure Athanasius's deposition.

The Arsenius affair was then raised once again by the Meletians. Sozomen indicates that Athanasius was surprised that many of his supposed friends became his accusers in regard to the missing bishop of Hypsele.[320] The Meletians certainly claimed popular support for their allegations. A document was presented to the synod which purported to contain public complaints from the people of Alexandria concerning Athanasius's conduct in regard to Arsenius.[321]

Athanasius and the Egyptian bishops then began the lengthy process of refuting the charges which had been presented.[322] Certain of the accusations were dealt with out of hand, while others were referred to future sessions of the synod.[323] In a dramatic gesture, Athanasius brought Arsenius out of hiding and presented him alive, with both arms, before the assembled bishops, asking his opponents to explain where they had secured their evidence of the severed limb in the wooden box.[324]

Perhaps suspecting that Athanasius would have access to Arsenius, his opponents had already framed their reply. They stated that Athanasius had ordered a suffragan bishop, Plusianus, to burn the house of Arsenius, and to arrest, imprison, and maltreat the bishop of Hypsele. Arsenius, however, had

---

[318] ... κοινῇ δὲ πάντες, ὡς δι ' ἐπιορκίας τινῶν εἰς τὴν ἐπισκοπὴν παρῆλθεν, συνθεμένων πάντων μηδένα χειροτονεῖ, πρὶν τὰ ἐν αὑτοῖς ἐγκλήματα διαλύσωσιν ...; Sozomen, HE II, 26, 6 (Bidez, 84, 25-27). Cf. section I.3.2 of this present study for a more in-depth discussion of the controversy concerning Athanasius's consecration and the involvement of the Meletians.

[319] Sozomen, HE II, 25, 6 (Bidez, 84, 27-29).

[320] Ibid. 25, 7 (Bidez, 85, 1-2).

[321] Ibid. 25, 7 (Bidez, 85, 3-4).

[322] Ibid. 25, 8ff., Sozomen includes a charge of fornication which seems to be apocryphal and was not included in the acts of synod of which he made use (ibid. 25, 11). In making use of this story there appears to be a dependence upon Rufinus (HE I, 17), who may well have copied the information from Gelasius, cf. Gwatkin, op. cit., 89, fn. 3.

[323] Sozomen, HE II, 25, 8 (Bidez, 85, 5-7).

[324] Ibid. 25, 10 (Bidez, 85, 17-23).

escaped from Plusianus and had gone into hiding. The Meletians concluded that he had been killed on the orders of Athanasius and, because Arsenius was well loved by his fellow bishops and had been a confessor, they had notified the magistrates.[325] The inclusion of Plusianus, who was probably a former Meletian, in their explanation concerning Arsenius, strengthens the argument that much of what took place in Tyre was the result of an extended rivalry between those Meletians who had regularized their relationship with Alexandria and those who had remained schismatic.[326]

With so many Egyptian bishops present, many of them former Meletians, Athanasius was able to show through the course of several sessions that the majority of the charges which had been brought against him were groundless. The structure of the synod and due regard for proper procedure, however, had already begun to break down. Dionysius, who may have regarded the assembly as little more than an imperial commission, began to use the troops which were present to maintain order and appears to have limited the scope of the debate.[327] As Arsenius was certainly alive and active in accusing his former brethren, and as the other issues had been set aside, all that remained was the case of Ischyras. Macarius had remained adamant in his denial of the charge and, presumably, Athanasius had presented the schedule of Meletian clergy from the time of Alexander to the synod, showing that Ischyras had not been ordained by Meletius and, therefore, was not a presbyter in the village of Secontarurus. The logical consequence of this evidence, at least for the Athanasians, was that Ischyras would not have, therefore, been in possession of a church and altar, much less an episcopal throne, and Macarius could not be accused of sacrilege in the matter of the chalice.

2.4 The Mareotic Commission, August/September AD 335

The Eusebians suggested to Dionysius that a commission of inquiry should be sent to the Mareotis to secure additional evidence. Athanasius considered such an undertaking to be "superfluous," perhaps because the bishop of the Mareotis, Agathammon (yet another former Meletian) was already present at the synod and was well acquainted with the case.[328] Nevertheless, Athanasius suggested that if such a commission was to be sent, its members should be impartial and, therefore, exclude those bishops

---

[325]*Ibid*. 25, 12 (Bidez, 85, 26-86, 4).

[326]*Apol*. 69, 2 (Opitz, 147, 21).

[327]*Apol*. 8, 3 (Opitz, 94, 11-13). Because of the letters which are exchanged between *comes Dionysius* and the members of the Synod of Tyre, Girardet has made the assumption that Dionysius was not actually present at the deliberations of the assembly in Tyre (*op. cit.*, 68). This approach must be regarded as incorrect in the light of the statements issued by the Egyptian bishops who were only three years distant from the event at the time of their encyclical letter in AD 338/339 which has been cited above.

[328]*Apol*. 72, 3 (Opitz, 151, 20-22).

who had already shown themselves to be hostile in regard to his own position. Although Athanasius believed that he had persuaded Dionysius to follow this course of action, the commission which was appointed included the very persons Athanasius had suggested should be excluded.[329]

Dionysius, rather than selecting the commission himself, had directed the synod to make the appointments by a unanimous vote, probably under the direction of Flacillus of Antioch rather than Eusebius of Caesarea, who had already come under attack from the Egyptians.[330]   The commission, probably elected by a simple majority vote of the accredited members of the synod (which excluded the greater portion of the Egyptian delegation), consisted of Theognis of Nicaea, Maris of Chalcedon, Theodorus of Heraclea (in Thrace), Macedonius of Mopsuestia (in Cilicia), Ursacius of Singidunum, and Valens of Mursa.[331]   All of the members were open Arian sympathizers and all were intractably opposed to Athanasius.   Although Ischyras, the complainant in the matter, accompanied the commission to Egypt as a material witness, Macarius, the accused party, was left in custody at Tyre. With a military guard at their disposal and a letter requesting the assistance of the prefect of Egypt in hand, they arrived in the Mareotis in late August AD 335.[332]

The proceedings of the commission in the Mareotis were openly biased and partisan.   As has been mentioned above, the prefect of Egypt, Philagrius, was no friend to the church in Alexandria.   He met the commission from Tyre and may have supplemented their military escort with other soldiers under his direct command.[333]   As the commission began its inquiries, a good number of Alexandrian presbyters and deacons made their way to the Mareotis in order to set forth evidence on behalf of Macarius and to "claim the right of being present at the investigation" since Athanasius's interests were not represented in its membership.[334]   Their presence, however, was not welcomed by the commission, and they were turned away.   In consequence, the sixteen presbyters and five deacons from Alexandria presented the commission with a written protest concerning their exclusion

---

[329]*Apol.* 72, 4 (Opitz, 151, 24-26).

[330]*Apol.* 81, 1-2 (Opitz, 161, 5-16).

[331]*Apol.* 72, 4 (Opitz, 151, 25-26).

[332]*Apol.* 72, 4-5 (Opitz, 151, 25-152, 1). The letter from the clergy of the Mareotis affirming their loyalty to Athanasius which was sent to Dionysius was dated 8 September AD 335. By the time the letter was sent, the Mareotic commission had already arrived in Egypt and was pursuing its investigation, *cf. Apol.* 76, 5 (Opitz, 156, 18).

[333]*Apol.* 83, 3 (Opitz, 162, 17).

[334]ἐπειδὴ δὲ οὔτε Μακάριον ἠγάγετε οὔτε ὁ αἰδεσιμώτατος ἡμῶν ἐπίσκοπος ᾽Αθανάσιος μεθ᾽ ὑμῶν εἰσῆλθεν, ἠξιώσαμεν κἂν αὐτοὶ παρεῖναι ἐν τῇ κρίσει, ἵνα παρόντων ἡμῶν ἀσφαλὴς ἡ ἐξέτασις γένηται καὶ πεισθῶμεν καὶ ἡμεῖς. ; *Apol.* 73, 2 (Opitz, 152, 15-18).

and, "so that it would not be kept secret," sent a further copy to the *curiosus* Flavius Palladius, presumably to be sent on to Constantine.[335]

Philagrius and the commissioners set to the task of interrogating witnesses within the region. The catholic presbyters and deacons of the Mareotis attempted to appear before the inquiry with the intention of presenting firsthand accounts of the incident involving Ischyras but were, like their Alexandrian colleagues, turned away.[336] As a result of this exclusion, the fifteen presbyters and fifteen deacons presented a written statement to Philagrius, Palladius, and Flavius Antoninus (a *biarchus* of the praetorian prefects), stating that Ischyras had been ordained invalidly by Colluthus and possessed no church, that no chalice had been broken, and that the whole story was false and an invention. Furthermore, they swore before almighty God and Constantine and his sons that this was the truth of the matter.[337]

The commission, however, had begun to use other methods to obtain information. According to Athanasius, they began to make use of duress and violence in order to gain the cooperation of witnesses.[338] Persons who would have had little, if any, knowledge of the affair, including catechumens (excluded from the offering of the oblation), Jews, and those outside the church, were persuaded to confirm the allegations against Athanasius and Macarius.[339] Nevertheless, contradictions remained apparent. It was learned that Macarius had visited the village on a weekday when the Eucharist would not have been celebrated.[340] Ischyras had not encountered Macarius at the time of the alleged incident, for he had been ill and in bed.[341] Even the witnesses against Athanasius, whom he had been accused of hiding, added information which helped to prove his innocence.[342]

The Mareotic clergy, witnessing the proceedings from a distance, wrote yet another letter, this one to the members of the synod in Tyre. In it they complained of "the conspiracy which has been formed against our bishop Athanasius" and the obvious bias of the commissioners in the Mareotis.[343] After again rehearsing the facts concerning the career of Ischyras and condemning the methods of the commissioners, the letter ended by encouraging the members of the synod to consider that there will also "be a

---

[335]*Apol.* 72, 4 (Opitz, 152, 23-153, 1).

[336]*Apol.* 74, 3 (Opitz, 154, 27-28).

[337]*Apol.* 76, 1-5 (Opitz, 155, 34-156, 18).

[338]*Apol.* 83, 3 (Opitz, 162, 16-18).

[339]*Apol.* 72, 6 (Opitz, 152, 5-6); *Apol.* 31, 1 (Opitz, 110, 9).

[340]*Apol.* 11, 5 (Opitz, 96, 24-25).

[341]*Apol.* 83, 2 (Opitz, 162, 8-9).

[342]*Apol.* 83, 3 (Opitz, 162, 13-16).

[343]... μάλιστα ὅτι ἀναγκαίαν ἡμῶν ἐποίησεν εἶναι τὴν μαρτυρίαν ἡ γενομένη συσκευὴ κατὰ τοῦ ἐπισκόπου ἡμῶν ᾽Αθανασίου., *Apol.* 74, 2 (Opitz, 153, 31-32).

judgment held by God."[344]   The commission itself, having completed its inquiry, began the journey back to Tyre, probably during the latter portion of September AD 335.[345]

2.5 The Judgment at Tyre, October AD 335

While the Mareotic commission was holding its enquiry in Egypt, protests against their conduct and the procedures followed by the synod were being mounted in Tyre. Athanasius lodged a complaint with Dionysius concerning the composition of the commission.[346]   The forty-seven Egyptian bishops at Tyre delivered a petition to the assembled bishops in which they described the Mareotic commission as having been selected "without our consent"[347] and as having sent out couriers in order to bring Meletians into the Mareotis to testify against Athanasius.[348]   They followed this communication with an almost identical letter to Dionysius and, finally, with a third petition in which they made a formal appeal that the case be referred to the emperor himself.[349]   When Alexander of Thessalonica had been informed as to the biased actions of the commission, he likewise wrote to Dionysius warning him that a conspiracy had been formed against Athanasius which involved the Arians, the Meletians, and the Colluthians regarding the future of the Egyptian church.[350]   For his part, Dionysius wrote to the Eusebians and informed them that both Alexander and Athanasius had questioned the procedural conduct of the synod. He also provided them with a copy of the letter from Alexander, with the warning

---

[344]*Apol.* 75, 5 (Opitz, 154, 36).

[345]Athanasius implies that before returning to Tyre, the commission first went to Alexandria as guests of the prefect Philagrius: Καὶ τίνα τὰ παρ' αὐτῶν εἰς τὴν 'Αλεξάνδρειαν τολμηθέντα, νομίζομεν ὑμᾶς μὴ ἀγνοεῖν, πανταχοῦ γὰρ διαδέδοται.. ; *Apol.* 15, 1 (Opitz, 98, 29-30). In Athanasius's description of the "outrages" which were committed, the bishop of Alexandria indicates that the crowds were used by Philagrius and the bishops as an instrument of intimidation against the catholics in the city, especially against the ἁγίων παρθένων καὶ τῶν ἀδελφῶν. This account is ignored by T.D. Barnes in his description of the events surrounding the Synod of Tyre (Barnes, *Constantine and Eusebius*, 236-239) despite its importance for understanding the later flight of Athanasius to appear before the emperor in Constantinople. For a full account of the incidents in Alexandria, *cf. Apol.* 15, 1ff. (Opitz, 98, 29-99, 9).

[346]*Apol.* 81, 1 (Opitz, 161, 6-8).

[347]*Apol.* 77, 6 (Opitz, 157, 20-21).

[348]*Apol.* 77, 5 (Opitz, 157, 10-12).

[349]*Cf. Apol.* 78, 1ff. (Opitz, 158, 1-159, 48). καὶ γὰρ εὔλογον ἀποσταλέντα σε παρὰ τῆς βασιλείας αὐτοῦ καὶ ἡμῶν ἐπικαλεσαμένων τὴν εὐσέβειαν αὐτοῦ αὐτῷ τηρῆσαι τὸ πρᾶγμα., ; *Apol.* 79, 2 (Opitz, 160, 8-9).

[350]*Apol.* 80, 1ff. (Opitz, 160, 21-161, 4).

that care should be taken not to provide grounds for an appeal by the accused parties.[351]

The majority of the bishops in Tyre had, early in September, made their way to Jerusalem for the dedication of the Church of the Holy Sepulchre and an enlarged synodal gathering which formally readmitted Arius and Euzoius (and others of their party) to the communion of the church.[352] The unity of the church, which Constantine had longed for, was now almost completely accomplished. Following a week of celebrations which lasted from 13 to 20 September AD 335, the bishops reassembled in Tyre to hear the report of the Mareotic commission and to pass judgment on Athanasius. The bishop of Alexandria, however, had already fled. Sozomen indicates that Athanasius had, sometime earlier, been forced to withdraw from the public sessions of the synod owing to the unruliness of the proceedings and fears for his safety on the part of the authorities.[353] It is likely that, following the appeal to the emperor which the Egyptian bishops had submitted to Dionysius, Athanasius had decided (or was convinced) to make his way from Tyre to appear before the emperor in Constantinople, probably departing before the synod reconvened to hear the report of the commission.[354]

In his absence, the synod considered the report of the Mareotic commission. The full report of the commission doubtless contained a large number of irregularities and inconsistencies which were omitted from the formal summary presented to the synod, although Julius, the bishop of Rome, would later make use of these omissions in his defense of Athanasius.[355] The particular charge which continued to receive the greatest attention was the destruction of the chalice of Ischyras, which was attested to by the leading members of the commission.[356] The accusations surrounding the treatment of Arsenius were passed over in silence.[357] Athanasius was thereupon condemned by the synod, deposed from his episcopate, and forbidden to return to Alexandria in order that further divisions and disturbances might be avoided.[358]

---

[351]*Apol.* 81, 1ff. (Opitz, 161, 5-16).

[352]Sozomen, *HE* II, 27, 1ff. (Bidez, 88, 4-91, 2). For further elaboration on the reception of Arius and Euzoius at the Synod of Jerusalem, *cf.* Williams, *Arius, op. cit.,* 79. *Cf.* Schwartz, *GS* III, *op. cit.,* 247ff.

[353]Sozomen, *HE* II, 25, 13 (Bidez, 86, 6-12).

[354]Τούτων οὕτω πραττομένων ἀνεχωρήσαμεν ἀπ᾽ αὐτῶν ὡς ᾽ἀπὸ συνόδου τῶν ἀθετούντων· ἃ γὰρ ἐβούλοντο, ταῦτα καὶ ἔπραττον. ὅτι μὲν οὖν τὰ πραττόμενα κατὰ μονομέρειαν οὐδεμίαν ἔχει δύναμιν, οὐδείς ἐστιν, ὅστις ἀγνοεῖ τῶν πάντων ἀνθρώπων., ; *Apol.* 82, 1 (Opitz, 161, 17-19).

[355]*Cf. Apol.* 27, 3ff. (Opitz, 107, 13-27); 83, 4 (Opitz, 162, 18ff.).

[356]Sozomen, *HE* II, 25, 19 (Bidez, 87, 2).

[357]Socrates, *HE* I , 32 (PG 67, 164B).

[358]Sozomen, *HE* II, 25, 15 (Bidez, 86, 14-17).

Sozomen reports that following this sentence of deposition "John [Archaph] and his followers were reinstated in fellowship. . . and each was placed again in his own clerical rank."[359] This, however, would seem to be somewhat of an anomaly, as John had earlier been received by the emperor and, perhaps, temporarily by Athanasius. Socrates, while not mentioning John Archaph, states that Arsenius was restored to communion.[360] Again, such a report is probably unfounded, as Arsenius had already been reconciled to Athanasius before the synodal sessions at Tyre. In both instances the intent of the historians appears to be intertwined with the polemical device of showing the contrast between the reception of Athanasius's accusers while the bishop himself is unjustly condemned. Nevertheless, it is possible that the bishops at Tyre did make a special effort to affirm publicly the validity of the clerical status of the Meletians who were in attendance at the synod.

An account of the proceedings and the subsequent judgment of the assembled bishops was prepared and sent to Constantine.[361] Further, a similar account of the actions of the synod was included in a circular letter which was sent to "the bishops of all regions" enjoining them not to receive Athanasius in fellowship or to communicate with him by letter.[362] Both of these letters contained and affirmed the multitude of charges that had been brought against Athanasius both before and after his flight from Tyre. Included in the list of accusations was the particular indictment that Athanasius has disobeyed the emperor by his failure to appear at Caesarea the previous year. The inclusion of this charge, which apparently had not been raised during the general sessions of the synod, appears to have been a blatant attempt on the part of the pro-Arian bishops to contrast Athanasius's disobedience to Constantine's wishes with Arius's recent submission. Sozomen's summary of the synodal letter of condemnation is as follows:

> They also declared in this letter that they had been forced to bring this condemnation upon him [*i.e.,* Athanasius] because when commanded by the emperor the preceding year to appear before the eastern bishops who were gathered at Caesarea, he disobeyed the summons, kept the bishops waiting for him, and set aside the commands of the ruler. They also stated that when the bishops had assembled at Tyre, he went to the city intending to cause disturbances and riots at the synod, bringing with him a large retinue for this purpose; that when there he often refused to reply to the accusations brought against him, insulted individual bishops, and when called before them he sometimes obeyed, and at other times did not allow himself to be judged. In the same

---

[359]Sozomen, *HE* II, 25, 15 (Bidez, 86, 17-19).
[360]Socrates, *HE* I, 32 (PG 67, 164B).
[361]Sozomen, *HE* II, 25, 16 (Bidez, 86, 19-22).
[362]*Ibid.*

letter they specifically stated that he was without doubt guilty of having broken a sacred cup . . .[363]

The language used in this declaration of guilt was intended to be inflammatory, and only two specific items are mentioned. First, and probably most importantly, Athanasius is presented as one who willfully disobeyed Constantine's summons to appear at Caesarea. Second, the accusation concerning the chalice of Ischyras is specified. The other portions of the letter are devoted to presenting the bishop of Alexandria as being a disruptive individual within the life of the church, this being exemplified by his unwillingness to accept the actions of his opponents at the synod. The lack of substance in their verdict and the absence of Athanasius at its pronouncement clearly indicated that the matter of the bishop's ultimate fate was not yet fully decided. Further, in the presence of the Egyptian bishops, Marcellus of Ancyra, and other "pro-Athanasian" bishops, the verdict, despite Constantine's later assertion to Antony the Hermit, could scarcely have been unanimous.

2.6 The Flight to Constantinople and Exile, November AD 335

The circumstances and manner of Athanasius's flight from Tyre has remained, despite numerous studies, a vexed question. The Egyptian bishops, writing within half a decade after the event, state that, "the *comes* threatened" Athanasius "with violence and was excited against him; the bishop fled from this violence and went before the most religious emperor" in order to protest against the actions of Dionysius and the synod at Tyre.[364] Athanasius himself wrote that the decision to go before the emperor was made after the initial protests by Alexander of Thessalonica and the Egyptian bishops had been presented to Dionysius and had, apparently, been set aside: "While matters were proceeding in this manner, we withdrew from them, as from a gathering of duplicitous men, for they did whatever they wished, and there is no man in the world who does not know that proceedings favoring a single party cannot be upheld as good."[365]

The placement of this passage precedes Athanasius's recapitulation of the proceedings at Tyre and his narrative of the reception of the Arians in Jerusalem. From the context of his account it has been assumed that Athanasius secretly departed Tyre during the last days of August or the early part of September.[366] Although no exact date for his departure has been

---

[363]Sozomen, *HE* II, 25, 17-19a (Bidez, 86, 23-87, 3).

[364]*Apol.* 9, 2 (Opitz, 95, 4-8).

[365]*Apol.* 82, 1 (Opitz, 161, 17-19).

[366]*Cf.* P. Peeters, "Comment s. Athanase s'enfuit de Tyr en 335," *Bulletin de la classe des lettres de l'Academie royale de Belgique* 30 (1944): 148ff.; and "L'Epilogue du Synode de Tyr en 335," *Anal Boll* 63 (1945): 133-134; Epiphanius, *Haer.* 68, 9, 4.

established, it is known that Athanasius arrived in Constantinople on 30 October AD 335.[367] This dating, however, presents some difficulties. The journey from Tyre to the port of Gaza, which constitutes a distance similar to the trip from Tyre to Constantinople, took only about twenty days. Athanasius's journey, however, is approximated as having lasted fully two months.

This inconsistency has encouraged a perhaps overly dramatic reconstruction of events on the part of certain scholars. For example, P. Peeters, building upon the evidence marshaled by E. Schwartz, suggests that the length of the voyage had much to do with Athanasius's mode of transportation. Peeters translates the Syriac *tophā* within the narrative of the *Festal Letter Index* VIII as "raft" and opines that Athanasius found "a timber raft floating . . . in the port" and made his way out of the harbor, "resembling a prisoner making his escape."[368] T.D. Barnes has followed this tradition and evokes an even greater sense of adventure when he states that "Athanasius fled from Tyre in an open boat and under the cover of darkness, evading the soldiers who doubtless patrolled the harbor."[369] A. Martin is certainly correct in suggesting that "it is perhaps not necessary to dramatize any further the sailing from Tyre of which we do not know the date as surely as that of the arrival at Constantinople."[370]

In any case, there are certain difficulties with these dramatic reconstructions, and other possible explanations should be brought forward. It is clear from the account of Sozomen that the first withdrawal of Athanasius from the sessions of the Synod of Tyre was at the instigation of "the officers who had been appointed by the emperor," who were concerned for the safety of the bishop.[371] In this narrative, Athanasius's flight from Tyre immediately follows his removal from the proceedings by these officers. R.I. Frank, in his study of the *scholae palatinae*, writes that

> when questions of security and order arose it was quite natural for *scholares* to be used.
> Security was most notably a problem at the Council of Tyre, undoubtedly the most disorderly—one might even say uproarious—of all the councils. . . . Dionysius had at his command a detachment of soldiers. They are variously called "military guards," "foreigners" (that is, *gentiles*), "an imperial detachment," and "those whom the emperor had sent to maintain order." It is clear that they were imperial guards.
> Events showed that the guards were needed. . . . The bishops hostile to Athanasius were so incensed . . . that they attacked him in a

---

[367]*Festal Letter Index* VIII (*Histoire*, A. Martin, 233).

[368]*Ibid.*; Peeters, "L'Epilogue," *op. cit.*, 134-135.

[369]Barnes, *Constantine and Eusebius*, 239.

[370]*Histoire*, A. Martin, 284.

[371]Sozomen, *HE* II, 25, 13 (Bidez, 86, 5-12).

body, and only the intervention of the guards on duty saved the patriarch from a violent death. The officers in charge took him out of the hall by a secret exit and that night sent him away on board a ship in order to avoid further danger.[372]

Is it then possible to postulate that Athanasius's flight from Tyre was not that of an escaping prisoner, but rather of one who was sent to Constantinople in some manner of protective custody? Certainly, the adventurous escape on a raft or small open boat becomes even more problematic when Athanasius states that five Egyptian bishops, Adamantius, Anubion, Agathammon, Arbethion, and Peter, all of whom had been at Tyre, were present at Constantinople, having apparently accompanied him on his journey.[373] If the sessions of the synod had, in fact, been suspended to allow the bishops to make their way to the celebrations in Jerusalem (13-20 September) it may be possible to suggest that Athanasius and his companions left Tyre under the protection of Dionysius at about the same time. The length of the journey would thereby be shortened to about forty days or less and would allow for Athanasius's retinue traveling with him.

Admittedly, such a revisioning of these tangled and ill-reported events is hypothetical, but one may note that in the later letter of Constantine II which restored Athanasius to his see, the reason imputed to Constantine for the bishop's exile was one of protection from his enemies.[374] Despite later assertions to the contrary, one may, therefore, possibly question whether or not Athanasius's flight from Tyre was under the protection of imperial authority and may have provided the genesis for what has always been considered a face-saving literary device. If this is allowed as a possibility, the account in the letter of Constantine II may be seen as something other than a polite fiction.

When Athanasius and his companions arrived in Constantinople during the latter portion of October, Constantine was not in the city. The emperor appears to have left the capital for Nicopolis on or about 21 October and returned to Constantinople, according to A. Martin's calculations, on 30 October, whereupon he encountered Athanasius.[375] Athanasius had most

---

[372]R.I. Frank, *Scholae Palatinae: The Palace Guards of the Later Roman Empire,* Papers and Monographs of the American Academy in Rome, Vol. 23, Rome, 1969, 116-117.

[373]*Apol.* 87, 2 (Opitz, 166, 4-6). For the presence of these bishops in Tyre before accompanying Athanasius on the journey to Constantinople, *cf. Apol.* 78, 7 (Opitz, 159, 1, 4, 13, 17, and 22).

[374]*Apol.* 87, 4-7 (Opitz, 166, 11-29).

[375]*Festal Letter Index* VIII (*Histoire,* A. Martin, 234-235). T.D. Barnes, however, holds to the traditional interpretation of the Index and contends that Athanasius arrived in the capital on 30 October AD 335 and did not see the emperor until 7 November, with the Eusebian party from Tyre arriving within

probably been apprised of the time and place of the emperor's return, for as Constantine entered the city on horseback, the bishop of Alexandria and his companions blocked the way and approached the emperor in "the middle of the road." Athanasius's appearance was such that Constantine did not recognize him at first. It is likely that the bishop had dressed himself in mourning and, although he later attempted by editing to downplay his pitiable condition, it is clear that he presented himself as a wronged and utterly dependant supplicant in the emperor's presence.[376]

After the emperor's attendants had ascertained the bishop's identity and complaint, however, Constantine refused to grant Athanasius a personal hearing and came close to having the bishop forcibly removed from the roadway. At the last moment, Athanasius declared that he asked only one favor, that he might make his complaint to the emperor in the presence of the bishops from Tyre who had wronged him. Constantine relented: "As this appeared to me to be a reasonable request, I commanded this letter to be written to you," the bishops at Tyre, "so that all of you who made up the synod which was held at Tyre might quickly and without delay come to the court of my clemency, in order to prove by evidence that you have passed an impartial and sound judgment."[377]

Constantine was apparently as yet uncertain as to what had transpired at Tyre and does not seem to have been in possession of the synodal letter of condemnation. By making use of Martin's calculations, we know that Athanasius could have had several days in which to convince Constantine that he had been unjustly dealt with at Tyre. What happened next is uncertain, but it is argued by some, like Peeters and Barnes, that Eusebius of Nicomedia, accompanied by Theognis, Patrophilus, Eusebius of Caesarea, Ursacius, and Valens, arrived in the capital on 6 November, the very day that

---

hours of this initial interview (*The New Empire*, 79; *Constantine and Eusebius*, 240).

[376]Athanasius's editing of Constantine's description of the encounter is evident when *Apol.* 86, 6 (Opitz, 165, 5-8) is compared with the record preserved in Gelasius, *HE* III, 18, 4. The two accounts are as follows:

... ἐπιβαίνοντί μοι λοιπὸν τῆς ἐπωνύμου ἡμῶν καὶ πανευδαίμονος πατρίδος τῆς Κωνσταντινουπόλεως (συνέβαινε δὲ τηνικαῦτα ἐφ᾽ ἵππου ὀχεῖσθαι) ἐξαίφνης 'Αθανάσιος ὁ ἐπίσκοπος ἐν μέσῃ τῇ λεωφόρῳ μετὰ ἑτέρων τινῶν, οὕς περὶ αὐτὸν εἶχεν ... (*Apol.* 86, 6).

... εἰσιόντι μοι ἀπὸ προκέσσου ἐπὶ τὴν ἐπώνυμον ἡμῶν καὶ πανευδαίμονα Κωνσταντινούπολιν πρόσεισιν ἐν μέσῳ τῆς λεωφόρου ... (Gelasius, *HE* III, 18, 4).

For further comments on these passages, *cf.* N.H. Baynes, "Athanasiana," *JEA* 11 (1925): 61ff.

[377]*Apol.* 86, 9 (Opitz, 165, 16-20).

Constantine was preparing his letter.[378]   This convenient and dramatic scenario, however, is based entirely on circumstantial evidence.

The *Festal Letter Index* VIII informs us that Athanasius arrived in the capital on 30 October but had to wait eight days before presenting himself before Constantine, that is, until 6 November. The *Index* also indicates that Athanasius was sent into exile on the following day, 7 November.[379] Although G.R. Sievers argued that this date is incorrect and should be amended to 5 February AD 336, the transmitted date of 7 November AD 335 has been defended well by P. Peeters and is consistent with the witness of the *Acephale,* which indicates that the duration of Athanasius's first exile was twenty-eight months and eleven days, a time which corresponds with the bishop's banishment from the capital on this day.[380]   If Sievers is indeed incorrect, and the circumstantial evidence does seem to indicate that this is the case, it must be allowed that the Eusebian party was probably already present in the capital on 6/7 November.

A. Martin, however, has argued that 30 October was the date of Athanasius's first meeting with Constantine "and not the date of his arrival in the capital, as the *Index* would have us to believe."[381] This would allow for a period of several days, during which Athanasius might have met with the emperor and the letter of Constantine could have been prepared for dispatch. Within this first week of November, the Eusebian party from Tyre could also have arrived and learned of what was taking place.   Although somewhat less dramatic, such a sequence does seem somewhat more realistic.

It is slightly less puzzling, therefore, why Athanasius indicates that Eusebius and his confederates had read the letter of Constantine prior to their journey to the capital and prevented any other bishops than themselves from attending upon the emperor.[382]   Athanasius's narrative simply compresses events past the point of chronological accuracy. The subsequent actions of the Eusebians at court would have certainly convinced Athanasius that they had been informed beforehand of the contents of Constantine's letter. Had the Eusebians been in the capital for even a few days, it is difficult to believe that they would not have had access to such information. Such knowledge, however, could only have been obtained after their arrival in Constantinople.

It is entirely likely that T.D. Barnes is correct in his assertion that, by the time of Athanasius's arrival in Constantinople, the six Eusebian bishops were already enroute to the capital bearing the synodal letter of condemnation

---

[378]Barnes, *Constantine and Eusebius, op. cit.,* 240; Peeters, "L'Epilogue," *op. cit.,* 137.

[379]*Festal Letter Index* VIII (*Histoire,* A. Martin, 233).

[380]G.R. Sievers, "*Athanasii Vita Acephala:* Ein Beitrag zur Geschichte des Athanasius," *Zeitschrift für historische Theologie* 38 (1868): 98; *cf.* Peeters, "Comment," *op. cit.,* 166ff., and *Histoire,* A. Martin, 285, note 24.

[381]*Histoire,* A. Martin, 285, note 22b.

[382]*Apol.* 87, 1 (Opitz, 165, 36-166, 2).

from Tyre in order to deliver it in person to the emperor.[383]   If, as E. Schwartz suggests, the final session of Tyre took place after the Synod of Jerusalem (13-20 September), Eusebius and his companions could easily have left Tyre during the early portion of October and made the twenty days' journey to Constantinople, with their arrival falling within the first week of November, that is, a short time after Athanasius's first meeting with Constantine.[384]   That they carried with them the letter from the Synod of Tyre may be indicated by Athanasius when he specifically states within the context of the passage relating their arrival in the capital that "they no longer said anything about the cup and Arsenius," having perceived that the situation had now changed.[385]

According to Barnes, the change that had taken place was that the emperor had ordered the bishops from Tyre to reassemble in Constantinople and "by implication, therefore, Constantine annulled the decisions already made by the council."[386]   This view contrasts to that of K. Girardet, who contends that Athanasius's exile subsequent to his last interview with Constantine was the emperor's legal "execution of the judgment of Tyre."[387] Each of these views presupposes that the Synod of Tyre possessed a substantially more than advisory authority. Whatever the true extent of this authority was, however, subsequent events show clearly that Constantine considered the judgment of the synod to be subject to his review and, as matters transpired, all of the primary sources appear to be in agreement that Athanasius's banishment was based upon an accusation which had not been brought forward at Tyre or included in the synodal letter of condemnation. To this extent it would seem that Barnes is substantially closer to the truth of the matter in his assertion that Constantine annulled the judgment which had been promulgated by the synod.

Both Socrates and Sozomen, while following the chronologically inaccurate narrative of Athanasius, indicate the consternation of the bishops at Tyre over the setting aside of their judgment by the emperor.[388]   Socrates indicates that the Eusebians who journeyed to the capital decided not "to allow any further inquiry . . . concerning the broken cup, the overthrown altar, or the killing of Arsenius," that is, those very charges included in the synodal letter of condemnation.[389]   Sozomen, however, while emphasizing the fear of the bishops at Tyre over the emperor's reversal, claims that the

---

[383]Barnes, *Constantine and Eusebius, op. cit.*, 239.

[384]Schwartz, *GS* III, 247ff.

[385]*Apol.* 87, 1, *loc. cit.*

[386]Barnes, *Constantine and Eusebius, op. cit.*, 240.

[387]Girardet, *Kaisergericht und Bischofsgericht, op. cit.*, 73.

[388]Socrates, *HE* I, 35, 1 (PG 67, 169C); Sozomen, *HE* II, 28, 13 (Bidez, 93, 5-8).

[389]Socrates, *loc. cit.*

Eusebians who had made their way to Constantinople simply added a further accusation to those which had been advanced at the synod.[390]

With the original synodal condemnation of Athanasius now, for all intents and purposes, set aside and the emperor requiring the recall of the bishops to a new session in Constantinople, Eusebius of Nicomedia and the other five bishops decided upon a new course of action. In an interview with Constantine, probably on 6 November, at which the pro-Athanasian Egyptian bishops were also present, they accused the bishop of Alexandria of treason.[391] The substance of the charge was that Athanasius had threatened to prevent the transportation of grain from Egypt to Constantinople.[392]

Whether Athanasius was given the opportunity to answer this charge is uncertain. When the bishop of Alexandria related the incident almost twenty years after the event, he stated that the emperor "was quickly angered, and instead of allowing me a hearing, he sent me away into Gaul."[393] In the letter of the Egyptian bishops, however, written only three years after the confrontation, Athanasius seems to be present when the accusation is made by Eusebius of Nicomedia, for upon hearing the charge he wept and cried out that he was incapable of making such a threat as he was a poor man without such power in his position.[394] Eusebius's rejoinder, as recorded in this narrative, was to repeat publicly the charge and state that Athanasius was a rich and powerful man who was able to do anything.[395] Epiphanius relates that Athanasius was indeed present and ordered by Constantine to answer this new accusation. In the course of the interview, according to this account, both Constantine and Athanasius became increasingly angry until, at the last, the bishop of Alexandria invoked divine judgment and stated that God would decide between them.[396]

Taking these accounts together, it seems likely that Athanasius was present for at least some portion of this final interview with Constantine. When Athanasius states that he was sent into exile without a hearing, it may be that the bishop had requested a formal session before the emperor in which he would have had the opportunity to advance evidence on his behalf in order to disprove the accusation. Clearly, no such formal enquiry took place. It may also be noted that while the letter of the Egyptian bishops included Athanasius's emotional denials, the bishop himself makes no mention of the scene. The description of Epiphanius, while the most dramatic and likely

---

[390]Sozomen, *HE* II, 28, 13 (Bidez, 93, 5-10).

[391]*Apol.* 87, 1-2 (Opitz, 165, 36-166, 6).

[392]*Ibid.*; *Apol.* 9, 4 (Opitz, 95, 14-20).

[393]*Apol.* 87, 2 (Opitz, 166, 6-8).

[394]... γὰρ ἂν ἰδιώτης ἄνθρωπος καὶ πένης τηλικαῦτα δύναιτο; *Apol.* 9, 4 (Opitz, 95, 15-16).

[395]... πλούσιον καὶ δυνατὸν καὶ ἱκανὸν πρὸς πάντα; *Apol.* 9, 4 (Opitz, 95, 17).

[396]Epiphanius, *Haer.* 68, 9, 5 (PG 42, 197D).

conveying the spirit of the encounter, is without corroboration as to the details presented.

All of the narratives agree on one point in particular, the anger of Constantine. Whether this anger was owing to exasperation or the provocation of Athanasius or Eusebius will likely remain an unanswered question. What is certain, however, is that Constantine acted decisively. No further trial was held. No further synod was called to consider the matter. Athanasius was not even formally deposed as the bishop of Alexandria but was banished to Trier in Gaul. On 7 November AD 335, almost immediately after this last interview, Athanasius set sail from Constantinople, possibly making his way to Trier by way of Rome.[397]

What then was the reason for Athanasius's first exile? All of the narratives agree that the primary cause of Constantine's anger had to do, in one way or another, with the alleged threat of Athanasius concerning the delay of grain shipments from Alexandria to Constantinople. According to Socrates, Constantine had issued a daily allowance of eighty thousand measures of grain to the citizens of the capital. He further states that this grain was brought directly from Alexandria.[398] The delay or impeding of these shipments would have been a disaster of the first rank for Constantine's fledgling capital. At very nearly the same time as Athanasius's first exile, another incident took place which illustrates the importance that Constantine placed upon these regular deliveries from Egypt. Barnes describes the incident as follows:

> Sopater, a pupil of Iamblichus, had frequented the court of Licinius; he came to the court of Constantine after his master's death. Despite Sopater's paganism, the emperor held him in high esteem, conversed long with him, and used him as an adviser when conducting public business. However, one autumn the grain ships were delayed by the weather, and the hungry crowd in the hippodrome evinced its displeasure with the emperor. Sopater's enemies pounced. They accused the philosopher of fettering the winds. Constantine condemned Sopater to be beheaded (perhaps about the same time as Athanasius's enemies secured his removal by accusing him of threatening the grain supply).[399]

From the account related above, it is perhaps easier to understand what might otherwise appear to be merely a rhetorical remark in the letter of the Egyptian bishops written three years later, which states that "the grace of God ...

---

[397]Cf. C. Pietri, "La Question d'Athanase vue de Rome," *Politique et théologie,* 96.

[398]Socrates, *HE* II, 13, 5 (PG 67, 209A).

[399]Barnes, *Constantine and Eusebius, op. cit.,* 253.

moved the pious emperor to mercy for he sentenced" Athanasius "to banishment instead of death."[400]

It is known that Athanasius did have control over some grain supplies in Egypt which Constantine had allocated to the bishops of Egypt and Libya for the support of widows and the poor. The bishop of Alexandria as metropolitan most probably supervised the distribution of this supply. There were past allegations by his enemies that Athanasius had been involved in the illegal sale of this grain, but these accusations had been dismissed.[401] In any case, the amount of grain involved would have been very small in comparison to the shipments bound for the capital. In a slightly different connection, H.G. Opitz opined that Athanasius maintained a particular influence among the sailors and dockworkers of Alexandria.[402] It is, however, difficult to connect either his control of a charitable stock of grain or his possible popularity at the Alexandrian docks with the ability to prevent the regular shipments from Egypt to the capital.

When considering Athanasius's actual power with regard to his extensive see, it should also be remembered that the bishop, while in Tyre, was unable to influence or to control the activities of the Mareotic commission either in the hinterlands of lower Egypt or in Alexandria itself. Furthermore, it is difficult to believe that after so many interviews with the emperor in which Athanasius was able to turn the tables on his enemies by persuasion, he would have resorted to threats, such as the one which has been alleged, as a means of bargaining or escape. If, however, the case of Athanasius is compared with that of Sopater, it seems possible that the emperor may only have needed to believe that Athanasius could influence the shipments (or to have claimed such ability) in order to be moved to pronounce a sentence of banishment upon the bishop. In either case, there is no evidence apart from the Eusebian accusation that Athanasius actually conspired to cause such delays or threatened to do so. At this particular time, given Athanasius's weakened position, such a course of action seems very unlikely.

There is, however, another possible cause for Constantine's banishment of Athanasius. Socrates states that "some affirm that the emperor came to this decision in order to establish unity in the church," which would have been impossible since Athanasius refused to accept the readmission of Arius and his companions.[403] Sozomen echoes this assertion but comments that it is uncertain whether or not the emperor believed any of the accusations or simply imagined that "unity would be restored among the bishops if Athanasius were removed."[404] Considering

---

[400]*Apol.* 9, 4 (Opitz, 95, 18-20).

[401]*Apol.* 18, 1-2 (Opitz, 100, 25-32).

[402]*Ep. encycl.* 5, 5 (Opitz, 175, note to line 5).

[403]Socrates, *HE* I, 35, 1 (PG 67, 171A).

[404]Sozomen, *HE* II, 28, 14 (Bidez, 93, 11-13).

the crime(s) with which Athanasius was accused, mere banishment to a provincial capital with the retention of his dignity as a bishop was slight punishment. The sentence in itself may argue that Constantine was convinced less of the bishop's wrongdoing than of his being an impediment to structural unity within the church.

Such a view might be strengthened by the fact that the anti-Athanasian Meletian faction also experienced a substantial defeat after Tyre. Sozomen reports that following the banishment of Athanasius the Egyptian church became factionalized, with some supporting Athanasius while the Meletians had apparently put forward John Archaph as the *de facto* bishop of Alexandria. When Constantine became aware of this situation, he immediately exiled the Meletian leader, imposing upon him the same sentence of banishment which had been received by Athanasius. The reason given by the historian was that the emperor was unwilling to receive the requests or petitions of "any person who was suspected of causing dissension or strife" within the Christian community.[405] Sozomen, by way of an editorial comment, also relates that the decrees of the Synod of Tyre "did not bring any benefits" to John Archaph and, by implication, the Meletian community in Egypt.[406] Such a statement lends greater weight to the view that the decrees of Tyre were never recognized by either Constantine or a good many others within the church as being binding or conclusive. Furthermore, although Constantine would enjoin Antony the Hermit not to "overlook the decrees of the synod" of Tyre in regard to Athanasius, it is clear that the emperor himself treated them very lightly in practice, if, in fact, he took them into account at all.[407]

Athanasius himself would later contend that Constantine had banished him so that he would be protected from the hostility and hatred of his enemies. It is important, however, to note that he makes this claim first in connection with the letter of Constantine II which was written on the occasion of the bishop's return from his first exile, 17 June AD 337, and second in connection with his contention that Constantine did not exile him in order to please the Eusebians, for the emperor did not replace him as the bishop of Alexandria with a candidate of their choice.[408] In each case the emphasis has been placed upon the decision of the emperor alone over against the so-called judgment of the Synod of Tyre. Moreover, the fact that Constantine did not accede to the wishes of the Eusebian bishops in regard to the vacant see of Alexandria may indicate that the exile of Athanasius was intended by the emperor to be a temporary measure, as stated by Constantine

---

[405]Sozomen, *HE* II, 31, 4-5 (Bidez, 96, 20-29).

[406]... καὶ οὐδὲν ὤνησεν ’Ιωάννην τὰ δεδογμένα τοῖς ἐν Τύρῳ συνεληλυθόσι; Sozomen, *HE* II, 31, 5 (Bidez, 96, 26-27).

[407]Sozomen, *HE* II, 31, 3 (Bidez, 96, 14-18).

[408]*Apol.* 88, 1-3 (Opitz, 167, 1-10); *Hist. arian.* 50, 2 (Opitz, 212, 4-9).

II in his letter.[409] The possibility remains, as has been stated above, that Athanasius was removed from Tyre for his own protection. In the intense polemical atmosphere which surrounded his return from exile and continued into future years, this explanation may well have been extended by the bishop and his supporters to cover the whole of the first exile.

The fact remains that the see of Alexandria did remain vacant throughout Athanasius's first exile. In addition to the intrusion of John Archaph, it is possible that Secundus of Ptolemais, following his own restoration, attempted to consecrate Pistus, an Arian presbyter of Alexandria, as bishop in Athanasius's stead.[410] E. Schwartz, however, is of the opinion that Pistus was only made bishop of the Mareotis, although this seems unlikely, as Ischyras appears to have been elevated to this honor as a reward for his service at Tyre.[411] In any case, Pistus does not seem to have been recognized by either his fellow clergy or the imperial authorities and soon fades from view. Although banished to "the ends of the earth" in Trier, Athanasius remained the bishop of Alexandria, notwithstanding the actions of the Synod of Tyre.[412]

From all of the evidence gathered above, it is not unreasonable to conclude that the banishment of Athanasius by Constantine was not a direct result of the charges brought against him at Tyre, much less of the synodal letter of condemnation which the bishops at Tyre put forward. Possibly intended to be a temporary measure, the exile was the result of an imperial edict issued in an effort to restore peace within the Christian community. The issue of the validity of the decisions made at the Synod of Tyre, however, would continue to follow Athanasius throughout his remaining episcopal career.

---

[409]*Apol.* 87, 6 (Opitz, 166, 20-25).

[410]*Apol.* 24, 2 (Opitz, 105, 11-14).

[411]Schwartz, *GS* III, 98; *Apol.* 85, 3-7 (Opitz, 163, 19-164, 3).

[412]*Festal Letter* X, 1.

CONCLUSION

And yet one would not "willing let die" the words in which so many writers have felt constrained to do homage to such a life and such a soul. If Gregory Nazianzen's eulogy is too rhetorically gorgeous for modern taste, Hooker's will live while English is spoken: and Gibbon's admiration for Athanasius as a born ruler of men is the more significant as coming from one who could have no tenderness for Church heroes . . . his character may be thought specifically worthy of recollection . . . the deep religiousness . . . the unwearied persistency . . . the many-sidedness, and harmonious "combination of excellences" . . . the affectionateness which made him so tender and generous . . . endowed the great theologian and Church-ruler with the capacities and opportunities peculiar to a truly loveable man.[1]

In Alexandria itself, he maintained the popular support which he enjoyed from the outset and buttressed his position by organizing an ecclesiastical mafia. In later years, if he so desired, he could instigate a riot or prevent the orderly administration of the city. Athanasius possessed a power independent of the emperor which he built up and perpetuated by violence . . . Like a modern gangster, he evoked widespread mistrust, proclaimed total innocence—and usually succeeded in evading conviction on specific charges.[2]

These irreconcilable views of Athanasius are extreme expressions of two schools of thought. To the first have belonged nearly all of the historians of Athanasius previous to the early twentieth century, as well as a small group of modern authors. The majority of these, however, it should be remembered, were (or are) themselves connected with religious traditions which have looked with reverence upon Athanasius. To the second has

---

[1]W. Bright, *The Orations of St. Athanasius against the Arians*, second edition, Oxford, 1884, c-ci.

[2]T.D. Barnes, *Constantine and Eusebius*, London, 1981, 230.

subscribed, to greater or lesser degrees, the vast majority of modern church historians.

The supporters of the first argue that Athanasius, even with minor character flaws, was a robust exponent of the faith of the church and a champion of the Nicene definition. While admitting that he was often rash and impetuous or imprecise in his theological terminology, they believe that his qualities as a writer and churchman far outweigh any defects of thought or character which he may have possessed. In short, many, especially among the writers of the nineteenth century, took too uncritical a view of Athanasius, who, it must be admitted, is not at first sight a wholly attractive personality. Intrigue seems to have surrounded him from the earliest days of his episcopate. As a young and relatively powerful bishop, he may have done less than was required for the reconciliation of the Meletian community in Egypt. He shared many of the aggressive qualities of his age. Too often Egyptian ecclesiastical disputes dissolved into fratricidal violence, with the possibility of outrages being committed by all involved. I would argue, however, that much of the evidence provided by Athanasius himself has often been discounted, and greater weight has been given to material from sources which upon thoughtful investigation do not always present the clear picture of misconduct on the part of Athanasius in the early years of his episcopate that is often claimed. Furthermore, the application of modern standards of conduct upon fourth-century personalities is sometimes less than helpful in an enquiry of this sort.

The second school of thought maintains that Athanasius was wholly driven by a "Wille zur Macht," entirely consumed by greed and ambition, and consistently prone to resort to violence, especially in the early years of his episcopate. Concerned only with self-aggrandizement, he was too shortsighted to attend to the true interests of the church as an international and cosmopolitan entity. This view, however, ignores the serious manner with which Athanasius approached his responsibilities as he perceived them. Very few can question the support which Athanasius enjoyed within the Egyptian church almost from the outset, or the large number of Meletian clergy who supported him even against their former coreligionists. In synodal gatherings and in the presence of the emperor, Athanasius time and time again frustrated the attempts of his enemies to remove him by means of demonstrable evidence which proved the falsity of their accusations. His means of defense in such situations was often pragmatic and, although unpopular with his opponents, proved to be convincing to the emperor, the Western bishops, the Egyptian monastic communities, his own clergy, and even some of those who had once brought charges against him. It may be argued reasonably that Athanasius went to extreme lengths to maintain his position and that his basic motivation was, therefore, selfish; but the consistency with which he proclaimed his innocence and marshaled documents and witnesses to support his claims does suggest some degree of confidence on his part which goes beyond mere bravado or a gangsterlike mentality. The survival of the church as he perceived it lay at the heart of his struggle. This, even in the early years of his episcopate, he knew well. He also knew, having seen the deposition of Eustathius and having witnessed the other activities of Eusebius of Nicomedia, how ruthless his enemies could be in achieving their ends. It seems reasonable to argue, therefore, that he would not have lightly taken a position or undertaken an extremely provocative action which could have been used later to remove him; it is arguable from the investigations undertaken in this study that he never did so.

In fact, both views of Athanasius have often oversimplified a complex sequence of events generated by equally complex personalities. One too partisan, the other too critical, both views share a fundamental failing in crediting Athanasius during the early years of his episcopate with more efficiency and power, more influence and ambition (for good or for ill), than he actually possessed. Both views also attribute to the bishop less local pastoral concern than he obviously exercised in maintaining his support within Egypt and clearly demonstrated in so many of his extant writings.[3] This distortion of history is excusable, for the near contemporaries of Athanasius, Gregory and the historians, for example, may themselves have exaggerated the bishop's influence and power in the interests of hagiography or their own immediate doctrinal and ecclesiastical concerns.

In a similar manner, the circumstances surrounding the Synod of Tyre and Athanasius's banishment by Constantine have also been oversimplified. By the year AD 338, the Eusebians appear to have begun a campaign to have the deposition of Athanasius at Tyre recognized by the Western bishops (especially Julius of Rome) and the new secular authority which had been vested in Constantine II, Constans, and Constantius II following the death of Constantine the Great on 22 May AD 337 and their proclamation as *augusti* on 9 September of that same year.[4]   An answer to the letters of the Eusebians to the three emperors was undertaken by the Synod of Alexandria in AD 338/339. The Egyptian bishops specifically answered the charges which led to the Synod of Tyre and the subsequent actions of that gathering with regard to the innocence of Athanasius with the strong assertion that the bishops at Tyre lacked the authority and the means to depose the bishop of Alexandria.[5] They appear to maintain Athanasius's own claim that he had been exiled by imperial authority alone and could, therefore, rightly and legally be returned to his city by a subsequent imperial decree, this time

---

[3]This pastoral concern of Athanasius has recently been highlighted in C. Kannengiesser, *Athanase d'Alexandrie évêque et écrivain,* Théologie historique 70, Paris, 1983; and in C. Kannengiesser, "St. Athanasius of Alexandria Rediscovered: His Political and Pastoral Achievement," *Coptic Church Review* vol. 9, no. 3 (Fall 1988): 68-74.

[4]*Cf. Apol.* 3: 5-7 (Opitz, 89, 19-90, 15), and *Hist. Arian.* 9, 1 (Opitz, 188, 3-5).

[5]*Cf. Apol.* 7, 2-8, 5 (Opitz, 93, 18-94, 30).

issued by the eldest of Constantine's sons, Constantine II, on 17 June AD 337.[6]

It seems reasonable to assume that this action had the initial consent of Constantius, as he had been appointed Caesar of the entire East, including Egypt and Libya.[7] Moreover, Athanasius probably had at least one meeting with Constantius at Viminacium, either before the bishop's triumphal entry into Alexandria on 23 November AD 337 or very soon thereafter.[8] It also appears that at least two of the *augusti* were convinced, or chose to believe as a matter of expediency, that Athanasius's first exile was the result of an exercise of imperial authority and not the execution of a synodal sentence. The Eusebian claim to the contrary would provide the background for both the second exile of Athanasius and the Synod of Sardica, where the charges from Tyre would be revived. Nevertheless, it is important to note that it was not until Athanasius's reinstatement at the hands of the *augusti* that the issue of Tyre's authority became central. Furthermore, it was only after Athanasius's return and the translation of Eusebius from Nicomedia to Constantinople that the authority of Tyre became a point of contention between the Eastern and Western bishops. To claim, therefore, that the judgment of the Synod of Tyre was universally recognized from the beginning is to dismiss those circumstances which actually surrounded the synod and to view its proceedings only from the Eusebian vantage point of the later synods at Antioch and Sardica. Such an outlook runs the risk of oversimplification and, perhaps, of accepting a Eusebian interpretation of events which was already anachronistic by the time of Sardica.[9]

A study of the early episcopate of Athanasius does, however, reveal inherent contradictions. As the bishop of Alexandria he possessed an established and seemingly highly organized ecclesiastical structure. The unique position of the Alexandrian church as a pivot between East and West cannot be questioned. Yet Arius arose out of Alexandria, Libya often sought

---

[6]For this decree, *cf. Apol.* 87, 4-7 (Opitz, 166, 11-29).

[7]Schwartz, *GS* III, 268.

[8]*Cf. Ad Const.* 5 (Szymusiak, SC 56, 93). Although the evidence for Athanasius's return to Alexandria in November AD 337, rather than November AD 338, is circumstantial, the arguments of A. Martin, *Histoire,* 75, 78-89, are convincing. The earlier argument of Baynes, "Athanasiana," *JEA* 2 (1925): 58-69, is based largely upon the time which Athanasius would have needed to commit the many outrages of AD 337 which were alleged by the Eusebians at Sardia and his assumptions concerning the writing of the *Festal Letter* for AD 338. The first contention might appear to be a matter of presuppositions influencing the dating of events, while the second argument has been effectively answered by Martin. We have, therefore, rejected Baynes's claim that Athanasius returned in November AD 338.

[9]How this Eusebian view concerning Tyre and the guilt of Athanasius effected subsequent events at Sardica is developed by H. Hess, *The Canons of the Council of Sardica,* Oxford, 1958, 9ff.

a semi-independent status, the monastic communities were unruly, schismatic groups like the Colluthians and Meletians held sway in some rural regions, and from the mid-third century the attitude of both Eastern and Western bishops toward Alexandria can only be described as ambiguous. Much of what Athanasius was in his early years as a bishop resulted from this environment. That he was a controversial figure, even in the early years of his episcopate, cannot be denied. That many of the controversies were inherited must also be accepted.

The question of Athanasius's character in these early years, however, remains. As this study was being completed, the long-awaited study of the fourth-century doctrinal controversies by the late R.P.C. Hanson, *The Search for the Christian Doctrine of God,* was published.[10] Although it is not possible to do full justice here to the material put forward by Hanson, some mention must be made of those points which are particularly germane to the issues which have been raised in the main body of this thesis. First, in what is a masterful compilation of materials and sources, Hanson rightly perceives the character of Athanasius in the early years of his episcopate as being crucial to our understanding of the period.[11] Unfortunately, Hanson has accepted, albeit with some reservations, the estimates of Athanasius by Schwartz, Barnes, and Klein.[12] Furthermore, the accounts of Philostorgius, whom Hanson recognizes as "an extreme Arian," are considered to be "moderate" and "consequently all the more worth considering."[13] Concerning Athanasius's election to the see of Alexandria, Hanson writes that the bishop "was indeed elected, but not by an immediate and unanimous acclamation, and not without suspicion of sharp practice."[14] He does accept, however, that the Meletian bishops were probably excluded from the election, although this situation is not connected with the resurgence of the schism.[15]

Although much more could be said about the particulars of his estimate of Athanasius and the circumstances surrounding the Synod of Tyre, Hanson has himself provided an instructive synopsis of the material: "When therefore we try to reconstruct the events which concerned Athanasius from his election in 328 until the Council of Tyre in the summer of 335, we must bear in mind that our main informant (Athanasius himself) is determined to conceal his violent behavior by alleging that all was invented by people who were dangerous heretics, and that most of the rest of the sources, and most

---

[10]R.P.C. Hanson, *The Search for the Christian Doctrine of God,* Edinburgh, 1988.

[11]Hanson, *op. cit.,* 239-273.

[12]*Ibid.,* 240-246; Hanson, however, mitigates the evaluation of Schwartz in his estimate of Athanasius as a theologian (*ibid.,* 421-422).

[13]Hanson, *op. cit.,* 241.

[14]*Ibid.,* 249.

[15]*Loc. cit.*

writers since, have taken this plea at face value."[16]   Hanson, however,
believed that one piece of evidence, "the significance" of which "has not yet
sunk in everywhere," must cause us to accept the thesis that "Athanasius's
first efforts at gangsterism in his diocese had nothing to do with difference of
opinion about the subject of the Arian Controversy, but were directed against
the Meletians."[17]

The evidence which Hanson brings forward is LP 1914. He introduces
his case for the acceptance of this document as follows:

> We might dismiss the accusations against Athanasius detailed by
> Sozomenus and Epiphanius as the product of sheer partisanship and not
> worthy of credence, as, for instance, Gwatkin does, and many a church
> historian before and after him who was willing to take Athanasius'
> protestations of his innocence at their face value. We might believe
> the direct denial that Athanasius ever hurt or imprisoned anyone made
> by the Egyptian bishops in 338. We might dismiss the allegations of
> the Council of Tyre, and treat the accusations made against Athanasius
> by the Eastern bishops, at Sardica in 343, with the same skepticism as
> we read the defence of him made at the same moment by the Western
> bishops, or with even more. All these are statements made for
> propaganda purposes by very much interested parties, though even in
> those circumstances it would be unwise to refuse all credit to them.
> But, accidentally or providentially, we have available to us
> contemporary evidence which we cannot possibly dismiss as invention
> or exaggeration or propaganda, to decide this point.
>
> The evidence consists of papyrus letters discovered by British
> archaeologists and published by H.I. Bell in his book *Jews and
> Christians in Egypt.*[18]

Hanson accepts LP 1914 as Bell published it, without any critical
evaluation of the document save for that of the letter's distinguished editor.
For Hanson, the letter shows "Athanasius behaving like an employer of
thugs hired to intimidate his enemies."[19]   One may note, however, almost in
contradiction to his earlier statement, that Hanson comments in a footnote
that "it should be pointed out that these papyri are by no means the only
evidence for the case against Athanasius."[20]   Yet, even Hanson has admitted

---

[16]*Ibid.,* 255.

[17]*Ibid.,* xx; 254.

[18]*Ibid.,* 251.

[19]*Ibid.,* 254.

[20]*Ibid.,* 252, fn. 63. To the present author's communication at the Tenth
International Conference on Patristic Studies held in Oxford in August 1987
Hanson has provided the following response in his study: the "arguments were
well presented, but were all hypothetical and tentative." The material presented at

that there is little clear evidence that is not contradicted by other sources to make such certain claims against the bishop of Alexandria. At this point, I believe, Hanson has followed a traditional approach to LP 1914 which, as has been shown in this present study, is less than helpful in an evaluation of the events which it claims to report. Many questions, both contextual and textual, remain unanswered in regard to LP 1914. In addition to those issues which have been considered here, other concerns may be raised. As E.A. Judge has wondered "what kind of solitaries" the persecuted Meletian monks who lived in Alexandria were, a further question might be, What sort of Egyptian monastic community in AD 334 is placed by the eastern gate of the old city wall, well to the west of the hippodrome, effectively within the city itself?[21] Furthermore, did H.I. Bell notice such an inconsistency when he chose to translate μονῇ in LP 1914 as "hostel" rather than "monastery," as he did in LP 1913?[22]   Clearly this papyrus poses more questions than it answers with any degree of certainty. Hanson's overdependence upon this document must place in some doubt many of his conclusions concerning Athanasius's character and behavior during the early years of his episcopate.

Hanson's treatment of the Synod of Tyre is somewhat more evenhanded, although he provides a very brief account of the proceedings.[23] He acknowledges that "ecclesiastical councils were, and long continued to be, intensely unsatisfactory organs of justice, without forms or standing orders or presidents who could control them or even counting of votes."[24] Once more, however, he accepts the testimony of Athanasius's enemies with little regard for context and states that the bishop of Alexandria's supporters "behaved during the session of Council in a disturbing and threatening manner" and that "his encouragement over several years to his supporters to behave like hooligans was now recoiling on his own head."[25]   Although

---

Oxford in 1987, however, was concerned only with the textual difficulties in LP 1914, of which Hanson makes no mention, and were set forward without the contextual material presented in this thesis.

[21]E.A. Judge, "The Earliest Use of *Monachos* for 'Monk' (P. Coll. Youtie 77) and the Origins of Monasticism," *Jahrbuch für Antike und Christentum* 20 (1977): 84. This mystery is compounded when one considers the geography described as being near to the "Gate of the Sun" (LP 1914, ll. 15-16), the eastern gate of the old Roman wall of Alexandria, but the reader is asked to believe that the attackers, already in a drunken state (LP 1914, l.9), covered 10-14 kilometers, from the Nicopolis to the wall and back again, in about three hours. During this time they are also alleged to have committed at least two beatings and to have carried away five prisoners. Although such a scenario is not impossible, it does strain credulity.

[22]LP 1914, 1.16, and LP 1913, 1.2; the translations are provided, respectively, from Bell, *Jews and Christians,* 62 and 50.

[23]Hanson, *op. cit.,* 259-262.

[24]*Ibid.,* 260.

[25]*Ibid.*

Hanson allows that there was "an air of nemesis" about the Synod of Tyre with regard to its proceedings, an impression is given that there was (and is) little doubt about Athanasius's guilt.[26] Hanson summarizes the actions of the synod:

> Nobody can pretend that the proceedings at Tyre were a model of just dealing. The difficulty facing the bishops gathered there was that they could only condemn on specific, not on general, charges, and it was difficult to obtain evidence on specific charges. But they had given Athanasius an opportunity to defend himself. The behavior of his supporters during the trial was menacing and exasperating and suggested that he was more concerned with coercion than with justice. It must have been clear to everybody that he had been for some time using indefensible violence in the administration of his see, even though it was not very easy to bring him to book on exact charges.[27]

Yet Hanson fails to mention the attacks upon Athanasius, the interference of Dionysius, the protests of bishops from outside of Egypt, and the false charge of murder; the violence of the Mareotic commission is considered only in an aside. The argument presented is one based upon silence and presuppositions concerning the character of the bishop of Alexandria.

In concluding his evaluation of the behavior of Athanasius, Hanson alleges that the "misconduct" of the bishop of Alexandria was the most serious cause of the breach between the East and West that became apparent at Sardica. He characterizes Athanasius's behavior as follows: "Even if some of the proceedings of the Council of Tyre were highhanded, it was beyond doubt that Athanasius had behaved with violence against the Meletians and evinced in his general conduct an authoritarian character determined to exploit the influence of his see."[28] Despite Hanson's assertions to the contrary, such an indictment of Athanasius differs very little from those of O. Seeck and E. Schwartz. For Hanson, Athanasius, while a genuine theologian, remained "an unscrupulous politician."[29]

---

[26]*Ibid.*, 262.

[27]*Ibid.*

[28]*Ibid.*, 272; Hanson also accepts the claim of M. Simonetti, *La crisi Ariana nel quarto secolo,* Rome, 1979, 153, that "Athanasius was a person to be held at arm's length as much as possible" (Hanson's translation) as far as the Eastern bishops were concerned. Such a view, however, is more appropriate to the situation following Sardica. Previous to that time Athanasius had enjoyed the support of a number of Eastern bishops, including Alexander of Thessalonica and Marcellus of Ancyra. The depositions in the east, along with the changing political situation cut away much of the support which Athanasius had previously enjoyed.

[29]Hanson, *op. cit.*, 422.

The picture of Athanasius which has emerged in the course of the research presented in this study is, admittedly, far different from what has been outlined above. I believe that certain assertions concerning Athanasius may be made on the basis of this research. Preeminent among these assertions is the conclusion that there is far less evidence for the violent and duplicitous character of Athanasius than might be supposed from a cursory reading of Hanson, Barnes, or the other current critics. Many of the contemporary views concerning Athanasius have less to do with documentary evidence than with an historical literary tradition that grew out of the first attempts of O. Seeck to prove the bishop of Alexandria to be a forger.[30] The change from the nineteenth-century view of Athanasius has been influenced more by a climate of criticism than with new documentary sources. Such a process may be plainly seen in the controversy surrounding Athanasius's election and consecration as bishop of Alexandria. The Philostorgian material has been well known for many years, but its value was measured over against more reliable sources and its inherent contradictions and interpolations caused it to be considered, I believe rightly, as being of little help in reconstructing the events of AD 328. Yet the work of W. Rusch endeavors to convince the reader that this material must be considered as being of equal importance to other well-established sources.[31]

The question of the Meletians and LP 1914 is somewhat different. In this case, very little critical textual or contextual evaluation has taken place. This has led to a blind acceptance of a document which must be considered enigmatic, to say the very least. On the basis of the research undertaken thus far, LP 1914 appears to be out of place with regard to context, and inexact (if not wholly suspect) in regard to its content.[32] In connection with this document, however, it is clear that the major controversy in Egypt from AD 328 to AD 335 was almost completely concerned with the Meletians and, perhaps, lesser schismatic groups such as the Colluthians rather than with the Arian party whose alliance with the schismatic groups was gradual and probably unknown to Athanasius until AD 334/335.[33] It is also certain that Athanasius enjoyed far greater support from Meletians who had reconciled themselves to the see of Alexandria than has been previously thought. This support continued through to the Synod of Tyre and may well have been instrumental in his winning over the Egyptian monastic communities, many of which had Meletian leanings.[34] Furthermore, there is very little evidence, apart from the accusations of his opponents, that Athanasius engaged in widespread or systematic violence within his see. Certainly, the oration of Gregory Nazianzen provides no such suggestion, even beneath the veil of its

---

[30]*Vide supra*, 11-14.

[31]*Vide supra*, 25ff.

[32]*Vide supra*, 62ff.

[33]*Vide supra*, 62-65, 143ff.

[34]*Vide supra*, 66ff.

expansive rhetoric.[35] It is, however, likely that a good deal of violence between various factions of the Egyptian church may have taken place during the course of this turbulent period, but the evidence indicates that no particular party, much less any one person, was exclusively responsible.[36]

Finally, some evaluation must be made of those events and circumstances which led to the Synod of Tyre and the first exile of Athanasius. This study contends that those events and circumstances which led to the Synod of Tyre must be considered as important as the gathering itself and, therefore, provide the necessary background for understanding what took place in the summer and autumn of AD 335. Any historical narrative is more than its constituent elements, more than information about places, dates, and situations: it is a chronological account of actions by persons with motives, these actions and motives coming together in particular events. To understand the motives and their outcome certainly requires knowledge about the persons involved, chronology, institutions, and documents, but unless a synthesis is made of these elements with each other and with the element of time, we are left without a true historical narrative. Tyre, therefore, cannot be viewed in isolation.

To this end I have attempted to place the Synod of Tyre within the context of the many earlier accusations of Athanasius before the emperor, the Meletian schism in Egypt, the evolution of canon law, synodal procedures and authority, and the earlier, but similar, deposition of Eustathius of Antioch. To these varied contextual elements comments have also been added concerning imperial authority and its relationship with synodal decrees. It is clear that the calling of the Synod of Tyre was concerned less with Athanasius's alleged misconduct in Egypt than with the Eusebian party's desire to rid itself of its opponents and secure the readmission of Arius and his fellows within the Egyptian church. It also seems probable that Athanasius was unaware of the Arian influence upon the machinations of the Meletians and that the Arian party within Egypt posed no real threat in the early years of his episcopate, although the situation in Libya may have been different. I would contend that these hypotheses are supported not only by the internal evidence of the documentary sources themselves but also by the external evidence of other, corroborating sources that surround the controversy. In the end, Athanasius's banishment was the result of an imperial decree on the basis of an accusation which had not even been raised at Tyre and which seems to have been improbable with regard to its content.

The many accusations made against Athanasius, before, during, and after Tyre have often been considered as evidence that some truth must stand behind the charges, even if particular indictments cannot be proved.[37] It must be said, however, that even a close examination of the accusations

---

[35]*Vide supra*, 87-94.

[36]*Vide supra*, 78.

[37]Hanson, *op. cit.*, 262.

against Athanasius provides little consistent evidence to indicate his guilt. On the contrary, the inconsistency of the accusations made by his opponents should cause one to question the veracity of such charges and the motives of his accusers. If the internal evidence of the indictments is unproductive, so too is the search for material evidence of guilt, for apart from the disputed claims of LP 1914 and the confused accounts of Philostorgius, little else emerges. On the contrary, Meletian and monastic support of Athanasius appears to grow within the very period of time during which Athanasius is supposed to be the most active in his alleged persecutions. The increasingly civil and secular nature of the charges made against Athanasius through the years, however, and indeed the civil quality of the final accusation made against him in Constantinople in AD 335, would indicate an attempt to play upon the deep-seated concerns of Constantine, especially concerning the unity of the empire and the economic health of his capital.

If the many accusations against Athanasius are essentially unproved and the actions of the Synod of Tyre so suspect that Constantine was convinced to recall the gathering to Constantinople, the motivation of the emperor in exiling both the bishop of Alexandria and John Archaph must be considered. The most immediate and obvious motive was a desire for unity within the Eastern church. However, while this may remain the prime reason for Constantine's actions, it does not exclude the possibility that there were other minor factors, possibly political and economic, which were of some importance. The combination of imperial respect and frustration with Athanasius which culminated in his banishment, while difficult for the modern reader to understand, does seem to have been a consistent trait of Constantine which was exercised in his relationship with a wide variety of church leaders. T.D. Barnes has commented upon this facet of Constantine's character:

> Official pronouncements by any autocrat deserve to be treated with a certain skepticism. But Constantine's letters to bishops, priests, and churches, fall into so consistent a pattern of respect tempered with frustration that it is difficult to regard them as mere products of tact, diplomacy, or policy. The emperor's personal attitudes and convictions constantly obtrude, and he speaks as one conversant with philosophy and theology who nevertheless believes the conversion of the Roman Empire to worship of the Christian God far more important than a precise (and potentially exclusive) definition of the intellectual content of Christianity.[38]

For the emperor, the exile of Athanasius, as well as of John Archaph, probably had little to do with the with the decrees of Tyre; instead, both Athanasius and the schismatics in Egypt were impediments to the unity of the Eastern church and the inclusiveness which the emperor desired.

---

[38]Barnes, *Constantine and Eusebius, op. cit.*, 242.

Although he may have hoped that the Synod of Tyre would settle the issue of Egypt, when it failed to do so he took matters into his own hands. Yet it remains significant that Constantine apparently refused to depose Athanasius, who remained "technically bishop of Alexandria" though exiled to Trier.[39] Banished by imperial decree, apart from the judgment of the Synod of Tyre, Athanasius would also return from exile to Alexandria under the patronage of imperial authority.

If the many accusations against Athanasius during the early years of his episcopate cannot be dismissed out of hand, they must at least be considered unproved. The persistence of these charges and, indeed, the fiasco of the Synod of Tyre may be explained in terms of factors external to the Egyptian church rather than through any of its internal failings or the misconduct of its bishop. The internal dissension in Egypt, especially among the Meletian and Colluthian schismatics, was undoubtedly a contributing factor, but the evidence shows that these discontented schismatics were encouraged and assisted by the Eusebians as part of a larger plan to have Arius readmitted within the Egyptian church. Recourse to the emperor was first employed by this alliance, before whom time after time the charges against Athanasius were refuted. The desire to have Athanasius appear before a synod, in a manner reminiscent of Eustathius, was but another part of this same process. The calling of the synods of Caesarea and Tyre, therefore, cannot be viewed in the conventional sense of tests of guilt or innocence but as tragic show trials, so familiar to our own century, the verdicts of which had been decided far in advance of their meeting.

In closing this study of the early episcopal career of Athanasius of Alexandria, I confess that there is still much to learn concerning this vitally important period of the bishop's life and career. Perhaps new sources will come to light, or further investigations of present sources may yield new insights. Yet I cannot but feel that the bishop deserves a better fate than to serve future generations continually as an example of a fourth-century gangster or an unscrupulous church politician of the late Constantinian epoch. For although there may have been times when Athanasius was rash or his movements ill judged, there is little solid evidence from the early years of his episcopate that he behaved in the manner which has been suggested by so many studies over the past three generations. It seems to me rather that the comment of Harnack, although slightly overstated as was the manner of his own time, may yet prove to be a more accurate epitaph for Athanasius than the vilification of many contemporary critics: "If we measure him by the standards of his time, we can discover nothing ignoble or weak about him."[40]

---

[39]*Ibid.*, 240.

[40]A. von Harnack, *History of Dogma* (English trans.), vol. 3, third edition, Edinburgh, 1898, 62.

APPENDIX: LONDON PAPYRUS 1914

1 Τῷ ἀγαπητῷ ἀδελφῷ ἆπα Παιηοῦ καὶ Παταβεῖτ πρεσβυτέροις
  Κάλλιστος ἐν

2 Κ(υρί)ῳ θ(ε)ῷ χαίρειν. Γινόσκιν ὑμᾶς θέλομεν τὰ πραχθέντα
  ἐνταῦθα

3 πράγματα· ἐξάφινα γάρ ἠκούσατε τὰ ἐπάθαμεν ἐν τῇ νυκτὶ
  ἐκίνῃ ἐν τῇ οἰκίᾳ Ἡρα-

4 κλέου τοῦ κομμενταρησίου. Εἰσὶν γὰρ καί τινες ἀδελφοὶ ἐκ
  τῶν ἐλ[θ]όντων πρὸς ὑμᾶς

5 μεθ᾽ ἡμῶν ἐν τῇ οἰκίᾳ καὶ δύνονται καὶ αὐτοὶ τὰ πραχθέντα
  [ὑ]μῖν ἀναγγῖλαι. Μετὰ

6 γὰρ τὴν ἡμέραν ἐκίνη⟨ν⟩ ἐν τῇ τ(ρ)ετράδι καὶ εἰκάζι τοῦ
  Παχ[ὼ]ν μηνὸς Ἰσὰκ

7 ὁ ἐπίσκοπος ἀπὸ Λητοῦς ἦλθεν πρὸς Ἡραείσκον ἐν
  Ἀλεξα[ν]δρ[ί]ᾳ, καὶ ἠθέλησεν

8 γεύσασθαι μετὰ τοῦ ἐπισκόπου ἐν τῇ παρεμβολῇ.
  Ἀκούσα[ντε]ς οὖν οἱ διαφέρον-

9 τες Ἀθανασίου καὶ ἦλθασιν φέροντες μεθ᾽ ἑαυτῶν
  στρατιότας τοῦ δουκὸς καὶ τῆς

10 παρεμβολῆς, οἰνόμενοι ἦλθασιν ὥρᾳ ἐνάτῃ συνκλίσαντες τὴν
   [π]αρεμβολὴν βουλόμε⟨νοι⟩

11 καὶ αὐτὸν καὶ τοὺς ἀδελφοὺς πιάσαι. Ἀκούσαντες οὖν τινὲς
   στρατιόται [ο]ἱ ἐν τῇ παρεμβολῇ καὶ

12 φόβον θεοῦ ἔχουτες ἐν τῇ καρδίᾳ ἦρκαν αὐτοὺς καὶ ἔκρυψαν
   ἐν ταῖς κέλλαις ἐν τῇ παρεμβολῇ·

13 καὶ ἐκίνων μὴ εὑρεθέντων ἐγβάντων αὐτῶν εὗραν τέσσαρες
   ἀδελφοὺς ἐρχομένους ἐν τῇ πα-

14 ρεμβολῇ, καὶ κατακόψαντες αὐτοὺς καὶ ἐμαρώεις ποιησάμενοι
   ὥστε αὐτοὺς κινδυνεῦσαι καὶ ἐξέβαλαν

15 αὐτοὺς ἔξω τῆς Νικοπώλεως. Καὶ μετὰ ⟨τὸ⟩ τούτους ἐγβαλῖν
   ἀπήλθασιν πάλιν ἐπὶ τὴν πύλην τοῦ

16 Ἡλίου ἐν τῇ μονῇ ἐν ᾗ ἠσὶν ἐπιξενούμενοι οἱ ἀδελφοὶ καὶ
   πιάσαντες ἄλλους πέντη ἐκῖ εἷ⟨ρ⟩ξαν

17 αὐτοὺς ἐν τῇ παρεμβολῇ ὀψίας, καὶ συνκλίσαντες αὐτοὺς
   μέχρις τοῦ τ[ὸ]ν πραιπόσιτον προερθῖν

18 ἐν τοῖς σίγνοις τὸ πρὸς πρφεὶ καὶ λαβὼν αὐτοὺς ὁ
   πραιπόσιτος καὶ ὁ σκρίβας καὶ αὐτοὺς ἐκέλευ-

19 σεν ἐγβληθῆαι ἐκτὸς τῆς Νικοπόλεως· καὶ τὸν μονάριν
   Ἡρακλίδην δύ[σα]ντες καὶ ὑβρίσαντες

20 ἐνέτιλαν τῷ αὐτῷ ἐπαπιλούμενοι, ὅτι "κατὰ ποίαν ἐτίαν τοὺς
μ[ο]ναχοὺς τῶν Μελιτανῶν
21 ἧασας ἐν τῇ μωνῇ;" καὶ ἀδελφὸν Ἄμμωνα ἐν τῇ παρεμβ[ο]λῇ
[κ]αὶ αὐτὸν ὑποδεχόμενον
22 τοὺς ἀδελφοὺς συνέκλισαν ἐν τῇ παρεμβολῇ, παρήγγιλαν δὲ
αὐτοῦ ὥστε μὴ ὑποδέχεσθαι αὐ
23 τὸν μοναχοὺς ἐν τῇ οἰκίᾳ αὐτοῦ. Ἄλλος γὰρ ἀδελφὸς οὐκ
ἔστιν ἰ μὴ ῥ̣ῦτοι οἰ] δ̣ρο ὑποδέχομενοι τοὺς
24 ἀδελφούς· ἐποίησαν αὐτοὺς διλανθῆναι. Θλιβόμεθα οὖν πάνυ
διειρ̣[γμέ]νοι ὑπὸ αὐτῶν κατὰ τό
25 πον. Ἐπιλοιπούμεθα οὖν [οὐν̣ ὅτι οὐκ ἐπιτρέπουσιν ἡμῖν
πρὸς τ̣[ὸ̣ν] πάπαν Ἡραεῖσκον ἀπελθίν
26 καὶ ἐπισκέψασθαι αὐτόν. Ἐν τῇ νυκτὶ γάρ ἐν ᾗ ὑβρίσθησαν
οἱ ἀδελφοὶ ὁ πραι[π]όσιτος τῶν στρατιοτῶν ἔπεμ
27 σεν φάσιν τῷ ἐπισκόπῳ λέγων ὅτι "ἡμάτησα καὶ ἐπαρυνήθην
ἐν τῇ νυκτὶ ὅτι τοὺς ἀδελφοὺς
28 ὕβρισα". Ἐποίησεν δὲ καὶ ἀγάπην ἐν ἐκίνη τῇ ἡμέρᾳ
Ἕλλην ὢν δ̣[ιὰ] τ̣ὸ ἁμάρτημα ὃ ἐποίησεν.

In the left margin, from top to bottom of the papyrus:

29 Ἀθανάσιος δὲ μεγάλως ἀθυμῖ καὶ αὐτὸς παρέχι ἡμῖν κάματον
διὰ τὰ γραφώμενα καὶ τὰς
30 φάσις τὰς ἐρχομένας αὐτ̣[ῷ] ἀ̣[πὸ] ἔξωθεν, ἐπιδὴ ὁ β̣[α]σιλεὺς
Μακάριον εὑρὼν ἔξω ἐν τῷ
31 κομιδάτῳ ....]υρῳ γράψας [.....] . ανιρυς ὅτι δήσας αὐτὸν
κα̣ὶ . επι
32 . α ἀπο . [................]α ἵνα α̣ῦτο . . . . .] . εσται.
Ἀπελθόντων οὖν Ἀρχελά
33 ου τοῦ [. . . . . . . καὶ . . . . .] . μετὰ Ἀθανασίου το̣ῦ υἱοῦ
Καπίτωνος,

Verso:

34 Βουλόμενοι ἀποσπάσε Μακάριον, ἡ φάσις οὖν ἀπελθην πρὸς
ἀπα Ἰωάννην ἐν Ἀντιοχίᾳ·
35 ἦλθεν καὶ πιάσας αὐτοὺς κατέσχεν αὐτούς, ἐπιδὴ ἐπὶ
συκοφαντίᾳ καὶ δινὰ ἦσαν γράψαν
36 τες κατὰ Ἡραεῖσκου, καὶ αὐτὸς Ἀρχέλαος τὰ γρ̣άμματα
ἦρκεν ἔξω. Ὁ θεὸς οὖν ἐποίησεν
37 καὶ τοὺς τρῖς ἔξω καὶ ἔχι ἔξω. Τοῦτ' οὖν ἤκουσεν
Ἀθανάσιος ὅτι Ἀρχέλαος
38 συνεσχέθη, πάνυ ἀθυμεῖ Ἀθανάσιος. Πολλαχῶς οὖν ἦλθαν
ἐπὶ
39 αὐτὸν καὶ μέχρις νῦν οὐκ ἀπεδήμησεν· ἐνεβάλετο δ̣[ὲ] τὰσκεύη
αὐτοῦ ἐν τῇ θα
40 λάσσῃ ὡς αὐτοῦ ἀπωδημοῦτος, καὶ πάλιν εἰς δεύτερον
ἤνε<γ>κεν τὰ σκεύη
41 ἀπὸ τοῦ πλοίου, μὴ βουλόμεν̣ος ἀ̣[π]ο̣δημ̣η̣[σ]α[ι] . . . . ψαι
. . ἔγρ̣α̣ψα εἴνα

42 γνοῖται ἐν ποίᾳ θλίψι ἐσμέν· ἤνεγκεν γὰρ ἐπίσκοπον τῆς
    κάτω χώρας
43 καὶ συνέκλισεν αὐτὸν ἐν τῷ μακέλλῳ, καὶ πρεσβύτερον τῶν
    αὐτῶν μερῶν
44 συνέκλισεν καὶ αὐτὸν ἐν τῷ ἀπλικίτῳ καὶ διάκωνα ἐν τῇ
    μεγίστῃ φοιλακῇ, καὶ μέχρις
45 τῆς ὀγδόης καὶ εἰκάδος τοῦ Παχὼν μηνὸς καὶ Ἡραείσκος
    συνκεκλισμέ-
46 νος ἐστὶν ἐν τῇ παρεμβολῇ — εὐχαριστῶ μὲν τῷ δεσπότῃ θεῷ
    ὅτι ἐπαύθησαν ἐ πλη
47 γαὶ ἃς εἶχεν—καὶ ἐπὶ τῇ ἐνδόμῃ καὶ εἰκάδι ἐποίησεν
    ἐπισκόπους ἔπτα ἀποδη
48 μῆσαι· Ἔμις καὶ Πέτρος εἰς αὐτούς ἐστιν, υἱὸς Τουβέστις.
    Μὴ ἀμελήσηται θὺν
49 περὶ ἡμῶν, ἀδελφοί, ἐπιδὴ τὰ ψωμία ἀφῆκαν ὀπίσω, ἵνα διὰ
    τὸν ἐπί·σκοπον μή
50 πως ἔξω ἀρθῇ ἵνα πυρῇ αὐτὰ μετ' αὐτοῦ. Ἐγὼ γὰρ ἀγοράζων
    ἄρτους εἰς διασ
51 τροφὴν ἠγώρασα ἀπτάβην σίτου (ταλάντων) ιδ. Ἐπὰν οὖν
    εὕρηται εἰδήμωνα ἀποσ
52 στίλατέ μοι ὀλίγα ψωμία. Ἀσπάζομε τὸν πατέραν μου
    Πραγοῦν καὶ πάντας τοὺς
53 ἀδελφοὺς τοὺς ὄντας μετ' αὐτοῦ καὶ Θέονα τὸν διάκωνα καὶ
    Σαπρίωνα καὶ Ὡρίωνα
54 καὶ Παπνούτιν καὶ ἄπα Σαρμάτην καὶ Παώμιν καὶ Πιὸρ καὶ
    Εὐδαίμωνα καὶ ἄπα Τρύφωνα
55 καὶ Γερόντιον καὶ ἄπα Ἱέρακαν καὶ ἄπα Ἐλεγᾶν καὶ ἄρα
    Ἀρηοῦν καὶ ἄπα Πιὰμ καὶ Κορνήλιν
56 καὶ Πισάτιν καὶ Κολλοῦθον καὶ Ἰωσῆπ καὶ τὰ παιδία αὐτοῦ
    καὶ Φίνες. Μὴ ἀμελήσῃς οὖν,
57 πατήρ, ἀποστῖλαι πρὸς Ψαεῖν ἀπὸ Τερὸτ ἕνεκεν τῆς ἀρτάβης
    τοῦ σίτου, καὶ ποίησον
58 Τουᾶν ἀπὸ Ταμούρω ἵνα καὶ αὐτὸς ἀπέλθῃ εἰς Ταμούρω
    ἕνεκεν τῆς ἀρτάβης τοῦ σίτου·
59 ἡ ἡμέραι γάρ εἰσιν τοῦ λαβῖν αὐτοὺς αὐτάς. Ἀσπάζομε
    Παῦλον τὸν ἀναγνώστην καὶ ἄπα
60 Ἡλί‹α›ν καὶ Ἀνουβᾶν μέγαν καὶ Ἀνουβᾶν μικρὸν καὶ
    Παμούτιν καὶ Τιτρύην καὶ τὰ παιδία αὐτοῦ καὶ Ὁρ
61 ἀπὸ Τουμνακὼν καὶ πάντας τοὺς ἀδελφοὺς αὐτοῦ τοὺς μετ'
    αὐτοῦ καὶ Παπνούτιν καὶ Λεσ
62 νίδην τὸν ἀδελφὸν α‹ὐ›τ[οῦ] καὶ τὸν ἀδελφὸν τὸν ἄλλον τὸν
    μετ' αὐτῶν.

At the foot, the opposite way up:

63 Ἄ[πα Παιηοῦ καὶ Παταβεῖτ]   [π‹απὰ›] Κα‹λ›λίστου.

BIBLIOGRAPHY

PRIMARY SOURCES

Editions and Translations
Ammianus Marcellinus
Ammiani Marcellini rerum Gestorum. Edited by C.U. Clark. Vols. 1 and 2. Berlin, 1963.
Athanasius of Alexandria
Ἀπάντα Μεγάλου Ἀθανασίου, ἀπάντα τῶν ἁγίων Πατέρων. Vols. 1-12. Athens, 1974-77.
Apologie à l'Empereur Constance et Apologie pour sa fuite. Introduction, critical text, translation, and notes by J.M. Szymusiak, S.J. SC 56. Paris, 1958.
The Armenian Version of the Letters of Athanasius to Bishop Serapion Concerning the Holy Spirit. Edited and translated by G.A. Egan. Studies and Documents. Salt Lake City, 1968.
Athanasiana Syriaca. Edited and translated by R.W. Thomson. 4 vols. CSCO 257-258, 272-273, 324-325, 386-387. Louvain, 1965-77.
Atanasio: Lettere a Serapione lo Spirito Santo. Translation, introduction, and notes by E. Cattaneo. Rome, 1986.
Athanasius' Orations against the Arians, Book I. Translated and edited by W.G. Rusch. Sources of Early Christian Thought. Philadelphia, 1980.
Ausgewählte Schriften des heiligen Athanasius. Translated by J. Fisch. Bibliothek der Kirchenväter. Kempten, 1872-75.
Contra gentes and *De incarnatione.* Edited and translated by R.W. Thomson. Oxford Early Christian Texts. Oxford, 1971.
Discours contre les païens. Edited and translated by P.T. Camelot. SC 18. 2d edition. Paris, 1977.
La 10e lettre festale d'Athanase d'Alexandrie. Translation and commentary by M. Albert. In *Parole de l'Orient 6-7, Mélanges offerts au R.P. François Graffin, S.J.* Paris, 1976.
Die *Fest-Briefe des heiligen Athanasius Bischofs von Alexandrien aus dem Syrischen übersetzt und durch Anmerkungen erläutert.* Edited and translated by F. Larsow. Leipzig, 1852.

Des heiligen Athanasius ausgewählte Schriften aus dem Griechischen übersetzt. Edited and translated by J. Lippl, A. Stegmann, and H. Mertel. Bibliothek der Kirchenväter, second series, vols. 13 and 31. Kempten, 1913-17.

The Incarnation of the Word of God (De incarnatione). Translated by a religious of CSMV. London, 1953.

The Letters of Saint Athanasius Concerning the Holy Spirit. Translated by C.R.B. Shapland. London, 1951.

The Life of Antony and the Letter to Marcellinus. Translated by R.C. Gregg. Classics of Western Spirituality. New York, 1980.

The Life of St. Antony. Translated by R.T. Meyer. Ancient Christian Writers 10. Westminster, Md., 1950.

Μέγας Αθανάσιος. BEPES 30-37. Athens, 1962-1968.

Opera omnia quae exstant. Edited by B. de Montfaucon (J.P. Migne). PG 25-28. Paris, 1884-1887.

Orations against the Arians. Book III, 26-41. In *The Christological Controversy.* Translated and edited by R.A. Norris. Sources of Early Christian Thought. Philadelphia, 1980.

The Orations of St. Athanasius. The Ancient and Modern Library of Theological Literature. London, no date.

Osterfestbrief des Apa Athanasius aus dem Koptischen übersetzt und erläutert. Edited and translated by P. Merendino. Düsseldorf, 1965.

St. Athanasius' Orations against the Arians. Introduction, edition, and translation by W. Bright. Oxford, 1884.

Select Writings and Letters of Athanasius, Bishop of Alexandria. Edited by A. Robertson. LNPF, second series, vol. 4. Reprint ed. Grand Rapids, Mich., 1974.

Sur l'incarnation du verbe. Critical text, translation, introduction, notes, and index by C. Kannengiesser. SC 199. Paris, 1972.

Werke, hrsg. im Auftrage der Kirchenväter-Kommission der Preussischen Akademie der Wissenschaften. Edited by H.G. Opitz. Vol. II, 1, 1-280: *Die Apologien.* Berlin, 1935.

Athanasius of Alexandria (Spurious)

The Canons of Athanasius. Edited and translated by W. Reidel and W.R. Crum. London, 1904.

Five Homilies; Exposito fide; sermo major. Edited by H. Nordberg. Societas Scientarum Fennica: Commentationes Humanarum Literarum 30, 2. Helsinki, 1962.

Epiphanius

Adversus Octoginta Haereses. PG 41 and 42. Paris, 1864.

Ancoratus und *Panarion.* Edited by K. Holl. GCS 25, 31, 37. Leipzig, 1915, 1922, 1933.

Eusebius of Caesarea

Church History, Life of Constantine, and Oration in Praise of Constantine. Translated by A.C. McGiffert and E.C. Richardson. LNPF, second series, vol. 1. Reprint. ed. Grand Rapids, Mich., 1974.

Ecclesiastical History [with Greek text]. Translated and edited by K. Lake and J.E.L. Oulton. Loeb Classical Library 1 and 2. London and New York, 1926-1932.

Eusebius Bishop of Caesarea: The Ecclesiastical History and the Martyrs of Palestine. Translation, introduction, and notes by H.J. Lawlor and J.E.L. Oulton. 2 vols. London, 1927-1928.

Historia Ecclesiastica. Edited by E. Schwartz. GCS 9: *Eusebius Werke* 2, 1 and 2. Leipzig, 1903-08.

Historia Ecclesiastica. PG 20. Paris, 1864.

The History of the Church from Christ to Constantine. Translated by G. Williamson. New York, 1966.

In Praise of Constantine: A Historical Study and New Translation of Eusebius' Tricennial Orations. Translation, introduction, and notes by H.A. Drake. Berkley, California, 1976.

Laudes Constantini. PG 20. Paris, 1864.

Laus Constantini. Edited by I. Heikel. GCS 7: *Eusebius Werke* 1. Leipzig, 1902.

Vita Constantini. PG 20. Paris, 1864.

Vita Constantini. Edited by F. Winkelmann. GCS 7: *Eusebius Werke*, 1, 1. Berlin, 1975.

Hilary of Poitiers.
S. Hilarii Episcopi Pictaviensis Opera, Pars Quarta [Including *Fragmenta historica*]. Edited by A. Feder. Vienna and Leipzig, 1916.

Palladius
Palladius: The Lausiac History. Translated by R.T. Meyer. Ancient Christian Writers 34. Westminster, Md., 1965.

Philostorgius
Philostorgius Kirchengeschichte. Edited by J. Bidez. GCS. 2d edition, revised by F. Winkelmann. Berlin, 1972.

Severus of El-Eschmounein
The History of the Patriarchs of the Coptic Church of Alexandria. Edited, translated, and annotated by B. Evetts. PO 3, 4.

Socrates
Ecclesiastica Historia. PG 67. Paris, 1864.

The Ecclesiastical History of Socrates Scholasticus. Translated and annotated by A.C. Zenos. LNPF, second series, vol. 2. Reprint ed. Grand Rapids, Mich., 1974.

Socrates Scholasticus, Ecclesiastica Historia. Edited by R. Hussey. Vols. 1 and 3. Oxford, 1853.

Sozomen
Ecclesiastica Historia. PG 67. Paris, 1864.

The Ecclesiastical History of Sozomen Comprising a History of the Church from AD 323 to AD 425. Translated by D.D. Hartranft. LNPF, second series, vol. 2. Reprint ed. Grand Rapids, Mich., 1974.

Histoire ecclésiastique. Vols. 1 and 2. Greek text from the edition by J. Bidez. Introduction by B. Grillet and G. Sabbah. Translated by A.J. Festugière. Annotation by G. Sabbah. SC 306. Paris, 1983.
Sozomenus Kirchengeschichte. Edited and translated by J. Bidez and G.C. Hansen. GCS 50. Berlin, 1960.
Sulpicius Severus
Chronicorum libri duo. Edited by C. Halm. CSEL 1. Vienna, 1866.
Theodoret
Historia ecclesiastica. PG 82. Paris, 1864.
Historia ecclesiastica. Edited by L. Parmentier. GCS 14. 2d edition, revised by F. Scheidweiler. Berlin, 1954.

Collections of Ancient Source Documents

Athanasius Werke. Hrsg. in Auftrage der Kirchenväter-Kommission der Preussischen Akademie der Wissenschaften. Vol. 3, 1, 1-76: *Urkunden zur Geschichte des arianischen Streites 318-328.* Edited by H.G. Opitz. Berlin, 1934.
Conciliorum Oecumenicorum Decreta. Edidit Instituto per le Scienze Religiose. 3d edition. Bologna, 1973.
Sacrorum Conciliorum Nova et Amplissima Collectio. Edited by J.D. Mansi. vol. 2. Florence, 1762.

Bibliographies

Bibliographia Patristica. Vols. 1-29. Edited by W. Schneemelcher. Berlin, 1959.
Bibliographie de la Revue d' histoire ecclésiastique. Louvain.
Clavis Patrum Graecorum. Vol. 2: *Ab Athanasio ad Chrysostomun.* Edited by M. Geerard. Brepols-Turnhout, 1974.

SECONDARY SOURCES

Currently there exists no extensive bibliography in print which is devoted to the subject of Athanasius of Alexandria. Certain works of bibliographic reference, however, have been listed in the previous section. In addition to these purely bibliographic resources two other works have been of great help in the preparation of this study. The Athanasian references listed in J. Quasten, *Patrology*, vol. 3, Westminster, Md., 1975, 20-79, have been extremely helpful. More current listings were found in the bibliographical sections of Frances Young, *From Nicaea to Chalcedon*, SCM Press, 1983.

Abramowski, L. "Die Synode von Antiochen 324/25 und ihr Symbol." *ZKG* 86 (1975): 356-366.

————. "Dionys von Rom (†268) und Dionys von Alexandrien (†264/5) in den arianischen Streitigkeiten des 4. Jahrhunderts." *ZKG* 93 (1982): 240-272.

Ackroyd, P.R., and C.F. Evans, eds. *Cambridge History of the Bible*. Vol. 1. Cambridge, 1970.

Ahrens, D. "Geometric Patterns of 'Athanasian' Origin on Early Coptic Textiles: A Recent Acquisition of the Trierer Museum." *Bulletin de la Société d'archéologie copte* 25 (1983): 77-81.

Albertz, M. "Zur Geschichte der jung-arianischen Kirchengemeinschaft." *ThStKr* 82 (1909): 205-278.

d'Ales, A. "Pour le texte de Saint Athanase (de Decretis 27)." *RSR* (1924): 61.

Altaner, B. *Patrologie: Leben, Schriften und Lehre der Kirchenväter*. Freiburg, 1951.

Amidon, P.R. "The Procedure of St. Cyprian's Synods." *VC* 37 (1983): 328-339.

Ariès, P., and G. Duby, eds. *A History of Private Life*. Vol. 1: *From Pagan Rome to Byzantium*. Edited by P. Veyne. Translated by A. Goldhammer. London, 1987.

Armstrong, C.B. "The Synod of Alexandria and the Schism at Antioch in AD 362." *JThS* 22 (1921): 206-221, 347-355.

Arnou, R. "Arius et la doctrine des relations trinitaires." *Gregorianum* 14 (1933): 269-272.

Atzberger, L. *Die Logoslehre des Athanasius*. Munich, 1880.

Aubineau, M. "Une homélie pascale attribuée à s. Athanase d'Alexandrie dans le Sinaïticus gr. 492." *Zetesis: Album amicorum Prof. Dr. E. de Strycker*. Utrecht (1973): 668-678.

Auf der Maur, H. *Die Osterhomilien des Asterios Sophistes*. Trierer Theologische Studien 19, 1967.

Azkoul, M. "*Sacerdotium et imperium*: The Constantinian *Renovatio* According to the Greek Fathers." *ThSt* 32 (1971): 431-464.

Backes, I. "Das trinitarische Glaubensverständnis beim hl. Athanasius dem Grossen." *Trierer Theologische Zeitschrift* 82 (1973): 129-140.

Bardenhewer, O. *Geschichte der altkirchlichen Literatur*. Vol. 2. 2d ed. Freiburg, 1914.

————. *Patrology*. 2d ed. Translated by T.J. Shahan. Freiburg, 1908.

Bardy, G. "Alexandrie, Antioche, Constantinople (325-451)." In *L'Eglise et les eglises*, edited by O. Rousseau, vol. 1, 183-207. Chevetogne, 1954.

————. "The Arian Crisis." In *The Church in the Christian Roman Empire*, Palanque et al., vol. 1. London, 1949.

————. "Athanase." *Dictionnaire de la spiritualité* 1 (Paris, 1937), cols. 1047-1052.

————. "Athanase d'Alexandrie (saint)." *DHGE* 4, col. 1313-1340.

————. "Aux origines de l'école d'Alexandrie." *RSR* 27 (1932): 65-90.

————. "La Crise arienne." In *Histoire de l'église,* edited by A. Fliche and V. Martin, vol. 3, 69f. Paris, 1950.

————. "L'Héritage littéraire d'Aetius." *RHE* 24 (1928): 809-827.

————. "La Politique religieuse de Constantin après le concile de Nicée." *RSR* 8 (1928): 516-551.

————. *Recherches sur saint Lucien d'Antioche et son école.* Paris, 1936.

————. "Saint Alexandre d'Alexandrie a-t-il connu la 'Thalie' d'Arius?" *RSR* 6 (1926): 527-532.

————. *Saint Athanase (296-373).* 2d. ed. Paris, 1914.

————. "Sur la réitération du concile de Nicée." *RSR* 23 (1933): 430-450.

Barnard, L.W. "The Antecedents of Arius." *VC* 24 (1970): 172-188.

————. "Athanase et les empereurs Constantin et Constance." In *Politique et théologie,* edited by C. Kannengiesser, 127-143. Paris, 1974.

————. "Athanasius and the Meletian Schism in Egypt." *JEA* 59 (1975): 183-189.

————. "Athanasius and the Roman State." *Latomus* 36 (1977): 422-437. Reprinted in *Studies in Church History and Patristics. Ἀναλέκτα Βλατάδων* 26 (Thessalonica, 1978): 312-328.

————. "The Date of S. Athanasius' *Vita Antonii.*" *VC* 28 (1974): 169-175.

————. "Edward Gibbon on Athanasius." In *Arianism,* edited by R.C. Gregg, 361-369. Philadelphia, 1985.

————. "The Figure of 'Trumpets' in Syriac Tradition: An Egyptian Parallel." *Le Muséon* 88 (1975): 327-329.

————. "The Site of the Council of Sardica." *StP* 17/1 (1982): 9-13.

————. "Some Liturgical Elements in Athanasius' *Festal Epistles.*" *StP* 13 (1975): 337-342.

————. "Some Notes on the Meletian Schism in Egypt." *StP* 12, TU 115 (1975): 399-405.

————. "Two Notes on Athanasius. 1. Athanasius' Election as Archbishop of Alexandria. 2. The Circumstances Surrounding the Encyclical Letter of the Egyptian Bishops (Apol. c. Ar. 3.1-19.5)." *OrChP* 41 (1975): 344-356. Reprinted in *Studies in Church History and Patristics. Ἀναλέκτα Βλατάδων* 26 (Thessalonica, 1978): 329-340.

————. "What was Arius' Philosophy?" *ThZ* 28 (1972): 110-117.

Barnes, J.W.B., and H. Chadwick. "A Letter Ascribed to Peter of Alexandria." *JThS,* NS 24 (1973): 443-455.

Barnes, T.D. "Angel of Light or Mystic Initiate? The Problem of the *Life of Antony.*" *JThS,* NS 37 (1986): 353-368.

————. *Constantine and Eusebius.* Cambridge, Mass., 1981.

————. *Early Christianity and the Roman Empire.* London, 1984.

————. "Emperor and Bishops, A.D. 324-344: Some Problems." *AJAH* 3 (1978): 53-75.

————. *The New Empire of Diocletian and Constantine.* Cambridge, Mass., 1982.

Barnes, W.E. "Arius and Arianism." *Expository Times* 46 (1934): 18-24.

Bartelink, G. "Die literarische Gattung der *Vita Antonii*: Struktur und Motive." *VC* 36 (1982): 38-62.

————. "Observations de critique textuelle sur la plus ancienne version latine de la *Vie de s. Antoine* par s. Athanase." *Revue Bénédictine* 81 (1971): 92-95.

Batiffol, P. "Le περὶ παρθενίας du Pseudo-Athanase." *Römische Quartalschrift für christliche Altertumskunde und für Kirchengeschichte* 7 (1893): 275ff.

————. "Les Sources de l'histoire du concile de Nicée." *Echos d'Orient* 28 (1925): 385-402; 30 (1927): 5-17.

————. "Le Synodikon de S. Athanase." *ByZ* 10 (1901): 128-143.

Bauer, W. *Orthodoxy and Heresy in Earliest Christianity.* Philadelphia, 1971.

Baus, K. "Meletius of Lycopolis." *LThK* 7, n.d.

Baynes, N.H. "Athanasiana." *JEA* 11 (1925): 58-69.

————. "Athanasius." Review of *The Study of St. Athanasius* by F.L. Cross (Oxford, 1945). *Journal of Roman Studies* 35 (1945): 121-124.

————. *Byzantine Studies and Other Essays.* London, 1955.

————. *Constantine the Great and the Christian Church.* The British Academy Raleigh Lecture on History, 1929. 2d ed. Preface by H. Chadwick. London, 1972.

————. "Eusebius and the Christian Empire." *Mélanges Bidez* (1934): 13-18.

————. "St. Antony and the Demons." *JEA* 40 (1954): 7-10.

————. "Sozomen, Ecclesiastica Historia I.15." *JThS* 49 (1948): 165-168.

Bebawi, G. "St. Athanasios: The Dynamics of Salvation." *Sobornost* 8, 2 (1986): 24-41.

Bell, H.I. "Athanasius: A Chapter in Church History." *Congregational Quarterly* 2 (1925): 158-176.

————. "Bibliography of Sir Harold Idris Bell." *JEA* 40 (1954): 3-6.

————. *Cults and Creeds in Graeco-Roman Egypt.* London, 1953.

————. *Egypt from Alexander the Great to the Arab Conquest: A Study in the Diffusion and Decay of Hellenism.* Oxford, 1948.

————. "The Gospel Fragments P. Egerton 2." *HTR* 42 (1949): 53-63.

————. "New Lights on St. Athanasius." *The Adelphi* (1924): 1006-1009.

————. "The Problems of Translation." In *Literature and Life, Addresses to the English Association.* H.I. Bell, G. Boas et al. London, 1948.

————, ed. *Jews and Christians in Egypt.* Oxford, 1924.

"Bell, Sir Harold Idris."*Dictionary of National Biography,* 8th supplement (1981 ed.).

Bellini, E. *Alessandro e Ario: Un esempio di conflitto tra fede e ideologia. Documenti della prima controversia ariana.* Milan, 1974.

Berchem, J.B. "L'Incarnation dans le plan divin d'après saint Athanase." *Echos d'Orient* 33 (1934): 316-330.

————. "Le Rôle du verbe dans l'oeuvre de la création et de la sanctification d'après saint Athanase." *Angelicum* 15 (1938): 201-232, 515-558.

Berkhof, H. *Kirche und Kaiser.* Translated by G.W. Lorcher. Zürich, 1947.

————. *Die Theologie des Eusebius von Caesarea.* Amsterdam, 1939.

Bernard, R. "L'Image de Dieu d'après saint Athanase." *Théologie* 25 (1952).

Beskow, P. *Rex Gloriae: The Kingship of Christ in the Early Church.* Translated by E.J. Sharpe. Uppsala, 1962.

Bienert, W. *Dionysius von Alexandrien: Zur Frage des Origenismus im dritten Jahrhundert.* Berlin, 1978.

————. "Neue Fragmente des Dionysius und des Petrus von Alexandrien aus Cod. Vatop. 236." *Kleronomia* 5 (1973): 308-314.

————. "The Significance of Athanasius." *Irish Theological Quarterly* 48 (1981): 181-195.

Blane, A., and T.E. Bird, eds. *The Ecumenical World of Orthodox Civilization: Russia and Orthodoxy, 3. Essays in Honour of Georges Florovsky.* The Hague, 1974.

Borchardt, C.F.A. *Hilary of Poitiers' Role in the Arian Struggle.* The Hague, 1966.

Bornhäuser, K. *Die Vergottungslehre des Athanasius und Johannes Damascenus.* Gütersloh, 1903.

Botte, B. "L'Euchologe de Sérapion est-il authentique?" *Oriens Christianus* 48 (1964): 50-56.

Boularand, E. "Aux sources de la doctrine d'Arius." *BLE* 68 (1967): 241-272.

————. "Les Débuts d'Arius." *BLE* 65 (1964): 175-203.

————. "Denys d'Alexandrie et Arius." *BLE* 67 (1966): 162-169.

————. *L'Hérésie d'Arius et la "foi" de Nicée.* 2 vols. Paris, 1972.

Bouyer, L. *L'Incarnation et l'église-corps du Christ dans la théologie de saint Athanase.* Paris, 1943.

————. *La Vie de s. Antoine.* Wandrille, 1950.

Bowman, A.K. *Egypt after the Pharaohs, 332 B.C.-A.D. 642.* Los Angeles, 1986.

Brakmann, H. "Alexandrie und die Kanones des Hippolyt." *Jahrbuch für Antike und Christentum* 22 (1979): 139-149.

Breckenridge, J. "Julian and Athanasius: Two Approaches to Creation and Salvation." *Theology* 76 (1973): 73-81.

Brennan, B.R. "Dating Athanasius' *Vita Antonii.*" *VC* 30 (1976): 52-54.

Brennecke, H.C. *Hilarius von Poitiers und die Bischofsopposition gegen Konstanius II: Untersuchungen zur dritten Phase des arianishen Streites (337-361).* Patristische Texte und Studien 26. Berlin, 1984.

Bright, W. *The Age of the Fathers.* 2 vols. London, 1903.

————. "Athanasius." In *Dictionary of Christian Biography* 1, 179-203.

————. *Lessons from the Lives of Three Greek Fathers.* London, 1891.

————. *The Roman See in the Early Church.* London, 1896.

Brock, S. "A Baptismal Address Attributed to Athanasius." *Oriens Christianus* 61 (1977): 92-102.

Brooks, E.W. "The Ordination of the Early Bishops of Alexandria." *JThS* 2 (1901): 612-613.

———, ed. *The Sixth Book of the Select Letters of Severus Patriarch of Antioch in the Syrian Version of Athanasius of Nisibis.* Vol. 2. London, 1903.

Brown, P. "The Rise and Function of the Holy Man in Late Antiquity." In *Society and the Holy in Late Antiquity,* 103-152. Berkeley, 1982.

———. *The World of Late Antiquity A.D. 150-750.* London, 1971.

Budge, E.A.W. *The Paradise of the Holy Fathers.* 2 vols. London, 1907.

———, ed. *Coptic Homilies in the Dialect of Upper Egypt.* London, 1910.

Burn, A.E. *The Council of Nicaea.* London, 1925.

Burns, P.C. *The Christology in Hilary of Poitiers' Commentary on Matthew.* Rome, 1981.

———. "Hilary of Poitiers' Confrontation with Arianism in 356 and 357." In *Arianism,* edited by R.C. Gregg, 287-301. Philadelphia, 1985.

Bury, J.B. *History of the Later Roman Empire.* 2 vols. New York, 1958.

Bush, R.W. *St. Athanasius: His Life and Times.* London, 1888.

Butcher, E.L. *The Story of the Church of Egypt.* 2 vols. London, 1887.

Camelot, P. *Le Concile et les conciles.* Edited by Botte et al. Paris, 1960.

Campbell, T.C. "The Doctrine of the Holy Spirit in the Theology of Athanasius." *Scottish Journal of Theology* 27 (1974): 408-440.

von Campenhausen, H. "Das Bekenntnis des Eusebius v. Caesarea (Nicaea 325)." *ZNW* 67 (1976): 123-139.

———. *Ecclesiastical Authority and Spiritual Power in the Church of the First Three Centuries.* London, 1969.

———. *The Fathers of the Greek Church.* Translated by S. Godman. New York, 1959.

———. *Tradition and Life in the Church.* Translated by A.V. Littledale. Philadelphia, 1968.

Carrington, P. *The Early Christian Church.* 2 vols. Cambridge, 1957.

Case, R.A. "Will the Real Athanasius Please Stand Up?" *Journal of the Evangelical Theological Society* 19 (1976): 283-295.

Casey, R.P. "Armenian Manuscripts of St. Athanasius of Alexandria." *HTR* 24 (1936): 43-59.

———. "An Armenian Version of Athanasius' Letter to Epictetus." *HTR* 26 (1933): 127-150.

———. "The Athens Text of Athanasius' *Contre Gentes* and *De Incarnatione.*" *HTR* 23 (1930): 51-89.

———. *The De incarnatione of Athanasius, Part 2: The Short Recension.* Studies and Documents 14. London, 1946.

———. "Greek Manuscripts of Athanasian Corpora." *ZNW* 30 (1931): 49-70.

———. "A Syriac Corpus of Athanasian Writings." *JThS* 35 (1934): 66-67.

Caspar, E. *Geschichte des Papsttums von den Anfängen bis zur Höhe der Weltherrschaft.* Vol. 1. Tübingen, 1930.

Cataneo, E. "Il tema della grazia in s. Atanasio d'Alessandria." In *Una Hostia, Studi in Onore del Card. Corrado ursi,* edited by S. Muratore and A. Rolla, 163-186. Naples, 1983.

Cavallera, F. *Saint Athanase.* Paris, 1908.

──────. *Le Schisme d'Antioche.* Paris, 1905.

Cave, W. *Ecclesiastici: Or, the History of the Lives, Acts, Death, and Writings of the Most Eminent Fathers of the Church.* London, 1683.

Ceillier, R. "Saint Athanase, archevêque d'Alexandrie, docteur de l'église et confesseur." In *Histoire des auteurs sacrés et ecclésiastiques,* vol. 4, 89-233. Paris, 1860.

Ceska, J. "Die politischen Hintergründe der Homoousioslehre des Athanasius." In *Die Kirche angesichts der konstantinischen Wende,* edited by G. Ruhbach, 297-321. Darmstadt, 1976.

Chadwick, H. "Athanasius, De decretis 40,3." *JThS* 49 (1948): 168-169.

──────. *The Early Church.* Pelican History of the Church 1. New York, 1976.

──────. "Faith and Order at the Council of Nicaea: A Note on the Background of the Sixth Canon." *HTR* 53 (1960): 171-195.

──────. "The Fall of Eustathius of Antioch." *JThS* 49 (1948): 27-35.

──────. *History and Thought of the Early Church.* London, 1982.

──────. "The Origin of the Title 'Oecumenical Council'." *JThS* 23 (1972): 132-135.

──────. "Ossius of Cordova and the Presidency of the Council of Antioch 325." *JThS,* NS 9 (1958): 292-298.

──────. *The Role of the Christian Bishop in Ancient Society.* Colloquy 35 of the Center for Hermeneutical Studies in Hellenistic and Modern Culture. Berkeley, 1980.

Chestnut, G.F. *The First Christian Histories.* Paris, 1977.

──────. "Kairos and Cosmic Sympathy in the Church Historian Socrates Scholasticus." *ChH* 44 (1975): 161-166.

Chitty, D. *The Desert a City.* Oxford, 1966.

Christou, P. "Uncreated and Created, Unbegotten and Begotten in the Theology of Athanasius of Alexandria." *Augustinianum* 13 (1973): 399-409.

Clarke, F.S. "Lost and Found: Athanasius' Doctrine of Predestination." *Scottish Journal of Theology* 29 (1976): 435-450.

Clayton, A. "The Orthodox Recovery of a Heretical Proof Text: Athanasius of Alexandria's Exegesis of Proverbs 8.22f in Conflict with the Arians." Ph.D. diss., Perkins School of Theology, 1987.

de Clerq, V.C. *Ossius of Cordova: A Contribution to the History of the Constantinian Period.* CUA Studies in Christian Antiquity 13. Washington, 1954.

Coiderakis, H. "Τι Διδασκει ο Μ. Αθανασιος περι 'Αρειου και 'Αρειανισμου." *Ekklesiastikos Pharos* 29 (1930): 496-516.

Coleman-Norton, P.R. *Roman State and Christian Church*. Vol. 1. London, 1966.

Congar, Y. *Diversity and Communion*. Translated by J. Bowden. London, 1984.

Connolly, R.H. *The So-called Egyptian Church Order and Derived Documents*. Cambridge, 1916.

Constantinides, M. *'O Μέγας 'Αθανάσιος καὶ ἡ ἐποχὴ αὐτοῦ*. Athens, 1937.

Conybeare, F.C. "On the Sources of the Text of S. Athanasius." *Journal of Philology* 24 (1896): 285-300.

Cook, S.A., F.E. Adcock, and M.P. Charlesworth, eds. *Cambridge Ancient History*. Vol. 1. 2d ed. Cambridge, 1954.

Coulange, L. "Métamorphose du consubstantiel: Athanase et Hilaire." *Revue d'histoire et de littérature religieuse* (1922): 168-214.

Cox, P. *Biography in Late Antiquity: A Quest for the Holy Man*. Berkeley, 1983.

Cranz, F.E. "Kingdom and Polity in Eusebius of Caesarea." *HTR* 45 (1952): 47-66.

Cremers, V. *De Verlossingsidee by Athanasius den Groote*. Turnhout, 1921.

Cross, F.L. "Council of Antioch in 325 A.D." *Church Quarterly Review* 128 (1938): 49-76.

————. Review of *The De incarnatione of Athanasius, Part 2: The Short Recension*, by R.P. Casey. *JThS* 49 (1948): 88-95.

————. *The Study of Athanasius*. Oxford, 1945.

Cummings, D., ed. and trans. *The Rudder*. Chicago, 1957.

Cunningham, A. *The Bishop in the Church: Patristic Texts on the Role of the Episkopos*. Theology and Life 13. Wilmington, Del., 1985.

Curti, G. "Il linguaggio relativo al Padre e al Filio in alcuni passi dei 'Commentarii in Psalmos' de Eusebio di Cesarea." *Augustinianum* 13 (1973): 483-506.

Daniélou, J. *Gospel and Hellenistic Culture*. Vol. 2 of *A History of Early Christian Doctrine before the Council of Nicaea*. Edited and translated by J.A. Baker. London, 1973.

Daniélou, J., and H. Marrou. *The First Six Hundred Years*. Vol. 1 of *The Christian Centuries: A New History of the Catholic Church*. Edited by Rogier et al. Translated by V. Cronin. London, 1964.

Davis, L.D. *The First Seven Ecumenical Councils (325-787): Their History and Theology*. Theology and Life 21. Wilmington, Del., 1987.

Delhougne, H. "Autorité et participation chez les pères du cénobitisme." *Revue d'ascétique et de mystique* 45 (1969): 369-394.

Dempf, A. *Eusebius als Historiker*. Munich, 1964.

Devos, P. "Une passion grecque inédite de saint Pierre d'Alexandrie et sa traduction par Anastase le bibiothécaire." *AnalBoll* 85 (1965): 157-187.

Dimitrijevic, D. "Die Christologie des hl. Athanasius und ihre Bedeutung für die Auffassung der Eucharistie." *Kyrios* 14 (1974): 61-84.

Dix, G. *The Apostolic Tradition.* London, 1968.

──────. *Jurisdiction in the Early Church.* London, 1975.

Dorner, I.A. *History of the Development of the Doctrine of the Person of Christ.* 3 vols. Translated by P. Simon. Edinburgh, 1897.

Dörries, H. "Die *Vita Antonii* als Geschichtsquelle." *Nachrichten der Akademie der Wissenschaften in Göttingen,* philologisch-historische Klasse (1949): 357-410.

Downey, G. "The Perspective of the Early Church Historians." *Greek, Roman, and Byzantine Studies* 6 (1965): 57-70.

Dragas, G.D. *Athanasiana.* Vol. 1. London, 1980.

──────. "Conscience and Tradition: Newman and Athanasius in the Orthodox Church." *Internationale Cardinal Newman Studien.* Nürnberg, 1980.

──────. "The Eternal Son: An Essay in Christology with Special Reference to St. Athanasius." *Abba Salama* 9 (1979): 18-54.

──────. "He Became Man." *StP* 16 (1975): 281-294.

──────. "Holy Spirit and Tradition: The Writings of St. Athanasius." *Sobornost* 1.1 (1979): 51-72.

──────. "The Homoousion in Athanasius' *Contra Apollinarem I.*" In *Arianism,* edited by R.C. Gregg, 233-241. Philadelphia, 1985.

──────. *The Meaning of Theology.* Darlington, 1980.

──────. "Nature and Grace According to St. Athanasius." *Church and Theology* 1 (1980): 513-554.

──────. "A Note Concerning Athanasius' Soteriology." *Ekklesiastikos Pharos* 61 (1979): 210-220.

──────. *St. Athanasius Contra Apollinarem.* Athens, 1985.

──────. "The Two Treatises of St. Athanasius 'Contra Apollinarem': Second Thoughts on the Research of the Critics." *Abba Salama* 6 (1975): 84-96.

Duchesne, L. *The Early History of the Christian Church from Its Foundation to the End of the Fifth Century.* 3 vols. New York, 1922.

──────. *Histoire ancienne de l'église.* Vol. 2. 5th ed. Paris, 1911.

Duval, Y.M. "La Problématique de la 'Lettre aux vierges' d'Athanase." *Le Muséon* 88 (1975): 405-433.

Ebied, R.Y., and L.R. Wickman. "A Note on the Syriac Version of Athanasius *Ad Epictetum* in Ms. BM add. 14557." *JThS,* NS 23 (1972): 144-154.

Echternach, H. *Kirchenväter, Ketzer und Konzilien.* Göttingen, 1962.

Egan, G. *The Armenian Version of the Letters of Athanasius to Bishop Serapion Concerning the Holy Spirit.* Studies and Documents 37. Salt Lake City, 1968.

──────. "A Treatise Attributed to Athanasius." *Le Muséon* 80 (1967): 139-151.

Ehrman, B.D. "The New Testament Canon of Didymus the Blind." *VC* 37 (1983): 1-21.

Eichhorn, A. "Athanasii de vita ascetica testimonia collecta." Diss., Halle, 1886.

Elert, W. *Eucharist and Church Fellowship in the First Four Centuries.* Translated by N. Nagel. St. Louis, 1966.

Elliger, W. "Bemerkungen zur Theologie des Arius." *ThStKr* 103 (1931): 244-251.

Eustratiades, S. "᾿Αθανάσιος ὁ Μέγας, Πατριάρχης ᾿Αλεξανδρείας." *Romanos* 1 (1932-33): 55-58.

Fairweather, E.R., and E.R. Hardy. *The Voice of the Church: The Ecumenical Council.* Greenwich, Conn., 1962.

Farrar, F.W. *Lives of the Fathers, Sketches of Church History in Biography.* 2 vols. Edinburgh, 1889.

Feidas, V. *Τὸ Κολλουθιανὸν σχίσμα καὶ αἱ ἀρχαὶ τοῦ ᾿Αρειανίσμου.* Athens, 1973.

Ferguson, E. "Athanasius, *Epistola ad Marcellinum in interpretationem psalmorum.*" *Ekklesiastikos Pharos* (1978): 378-403.

———. "Athanasius, *Epistola ad Marcellinum in interpretationem psalmorum.*" *StP* 16 (1985): 295-308.

———. "Attitudes to Schism at the Council of Nicaea." In *Schism, Heresy, and Religious Protest,* 57-63. Edited by D. Baker. Cambridge, 1972.

Fernandez, G. "Athanasius of Alexandria and Liberius of Rome: Analysis of the Letter *Pro deifico timore* of Liberius in the Light of the Edict of Arles of 358." In *Arianism,* edited by R.C. Gregg, 303-311. Philadelphia, 1985.

Fialon, E. *Saint Athanase: Etude littéraire suivie de l'Apologie à l'Empereur Constance et de l'Apologie de sa fuite traduites en français.* Paris, 1877.

Flesseman-van Leer, E. *Tradition and Scripture in the Early Church.* Assen, 1954.

Fliche, A., and V. Martin, eds. *Histoire de l'église.* 21 vols. Vol. 3: *De la paix constantinienne à la mort de Théodose,* by J.R. Palanque, G. Bardy, and P. de LaBriolle. Paris, 1950.

Florovsky, G. "The Authority of the Ancient Councils and the Tradition of the Fathers." In *Glaube, Geist, Geschichte: Festschrift für Ernst Benz.* Leiden, 1967.

———. "The Concept of Creation in Saint Athanasius." *StP* 6 (1962): 36-57.

———. *The Eastern Fathers of the Fourth Century.* Paris, 1931.

———. "The Fourth Century: An Introduction." *Sobornost* 7 (1977): 241-252.

———. "The Function of Tradition in the Early Church." *Greek Orthodox Theological Review* 9.2 (1963): 73-125.

Foakes-Jackson, F.J. *Eusebius Pamphili, Bishop of Caesarea and First Christian Historian: A Study of the Man and His Writings.* Cambridge, 1933.

Fouyas, M. *The Person of Christ in the Decisions of the Ecumenical Councils.* Addis Ababa, 1976.

Fox, R.L. *Pagans and Christians.* New York, 1986.

Fraser, P.M. *Ptolemaic Alexandria.* 2 vols. Oxford, 1972.

Frend, W.H.C. "Athanasius as an Egyptian Christian Leader in the Fourth Century." In *Religion Popular and Unpopular in the Early Christian Centuries,* 20-37. London, 1976.

————. *The Rise of Christianity.* Philadelphia, 1984.

Fromen, H. "Athanasii historia acephala." D. Phil. diss., Münster, 1915.

Gallay, P. *La vie de saint Grégoire de Nazianze.* Paris and Lyon, 1943.

Galtier, P. "Saint Athanase et l'âme humaine du Christ." *Gregorianum* 36 (1955): 553-589.

Garitte, G. *Un témoin important du texte de la vie de s. Antoine par s. Athanase.* Etudes de philologie, d'archéologie et d'histoire ancienne publiées par l'Institut historique belge de Rome 3. Bruxelles, 1939.

Gaudel, A. "La date des trois discours contre les Ariens." *RSR* 9 (1929): 524-539.

————. "La Théologie du Λόγος chez saint Athanase." *RSR* 11 (1931): 1-26.

Gaudemet, J. *Conciles Gaulois du IVe siècle.* SC 241. Paris, 1977.

————. *L'Eglise dans l'empire roman, IVe-Ve siècles.* Paris, 1958.

Gericke, W. *Marcell von Ancyra: Der Logos-Christologe und Biblizist.* Halle, 1940.

Gero, S. "The True Image of Christ: Eusebius' Letter to Constantia Reconsidered." *JThS,* NS 32 (1981): 460-470.

Gessel, W. "Das primatiale Bewusstsein Julius I. im Lichte der Interaktionen zwischen der Cathedra Petri und den zeitgenössischen Synoden." In *Konzil und Papst: Festgabe für Hermann Tüchle,* edited by G. Schwaiger, 63-74. Munich, Paderborn, and Vienna, 1975.

de Ghellinck, J. "Qui sont les ὥς τινες λέγουσι de la lettre d'Arius?" *Miscellanea Mercati* 1 (1946): 127-144.

Giardini, F. "Doctrina espiritual en la *Vita Antonii* de san Atanasio." *Teologia espiritual* 4 (1960): 377-412; 7 (1963): 681-701.

Gilliard, F.D. "The Social Origins of Bishops in the Fourth Century." Ph.D. diss., University of California at Berkeley, 1966.

Gillman, I. "Eschatology in the Reign of Constantine." *Reformed Theological Review* 24 (1965): 40-51.

Girardet, K.M. "Appellatio: Ein Kapitel kirchlicher Rechtsgeschichte in den Kanones des vierten Jahrhunderts." *Historia* 23 (1974): 98-127.

————. "Constance II, Athanase et l'édit d'Arles (353): A propos de la politique religieuse de l'empereur Constance II." In *Politique et théologie,* edited by C. Kannengiesser, 65-91. Paris, 1974.

————. *Kaisergericht und Bischofsgericht: Studien zu den Anfängen des Donatistenstreites (313-315) und zum Prozess des Athanasius von Alexandrien (328-346).* Bonn, 1975.

Giuriceo, M.A. "The Church Fathers and the Kingly Office." Ph.D. diss., Cornell, 1955.

Goering, J.E. "Pachomius' Vision of Heresy: The Development of a Pachomian Tradition." *Le Muséon* 95 (1982): 241-262.

Goermans, M. "L'Exil du pape Libère." In *Mélanges offerts à Mademoiselle Christine Mohrmann*, 181-189. Utrecht, 1963.

von der Goltz, E. *De virginitate, eine echte Schrift des Athanasius.* TU 29, 2a. Leipzig, 1905.

Gore, C. "On the Ordination of the Early Bishops of Alexandria." *JThS* 3 (1902): 279-280.

Grant, R.M. "The Apostolic Fathers' First Thousand Years." *ChH* 31 (1962): 421-429.

——. "The Case against Eusebius or, Did the Father of Church History Write History?" *StP* 115 (1975): 413-421.

——. "Early Alexandrian Christianity." *ChH* 40 (1971): 133-144.

——. *The Early Christian Doctrine of God.* Charlottesville, Virginia, 1966.

——. "Eusebius and Church History." In *Understanding the Sacred Text: Essays in Honour of M.S. Enslin on the Hebrew Bible and Christian Beginnings,* edited by J. Reumann, 233-247. Valley Forge, 1972.

——. *Eusebius as Church Historian.* Oxford and New York, 1980.

——. "Religion and Politics at the Council of Nicaea." *JR* 55 (1975): 1-12.

Greenslade, S.L. *Church and State from Constantine to Theodosius.* London, 1954.

——, ed. *Schism in the Early Church.* London, 1953.

Gregg, R.C. "Arianism." In *New Dictionary of Christian Theology* (1983).

——, ed. *Arianism, Historical and Theological Reassessments: Papers from the Ninth International Conference on Patristic Studies, September 5-10, 1983. Oxford, England.* Patristic Monograph Series 11. Philadelphia, 1985.

Gregg, R.C., and D.E. Groh. "The Centrality of Soteriology in Early Arianism." *Anglican Theological Review* 59 (1977): 260-278. Reprinted in *StP* 15 (1984): 305-316.

——. *Early Arianism: A View of Salvation.* Philadelphia, 1981.

Gregory, T.E. *Vox Populi: Popular Opinion and Violence in the Religious Controversies of Fifth Century A.D.* Columbus, Ohio, 1979.

Griffiths, J.G. "Egyptian Influences on Athanasius." In *Studien zur Sprache und Religion Aegyptens* [Festschrift W. Westendorf], vol. 2, 1023-1037. Göttingen, 1984.

Griggs, C.W. "History of Christianity in Egypt to 451 A.D." Ph.D. diss., University of California, 1979.

Grillmeier, A. *Christ in Christian Tradition.* Vol. 2. 2d ed. Translated by J. Bowden. London and Oxford, 1975.

————. "Konzil und Rezeption." In *A. Grillmeier S.J., Mit ihm und in ihm: Christologische Forschungen und Perspektiven*, 303-412. Freiburg, Basel, and Vienna, 1975.

————. "Die Stellung des Tomus von Alexandrien 362 in der Christologie des hl. Athanasios." In *Das Konzil von Chalkedon, Geschichte und Gegenwart*, vol. 1, 91-99. Freiburg, 1954.

Groh, D.E. "New Directions in Arian Research." *Anglican Theological Review* 68, no. 4 (1987): 347-355.

Gryson, R. *Scolies ariennes sur le concile d'Aquilée*. SC 267. Paris, 1980.

Gummerus, J. *Die homöusianische Partei bis zum Tode des Konstantius*. Leipzig, 1900.

Gustafsson, B. "Eusebius' Principles in Handling His Sources, as Found in His *Church History* Books I-VIII." *StP* 4 (1961): 429-441.

Gwatkin, H.M. *The Arian Controversy*. London, 1898.

————. *The Knowledge of God and Its Historical Development*. 2 vols. Edinburgh, 1906.

————. *Studies of Arianism*. 2d ed. Cambridge, 1900.

van Haarlem, A. *Incarnatie en verlossing bij Athanasius*. Wageningen, 1961.

Hagedorn, D., ed. *Der Hiobkommentar des Arianers Julian*. Berlin, 1973.

Hagel, K.F. *Kirche und Kaisertum in Lehre und Leben des Athanasius*. Borna and Leipzig, 1933.

Hall, S.G. Review of *Early Arianism*, by Gregg and Groh. *King's Theological Review* 5 (1982): 28.

————. "The Thalia of Arius in Athanasius' Accounts." In *Arianism*, edited by R.C. Gregg, 37-57. Philadelphia, 1985.

Hamilton, A. "Athanasius and the Simile of the Mirror." *VC* 34 (1980): 14-18.

————. "Narrative in the Theology of St. Athanasius." *Colloquium* 10 (1977): 6-13.

Handspicker, M. "Athanasius on Tradition and Scripture." *Andover Newton Quarterly* 3.1 (1962): 13-29.

Hanson, R.P.C. "The Arian Doctrine of the Incarnation." In *Arianism*, edited by R.C. Gregg, 181-211. Philadelphia, 1985.

————. "The Doctrine of the Trinity Achieved in 381." *Scottish Journal of Theology* 36 (1983): 41-57.

————. "The Fate of Eustathius of Antioch." *ZKG* 95 (1984): 171-179.

————. *The Search for the Christian Doctrine of God*. Edinburgh, 1988.

————. *Tradition in the Early Church*. London, 1962.

————. "Who Taught 'Εξ οὐκ ὄντων?" In *Arianism*, edited by R.C. Gregg, 79-83. Philadelphia, 1985.

Hardy, E.R. *Christian Egypt: Church and People*. Oxford, 1962.

von Harnack, A. *Die Chronologie der altkirchlichen Literatur bis Eusebius*. 2 vols. Leipzig, 1904.

————. *History of Dogma*. Vols. 3 and 4. Translated by E.B. Speirs and J. Millar. London, Edinburgh, and Oxford, 1897-1898.

————. *Lehrbuch der Dogmengeschichte.* 3 vols. 3d ed. Freiburg and Leipzig, 1894-1897.

Harris, J.R. *The Apology of Aristides: Texts and Studies.* Edited by R.J. Armitage. Vol. 1. Cambridge, 1983.

Hauben, H. "On the Meletians in P. London VI: The Problem of Papas Heraiscus." In *Bibliography Papyrologie: Proceedings of the XVI International Congress of Papyrology,* 447-456. Chicago, 1981.

Haugaard, W.P. "Arius: Twice a Heretic?" *ChH* 29 (1960): 251-263.

Hauret, C. "Comment le 'défenseur de Nicée' a-t-il compris le dogme de Nicée?" Ph.D. diss., Rome, 1936.

Hauser-Meury, M.M. *Prosopographie zu den Schriften Gregors von Nazianz.* Bonn, 1960.

Haykin, M.A.G. "'The Spirit of God': The Exegesis of I Cor. 2:10-12 by Origen and Athanasius." *Scottish Journal of Theology* 35 (1982): 513-528.

Hefele, C.J. *Conciliengeschichte.* Vol. 1. Freiburg, 1855.

————. *Histoire des conciles d'après les documents originaux.* Vol. 1, parts 1 and 2. Translated by L. Leclerq. Paris, 1907.

————. *A History of the Christian Councils.* Vols. 1 and 2. Translated by W.R. Clark. Edinburgh, 1871.

Henry, P. "Why is Contemporary Scholarship so Enamoured of Ancient Heretics?" *StP* 17.1 (1982): 123-126.

Hernández, G.F. "El cisma meleciano en la iglesia egipcia." *Gerión* 2 (1984): 155-180.

————. "Problemas históricos en torno a la muerte de Arrio." *Erytheia: Revista de estudios byzantinos y neogriegos* 5 (1984): 95-103.

Heron, A. "'Logos, Image, Son': Some Models and Paradigms in Early Christology." In *Creation, Christ, and Culture: Studies in Honour of T.F. Torrance,* edited by R.W.A. McKinney, 43-62. Edinburgh, 1976.

————. "The Pseudo-Athanasian Works *De Trinitate et Spiritu Sancto* and *De incarnatione et contra Arianos:* A Comparison." In *Aksum Thyateira: A Festschrift for Archbishop Methodios of Thyateira and Great Britain,* edited by G.D. Dragas. London, 1985.

————. "Zur Theologie der 'Topici' in den Serapionbriefen des Athanasius." *Kyrios* 14 (1974): 3-24.

Herrmann, J. "Ein Streitgespräch mit verfahrensrechtlichen Argumenten zwischen Kaiser Konstantius und Bischof Liberius." In *Festschrift für Hans Liermann,* edited by V.K. Obermayer und H.R. Hagemann, 77-86. Erlangen, 1964.

von Hertling, L. *Antonius der Einsiedler.* Forschungen zur Geschichte des innerkirchlichen Lebens 1. Innsbruck, 1929.

————. *Communio: Church and Papacy in Early Christianity.* Translated by J. Wicks. Chicago, 1972.

Hess, H. *The Canons of the Council of Sardica A.D. 343: A Landmark in the Early Development of Canon Law.* Oxford, 1958.

Higgins, M.J. "Two Notes: 1. Athanasius and Eusebius on the Council of Nicaea; 2. The Pope's Right to Try a Patriarch on a Disciplinary Charge." In *Polychronion: Festschrift Franz Dölger*, 238-243. Heidelberg, 1966.

Holl, K. "Die Bedeutung der neuveröffentlichten melitianischen Urkunden für die Kirchengeschichte." *Sitzungsberichte der preussischen Akademie der Wissenschaften*. Philosophisch-historische Klasse 1925, 18-31. Reprinted in his *Gesammelte Aufsätze* 2 (1928): 283-297.

Holland, D.L. "The Creeds of Nicaea and Constantinople Revisited." *ChH* 38 (1969): 248-261.

―――. "Die Synode von Antiochen (324/25) und ihre Bedeutung für Eusebius von Caesarea und das Konzil von Nicäa." *ZKG* 81 (1970): 163-181.

Holland, J.A.B. "Athanasius and Arius II: Why the Impulse to Reduce?" *Reformed Theological Review* 30 (1971): 33-47.

―――. "Athanasius versus Arius: What Now?" *Reformed Theological Review* 28 (1969): 16-27.

―――. "The Development of the Trinitarian Theology of Athanasius in His Conflict with Contemporary Heresies." Ph.D. diss., University of Edinburgh, 1963.

―――. "The Implications of Athanasius for Us." *Reformed Theological Review* 31 (1972): 1-9.

―――. "III. The Solution of Athanasius." *Reformed Theological Review* 30 (1971): 69-78.

Honigmann, E. "La Liste originale des pères de Nicée." *ByZ* 14 (1939): 17-76.

Hoppenbrouwers, H. *La Plus Ancienne Version latine de la* Vie de s. Antoine *par s. Athanase*. Nijmegen, 1960.

Hoss, K. *Studien über das Schrifttum und die Theologie des Athanasius*. Freiburg, 1899.

Hugger, V. "Des hl. Athanasius Traktat in Mt. 11.27." *ZKTh* 42 (1918): 437-441.

―――. "Mai's Lukaskommentar und der Traktat *De passione* athanasianisches Gut?" *ZKTh* 43 (1919).

Hughes, P. *The Church in Crisis: A History of the General Councils 325-1870*. New York, 1961.

Hunger, H. *Die hochsprachliche profane Literatur der Byzantiner*. Munich, 1978.

Javierre, A.M. *El tema literario de la sucesión: Prolegómenos para el estudio de la sucesión apostólica*. Zurich, 1963.

Jedin, H. *Handbuch der Kirchengeschichte*. Vol. 2: *Die Reichskirche nach Konstantin dem Grossen*. Freiburg, 1975.

―――. *Handbuch der Kirchengeschichte*. Vol. 2/1: *Die Kirche von Nikaia bis Chalkenon*. Freiburg, 1975.

Joannou, P.P. *La Législation impériale et la christianisation de l'empire romain (311-476)*. Orientalia Christiana Analecta, no. 192. Rome, 1972.

―――. *Die Ostkirche und die Cathedra Petri im 4. Jahrhundert*. Revised by G. Denzler. Päpste und Papsttum 3. Stuttgart, 1972.

Jolowicz, H.F. *Historical Introduction to the Study of Roman Law*. Cambridge, 1954.

Jones, A.H.M. *Constantine and the Conversion of Europe*. London, 1948.

―――. "The Date of the *Apologia contra Arianos* of Athanasius." *JThS*, NS 5 (1954): 224-227.

―――. *The Later Roman Empire*. 2 vols. Oxford, 1964.

―――. "Notes on the Genuineness of the Constantinian Documents in Eusebius' Life of Constantine." *JEH* 5 (1954): 196-200.

Judge, E.A. "The Earliest Use of *Monachos* for 'Monk' (P. Coll. Youtie 77) and the Origins of Monasticism." *Jahrbuch für Antike und Christentum* 20 (1977): 72-89.

Judge, E.A., and S.R. Pickering. "Papyrus Documentation of Church and Community in Egypt to the Mid-Fourth Century." *Jahrbuch für Antike und Christentum* 20 (1977): 47-71.

Kannengiesser, C. "Arius and the Arians." *ThSt* 44 (1983): 456-475.

―――. *Athanase d'Alexandrie évêque et écrivain: Une lecture des traité 'Contre les Ariens.'* Théologie historique 70. Paris, 1983.

―――. "Athanase édité par R.W. Thomson." *RSR* 61 (1973): 217-232.

―――. "The Athanasian Decade 1974-84: A Bibliographical Report." *ThSt* (1985): 524-541.

―――. "Athanasius of Alexandria and the Foundations of Traditional Christology." *ThSt* 34 (1973): 103-113.

―――. "Athanasius of Alexandria and the Holy Spirit between Nicaea I and Constantinople I." *Irish Theological Quarterly* 48 (1981): 166-180.

―――. "Athanasius of Alexandria: A Paradigm for the Church of Today." *Pacifica* 1 (1988): 85-99.

―――. "Athanasius of Alexandria in East and West Revisited." Paper presented at the University of Virginia, 26 October 1987.

―――. "Athanasius of Alexandria Rediscovered: His Political and Pastoral Achievement." Paper presented at the Catholic University of America, Washington, D.C., 22 October 1987.

―――. "Athanasius of Alexandria—Three Orations against the Arians: A Reappraisal." *StP* 18 (1982): 981-995.

―――. "Athanasius of Alexandria vs. Arius: 'The' Alexandrian Crisis." In *The Roots of Egyptian Christianity*, edited by B. Pearson and J. Goehring, 204-215. Philadelphia, 1986.

―――. "Athanasius von Alexandrien." In *Gestalten der Kirchengeschichte*, edited by M. Greschat, 266-283. Vol. 1, Alte Kirche I. Tübingen, 1984.

————. "Athanasius von Alexandrien: Seine Beziehungen zu Trier und seine Rolle in der Geschichte der christlichen Theologie." *Trierer Theologische Zeitschrift* 82 (1973): 141-153.

————. "La Bible dans les controverses ariennes en occident." In *Le Monde latin antique et la Bible*, 543-564. Vol. 2: *Bible de tous les temps*, edited by J. Fontaine and C. Pietri. Paris, 1985.

————. "La Bible et la crise arienne." In *Le Monde grec ancien et la Bible*, 301-312. Vol. 1: *Bible de tous les temps*, edited by C. Mondésert. Paris, 1984.

————. "Les 'Blasphèmes d'Arius' (Athanase d'Alexandrie, *De synodis* 15): Un écrit néo-arien." In *Mémorial André-Jean Festugière: Antiquité païenne et chrétienne*, edited by E. Lucchesi and H.D. Saffrey, 143-151. Geneva, 1984.

————. "The 'Blasphemies of Arius': Athanasius of Alexandria *De synodis* 15." In *Arianism*, edited by R.C. Gregg, 59-77. Philadelphia, 1985.

————. "Les Citations bibliques du traité athanasien *Sur l' ncarnation du verbe* et les Testimonia." In *La Bible et le pères*, 135-160. Strasbourg, 1970.

————. "The Contemporary Task of Historical Theology." Paper presented as inaugural lecture as C.F. Huisking Professor of Theology at the University of Notre Dame, Notre Dame, Ind., 8 April 1983.

————. "La Date de *l'Apologie* d'Athanase *Contre les païens* et *Sur l'incarnation du verbe*." *RSR* 58 (1970): 383-428.

————. "Les Différentes Recensions du traité *De incarnatione verbi* de s. Athanase." *StP* 7 (1966): 221-229.

————. "L'Enigme de la lettre au philosophe Maxime d'Athanase d'Alexandrie." In *Ἀλεξανδρίνα: Mélanges offerts à Claude Mondésert, S.J.* Paris, 1987.

————. *Holy Scripture and Hellenistic Hermeneutics in Alexandrian Christology: The Arian Crisis.* Colloquy 41 of the Center for Hermeneutical Studies in Hellenistic and Modern Culture. Berkeley, 1982.

————. "L'Interprétation de Jérémie dans la tradition alexandrine." *StP* 12, TU 115 (1975): 317-320.

————. "*Logos* et *Nous* chez Athanase d'Alexandrie." *StP* 11, TU 108 (1972): 199-202.

————. "Le Mystère pascal du Christ selon Athanase d'Alexandrie." *RSR* 63 (1975): 407-442.

————. "Nicée 325 dans l'histoire du Christianisme." *Concilium* 138 (1978): 39-47.

————. "La Nouveauté chrétienne vue par Origène." In *L'Ancien et le nouveau*, edited by J. Doré, 111-135. Cogitatio Fidei 3. Paris, 1982.

————. "Origenes, Augustin und der Paradigmenwechsel in der Theologie." In *Theologie-Wohin?* edited by H. Küng and D. Tracy, 151-167. Oekumenische Theologie 2. Zürich, 1984.

————. "Où et quand Arius composa-t-il la *Thalie?*" In *Kyriakon,* edited by P. Granfield and J.A. Jungmann, 2 vols., 346-351. Münster, 1970.

————. "Le Recours au Livre de Jérémie chez Athanase d'Alexandrie." In *Epektasis: Festschrift Jean Daniélou,* edited by J. Fontaine and C. Kannengiesser. Paris, 1972.

————. "St. Athanasius of Alexandria Rediscovered: His Political and Pastoral Achievement." *Coptic Church Review* 9, 3 (Fall 1988): 68-74.

————. "Le Témoignage des *Lettres Festales* de s. Athanase sur la date de *l'Apologie contre les païens—Sur l'incarnation du verbe.*" *RSR* 52 (1964): 91-100.

————. "Théologie et patristique: Le Sens actuel de leur rapport verifié chez Athanase d'Alexandrie." In *Humanisme et foi chrétienne: Mélanges scientifiques du centenaire de l'Institut catholique de Paris,* edited by C. Kannengiesser and Y. Marchasson. Paris, 1976.

————. "Le Texte court du *De incarnatione* athanasien." *RSR* 52 (1964): 589-596; 53 (1965): 77-111.

————, ed. *Early Christian Spirituality.* Translated by P. Bright. Sources of Early Christian Thought. Philadelphia, 1986.

————, ed. *Politique et théologie chez Athanase d'Alexandrie.* Actes du Colloque de Chantilly, 23-25 Septembre 1973. Théologie historique 27. Paris, 1974.

Karakolas, K. *Ἡ ἐκκλησιολογία τοῦ Μεγάλου Ἀθανάσιου.* Thessaloniki, 1968.

Karpp, H. "Textkritische Bemerkungen zu Athanasius, *De decretis Nicaenae synodi* 27, 1." *VC* 28 (1974): 141-143.

Kaye, J. *Works of John Kaye.* London, 1876.

Kee, A. *Constantine versus Christ: The Triumph of Ideology.* London, 1982.

Kehrhahn, T. *De sancti Athanasii quae fertur "Contra gentes oratione."* Berlin, 1913.

Kelly, J.N.D. *Early Christian Creeds.* 2d ed. London, 1967.

————. *Early Christian Doctrines.* 4th ed. London, 1968.

Kemp, E.W. "Bishops and Presbyters at Alexandria." *JEH* 6 (1955): 125-142.

Kennedy, G.A. *The Art of Rhetoric in the Roman World, 300 B.C.-A.D. 300.* Princeton, 1972.

————. *Classical Rhetoric and Its Christian and Secular Tradition from Ancient to Modern Times.* Chapel Hill, N. C., 1980.

————. *Greek Rhetoric under Roman Emperors.* Princeton, 1983.

Kettler, F.H. "Der melitianische Streit in Ägypten." *ZNW* 35 (1936): 159-163.

Kidd, B.J. *A History of the Church to A.D. 461.* Oxford, 1922.

Klein, R. *Constantius II und die christliche Kirche.* W.B.G., Impulse der Forschung. Darmstadt, 1977.

————. "Zur Glaubwürdigkeit historischer Aussagen des Bischofs Athanasius von Alexandrien über die Religionspolitik des Kaisers Constantius II." *StP* 17 (1982): 996-1017.

Klijn, A.F.J. "Jewish Christology in Egypt." In *The Roots of Egyptian Christianity*, edited by B. Pearson and J. Goehring, 161-175. Philadelphia, 1986.

Klostermann, E., ed. *Eusebius Werke*. Vol. 4: *Die griechischen christlichen Schriftsteller der ersten Jahrunderte*. Berlin, 1972.

Kolp, A.L. "Partakers of the Divine Nature: The Use of II Peter 1:4 by Athanasius." *StP* 17 (1982): 1018-1023.

Kopecek, T.A. *A History of Neo-Arianism*. 2 vols. Patristic Monograph Series 8. Cambridge, Mass., 1979.

————. "Neo-Arian Religion: The Evidence of the *Apostolic Constitutions*." In *Arianism*, edited by R.C. Gregg, 153-179. Philadelphia, 1985.

————. "Professor Charles Kannengiesser's View of the Arian Crisis: A Critique and Counter-Proposal." Colloquy 41 of the Center for Hermeneutical Studies in Hellenistic and Modern Culture, 51-68. Berkeley, 1982.

Kraft, H. *Kaiser Konstantins religiöse Entwicklung*. Tübingen, 1955.

————. "Ὁμοούσιος." *ZKG* 66 (1954/55): 1-24.

Krause, M. "Das christliche Alexandrien und seine Beziehungen zum koptischen Aegypten." In *Alexandrien: Kulturbegegnungen dreier Jahrtausende im Schmelztiegel einer mediterranen Grossstadt*, edited by N. Hinske, 53-62. Aegyptiaca Treverensia 1. Mainz, 1981.

Kreilkamp, H. "The Origin of the Patriarchate of Constantinople and the First Roman Recognition of Its Patriarchal Jurisdiction." Ph.D. diss., the Catholic University of America, 1964.

Lake, K. "Some Further Notes on the Mss. of the Writings of St. Athanasius." *JThS* 5 (1903): 108-114.

Lake, K., and R.P. Casey. "The Text of the *De incarnatione* of Athanasius." *HTR* 19 (1926): 259-270.

Laminski, A. *Der Heilige Geist als Geist Christi und Geist der Gläubigen: Der Beitrag des Athanasios von Alexandrien zur Formulierung des trinitarischen Dogmas im IV. Jht.* Erfurter theologische Studien 23. Leipzig, 1969.

Larentzakis, G. *Einheit der Menschheit, Einheit der Kirche bei Athanasius: Vor- und nachchristliche Soteriologie und Ekklesiologie bei Athanasius von Alexandrien*. Graz, 1978.

————. "Einige Aspekte des hl. Athanasios zur Einheit der Kirche." *Κληρονομία* 6 (1974): 242-259.

Lassus, J. "L'Empereur Constantin, Eusèbe et les lieux saints." *Revue de l'histoire des religions* 171 (1967): 135-144.

Lauchert, F. *Leben des heiligen Athanasius des Grössen*. Cologne, 1911.

————. *Die Lehre des heiligen Athanasius des Grössen*. Leipzig, 1895.

Lawlor, H.J. "The Chronology of Eusebius." *Classical Quarterly* 19 (1924): 94-101.

————. *Eusebiana: Essays on the* Ecclesiastical History *of Eusebius.* New York, 1912.

Lebon, J. "Altération doctrinale de la 'Lettre à Epictète' de Saint Athanase." *RHE* 31 (1935): 713-761.

————. "Une ancienne opinion sur la condition du corps du Christ dans la mort." *RHE* 23 (1927): 5-43, 207-241.

————. "Athanasiana Syriaca." *Le Muséon* 40 (1927): 205-248.

————. "Athanasiana Syriaca." *Le Muséon* 41 (1928): 169-216.

————. "Pour une édition critique des oeuvres de S. Athanase." *RHE* 3 (1925): 524-530.

————. Review of H.G. Opitz, *Untersuchungen zur Überlieferung der Schriften des Athanasius. RHE* 31 (1935): 783-788.

————. "S. Athanase a-t-il employé l'expression ὁ κύριακος ἄνθρωπος?" *RHE* 31 (1935): 307-329.

Lebreton, J. "'Ἀγεννήτος dans la tradition philosophique et dans la littérature chrétienne du IIe siècle." *RSR* 16 (1926): 431-443.

Leclercq, H. "Alexandrie (Archéologie)." *DACL* 1, cols. 1098-1182.

Lecuyer, J. "Le Problème des consécrations épiscopales dans l'église d'Alexandrie." *BLE* 65 (1964): 241-257.

————. "La Succession des évêques d'Alexandrie aux premiers siècles." *BLE* 70 (1969): 81-99.

Lee, G.M. "Eusebius on St. Mark and the Beginnings of Christianity in Egypt." *StP* 12 (1975): 422-431.

L.T. Lefort. "A propos des Festales de s. Athanase." *Le Muséon* 67 (1954): 43-50.

————. "Athanase, Ambroise et Chenoute sur la virginité." *Le Muséon* 48 (1935): 55-73.

————. "Athanase écrivain copte." *Le Muséon* 42 (1933): 1-33.

————. "Athanasiana Coptica." *Le Muséon* 69 (1956): 233-241.

————. "La chasse aux reliques des martyrs en Egypte au IVe siècle." *La nouvelle Clio* 6 (1954): 225-230.

————. "L'Homélie de s. Athanase des papyrus de Turin." *Le Muséon* 71 (1958): 5-50, 209-239.

————. "Les *Lettres festales* de s. Athanase." *Bulletin de la classe des lettres de l'Academie royale de Belgique* 39 (1953): 643-656; 41 (1955): 183-185.

————. "Un nouveau 'De virginitate' attribué à s. Athanase." *AnalBoll* 67 (1949): 142-152.

————. "S. Athanase sur la virginité." *Le Muséon* 42 (1929): 197-274.

Leloir, L. "Premiers renseignements sur la *Vie d'Antoine* en éthiopien." In *Antidoros: Festschrift M. Geerard,* 9-11. Antwerp, 1984.

Leroux, J.M. "Athanase et la seconde phase de la crise arienne (345-373)." In *Politique et théologie,* edited by C. Kannengiesser, 145-156. Paris, 1974.

Leroy, F.J. "Une homélie nouvelle, origéno-arienne, issue de milieux anti-Marcelliens. BHG 1076z, in Lc I, 31-44." In *Epektasis: Festschrift pour J. Daniélou*, 343-353. Paris, 1972.

Lewis, N. *Life in Egypt under Roman Rule.* Oxford, 1983.

Lienhard, J.T. "The Epistle of the Synod of Ancyra, 358: A Reconsideration." In *Arianism*, edited by R.C. Gregg, 313-319. Philadelphia, 1985.

————. "Marcellus of Ancyra in Modern Research." *ThSt* 43 (1982): 486-503.

Lietzmann, H. "Die Anfänge des Problems Kirche und Staat." In *Die Kirche angesichts der konstantinischen Wende*, 1-13. Darmstadt, 1976.

————. "Chronologie der ersten und zweiten Verbannung des Athanasius." *ZWTh* 44 (1901): 380-390.

————. *A History of the Early Church.* 4 vols. New York, 1961.

————. "Symbolstudien XIII." *ZNW* 24 (1925): 193-202.

Lippold, A. "Bischof Ossius von Cordoba und Konstantin der Grosse." *ZKG* 92 (1981): 1-15.

Loeschke, G. "Zur Chronologie der beiden grossen anti-arianischen Schreiben des Alexander von Alexandrien." *ZKG* 31 (1910): 584-586.

Longosz, S. "Swiety Atanazy a Biblia." *Ruch Biblijny i Liturgiczny* 27 (1974): 237-296.

Loofs, F. "Arianismus." *RE* 3 (1897): 6-45.

————. "Athanasius von Alexandrien." *RHE* 3 (1897): 194-205.

————. "Die chronologischen Angaben des sog. 'Vorbericht' zu den Festbriefen der Athanasius." *Sitzungsberichte der königlichen preussischen Akademie der Wissenschaften* (1908): 1013-1022.

————. "Das Glaubensbekenntnis der Homoousianer von Sardica." *AAWB* (1909): 1.

————. "Das Nicäanum." In *Festgabe K. Müller*, 68-82. Tübingen, 1922.

Lorenz, R. *"Arius judaizans?" Untersuchungen zur dogmengeschichtlichen Einordnung des Arius.* Göttingen, 1980.

————. "Die Christusseele im arianischen Streit: Nebst einigen Bemerkungen zur Quellenkritik des Arius und zur Glaubwürdigkeit des Athanasius." *ZKG* 94 (1983): 1-51.

————. "Das Problem der Nachsynode von Nicäa (327)." *ZKG* 90 (1970): 22-40.

————. *Der zehnte Osterfestbrief des Athanasius von Alexandrien: Text, Übersetzung, Erläuterungen.* Berlin, New York, 1986.

Lorimer, W. "Critical Notes on Athanasius." *JThS* 40 (1939): 37-46.

Louth, A. "Athanasius' Understanding of the Humanity of Christ." *StP* 16 (1985): 309-318.

————. "The Concept of the Soul in Athanasius' *Contra gentiles—De incarnatione*." *StP* 13 (1975): 227-231.

————. *The Origins of the Christian Mystical Tradition.* Oxford and New York, 1981.

————. "Reason and Revelation in Saint Athanasius." *Scottish Journal of Theology* 23 (1970): 385-396.

————. "St. Athanasius and the Greek *Life of Antony*." *JThS*, NS 39, 2 (October 1988): 504-509.

Luibhéid, C. "The Alleged Second Session of the Council of Nicaea." *JEH* 34 (1983): 165-174.

————. "The Arianism of Eusebius of Nicomedia." *Irish Theological Quarterly* 43 (1976): 3-23.

————. *The Council of Nicaea*. Galway, 1982.

————. *Eusebius of Caesarea and the Arian Crisis*. Dublin, 1978.

————. "Eusebius of Caesarea and the Nicene Creed." *Irish Theological Quarterly* 39 (1972): 299-305.

————. "Finding Arius." *Irish Theological Quarterly* 45 (1978): 81-100.

Lyman, R.J. "Christology and Cosmology: Will and Substance Models in Origen, Eusebius, and Athanasius." D.Phil. diss., Oxford Univer-sity, 1983.

————. "Substance Language in Origen and Eusebius." In *Arianism*, edited by R.C. Gregg, 257-265. Philadelphia, 1985.

McCoy, J.D. "Philosophical Influences on the Doctrine of the Incarnation in Athanasius and Cyril of Alexandria." *Encounter* (Indianapolis) 38 (1977): 362-391.

McKean, W.H. *Christian Monasticism in Egypt*. London and New York, 1920.

Malone, E.E. *The Monk and the Martyr*. Washington, 1950.

Mansi, J.D. *Sacrorum Conciliorum Nova et Amplissima Collectio*. Florence, 1758-1798.

Mantzaridos, G. Τόμος Ἑορτίος. Χιλιοστῆς ἑξακοσιοστῆς ἐπετείου Μεγάλου Ἀθανασίου. Thessalonica, 1974.

Marangoni, V.O. "Juan 10, 30 en la argumentación escriturística de san Atanasio." *Stromata* 26 (1970): 3-57.

Marchasson, Y., and C. Kannengiesser, eds. *Humanisme et foi chrétienne: Mélanges scientifiques du centenaire de l'Institut catholique de Paris*. Paris, 1976.

de Margerie, B. "Exégèse polémique, doctrinale et spirituelle de saint Athanase." In *Introduction à l'histoire de l'église 1: Les Pères grecs et orientaux*, chapter 5. Paris, 1980.

Margull, H.J., ed. *The Council of the Church*. Philadelphia, 1966.

Markus, R.A. "Church History and the Early Church Historians." In *The Materials, Sources, and Methods of Ecclesiastical History*, edited by D.A. Baker, 1-17. Oxford, 1975.

Marot, Dom H. "Les conciles romains des IVe et Ve siècles et le développement de la primauté." *Istina* 4 (1957): 435-462.

————. "Vornicänische und ökumenische Konzile." In *Das Konzil und die Konzile*, 23-41. Stuttgart, 1962.

Marrou, H.I. "L'Arianisme comme phénomène alexandrin." *Académie des inscriptions et Belles Lettres*, (1973): 533-542.

Martin, A. "Athanase et les Mélitiens." In *Politique et théologie*, edited by C. Kannengiesser, 31-61. Paris, 1974.

―――. "Aux origines de l'église copte: L'Implantation et le développement du Christianisme en Egypte (Ie-IVe siècles)." *Revue des études anciennes* 88 (1981): 35-56.

―――. "Les Premiers Siècles du Christianisme à Alexandrie." *Revue des études Augustiniennes* 30 (1984): 211-225.

Mayer, J. "Über Echtheit und Glaubwürdigkeit der dem heiligen Athanasius d. Grossen zugeschriebenen *Vita Antonii*." *Der Katholik* (1886): Heft I, Neue Folge 55, Art. XXXII, 495-516, and Art. XXXIX, 619-636; Heft II, NF 56, Art. XI, 173-193.

Meijering, E.P. "The Doctrine of the Will and of the Trinity in the Orations of Gregory of Nazianzus." *NedThT* 27 (1973): 224-234.

―――. "῟Ην ποτε ὅτε οὐκ ἦν ὁ υἱός. A Discussion on Time and Eternity." *VC* 28 (1974): 161-169.

―――. *God, Being, History: Studies in Patristic Philosophy*. Amsterdam and Oxford, 1975.

―――. *Orthodoxy and Platonism in Athanasius: Synthesis or Antithesis*: 2d ed. Leiden, 1974.

O. Meinardus. *Christian Egypt, Ancient and Modern*. Cairo, 1965.

―――. *Christian Egypt, Faith and Life*. Cairo, n.d.

―――. "An Examination of the Traditions Pertaining to the Relics of St. Mark." *OrChP* 36 (1970): 348-376.

Meinhold, P. "Die gesamtchristliche Bedeutung des. hl. Athanasius." *Kyrios* 14 (1974): 97-114.

Meredith, A. "Emanation in Plotinus and Athanasius." *StP* 16 (1985): 319-323.

―――. "Orthodoxy, Heresy, and Philosophy in the Latter Half of the Fourth Century." *Heythrop Journal* 16 (1975): 5-21.

P. Merendino. *Paschale Sacramentum: Eine Untersuchung über die Osterkatechese des hl. Athanasius von Alexandrien in ihrer Beziehung zu den frühchristlichen exegetisch-theologischen Überlieferungen*. Münster, 1965.

Meslin, M. *Les Ariens d'occident*. Paris, 1967.

Milburn, R.L.P. *Early Christian Interpretations of History*. The Bampton Lectures of 1952. London, 1954.

Miller, M. "Archaic Literary Chronography." *Journal of Hellenic Studies* 75 (1955): 54-58.

Moehler, J.A. *Athanasius der Grosse und die Kirche seiner Zeit, besonders im Kampfe mit dem Arianismus*. 2d ed. Mainz, 1844.

―――. *Athanase le Grand et l'église de son temps en lutte l'arianisme*. Translated by Zickwolff and Cohen. 3 vols. Paris, 1849.

Molland, E. "La Développement de l'idée de succession apostolique." *RHPR* 34 (1954): 1-29.

Momigliano, A. "Pagan and Christian Historiography in the Fourth Century A.D." In *The Conflict of Paganism and Christianity in the Fourth Century,* 79-99. Oxford, 1963.

Monachino, V. "Communio e primato nella controversia ariana." *Archivum Historiae Pontificum* 7 (1969): 43-78.

Mönnich, C.W. "De Achtegrond van de arianse Christologie." *NedThT* 4 (1950): 378-412.

Montevecchi, O. *La Papirologia.* Torino, 1973.

Morard, F. "Encore quelques réflexions sur monachos." *VC* 34 (1980): 395-401.

Moreira, A.M. *Potamius de Lisbonne et la controverse arienne.* Louvain, 1969.

Mosshammer, A.A. *The Chronicle of Eusebius and Greek Chronographic Tradition.* Lewisburg, Pa., 1979.

Moutsoulas, E.D. 'H 'Αρειανή ἔρις καὶ ὁ Μέγας 'Αθανασιος. Athens, 1979.

――――. 'Ο Μέγας 'Αθανάσιος. Athens, 1974.

――――. "Le Problème de la date des 'Trois discours' contre les Ariens d'Athanase d'Alexandrie." *StP* 16 (1985): 324-341.

Mühlenberg, E. *Apollinaris von Laodicea.* Göttingen, 1959.

――――. "Vérité et bonté de Dieu." In *Politique et théologie,* edited by C. Kannengiesser, 215-230. Paris, 1974.

Müller, C.D.G. "Athanasius von Alexandrien als koptischer Schriftsteller." *Kyrios* 14 (1974): 195-204.

Nautin, P. "Deux interpolations orthodoxes dans une lettre d'Arius." *AnalBoll* 67 (1949): 131-141.

――――. "La Doctrine d'Arius." *Annuaire de l'Ecole pratique des Hautes Etudes,* V^e section: Sciences religieuses 83 (1974-75): 231f.

Neale, J.M. *A History of the Holy Eastern Church: The Patriarchate of Alexandria.* 2 vols. London, 1847.

Neander, A. *General History of the Christian Religion and Church.* Translated by J. Torrey. Edinburgh, 1859.

Newman, J.H. *Apologia Pro Vita Sua: Being a History of His Relgious Opinions.* London, 1890.

――――. *The Arians of the Fourth Century.* London, 1833.

――――. *Catholic Sermons of Cardinal Newman.* London, 1957.

――――. *An Essay on the Development of Christian Doctrine.* Rev. ed. London, 1878.

――――. *Lyra Apostolica.* 14th ed. London, 1867.

――――. *Select Treatises of St. Athanasius in Controversy with the Arians.* 2 vols. 2d ed. London, 1881.

de Nicola, A. "La concezione e la storia del male nel *Contra gentes—De incarnatione* de s. Atanasio." *Augustinianum* 16 (1976): 85-106.

Nordberg, H. *Athanasiana, I.* Helsinki, 1962.

――――. *Athanasius and the Emperor.* Commentationes Humanarum Litterarum 30.3. Helsinki, 1963.

————. *Athanasius' Tractates* Contra gentes *and* De incarnatione: *An Attempt at Redating.* Commentationes Humanarum Litterarum 28.3. Helsinki, 1961.

————. "On the Bible Text of St. Athanasius." Arctos. Acta philologica Fennica. *The New Scholasticism* 3 (1962): 119-141.

————. "A Reconsideration of the Date of Athanasius' *Contre gentes* and *De incarnatione.*" *StP* 3 (1961): 262-266.

Norden, E. *Die antike Kunstprosa.* 2 vols. Leipzig, 1898.

Norman, K.E. "Deification: The Content of Athanasian Soteriology." Ph.D. diss., Duke University, 1980.

Norris, F.W. "Gregory Nazianen's Opponents in Oration 31." In *Arianism,* edited by R.C. Gregg, 321-325. Philadelphia, 1985.

Nyman, J.R. "The Arian Controversy from Its Beginnings to the Council of Nicaea." D.Phil. diss., Oxford, 1960.

————. "The Synod of Antioch (324-325) and the Council of Nicaea." *StP* 4, TU 79 (1961): 483-489.

Opitz, H.G. "Euseb von Caesarea als Theologe: Ein Vortrag." *ZNW* 34 (1935): 1-19.

————. "Das Syrische Corpus Athanasianum." *ZNW* 33 (1934): 18-31.

————. *Untersuchungen zur Überlieferung der Schriften des Athanasius.* Arbeiten zur Kirchengeschichte 23. Berlin und Leipzig, 1935.

————. "Die Zeitfolge des arianischen Streites von den Anfängen bis zum Jahr 328." *ZNW* 33 (1934): 131-159.

Orlandi, T. "Sull'Apologia secundo (contra Arianos) di Atanasio di Alessandria." *Augustinianum* 15 (1975): 49-79.

Osborn, E. "Arian Obedience: Scouting for Theologians." Review of Gregg and Groh, *Early Arianism. Prudentia* 16 (1984): 51-56.

Papadopoulos, S. Ἀθανάσιος ὁ Μέγας καὶ ἡ θεολογία τῆς οἰκουμενικῆς συνόδου. Athens, 1975.

de Pauley, W.C. "The Idea of Man in Athanasius." *Theology* 12 (1926): 331-338.

Payne, R. *The Holy Fire: The Story of the Fathers of the Eastern Church.* London, 1958.

Pearson, B., and J. Goehring, eds. *The Roots of Egyptian Christianity.* Philadelphia, 1986.

Peeters, P. "Comment s. Athanase s'enfuit de Tyr en 335." *Académie royale de Belgique: Bulletin de la classe des lettres et des sciences morales et politiques,* series 5, vol. 30 (1945): 131-177.

————. "L'Epilogue du synode de Tyr en 335." *AnalBoll* 63 (1945): 131-144.

Pelikan, J. *The Christian Tradition: A History of the Development of Doctrine.* Vol. 1: *The Emergence of the Catholic Tradition.* London, 1971.

————. "Council or Father or Scripture: The Concept of Authority in the Theology of Maximus the Confessor." In *The Heritage of the Early*

Church: Essays in Honor of the V. Rev. Georges V. Florovsky, edited by D. Neiman and M. Schatkin, 277-288. Rome, 1973.

————. *The Excellent Empire: The Fall of Rome and the Triumph of the Church.* San Francisco, 1987.

————. *Historical Theology—Continuity and Change in Christian Doctrine.* New York, 1971.

————. *The Light of the World: A Basic Image in Early Christian Thought.* New York, 1962.

Pell, G.A. *Die Lehre des heiligen Athanasius von der Sünde und Erlösung.* Passau, 1888.

Percival, H.R., ed. *The Seven Ecumenical Councils of the Undivided Church, Their Canons and Dogmatic Decrees, Together with All the Canons of All the Local Synods Which Have Received Ecumenical Acceptance.* LNPF, 2d series, vol. 14. Reprint ed. Grand Rapids, Mich., 1974.

Peri, V. "La cronologia delle *Lettere festali* di sant' Atanasio e la quaresima." *Aevum* 35 (1961): 28-86.

Perichon, P. "Pour une édition nouvelle de l'historien Socrate: Les Manuscrits et les versions." *RSR* 53 (1965): 112-120.

Person, R.E. *The Mode of Theological Decision-Making at the Early Ecumenical Councils: An Inquiry into the Function of Scripture and Tradition at the Councils of Nicaea and Ephesus.* Basel, 1978.

Peterson, R.M. "The Gift of Discerning Spirits in the *Vita Antonii* 16-44." *StP* 17 (1982): 519-522.

Pettersen, A.L. "Christ's Death—A Liturgical Event for Athanasius of Alexandria?" *The Downside Review* 346 (1984): 22-31.

————. "Did Athanasius Deny Christ's Fear?" *Scottish Journal of Theology* 39 (1986): 327-340.

————. "The Questioning Jesus in Athanasius' *Contra Arianos* III." In *Ariansim,* edited by R.C. Gregg, 243-255. Philadelphia, 1985.

————. "A Reconstruction of the Date of the *Contra gentes—De incarntione* of Athanasius of Alexandria." *StP* 17 (1982): 1030-1040.

————. "'To Flee or Not to Flee': An Assessment of Athanasius' *De fuga sua.*" In *Persecution and Toleration,* edited by W.J. Sheils, 29-42. Oxford, 1984.

Pieper, M. "Zwei Blätter aus dem Osterbrief des Athanasius vom Jahre 364 (Pap. Berol. 11948)." *ZNW* 37 (1938): 73-76.

Pieszczoch, S. "Notices de la collégialité chez Eusèbe de Césarée (Histoire ecclésiastique)." *StP* 10 (1970): 302-305.

Pietri, C. "La Question d'Athanase vue de Rome (338-360)." In *Politique et théologie,* edited by C. Kannengiesser, 93-126. Paris, 1974.

Pollard, T.E. "Eusebius of Caesarea and the Synod of Antioch (324-25)." *Überlieferungsgeschichtliche Untersuchungen,* edited by Franz Paschke. Berlin, 1981.

————. "The Exegesis of John X 30 in the Early Trinitarian Controversies." *NTS* 3 (1957): 334-349.

————. "The Exegesis of Scripture and the Arian Controversy." *The Bulletin of the John Rylands Library of Manchester* 41 (1959): 414-429.

————. *Johannine Christology and the Early Church.* Cambridge, 1970.

————. "Logos and Son in Origen, Arius, and Athanasius." *StP* 2 (1957): 282-287.

————. "The Origins of Arianism." *JThS,* NS 9 (1958): 103-111.

Preisigke, F. *Namenbuch.* Heidelberg, 1922.

Prestige, G.L. " *'Aγέννητος* and *Γεν(ν)ητός* and Kindred Words in Eusebius and the Early Arians." *JThS* 24 (1923): 486-496.

————. " *'Aγέν(ν)ητος* and Cognate Words in Athanasius." *JThS* 34 (1933): 258-265.

————. *God in Patristic Thought.* London, 1952.

————. *Fathers and Heretics.* London and New York, 1940.

Prümm, K. "'Mysterion' und Verwandtes bei Athanasius." *ZKTh* 63 (1939): 350-359.

Pusey, E.B. *The Councils of the Church.* London, 1857.

Quasten, J. *Patrology.* 3 vols. Antwerp and Utrecht, 1975.

Radford, L.B. *Three Teachers of Alexandria: Theognostus, Pierus, and Peter.* Cambridge, 1908.

Rahner, H. *Kirche und Staat im frühen Christentum.* Munich, 1961.

Recheis, A. "Sancti Athanasii Magni Doctrina de primordiis seu quomodo explicaverit Genesim 1-3." *Antonianum* 28 (1953): 219-260.

Reitzen, R. *Des Athanasius Werk über das Leben des Antonius: Ein philologischer Beitrag zur Geschichte des Mönchtums.* Sitzungsberichte, Akadamie Heidelberg, 1914. Phil. Hist. Kl. Abh. 8.

Reynolds, H.R. *Athanasius: His Life and Work.* London, 1889.

Rezette, J. "Le Mystère de l'église dans la controverse anti-arienne chez saint Athanase." *Studii Biblici Franciscani Liber Annuus* 25 (1975): 104-118.

Richard, M. "Saint Athanase et la psychologie du Christ selon les Ariens." *Mélanges de science religieuse* 4 (1947): 5-54.

————., ed. *Asterii Sophistae Commentariorum in Psalmos quae supersunt.* Symbolae Osloenses, Fasc. Supplem. xvi. Oslo, 1956.

Ricken, F. "Nikaia als Krisis des altchristlichen Platonismus." *TP* 44 (1969): 321-341.

————. "Zur Rezeption der platonischen Ontologie bei Eusebius von Kaisareia, Areios und Athanasios." *TP* 53 (1978): 321-352.

Reidel, W., and W.E. Crum, eds. and trans. *The Canons of Athanasius of Alexandria.* London, 1904.

de Riedmatten, H. *Les Actes du procès de Paul de Samosate, étude sur la christologie du IIIe au IVe siècle.* Fribourg, 1952.

Ritschl, D. "Athanasius, Source of New Questions." In *Konzepte: Gesammelte Aufsätze,* vol. 1: *Patristische Studien,* 74-77. Bern, 1976.

————. *Athanasius: Versuch einer Interpretation.* Zurich, 1964.

Ritter, A.M. *Das Konzil v. Konstantinopel und sein Symbol.* Göttingen, 1965.

Robertson, A. "On Some Mss. of the Writings of St. Athanasius, Part I." *JThS* 3 (1902): 97-110.

————. *Select Writings and Letters of Athanasius, Bishop of Alexandria.* Prolegomena. LNPF, 2d series, vol. 4, 1891.

Roethe, G. *Zur Geschichte der römischen Synoden im 3. und 4. Jahrhundert.* Freiburg, 1937.

Rogala, S. *Die Anfänge des arianischen Streites.* Forschungen zur christlichen Literatur und Dogmengeschichte 7, 1. Paderborn, 1907.

Roldanus, J. *Le Christ et l'homme dans la théologie d'Athanase d'Alexandrie: Etude de la conjonction de sa conception de l'homme avec sa christologie.* Studies in the History of Christian Thought 4. Leiden, 1968.

Rondeau, M.J. "L'Epître à Marcellinus sur les Psaumes." *VC* 22 (1968): 176-197.

————. "Une nouvelle preuve de l'influence littéraire d'Eusèbe de Césarée sur Athanase: L'Interpretation des psaumes." *RSR* 56 (1968): 385-434.

Rordorf, W., and A. Schneider. *L'Évolution du concept de tradition dans l'église ancienne.* Traditio Christiana 5. Berne, 1982.

Reuther, R. *Gregory of Nazianzus: Rhetor and Philosopher.* Oxford, 1969.

Rusch, W.G. "A la recherche de l'Athanase historique." In *Politique et théologie,* edited by C. Kannengiesser, 161-177. Paris, 1974.

————. "Some Comments on Athanasius' *Contra Apollinarem* I,3." In *Arianism,* edited by R.C. Gregg, 223-231. Philadelphia, 1985.

————, ed. and trans. *The Trinitarian Controversy.* Sources of Early Christian Thought. Philadelphia, 1980.

Ryan, G.J. *De incarnatione of Athanasius.* Part I: *The Long Recension Manuscripts.* Studies and Documents 14. London, 1954.

Saake, H. *Pneumatologica: Untersuchungen zum Geistverständnis im Johannesevangelium bei Origenes und Athanasios von Alexandrien.* Frankfurt am Main, 1973.

————. "Das Präskript zum ersten Serapionbrief des Athanasios von Alexandrien als pneumatologisches Programm." *VC* 26 (1972): 188-199.

B. Salleron. *Matière et corps du Christ chez saint Athanase d'Alexandrie.* Rome, 1967.

Sample, R.L. "The Christology of the Council of Antioch (268 C.E.) Reconsidered." *ChH* 48 (1979): 18-26.

Sansbury, C.J. "Athanasius, Marcellus, and Eusebius of Caesarea: Some Thoughts on Their Resemblances and Disagreements." In *Arianism,* edited by R.C. Gregg, 281-285.

Sansterre, J.M. "Eusèbe de Césarée et la naissance de la théorie 'césaropapiste'." *ByZ* 42 (1972): 131-195, 532-594.

Sbodorne, S. "Caratteristiche stutturali di alcune vite di santi dei secoli III-IV." *Koinonia* 2 (1978): 57-67.

Scheidweiler, F. "Zur neuen Ausgabe des Athanasius." *ByZ* 47 (1954): 73-94.

Schneemelcher, W. "Athanasius von Alexandrien als Theologe und als Kirchenpolitiker." *ZNW* 43 (1950-51): 242-256.

──────. "Die Epistula Encyclica des Athanasius." In *Gesammelte Aufsätze*, 290-337. Thessalonica, 1974.

──────. "Kirche und Staat im 4. Jahrhundert." In *Die Kirche angesichts der konstantinischen Wende*, edited by G. Ruhbach, 220-235. Darmstadt, 1976.

──────. "Der Schriftgebrauch in den 'Apologien' des Athanasius." In *Text—Wort—Glaube*, edited by M. Brecht, 209-219. Arbeiten zur Kirchengeschichte 50. Berlin, New York, 1980.

──────. "Zur Chronologie des arianischen Streites." *ThLZ* 79 (1954): col. 393-400.

Schoemann, J.B. "Εἰκών in den Schriften des heiligen Athanasius." *Scholastik* 16 (1941): 335-350.

Schroeder, H.J. *Disciplinary Decrees of the General Councils*. London, 1937.

Schubart, W. "Alexandria." *RAC* 1, cols. 271-283.

Schwartz, E. "Das antiochenische Synodalschreiben von 325." *NGG* 1908, 305-374 [*GS* III, 169-187].

──────. "Die Dokumente des arianischen Streites bis 352." *NGG* 1905, 257-299 [*GS* III, 117-168].

──────. *Das Geschichtswerk des Thukydides*. Reprint ed., from the 3d edition of 1929. Hildesheim, 1969.

──────. "Die Quellen über den melitianischen Streit." *NGG* 1905, 164-187 [*GS* III, 87-116].

──────. *Der s.g.* Sermo major de fide *des Athanasius*. Munich, 1925.

──────. *Die Synode von Antiochien im Jahr 324/325: Ein Beitrag zur Geschichte des Konzils von Nicäa*. Berlin, 1913.

──────. "Von Konstantins Tod bis Sardica 342." *NGG* 1911, 469-522 [*GS* III, 265-334].

──────. "Von Nicaea bis zu Konstantins Tod." *NGG* 1911, 367-426 [*GS* III, 188-264].

──────. *Zur Geschichte der alten Kirche und ihres Rechtes*. [*GS* IV].

──────. *Zur Geschichte des Athanasius*. [*GS* III].

──────. "Zur Kirchengeschichte des 4. Jahrhunderts." *ZNW* 34 (1935): 129-213 [*GS* IV, 1-110].

Seeberg, E. *Die Synode von Antiochien in Jahren 324-25*. Berlin, 1913.

Seeck, O. *Geschichte des Untergangs der antiken Welt*. Stuttgart, 1920-1923.

──────. *Regesten der Kaiser und Päpste für die Jahre 311 bis 476 n. Chr. vorarbeit zu einer Prosopographie der christlichen Kaiserzeit*. Stuttgart, 1919. Reprint ed. Frankfurt, 1964.

————. "Untersuchungen zur Geschichte des nicäanischen Konzils." *ZKG* 17 (1896): 1-71, 319-362.

Seiler, R. "Athanasius' *Apologia contra Arianos*: Ihre Entstehung und Datierung." Ph.D. diss., University of Tübingen. Düsseldorf, 1932.

Sellers, R.V. *Eustathius of Antioch and His Place in the Early History of Christian Doctrine.* Cambridge, 1928.

Sesan, V. *Kirche und Staat im römisch-byzantinischen Reiche seit Konstantin dem Grossen und bis zum Falle Konstantinopels.* Vol. 1: *Die Religionspoloitik der christlichen römischen Kaiser von Konstantin dem Grossen bis Theodosius dem Grossen (311-380).* Leipzig, 1973.

Seston, W. "Constantine as Bishop." *JRS* 37 (1947): 127-131.

Setton, K.M. *Christian Attitude towards the Emperor in the Fourth Century.* New York, 1941. Reprint ed. New York, 1967.

Sieben, H.J. "Athanasius über den Psalter: Analyse seines Briefes an Marcellinus." *TP* 48 (1973): 157-173.

————. "Herméneutique de l'exégèse dogmatique d'Athanase." In *Politique et théologie,* edited by C. Kannengiesser, 195-214. Paris, 1974.

————. "Zur Entwicklung der Konzilsidee: Werden und Eigenart der Konzilsidee des Athanasius von Alexandrien." *TP* 45 (1970): 353-389.

Simonetti, M. *La crisi ariana nel IV secolo.* Studia Ephemeridis "Augustinianum" 11. Rome, 1975.

————. "Nota sull'ariano Candido." *Orpheus* 10 (1963): 151-157.

————. "Le origini dell'Arianesimo." *RSLR* 7 (1971): 317-330.

————. Review of Gregg and Groh, *Early Arianism. RSLR* 18 (1983): 304-306.

————. *Studi sull'arianesimo.* Rome, 1965.

————. "Teologia alessandrina e teologia asiatica al concilio di Nicaea." *Augustinianum* 13 (1973): 369-398.

Singer, C.G. "Athanasius." *Journal of Christian Reconstruction* 2 (1975): 163-178.

Skurat, K.E. "Die Heilsbedeutung der Menschwerdung Christi nach der Lehre des hl. Athanasius." *Stimme der Orthodoxie* 8 (1975): 46-50; 9 (1975): 53-57.

Slusser, M. "Athanasius, *Contra gentes* and *De incarnatione*: Place and Date of Composition." *JThS* 37 (1986): 114-117.

Smith, J.D. *The Death of Classical Paganism.* New York, 1976.

Smith, R.W. *The Art of Rhetoric in Alexandria.* The Hague, 1974.

Staniloae, D. "La Doctrine de saint Athanase sur le salut." In *Politique et théologie,* edited by C. Kannengiesser, 227-293. Paris, 1974.

————. "Die Erlösungslehre des hl. Athanasius des Grossen." *Kyrios* 14 (1974): 25-42.

Stanley, A.P. *Lectures on the History of the Eastern Church.* London, 1861.

Stead, G.C. "Atanasio." In *Dizionario patristico e di antichità cristiane* 1, edited by A. Di Berardino. 1983.

————. "Athanasius' *De incarnatione*: An Edition Reviewed." *JThS*, NS 31 (1980): 378-390.

————. "Athanasius' Earliest Written Work." *JTS*, NS 39, 1 (April 1988): 76-91.

————. "The Concept of Divine Substance." *VC* 29 (1975): 1-14.

————. *Divine Substance*. Oxford, 1977.

————. "Eusebius and the Council of Nicaea." *JThS*, NS 24 (1973): 85-100.

————. "The Freedom of the Will and the Arian Controversy." In *Platonismus und Christentum: Festschrift für Heinrich Dörrie*, edited by H.D. Blume and F. Mann. *Jahrbuch für Antike und Christentum*, supplement vol. 10 (1983): 245-257.

————. "'Homoousios' dans la pensée de saint Athanase." In *Politique et théologie*, edited by C. Kannengiesser, 231-253. Paris, 1974.

————. "The Platonism of Arius." *JThS*, NS 15 (1964): 16-31.

————. Review of G.D. Dragas, *St. Athanasius Contra Apollinarem*. *JThS*, NS 39, 1 (April 1988): 250-253.

————. "Rhetorical Method in Athanasius." *VC* 30 (1976): 121-137.

————. "The Scriptures and the Soul of Christ in Athanasius." *VC* 36 (1982): 233-250.

————. "The Significance of the Homoousios." *StP* 3 (1961): 397-412.

————. *Substance and Illusion in the Christian Fathers*. London, 1985.

————. "The *Thalia* of Arius and the Testimony of Athanasius." *JThS*, NS 29 (1978): 20-52.

Steenson, J.N. "Basil of Ancyra and the Course of Nicene Orthodoxy." D.Phil. diss., Oxford University, 1983.

Stegmann, A. "Zur Datierung der drei Reden des heiligen Athanasius gegen die Arianer." *ThQ* 96 (1914): 227-231.

Steidle, B. "*Homo Dei Antonius*. Zum Bild des *Mannes Gottes* im alten Mönchtum." *Studia Anselmiana* 38 (1956): 148-200.

Steigele, P. *Der Agennesiebegriff in der griechischen Theologie des vierten Jahrhunderts*. Freiburg, 1913.

Stevenson, J. *Studies in Eusebius*. Cambridge and New York, 1929.

Storch, R.H. "The 'Eusebian Constantine'." *ChH* 40 (1971): 145-155.

Strange, C. "Athanasius on Divinization." *StP* 16 (1985): 342-346.

Sträter, H. *Die Erlösunglehre des hl. Athanasius*. Freiburg, 1894.

Straub, J.A. "Constantine as Κοίνος 'Επίσκοπος: Tradition and Innovation in the First Christian Emperor's Majesty." *DOP* 21 (1967): 39-55.

————. "Kaiser Konstantin als Ἐπίσκοπος τῶν Ἐκτός." *StP* 1 (1957): 678-695.

Strohm, P.M. "Die Trinitätslehre des hl. Athanasius und ihr Missverstehen im Abendland." *Kyrios* 14 (1974): 43-60.

Stuelken, A. *Athanasiana: Literature und dogmengeschichtliche Untersuchungen*. TU 19, 4. Leipzig, 1899.

Telfer, W.R. "Arius Takes Refuge in Nicomedia." *JThS* 37 (1936): 60-63.

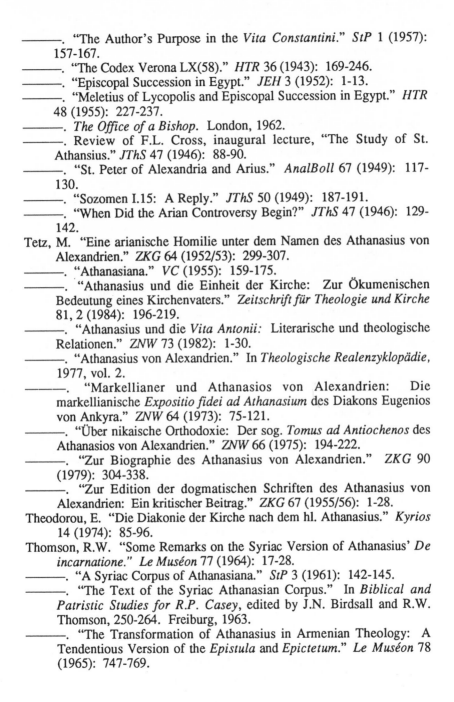

———. "The Author's Purpose in the *Vita Constantini*." *StP* 1 (1957): 157-167.

———. "The Codex Verona LX(58)." *HTR* 36 (1943): 169-246.

———. "Episcopal Succession in Egypt." *JEH* 3 (1952): 1-13.

———. "Meletius of Lycopolis and Episcopal Succession in Egypt." *HTR* 48 (1955): 227-237.

———. *The Office of a Bishop*. London, 1962.

———. Review of F.L. Cross, inaugural lecture, "The Study of St. Athansius." *JThS* 47 (1946): 88-90.

———. "St. Peter of Alexandria and Arius." *AnalBoll* 67 (1949): 117-130.

———. "Sozomen I.15: A Reply." *JThS* 50 (1949): 187-191.

———. "When Did the Arian Controversy Begin?" *JThS* 47 (1946): 129-142.

Tetz, M. "Eine arianische Homilie unter dem Namen des Athanasius von Alexandrien." *ZKG* 64 (1952/53): 299-307.

———. "Athanasiana." *VC* (1955): 159-175.

———. "Athanasius und die Einheit der Kirche: Zur Ökumenischen Bedeutung eines Kirchenvaters." *Zeitschrift für Theologie und Kirche* 81, 2 (1984): 196-219.

———. "Athanasius und die *Vita Antonii*: Literarische und theologische Relationen." *ZNW* 73 (1982): 1-30.

———. "Athanasius von Alexandrien." In *Theologische Realenzyklopädie*, 1977, vol. 2.

———. "Markellianer und Athanasios von Alexandrien: Die markellianische *Expositio fidei ad Athanasium* des Diakons Eugenios von Ankyra." *ZNW* 64 (1973): 75-121.

———. "Über nikaische Orthodoxie: Der sog. *Tomus ad Antiochenos* des Athanasios von Alexandrien." *ZNW* 66 (1975): 194-222.

———. "Zur Biographie des Athanasius von Alexandrien." *ZKG* 90 (1979): 304-338.

———. "Zur Edition der dogmatischen Schriften des Athanasius von Alexandrien: Ein kritischer Beitrag." *ZKG* 67 (1955/56): 1-28.

Theodorou, E. "Die Diakonie der Kirche nach dem hl. Athanasius." *Kyrios* 14 (1974): 85-96.

Thomson, R.W. "Some Remarks on the Syriac Version of Athanasius' *De incarnatione*." *Le Muséon* 77 (1964): 17-28.

———. "A Syriac Corpus of Athanasiana." *StP* 3 (1961): 142-145.

———. "The Text of the Syriac Athanasian Corpus." In *Biblical and Patristic Studies for R.P. Casey*, edited by J.N. Birdsall and R.W. Thomson, 250-264. Freiburg, 1963.

———. "The Transformation of Athanasius in Armenian Theology: A Tendentious Version of the *Epistula* and *Epictetum*." *Le Muséon* 78 (1965): 747-769.

Tillemont, L.S. *Mémoires pour servir à l'histoire ecclésiastique des six premiers siècles.* 16 vols. (Vol. 8: *Histoire de s. Athanase.*) Paris, 1693-1712.

Torjesen, K.J. "The Teaching Function of the Logos: Athanasius, *De incarnatione* XX-XXX, ii." In *Arianism,* edited by R.C. Gregg, 213-221. Philadelphia, 1985.

Torrance, T.F. "Athanasius: A Study in the Foundations of Classical Theology." In *Theology in Reconciliation,* 215-266. London and Grand Rapids, Mich., 1975.

————. "The Hermeneutics of Saint Athanasius." *Ecclesiastikos Pharo Alexandreias* 52 (1970): 446-468.

————. "Spiritus Creator: A Consideration of the Teaching of St. Athanasius and St. Basil." In *Theology in Reconstruction,* 209-228. London, 1965.

————, ed. *The Incarnation: Ecumenical Studies in the Nicene-Constantinopolitan Creed A.D. 381.* Edinburgh, 1981.

Trevijano, R. "The Early Christian Church of Alexandria." *StP* 12 (1975): 471-477.

Tsirpanlis, C.N. "Aspects of Athanasian Soteriology." Κληρονομία 8 (1976): 61-76.

Tuilier, A. "Les Évangelistes et les docteurs de la primitive église et les origines de l'école (didaskaleion) d'Alexandrie." *StP* 17, 2 (1982): 738-749.

————. "Le Sens de l'adjectif *oecumenique* dans la tradition apostolique et dans la tradition byzantine." *Nouvelle revue théologique* 86 (1964): 260-271.

————. "Le Sens du terme ὁμοούσιος dans le vocabulaire théologique d'Arius et de l'école d'Antioche." *StP* 3 (1961): 421-430.

Tulloch, J. "Athanasius." *Encyclopedia Britannica.* 9th ed. London, 1889.

Turner, C.H. "Notes on the *Apostolic Constitutions.*" *JThS* 16 (1914/1915): 54-61.

Turner, H.E.W. *The Pattern of Christian Truth.* London, 1954.

Twomey, V. *Apostolikos Thronos: The Primacy of Rome as Reflected in the Church History of Eusebius and the Historico-Apologetic Writings of St. Athanasius the Great.* Münster, 1982.

Ullmann, W. "The Constitutional Significance of Constantine the Great's Settlement." *JEH* 27 (1976): 1-16.

Unger, D. "A Special Aspect of Athanasian Soteriology." *Franciscan Studies* 6 (1946): 30-53, 171-194.

de Urbina, I.O. "L'anima umana di Cristo secondo S. Atanasio." *OrChP* 20 (1954): 27-43.

————. *Nicée et Constantinople.* Histoire des conciles oecumeniques, vol. 1. Paris, 1963.

————. *El Símbolo Niceno.* Madrid, 1947.

Van Haelst, J. "Les Sources papyrologiques concernant l'église en Egypte à l'époque de Constantin." In *Proceedings of the Twelfth International Congress of Papyrology*, 499, nos. 29-35. Toronto, 1970.

van Winden, J.C.M. "On the Date of Athanasius' Apologetical Treatises." *VC* 29 (1975): 291-295.

Vasiliev, A.A. *History of the Byzantine Empire 324-1453.* 2 vols. Reprint ed. Madison, Wis., 1958.

Viaud, G. *La Liturgie des Coptes d'Egypte.* Paris, 1978.

Voelkl, L. *Der Kaiser Konstantin: Annalen einer Zeitwende, 306-337.* Munich, 1957.

Vogt, H.J. "Parties in the History of the Church: Athanasius and His Contemporaries." Translated by F. McDonagh. *Concilium* (1973-1979): Pt. 1, 37-49.

Voisin, G. "La Doctrine christologique de saint Athanase." *RHE* 1 (1900): 226-248.

Vööbus, A. "Entdeckung einer unbekannten Biographie des Athanasios von Alexandrien." *ByZ* 71 (1978): 36-40.

———. *A History of Asceticism in the Syrian Orient.* 2 vols. Louvain, 1960.

de Vries, W. "Die Ostkirche und die Cathedra Petri im IV. Jahrhundert." *OrChP* 40 (1974): 114-144.

———. "Die Struktur der Kirche gemäss dem ersten Konzil von Nikaia und seiner Zeit." In *Wegzeichen: Festgabe zum 60. Geburtstag von Prof. Dr. Hermenegild M. Biedermann OSA,* edited by E. C. Suttner and C. Patock. Das östliche Christentum, N.F., vol. 25, 55-81. n.d.

Walker, J.B. "Convenance épistémologique de l'homoousion dans la théologie d'Athanase." In *Politique et théologie,* edited by C. Kannengiesser, 255-275. Paris, 1974.

Wallace-Hadrill, D.S. "The Eusebian Chronicle: The Extent and Date of Composition of Its Early Editions." *JThS,* NS 6 (1955): 248-253.

———. *Eusebius of Caesarea.* London, 1960.

Wallis, F. "On Some Mss. of the Writings of St. Athanasius: Part I and Part II." *JThS* 3 (1902): 97-111, 245-258.

Walters, C. *Monastic Archaeology in Egypt.* Warminster, 1974.

Wand, J.W.C. *Doctors and Councils.* London, 1962.

Weber, A. Ἀρχή: *Ein Beitrag zur Christologie des Eusebius von Cäsarea.* Rome, 1964.

Weigl, E. *Untersuchungen zur Christologie des hl. Athanasius.* Paderborn, 1914.

Weijenborg, R. "Apollinaristic Interpolations in the *Tomus ad Antiochenus* of 362." *StP* 3 (1961): 324-330.

Wells, J. "The Argument to Design in Athanasius and Maximus." *The Patristic and Byzantine Review* 8, 1 (1989): 45-54.

West, M.L. "The Metre of Arius' *Thalia.*" *JThS* NS 33 (1982): 98-105.

Wicks, J. *Communio, Church, and Papacy in Early Christianity.* Translated by L. Hertling. Chicago, 1972.

Wiles, M.F. "In Defence of Arius." *JThS*, NS 13 (1962): 339-347. Republished in *Working Papers on Doctrine*, 28-37. London, 1976.

————. *The Making of Christian Doctrine*. Cambridge, 1967.

Wiles, M.F., and R.C. Gregg. "Asterius: A New Chapter in the History of Arianism?" In *Arianism*, edited by R.C. Gregg, 153-179. Philadelphia, 1985.

Wilken, R.L. "Tradition, Exegesis, and the Christological Controversy." *ChH* 34 (1965): 123-142.

Williams, G.H. "Christology and Church-State Relations in the Fourth Century." *ChH* 20, 3 (1951): 3-33; 20, 4 (1951): 3-26.

Williams, R.D. "Arius and the Meletian Schism." *JThS*, NS 37, 1 (1986): 35-52.

————. *Arius: Heresy & Tradition*. London, 1987.

————. "The Logic of Arianism." *JThS*, NS 34 (1983): 56-81.

————. "The Quest of the Historical *Thalia*." In *Arianism*, edited by R.C. Gregg, 1-35. Philadelphia, 1985.

Winkelmann, F. "Der trinitarische Streit in zeitgenössischer Sicht." *Das Altertum* 13 (1967): 99-107.

Winter, H. "Recourse to Rome: Batiffol's Argument." *Revue de l'Université d'Ottawa* 37 (1967): 477-509.

Winter, J.G. *Life and Letters in Papyri*. Ann Arbor, Michigan, 1933.

Wojtowtsch, M. *Papsttum und Konzile von den Anfängen bis zu Leo I (440-461)*. Stuttgart, n.d.

Wolf, C.U. "Eusebius of Caesarea and the Onomasticon." *Biblical Archaeologist* 27 (1964): 66-96.

Wolfson, H.A. "Philosophical Implications of Arianism and Apollinarianism." *DOP* 12 (1958): 5-28.

————. *The Philosophy of the Church Fathers*. Vol. 1: *Faith, Trinity, Incarnation*. 2d ed. Cambridge, Mass., 1964.

Yanney, R. "The Church behind Saint Athanasius the Great." *Coptic Church Review* 9, 2 (1988): 35-44.

Young, F.M. *From Nicaea to Chalcedon*. London, 1983.

————. "A Reconsideration of Alexandrian Christology." *JEH* 22 (1971): 103-114.

————. *The Use of Sacrificial Ideas in Greek Christian Writers from the New Testament to John Chrysostom*. Patristic Monograph Series 5. Philadelphia, 1979.

Zahn, T. *Forschungen zur Geschichte des neutestamentlichen Kanons und der altkirchlichen Literatur*. Part 3: *Supplementum Clementinum*. Erlangen, 1884.

Zaphiris, G. "Connaissance naturelle de Dieu d'après Athanase d'Alexandrie." *Κληρονομία* 6 (1974): 61-96.

————. "Der Logos Gottes als Quelle des Lebens nach Athanasios dem Grossen." In *Philoxenia*, edited by A. Kallis. Münster, 1980.

————. "Reciprocal Trinitarian Revelation and Man's Knowledge of God According to St. Athanasius." In *Τόμος Ἑορτίος*, edited by G. Mantzarides, 287-373. Thessalonica, 1974.

Index